OTHER WORDS

American Indian Literature
and
Critical Studies Series
Gerald Vizenor, General Editor

OTHER WORDS

American Indian Literature, Law, and Culture

BY JACE WEAVER

UNIVERSITY OF OKLAHOMA PRESS : NORMAN

Also by Jace Weaver

Then to the Rock Let Me Fly: Luther Bohanon and Judicial Activism (Norman, 1993)

Defending Mother Earth: Native American Perspectives on Environmental Justice (Maryknoll, NY, 1996)

That the People Might Live: Native American Literatures and Native American Community (New York, 1997)

Native American Religious Identity: Unforgotten Gods (Maryknoll, NY, 1998)

American Journey: The Native American Experience (Detroit, 1998)

Library of Congress Cataloging-in-Publication Data

Weaver, Jace, 1957–
    Other words : American Indian literature, law, and culture / by Jace Weaver.
        p.   cm. — (American Indian literature and critical studies series ; v. 39)
    Includes bibliographical references (p.   ) and index.
    ISBN 0–8061–3352–X (alk. paper)
    1. Indians of North America—Social conditions.   2. Indians of North
America—Legal status, laws, etc.   3. Indians in literature.   I. Title.   II. Series.

E98.S67 W43 2001
973.0497—dc21

                                                                    2001027468

Other Words: American Indian Literature, Law, and Culture is Volume 39 in the American Indian Literature and Critical Studies Series.

The paper in this book meets the guidelines for permanence and durability of the Committee on Production Guidelines for Book Longevity of the Council on Library Resources, Inc. ∞

1 2 3 4 5 6 7 8 9 10

Blue

The sun crowns the horizon mountains
Like a child being pushed from its mother's womb.
Born out of the earth this day as any other,
A ceaseless cycle of birth, death, and rebirth.

The creatures of the night
Have packed away their voices.
And those of the day have yet to find their throats.

It is the time the French call "l'heure bleue,"
The blue hour.
But it is not an hour but a moment, an instant,
Suspended between night and dawn.

I stand stock-still in the California air.
Afraid to disturb the fragile communion,
Surely the same felt by our ancestors in the sheer silence
    as they greeted the new day.
Or by Elijah as he recognized the still small voice of his god.

A bird calls out,
As indifferent to my presence
    as he would be to my absence.
The blue hour is gone
    until tomorrow.

JACE WEAVER

CONTENTS

PREFACE

Almost ten years ago, I became what I like to term a "recovering lawyer." I left the daily practice of law to pursue a Ph.D. in religious studies. Nevertheless, the urge to "pick up" the law has never left me and remains something I struggle against one day at a time, sometimes successfully, sometimes less so. Well-meaning friends contact me to help with briefs on sacred sites and religious freedom, call me about the rights of prisoners to have access to traditional practices, even importune me to participate in a small criminal case on a western reservation. It has become clear to me that being a lawyer is like being a cannibal: Eat one arm and people will call you a cannibal for life. Ask Alferd Packer.

This is, to an extent, however, natural. The hand of congressional plenary power still rests heavy on American Natives. Aside from his or her relation to family, clan, or tribal nation, an Indian's most significant relationship is with the federal government. I still teach federal Indian and constitutional law, and the law continues to be an important part of my scholarship. So, as a professor of Native American Studies, my shackles to the law remain firmly in place and always will.

Native American Studies is by its nature two things, comparative and interdisciplinary. Though a given scholar's work may focus on a particular tribe, the field itself must take account of probably six hundred extant tribal traditions and eight major language families in the United States alone. A comparative approach is thus a simple reality. And so is interdisciplinarity. A single piece of scholarship may cut across not only law but history, literary criticism, religion, philosophy, sociology, and anthropology—and subdisciplines within them. Although as scholars we cannot hope to master all these fields—let alone be trained in them—we need at least some familiarity with their sources and methods if we are to do our work well. And when we read that not-so-hypothetical piece of scholarship, we can acknowledge that, in some sense, "this is what I do," regardless of whether our disciplinary home is Native American Studies, American Studies, Ethnic Studies, or any one of numerous other departments.

There are four fields in which Native American Studies has in the last decade begun to reach critical mass: history, literature, religious traditions and cultures (whether from the discipline of anthropology or religious studies), and law. Yet there have been few attempts to bridge these fields and bring to Native American Studies the intellectual coherence it needs if it is to take its place alongside other disciplines in the university. My own work has focused principally in three areas: religious traditions and cultures, law, and literature. By necessity, it also has a strong historical bent. The essays in this volume reflect this diversity, though pieces on literature (broadly defined) predominate. In a fall 1999 issue of *Wicazo Sa Review*, Robert Warrior and I implored those working in the field to take seriously the challenge of interdisciplinarity and the need for such coherence. We put the urgency of such developments in stark terms. It is my hope that with this book I can show one possible way forward, illustrating it with the various strands of my work. I do so, deliberately choosing a volume of essays over a book on a single topic, because I take this seriously and because I care deeply about Native American Studies and its future contours. Although I do not, in any way, mean to denigrate or devalue monographs (I have produced two and am working on a third), I believe that at present a book of essays such as this may be more important to the continued development of Native American Studies than a book on a single subject. While I would never put myself in the same category, I think here of the estimable work on critically important topics done in the essay form by scholars like Vine Deloria, Elizabeth Cook-Lynn, Jack Forbes, and Gerald Vizenor. The essays contained herein should not therefore be thought of as "occasional pieces," but considered as shorter treatments of specific themes, chapters on separate but related, often interlocking, topics. In this search for coherence and an interdisciplinary approach, I am hardly alone. Besides Warrior, Vizenor,

Cook-Lynn, Craig Womack, Joel Martin, and David Carrasco (to name only a few), broadly share this vision of our common enterprise.

Given the interdisciplinarity previously mentioned, there is no neat delineation between this volume's three parts. A given essay in one division often has elements perhaps best suited to one or both of the other sections. Some of the collected essays have appeared in some form in other venues. Most were written specifically for this project. Even when a piece has been previously published, it has been rewritten and updated to conform to the needs of this present project.

Chapter 1, "In Other's Words," is adapted from the first chapter of my book *That the People Might Live: Native American Literatures and Native American Community* and is used by permission of Oxford University Press. Chapter 2, "Trickster among the Wordies," combines and revises reviews that appeared in *Christianity and Crisis* (August 17, 1992) and *Wicazo Sa Review* (Fall 1997). A version of chapter 4, "Remnants of the First Earth," originally appeared in *Wicazo Sa Review* (Fall 1997). A very early version of chapter 6, "Clowns and Villains," appeared as "Ethnic Cleaning, Home-style" in *Wicazo Sa Review* (Spring 1994). Chapter 9, "Original Simplicities to Present Complexities," is a revision of an essay that originally appeared in the *Journal of the American Academy of Religion* (Summer 1995). Chapter 10, "Indian Presence with No Indians Present," and chapter 11, "Losing My Religion," are updated revisions of essays that appeared in my book *Native American Religious Identity: Unforgotten Gods* and are used by permission of Orbis Books.

I have tackled the subject of chapter 12, "Triangulated Power," twice previously: first in "Federal Lands: Energy, Environment and the States," in the *Columbia Journal of Environmental Law* 7:2 (1982) and later in an essay in my book *Defending Mother Earth: Native American Perspectives on Environmental Justice,* used with permission of Orbis Books. Chapter 12 combines elements of both essays but is also revised and updated. Chapter 13, "Scaling Ríos Montt," is based in part upon my own research during five trips to Guatemala, beginning in 1991. Because the political atmosphere in that country is still potentially unstable, I have not cited this material or identified those from whom I received it. Chapter 15, "Native Reformation and Indian Country," originally appeared in *Christianity and Crisis* (Feb. 15, 1993); a version of chapter 16, "A Biblical Paradigm for Liberation," originally appeared as a sidebar in the same article.

Chapter 18, "Reaching beyond Language," reflects work on my current monograph project, "Native American Eschatology and Apocalyptic Messianism: A Semiotics of Knowledge and Uncertainty." And a version of chapter 19, "From I-Hermeneutics to We-Hermeneutics: Native Americans and the Post-Colonial," appeared in *Semeia* (Fall 1997) and also in my book *Native American Religious Identity: Unforgotten Gods*, used by permission of Orbis Books. I am indebted for the title of that chapter to a paper delivered in 1988 at the Roundtable of Ethnic Minority Theologians by Stephen S. Kim of the Claremont Graduate School, entitled "From I-Hermeneutics to We-Hermeneutics: A Prolegomenon to Theology of Community from an Asian-American Perspective." That I find it applicable as a title for the present chapter attests to the many commonalities people of color have shared in the colonial experience.

Given the record of the last five hundred years, it is easy to lapse into a "litany of woes," cataloging the myriad dislocations and depredations that have been visited upon Indian peoples. Many Natives, accustomed to addressing the whitestream (a term I borrow from Claude Denis's *We Are Not You*, which Denis adapts from the feminist *malestream*, indicating that the dominant society, while "structured on the basis of the European, 'white' experience, is far from being simply 'white' in socio-demographic, economic, and cultural terms") readily assume a pose of anger in performance. In fact, we all know such persons, whose entire stock-in-trade is victimry and guilt. Although I do not want to belittle the justification for such an attitude—as Leslie Marmon Silko has written, "There were hundreds of years of blame that needed to be taken by somebody"—I nonetheless believe it to be a mistake. Whitestream audiences are likely to hear such an approach, feel momentarily remorseful, and then go home and wash it off, feeling that they have been granted a form of absolution. If, however, there are young Natives among the listeners, they internalize such words in a very different way. It is as likely to inculcate feelings of hopelessness and despair as it is defiance. Thus, though there is often anger in the essays that follow, I hope that I have been able to avoid trafficking in victimization and guilt. Such emotions are not only pedagogically unsound but ultimately unhealthy and self-defeating. All too often they are merely tropes to authenticity on the part of those assuming them in public presentation.

Some years ago, I was asked to contribute an essay to a volume on Native Americans and "success stories." No doubt fortunately, the book never eventuated. In thinking about it, however, I reflected upon a ledger-book drawing on the wall of my bedroom. I purchased it in Oklahoma and at the time knew nothing about its creator other than his name and the provenance that came with the picture. It stated that it was by Cohoe, a Cheyenne wolf soldier, who had been interned at Fort Marion. Later I picked up a copy of Stan Hoig's *Peace Chiefs of the Cheyennes*. Leafing through it, I discovered a photograph captioned, "Southern Cheyennes Henry Roman Rose, Yellow Bear, and Lame Man (also known as Cohoe) after their release from Fort Marion, Florida." After that, research allowed me to piece together the facts of the artist's life and put a story behind the art that had so long been on my wall. It seems to me that this search for Cohoe is a kind of metaphor for success. It involves a little luck, being in the right place at the right time, and a lot of hard work. The essays in this volume reflect that journey, as well.

In addition to *whitestream*, a couple of other notes on terminology are necessary. Although the University of Oklahoma Press style is to employ *American Indian* as a collective term for American indigenes, I use it along with *Native American*, and *Native*. All these generalized terms are, of course, social constructs and equally problematic. Whenever possible, I have used a given person's specific tribal affiliation as the best way of identifying him or her. Also, in my book *That the People Might Live* and in subsequent work, I have borrowed John Joseph Matthews's term *Amer-European* rather than *Euro-American* or *Euramerican*, a practice I follow here.

In closing, I need to thank the many friends and acquaintances who helped with this work and with my previous book, *American Journey: The Native American Experience*, during which the writing and editing of this present volume took shape: Betty Louise Bell, Vine Deloria, Jr., Armin Geertz, Paul Grant-Costa, Thomas King, Scott Momaday, Trudie Lamb Richmond, Elizabeth Theobald, Alan Velie, Gerald Vizenor, Robert Warrior, and Richard West. Special thanks to my research assistant at Yale Law School, John Cuero, without whose tireless help this book would not have come to fruition. Thanks to Vizenor, the general editor of the American Indian Literature and Critical Studies Series, and

John Drayton, director of the University of Oklahoma Press, for their faith in me. Finally, thanks to the students of the Association of Native Americans at Yale and the Yale chapter of NALSA, the best Native student groups I know, for their personal help and support. *Wado.*

JACE WEAVER

New Haven, CT

PART ONE

Literature

CHAPTER ONE

IN OTHER'S WORDS

Literature and Community

There's something about writing that's like armor to the soul.

ANONYMOUS

Leslie Marmon Silko has written:

> "The following statement, 'All existence is meaningless' is actually
> full of meaning; that is the irony of language. The act of stating what
> *is*, inevitably reminds us of what is *not*. Language forces meaning
> into existence. All barriers yield to language: distance, oceans, dark-
> ness, even time and death itself are easily transcended by language.
> We hear a story about a beloved ancestor from hundreds of years
> ago, but as we listen, we begin to feel an intimacy and immediacy
> of that long ago moment so that our beloved ancestor is very much
> present with us during the storytelling.[1]

Storytelling. At base that is what American Indian authors and poets are
doing—storytelling. According to Silko, when we use language to transcend humanly insurmountable barriers, we call that transcendent use
art. To the extent that it deals with transcendence, it also involves religion.
N. Scott Momaday states, "We have all been changed by words; we have
been hurt, delighted, puzzled, enlightened, filled with wonder. . . ."[2] This
power of language to transform has religious implications as well.

To discuss something labeled *Native American literature* is to enter a
thicket that would make Brer Rabbit (already an exercise in hybridity and

syncreticity, the melding of the Cherokee rabbit-trickster *Jisdu* into the culture of African slaves) envious. Almost immediately, briar-like questions arise. Who or what is a Native American? Louis Owens, at the beginning of his volume *Other Destinies: Understanding the American Indian Novel,* maps out this thicket: "Take one step into this region and we are confronted with difficult questions of authority and ethnicity: What is an Indian? Must one be one-sixteenth Osage, one-eighth Cherokee, one-quarter Blackfoot, or full-blooded Sioux to be Indian? Must one be raised in a traditional 'Indian' culture or speak a native language or be on a tribal roll? To identify as Indian—or mixedblood—and to write about that identity is to confront such questions."[3] In *Tribal Secrets,* as Gregory Gagnon points out, Robert Warrior avers that we often spend far too much time worrying about whether a given writer is "really an Indian."[4] Or, as Sherman Alexie states in his satiric poem "Introduction to Native American Literature": "Sometimes, it . . . talks too much about the color of its eyes & skin & hair."[5] Behind this wrangling is the seemingly constant, essentializing attempt by some activists and intellectuals to define "Indianness" while the majority of Indians live their lives as if such definitions were largely irrelevant, living out their own Indianness without a great deal of worry about such contestations over identity.[6] Few concern themselves with the delicate gymnastics of authenticity, such as those of Wub-e-keniew (Francis Blake, Jr.), who constructs a hierarchy of *Indian* (inauthentic), *Aboriginal Indigenous* (more authentic), and *tribal identification* (most authentic).[7]

Today there is, as Geary Hobson points out, "no universal agreement" as to who is a Native, a process rendered more dysfunctional by the fact that that for many years, for its own colonialist reasons, the United States government intruded itself into the question of definitions, an intrusion that still has a significant impact on Indian identity politics. Thomas King likewise acknowledges the difficulty in knowing who is Indian—the unspoken irony being that his citation for the proposition is Wallace Black Elk, who has been severely criticized by the Native community for peddling traditional spirituality to Amer-Europeans.[8] Persons are defined as Indian based upon a variety of often conflicting standards: 1) the tribe's or Native community's judgment, 2) the Amer-European community's judgment; 3) the federal government's (or, in some cases, a state's) judgment, or 4) self-identification.[9] One or more of these categories encompasses all Native peoples within the United States, including those that A. T. Anderson, in his report on the American Indian Policy Review Commission, called "the Uncounted," all those besides enrolled members of federally recognized tribes.[10]

In discussing the issue of identity and definition, Dennis McPherson and Douglas Rabb adopt the concept of the "outside view predicate," a notion derived from the Western philosophical schools of British conceptual analysis and European existential phenomenology. Coined by Phyllis Sutton Morris, the term means definitions "which, when applied to ourselves, imply an 'outside view' in either a literal or figurative sense." McPherson and Rabb elaborate:

> However, to apply an outside view predicate to yourself is much more than seeing yourself as others see you, though it is that as well. It is also allowing them to tell you who you are. It is in a sense giving up your freedom, your self determination to others; becoming what they want you to become rather than becoming what you have it within yourself to become. To accept an outside view predicate, such as ugly or ashamed . . ., is to fit into the plans and projects of others, to make it easy for them to manipulate you for their own ends, their own purposes. It is, in a very real and frightening sense, to lose yourself, to become alienated, to become a stranger, an alien to yourself.[11]

As can be seen, categories 2 and 3 above are outside view predicates. The need, McPherson and Rabb contend in the title of their volume, is for Natives to see, define, and be "Indian from the Inside."

In an often-cited passage from *The Names: A Memoir*, Scott Momaday writes that his mother, though just one-eighth Cherokee, reawakened her Native background by *imagining* herself Indian. He wrote that "she began to see herself as an Indian. That dim heritage became a fascination and a cause for her, inasmuch, perhaps, as it enabled her to assume an attitude of defiance, an attitude which she assumed with particular style and satisfaction; it became her. She imagined who she was. This act of imagination was, I believe, among the most important events of my mother's early life, as later the same essential act was to be among the most important of my own."[12] American Indian writers help Native readers imagine and reimagine themselves as Indian from the inside rather than as defined by the dominant society. Gerald Vizenor, especially, has been strident in his denunciation of the imaginary Indians that Natives too often become by capitulation to outside view predicates.

Today, notes Geary Hobson, "[p]eople are classified by their tribe, the family, or the government as 'full-bloods,' 'half-bloods,' 'one-fourths,' 'one-eighth,' and so on. This is the genetic distinction. Culturally, a person is characterized in terms of where he or she is from, who his or her people are and what [his or her] ways of life, religion, language are like. Socially (I believe there is a rather fine line between this and the cultural criterion), a person is judged as Native American because of how he or she views the world, his or her views about land, home, family, culture, etc."[13] Acknowledging that there are no easy answers, he goes on to discuss the case of John Ross, the great principal chief of the Cherokee Nation who led the tribe on the Trail of Tears and shepherded them through the Oklahoma reconstruction, and John Ridge. Though Ross was only one-eighth Cherokee and Ridge was seven-eighth, the former fought the tribe's dispossession from its homeland while the latter "collaborated," supported Removal, and was executed for cooperating in the alienation of tribal lands. Concludes Hobson, "Though genetically part Indian, of differing degrees, it was clear to the Cherokee people of the 1830s that John Ross was more 'one of themselves' than was John Ridge."[14] While Hobson is helpful in highlighting the limits of assimilation and the impulse toward Native identity,[15] his example ultimately does more to obscure than to illuminate: the situation of Ross and Ridge was more complex than he depicts it and the struggle between their two factions divided the Cherokee Nation for years. I agree with him, however, that simple essentialized identifications based on race are not adequate. Again, Vizenor has struggled against essentialism in notions of blood quantum identification with his coining of the neologism *crossblood* to replace the various *mixed-blood* categories delineated by Hobson above.

Ultimately, racially based definitions are insufficient; what matters is one's social and cultural milieu, one's way of life.[16] Hobson illustrates this with the case of Hispanic Americans: "While they are undeniably of Indian blood, and genetically Indian, they are nevertheless culturally and socially Spanish. Because of centuries of Catholicism, they are for the most part irrevocably alienated from the Native American portion of their heritage. Thus, to most Native Americans today, it is not merely enough that a person have a justifiable claim to Indian blood, but he or she must also be at least somewhat socially and culturally definable as a Native American."[17] Much the same could be said of most African Americans, many of whom, particularly in the South, have some degree of Native blood but nevertheless identify culturally and socially only as Black. Thomas King goes further, contending that definition on the basis of race is a kind of *dicto simpliciter*. He writes:

> It assumes that the matter of race imparts to the Native writer a tribal understanding of the universe, access to a distinct culture, and a literary perspective unattainable by non-Natives. In our discussions of Native literature, we try to imagine that there is a racial common denominator which full-bloods raised in cities, half-bloods raised on farms, quarter-bloods raised on reservations, Indians adopted and raised by white families, Indians who speak their tribal language, Indians who speak only English, traditionally educated Indians, university-trained Indians, Indians with little education, and the like all share. We know, of course, that there is not. We know that this is a romantic, mystical, and, in many instances, a self-serving notion that the sheer number of cultural groups in North America, the variety of Native languages, and the varied conditions of the various tribes should immediately belie.[18]

There are, alas, no stories carried in the blood.

In so stating, however, I do not join in the (I believe) erroneous and misguided criticism that Arnold Krupat voices of Scott Momaday. Krupat derides Momaday for his use of the phrases *racial memory* and *memory in the blood*. He professes ignorance as to precisely what the author meant but states that the evidence from his writing is that it is "overwhemingly if unfortunately" and "absurdly" racist. H. David Brumble III, in *American Indian Autobiography*, states that in Momaday's lexicon the terms are an "evocative synonym for 'culture.'" Given the previously cited statement by Momaday concerning his mother, one is tempted to agree with Brumble. Krupat, however, brushes his assessment aside as a reflection of his "charitably decent inability to believe that someone as talented and intelligent as Momaday could actually mean" the racist things he says. Paula Gunn Allen also uses the phrase, however, in *Spider Woman's Granddaughters*, when she writes, "The workings of *racial memory* are truly mysterious.

No Cherokee can forget the Trail of Tears. . . ." One can acknowledge the truth of Allen's statement—and Momaday's—without being "absurdly racist." The Cherokee can *never* forget the Trail of Tears—not because of some genetic determinism but because its importance to heritage and identity are passed down through story from generation to generation. I will always recall the unconveyable disdain and contempt in the voice of my grandmother, expressing a sentiment inherited from my grandfather, when she mentioned the name of Andrew Jackson. I would contend that what those like Momaday and Allen mean is the multiplicity of cultural codes that are learned and go toward shaping one's identity. As Ngugi points out, "[C]ulture does not just reflect the world in images but actually, through those very images, conditions a child to see the world in a certain way."[19] Such cultural coding exists finally beyond conscious remembering, so deeply engrained and psychologically imbedded as to be capable of being spoken of as "in the blood."

David Murray, in *Forked Tongues: Speech, Writing and Representation in North American Indian Texts*, states, "The question of whether Indian identity is measured by blood, expressed through kinship and genealogy, or through culture and place, remains a complex problem in Indian writing, reflecting the complexity of arguments over Indians' actual legal and cultural status in America, but in either case it is the problematic relation to the past and the role of the past in memory, personal and tribal, and in self-definition which continues as a major theme."[20] Thomas King succinctly summarizes: "One can become Canadian and a Canadian writer [or American and an American writer], for example, without having been born [there], but one is either born an Indian or one is not."[21] It is part of the distinction drawn by Edward Said between filiation and affiliation.[22] Joseph Conrad can become a part of English letters and Léopold Sédar Senghor a member of the French Academy, but Roger Welsch, for instance, can never become an Indian author.[23]

This is not to imply that Native identity, any more than any other element of Native culture, is forever static. It is important to insist that Native cultures be seen as living, dynamic cultures, "that they are able to adapt to modern life, and to *offer their members the basic values they need to survive in the modern world*."[24] In this process, as Louis Owens states, Native writers move beyond "ethnostalgia—most common to Euramerican treatments of Native American Indians—toward an affirmation of a syncretic, dynamic, adaptive identity in contemporary America"[25]—part of what Vine Deloria hinted at in the subtitle to his 1970 book, *We Talk, You Listen: New Tribes, New Turf.*[26]

Ultimately, for purposes of the study of Native literatures, I accept Hobson's definition: "Native American writers . . . are those of Native American blood and background who affirm their heritage in their individual ways as do writers of all cultures."[27] Such a definition is, admittedly, imperfect. It begs the question of what to do with writers who do not affirm such an identity or, more importantly, who affirm it at different times and in a multiplicity of ways. It also only hints at the perhaps even thornier definitional question of what is "Native American literature" or "literatures."[28]

Although, in my book *That the People Might Live: Native American Literature and Native American Community,* I have limned the difficulty of defining Native American literatures when nonfiction is included, I believe it must be included if the written output of a people is not to be fractured and compartmentalized. Indians have written books about Oliver La Farge, an Amer-European Native Americanist; E. W. Marland, oil tycoon and governor of Oklahoma; even about a non-Native federal judge.[29] Why were these authors drawn to these topics? What makes these writings Indian literature—if they are at all? One is tempted, with Tom King, to say that "[p]erhaps our simple definition that Native literature is literature produced by Natives will suffice for the while providing we resist the temptation of trying to define a Native."[30] Is Indian literature simply any writing produced by an American Indian? Thus, is Martin Cruz Smith's *Gorky Park,* about a KGB investigation of murders in Moscow, American Indian literature simply because its author is a Senecu del Sur/Yaqui Indian? Does the fact that Robbie Robertson of the folk rock group The Band is Mohawk make his songs, like "The Night They Drove Old Dixie Down" and "Up on Cripple Creek," Indian poetry or music? On the other hand, Smith has written works with Indian themes, most notably the anti-colonialist alternative history *The Indians Won;* and Robertson has produced music, in which he employs and adapts traditional chromatics and themes and which he vetted with elders on his reserve in Canada.[31]

Jack Forbes maintains that Native literature is that produced "by persons of Native identity and/or culture." The key question for him "is whether the work is composed or written to be received by a particular people. Is it internal to the culture?" What most fits his criteria, he concludes, is the discourse in "Indian published periodicals," the often topical, occasional, nonfiction writing that would not commonly be considered literature at all according to the Western purist standards discussed by Penny Petrone.[32] Krupat criticizes Forbes's attempt at an internally derived definition, in particular his inclusion of the "identity" of the author as a criterion, as "not only largely useless (e.g., a great many Indians, as a great many others, are persons of mixed racial origins) but obnoxious (e.g., it can tend to distinguish different percentages of 'blood,' ranking each a 'higher' or 'lower' type, depending on the context of concern)."[33] Involved in the gymnastics of authenticity, Krupat's critique is self-contradictory. On one hand, he labels Forbes's definition as offensive because of its potentially essentializing tendencies; on the other, however, he himself engages in such essentializing when he posits a pure, authentic Native identity counterposed to the "mixed blood" status of many Natives. Although I support Forbes's attempt to broaden the definition of Native literature by including nonfictional discourse, I agree that the boundaries which he ultimately sets are too restrictive, excluding too much writing by Natives. Reception and ownership within Native communities can serve to bring back much of what Forbes excludes. The issue of audience, as Forbes points out and as will be seen later, is a fundamental one in many respects. The reality of a non-Native (overwhelmingly Amer-European) controlled publishing industry and the limited potential for a Native readership (due to economics, small population base, etc.) renders the issue of audience more complex than Forbes acknowledges.

Conversely, LaVonne Ruoff includes within her bibliographic review a wide variety of literatures, both fiction and nonfiction, and with regard to the author's identity states, "Although I have generally accepted writers' designations of themselves as American Indian, I have respected the wishes of those who have indicated that their Indian ancestry was so marginal that they did not feel it appropriate to so define themselves."[34] She includes in her discussion not only the previously mentioned "non-Indian" works by Martin Cruz Smith but also works as diverse as the 1930s murder mysteries of Todd Downing, a Choctaw, primarily set in Mexico (*Murder in the Tropics, Death under the Moonflower*) with few or no Indian elements and Lynn Riggs's screenplay for the Arabian romance "Garden of Allah." The Amer-European critic Brian Swann concludes, "Native Americans are Native Americans if they say they are, if other Native Americans say they are and accept them, and (possibly) if the values that are held and acted upon are values upheld by the various native peoples who live in the Americas."[35] Perhaps, finally, one must be left in a sort of intellectual/critical limbo, floating along with Tom King who states that, in reality, we know neither what Native American literature is nor who Native writers are. He declares, "What we do have is a collection of literary works by individual authors who are of Native ancestry, and our hope, as writers and critics, is that if we wait long enough, the sheer bulk of this collection, when it reaches some sort of critical mass, will present us with a matrix within which a variety of patterns can be discerned."[36]

In their volume, *The Empire Writes Back*, Bill Ashcroft, Gareth Griffiths, and Helen Tiffin attempt to define "post-colonial literature," a category into which, at least arguably, Native American literatures fit. They contend that what all post-colonial literatures share is a certain relationship with the former colonizer, to the *métropole*. They note that these post-colonial literatures have emerged out of the experience of colonization and asserted themselves by foregrounding the tension with the former colonial power and by emphasizing their differences from the assumptions of the colonial *métropole*.[37]

Although some elements of this definition are helpful in coming to an understanding of Indian literature that, in part, asserts itself over and against the dominant culture, it nonetheless falls short because American Natives are not *post*-colonial peoples.[38] Instead, today they remain colonized, suffering from internal colonialism. The term *internal colonialism* was coined to characterize the subordination of the Scots and Welsh by the English and was first applied to the situation of American indigenes by anthropologist Robert Thomas.[39] It differs from classic colonialism in that, in classic colonialism, a small minority of colonizers from the *métropole* exert power over a large indigenous population in an area removed from the "mother country." By contrast, in internal colonialism, the autochthonous population is swamped by a large colonizer group, which, after several generations, no longer has a *métropole* to which to return.[40] The colony and the *métropole* are thus geographically coextensive. In post-colonial discourse, internal colonialism is often referred to as settler colonialism. Ashcroft, Griffiths, and Tiffin define *settler colonies* in contrast to *invaded colonies* as those in which the "land was occupied by European colonists who dispossessed and overwhelmed the indigenous populations. They established a transplanted civilization that eventually secured political independence while retaining a non-Indigenous language" and world-view.[41] Said recognizes the United States as a settler colony, which he sees as "superimposed on the ruins of considerable native presence."[42] Vizenor calls the phenomenon "paracolonialism."[43] Besides the indigenous peoples of the Americas, others in situations of internal colonialism include Palestinians, Maoris, and Australian Aborigines. For Natives, "the structures of colonialism will remain substantially intact if the institutionalized forms of racism, oppression and discrimination, which, as the solidified legacies of the colonial era, continue to bear uniquely on indigenous populations, are not also dismantled."[44]

If Indian literatures cannot be considered post-colonial literatures, are they then perhaps anti-colonial or resistance literature? The phrase *resistance literature,* according to Barbara Harlow in her book of the same name, was developed by Palestinian writer Ghassan Kanafani to describe the literature of that people. It presupposes a people's collective relationship to a common land, a common identity, or a common cause on the basis of which it is possible to distinguish between two modes of existence for the colonized, "occupation" or "exile." This distinction also presupposes an "occupying power" that has either exiled or subjugated—or, in the cases of Palestinians and Native Americans, exiled *and* subjugated—the colonized population and has, in addition, significantly intervened in the literary and cultural development of the people it has dispossessed and whose land it has occupied. In other words, literature becomes a critical arena for struggle.[45]

Once again, I believe that this definition by Harlow is useful in evaluating Native literatures. American Indians have been both subjugated and exiled from lands sacred to them, numinous landscapes where every mountain and lake held meaning for their identity and their faith. The dominant culture has intervened consequentially in their literature and culture. Today, Indians are indisputably an oppressed minority in the United States. "The result," as sociologist Menno Boldt puts it, "is a cultural crisis manifested by a breakdown of social order in Indian communities."[46] The statistics, which are often repeated, are staggering. The average yearly income is half the poverty level, and over half of all Natives are unemployed. On some reservations, unemployment runs as high as 85 to 90 percent. Health statistics chronically rank Natives at or near the bottom.

Male life expectancy is forty-four years, and female is forty-seven. Infant mortality is twice the national average. Diabetes runs six times the national average; alcoholism, five times; and cirrhosis of the liver is eighteen times higher than the national average. The worst part is that these statistics have not changed in thirty years. Substance abuse, suicide, crime, and violence are major problems among both urban and reservation populations. Increasingly, violence victimizes those with the least power—women, children, and the elderly.[47] Sexual abuse and violence against women have increased markedly. These problems did not occur, or occur to this degree, in traditional societies. Again, according to Boldt, "The problem is significantly attributable to cultural degeneration"—that process created by the compounded impact of genocide, colonialism, forced cultural and institutional assimilation, economic dependence, and racism.[48] The situation is not, however, as absolute as many, including some Indians, would suggest. Native survival in the face of internal colonialism and the revitalization of Native traditions attest to the truth of Said's repeated theme that there is always something beyond the reach of dominating systems, no matter how totally they saturate society, and that it is this part of the oppressed which the oppressor cannot touch that makes change possible: in "every situation, no matter how dominated it is, there's always an alternative."[49]

Ashcroft, Griffiths, and Tiffin observe that a distinctive characteristic of settler colonies is the maintenance of a non-autochthonous language following political independence from the *métropole*. They write, "Having no ancestral contact with the land, they [colonizers] dealt with their sense of displacement by unquestioningly clinging to a belief in the adequacy of the imported language—where mistranslation could not be overlooked it was the land or the season which was 'wrong.' Yet in all these areas [of the decolonized world] writers have come, in different ways, to question the appropriateness of imported language to place."[50] Some post-colonial theorists, following Fanon and Memmi, argue that colonization can only be put behind by achieving "full independence" of culture, language, and political organization. Thus, for example, Sukarno, realizing that Indonesia could not sever its colonial ties without ridding itself of Dutch, banned its teaching in all schools.[51] Others, like Guyanese Denis Williams, argue "that not only is this impossible but that cultural syncreticity is a valuable as well as an inescapable and characteristic feature of all post-colonial societies and indeed is the source of their peculiar strength."[52] Homi K. Bhabha agrees, averring that the "interstitial passage between fixed identifications opens up the possibility of a cultural hybridity that entertains difference without an assumed or imposed hierarchy."[53] Not all are so consistent: Ashis Nandy misguidedly criticizes Fanon (who, after all, averred that one must decolonize the mind or there is no true freedom) for attacking the West in French "in the elegant style of Jean-Paul Sartre," even though Nandy himself writes in English, for which he has "developed a taste" despite the fact that he forms his thoughts "in my native Bengali and then translate when I have to put them down on paper."[54]

One post-colonial theorist who has been consistent is Ngugi, who in his slim volume, *Decolonising the Mind: The Politics of Literature in African Literature,* wrote back to the *métropole* in English, the language of his colonizer, to explain why henceforth he would write only in his native African language. Although he would unquestionably eschew the characterization, Ngugi skirts the realm of religion and deals with the intricate web of issues central to Native literatures when he writes, "Culture embodies those moral, ethical and aesthetic values, the set of spiritual eyeglasses, through which [a people] come to view themselves and their place in the universe. Values are the basis of a people's identity, their sense of particularity as members of the human race. All this is carried by language. Language as culture is the collective memory bank of a people's experience in history. Culture is almost indistinguishable from the language that makes possible its genesis, growth, banking, articulation and indeed its transmission from one generation to the next." Language is both a shaper and a reflection of culture, and written and oral literatures are the primary means by which it does its work. Ngugi writes, "Language carries culture, and culture carries, particularly through orature and literature, the entire body of values by which we come to perceive ourselves and our place in the world. How people perceive themselves affects how they look at their culture, at their politics and at the social production of wealth, at their entire relationship to nature and to other beings. Language is thus inseparable from ourselves as a community of human beings with a specific form and character, a specific history, a specific relationship to the world."[55] Language as a bearer of culture and worldview is undisputed. In the Native community, Ngugi's words take on concrete form when one considers the Lumbees of North Carolina. With no language and little culture of their own, they borrow from pan-Indianism for their cultural expressions, leading Nick

Locklear, a Tuscarora, whom the Lumbees claim as one of their own, to state, "There ain't no such thing as a Lumbee. They made this thing up."[56]

The issue of language has been an important one in Native communities. The issue begins with the appellation *Indian*, an outside view predicate designed, according to Louis Owens, to impose a distinct alterity on indigenes. He writes, "To be 'Indian' was to be 'not European.' Native cultures—their voices systematically silenced—had no part in the ongoing discourse that evolved over several centuries to define the utterance . . . within the language of the invaders."[57] As part of its attempt at cultural genocide, the concerted assault on Native cultures and personhood, the dominant culture also sought to eradicate tribal languages. The "night of the sword and the bullet was followed by the morning of the chalk and blackboard. The physical violence of the battlefield was followed by the psychological violence of the classroom."[58] Boarding schools banned Native languages. In their place, they hoped to inculcate English, Amer-European values, and Christianity. Students routinely were punished for speaking "Indian." As a result entire generations were beaten into silence and through language and literature taken farther and farther from their world and themselves. Isabelle Knockwood describes the process: "When little children first arrived at the school we would see bruises on their throats and cheeks that told us that they'd been caught speaking [their Native language]. Once we saw the bruises begin to fade, we knew they'd stopped talking."[59]

Though Knockwood writes about her experiences in a Canadian residential school, her story could be replicated many times over for boarding schools in this country. Indians speak of being beaten or having their mouths washed out with yellow cake soap for talking in their own tongues. Jim McKinney, a Potawatomi, remembers being put in a dormitory room with three boys from three different tribes in order to force the speaking of English as a common language: the outcome was not that he learned much English but that he learned quite a lot of three other tribal languages. Quanah Tonemah, Kiowa and Comanche, says that, as a result, he and others became "lost generations," unable to speak their own languages and thus in large measure deracinated. With Tonemah, Knockwood concludes, "The punishment for speaking Mi'kmaw began on our first day at school, but the punishment has continued all our lives as we try to piece together who we are and what the world means to us with a language many of us have had to re-learn as adults."[60]

In light of such history, it is little wonder that, just as many Natives reject Christianity as the imported religion of the colonizer, many also question English (or Spanish or French) as the nonindigenous language of the invaders as well. Luci Tapahonso has written poetry in English but now prefers, like Ngugi, to express herself in Navajo, the native language that carries her culture and thoughtworld.[61] White critics, too, point to the use of English in their gymnastics of authenticity. David Murray, following Krupat, declares, "[T]o write about Indian experience and be published in English is inevitably to be involved in an ambiguous area of cultural identity [and runs] the risk of becoming yet another second-hand cultural identity." In a bizarre turn indicative of the gymnastics of authenticity that denigrates Native identity in favor of a "universal" humanity, he goes on to claim, "Another way of putting this is to say that modern Indian writers writing in English are not so very different from the white ethnopoets [who appropriate Native expressions and forms], in their relation to Indian cultures."[62]

Yet what is a viable option for Ngugi or Tapahonso is not always so for Native Americans. Publishing opportunities in most Native languages are nonexistent. Many Natives do not speak their tribal languages, and so as in Jim McKinney's dorm room at boarding school, the only real alternative in written literature is English if one wishes to communicate across the community. Owens writes that "[f]or the Indian author, writing within consciousness of the contextual background of a nonliterate culture, every word written in English represents a collaboration of sorts as well as a reorientation (conscious or unconscious) from the paradigmatic world of oral tradition to the syntagmatic reality of written language."

Ashcroft, Griffith, and Tiffin, while pointing up the limitations and difficulties in the use of English, note, "This is not to say that the English language is inherently incapable of accounting for post-colonial experience, but that it needs to develop an 'appropriate' usage in order to do so."[63] Thus Joy Harjo, who acknowledges language as a bearer of culture and worldview and the importance of literary creation in tribal languages for their renewal and revitalization but who does not know Muscogee, speaks of the poetry as a means of escaping the limitations and frustrations of English.[64] She now often talks in terms of "rewriting the enemy's language." Gerald Vizenor, who has rewritten a substantial amount of that language through his postmodernist wordplay and coining of neologisms, declares:

The English language has been the linear tongue of colonial discoveries, racial cruelties, invented names, the simulation of tribal cultures, manifest manners, and the unheard literature of dominance in tribal communities; at the same time, this mother tongue of paracolonialism has been a language of invincible imagination and liberation for many tribal peoples in the postindian world. English, a language of paradoxes, learned under duress by tribal people at mission and federal schools, was one of the languages that carried the vision and shadows of the Ghost Dance, the religion of renewal, from tribe to tribe on the vast plains at the end of the nineteenth century. . . . English, that coercive language of federal boarding schools, has carried some of the best stories of endurance, the shadows of tribal survivance, and now that same language of dominance bears the creative literature of distinguished postindian authors in the cities. The tribal characters dance with tricksters, birds, and animals, a stature that would trace the natural reason, coherent memories, transformations, and shadows in traditional stories. The shadows and language of tribal poets and novelists could be the new ghost dance literature, the shadow literature of liberation that enlivens tribal survivance.[65]

Today, many Native authors (as well as social scientists and historians) have, according to McPherson and Rabb, learned "to play the language-games of Europe" precisely because they, like Ngugi, "wish to tell *us* [Amer-Europeans] in language *we* will understand that *they* have no desire to become one of *us*, that assimilation is not the solution because they are not the problem. They have had to learn our language games because, with rare exceptions, in our ethnocentric arrogance we have not bothered to try to understand them in their own terms."[66]

Even Ngugi admits that language itself is not enough to bring renewal to a culture if the content of the literature produced in it is not liberative.[67] Every story—every myth—has "a pragmatic character." Every myth serves some purpose or end. The logical question, then, is to ask where a particular myth came from and what and whose purposes and ends it is designed to serve.[68] Traditional Native American tribal myths are communal in character, forming identity, explaining one's place in the cosmos, creating a sense of belonging. They serve as a countermythology to Amer-European myths that serve colonial interests—myths of discovery, conquest, lost tribes, nomadic savages perpetually involved in the chase and then quietly receding into the shadows until vanishing entirely from the stage of the New World Drama. The impulse to the myths of conquest in whitestream culture is so patent that even White theologian Achiel Peelman admits, "With respect to this native spirituality, the West is now forced to recognize that, notwithstanding its Judeo-Christian foundations (the Old Testament creation narratives), its true symbols are power (oppression), progress, conquest and individualism."[69] All the while murmuring in the ear of the Native, "Theft is Holy."[70]

Enrique Dussel links Amer-European myths of conquest of Indians with the metamyth of modernity. He writes,

> The birthdate of modernity is 1492, even though its gestation, like that of the fetus, required a period of intrauterine growth. Whereas modernity gestated in the free, creative medieval European cities, it came to birth in Europe's confrontation with the Other. By controlling, conquering, and violating the Other, Europe defined itself as discoverer, conquistador, and colonizer of an alterity likewise constitutive of modernity. Europe never discovered (*des-cubierto*) this Other as Other but covered over (*encubierto*) the Other as part of the Same: i.e., Europe. Modernity dawned in 1492 and with it the myth of a special kind of sacrificial violence which eventually eclipsed whatever was non-European."[71]

As Owens points out, these myths, which made sense of Amer-European responses to the "New World," had little or nothing to do with the actual inhabitants of the Americas.[72]

Upon discovery, the European's first response was not to define the indigenes they found in terms of alterity but in terms of sameness. March 1493 presented the Church, and therefore European civilization, with a terrible problem. That month Columbus arrived back in Spain with a number of indigenous captives who appeared to be human. At issue was how to account for these "man-like creatures inhabiting the Americas" when the biblical protology clearly spoke of only three continents (Europe, Africa, and Asia), each populated by the progeny of a different son of Noah after the Flood. Though ultimately the dilemma was resolved in 1512 when Pope Julius II declared Natives to be descended from Adam and Eve through the Babylonians, the first response was to postulate that the dark-skinned peoples who met Columbus were the Lost Tribes of Israel. Implicit in such a determination is that no people can achieve any level of civilization, even language, unless they are of the same stock as those already known. They are not Other but Same.[73]

In the myths of conquest, Columbus and those who followed discovered a vast, virginal, primeval wilderness, sparsely inhabited by a few roaming savages with no fixed abode. Amer-European pioneers conquered this land, impressing form on what previously had been formless, taking what had been held in escrow for them from the foundation of the world, becoming in the process a peculiarly chosen people, "God's American Israel," in their battle with the new frontier. This myth pervades the American psyche and was codified in Amer-European law. The reality was starkly different. Contrary to the myopic vision of European colonizers, America was an inhabited place. As historian Francis Jennings summarizes, "The American Land was more like a widow than a virgin. Europeans did not find a wilderness here; rather . . . they made one. . . . The so-called settlement of America was a *re*settlement, a reoccupation of a land made waste by the diseases and demoralization introduced by the newcomers."[74] Jennings conveniently omits that a great many original inhabitants were simply slaughtered as well. In the myths of conquest, Amer-Europeans did not commit such atrocities. When killings did occur, from Mystic Fort to the Marias, from Gnadenhutten to the Washita, they were tragic mistakes never to be replicated, the result of misunderstandings or madmen operating beyond their instructions. The question that Natives force upon Amer-European conscience and consciousness is: how many such incidents does it take before a pattern can be discerned and they are seen to be, however "tragic," more than "mistakes"? Terry Goldie notes that "a strong argument could be made that the white violence is, if not an essential, at least a systemic part of the imperial principle. Any opposition to the system of order imposed by the imperial invasion, an opposition which was inevitable given the different epistemes of the indigenous peoples, required the violent reaction of the white powers."[75]

Of course, even the few rude, scattered tribes could not be allowed to survive in the myths of conquest. To do so would be to pose an impediment to Amer-European designs on the continent. Extinction is a superior means of creating indigeneity. If all the indigenes are dead, there is no one to dispute the claim. In fact, guilt for wrongs done to the indigenous peoples in the past does not allow them to be other than *of* the past.[76] The myth of the Vanishing Indian was born. By the 1870s, D. P. Kidder of Drew Theological Seminary could explain the failure of Christian missions in North America to displace indigenous religious traditions:

> In no part of the world have there been greater personal sacrifices or more diligent toil to Christianize savages with results less proportioned to the efforts made. Without enumerating . . . causes, the fact must be recognized that throughout the whole continent the aboriginal races are dying out to an extent that leaves little present prospect of any considerable remnants being perpetuated in the form of permanent Christian communities. Still[,] missions are maintained in the Indian territories and on the reservations, and the government of the United States is effectively cooperating with them to accomplish all that may be done for the Christian civilization of the Indians and Indian tribes that remain.[77]

With the rise of the great rationalizing science of the nineteenth century, anthropologists rushed to study the remnants of Native cultures that remained. As improbable as it may now seem, until Margaret Mead packed her field kit and set her face toward Samoa in the twentieth century, American anthropologists almost exclusively studied Native Americans, motivated by a belief that such societies were dying out. As Joan Mark of the Peabody Museum at Harvard observes, "It was urgent to record as many of the old ways as possible before the last instance or even last memory of them disappeared completely. The reason it was considered urgent was that cultures represent alternative social arrangements from which we might learn something as well as clusters of irreplaceable historical data. For a culture to die out unrecorded, to become extinct, was analogous to a biological species becoming extinct. In each case it meant an irreparable loss of diversity and of scientific information."[78] By viewing the Indian as vanishing and the cultures as disintegrating, it was possible to view twentieth-century Indians who refused to vanish as degraded and inauthentic and to contrast them with stereotypes of the "pure," "authentic" *bon sauvage* or *sauvage noble* of the past and thus keep Indians safely in the stasis box of the nineteenth century. It is a version of the "Indian as corpse," the stasis box being only a thinly disguised coffin. An extinct people do not change. Their story is complete.[79] For most of America, the last Indian died on the frozen ground of Wounded Knee in 1890. Epitomizing this view was Henry Luce, publisher of *Time* and *Life*, who during the 1950s and 1960s forbade coverage of Indian stories and issues in his publications because he considered modern-day Natives to be, in his word, "phonies."[80] The closer an indigene is allowed to the coeval, the greater the perceived diminution in Indianness.

Thus, as Dussel makes clear in *The Invention of the Americas*, even the glorification of Natives as Noble Savages who are not allowed (alone of all minorities) to enter the twentieth century serves colonial interests, just as did the romanticized Arab world of Orientalism limned by Edward Said. It is no accident that avatar of imperialism, Karl May, chose as his twin subjects of colonial fantasias the American West of the noble Apache Winnetou and Old Shatterhand and the Arabia of Kara-ben-Nemsi. It did not matter that when he wrote of these exotic locales and peoples he had visited neither and, in fact, had spent the period of his purported travels in Germany's Zwickau prison, serving a sentence for fraud. May's colonialist fairy tales, like those of James Fenimore Cooper, were more authentic to White readers than anything dull reportage could offer.[81] By relegating Natives to an increasingly distant, and therefore comfortable, past, Amer-Europeans are freed to pursue there designs and complete their conquest of an ethnically cleansed America unimpeded. They can convince themselves of their own indigeneity. Memmi, Fanon, and Said all elaborate that it is not enough for the colonizer to control the present and the future of the colonized but, in the effort to prove his indigeneity, must also rewrite the past as well. According to Fanon, "Colonialism is not satisfied merely with holding a people in its grip and emptying the native's brain of all form and content. By a kind of perverted logic, it turns to the past of the people, and distorts, disfigures, and destroys it. This work of devaluing pre-colonial history takes on a dialectical significance today."[82] The Métis author Howard Adams elaborates on the meaning of Fanon's observation for American indigenes:

> The native people in a colony are not allowed a valid interpretation of their history, because the conquered do not write their own history. They must endure a history that shames them, destroys their confidence, and causes them to reject their heritage. Those in power command the present and shape the future by controlling the past,

particularly for the natives. A fact of imperialism is that it systematically denies native people a dignified history. Whites claim that Métis and Indians have no history or national identity, or, if they do, then it is a disgraceful and pathetic one. When natives renounce their nationalism and deny their Indianness, it is a sure sign that colonizing schemes of inferiorization have been successful.[83]

Myths of conquest must conquer other stories. Speaking of anthropology, the science that Claude Levi-Strauss called the "handmaiden of colonialism," Georges Sioui writes, "Far from bringing benefits to the people whose 'cultural conduct is being studied,' these scientific games have the unhappy effect of overshadowing their socio-economic condition and of dashing their efforts to restore their historic dignity," too often drowning out their attempts at assertion of their own subjectivity in a sea of "scientificity." Johannes Fabian, in his *Time and the Other: How Anthropology Makes Its Object*, agrees, noting the primitivism the discipline imposes on indigenous cultures: "Anthropology contributed above all to the intellectual justification of the colonial enterprise. It gave politics and economics—both concerned with human Time—a firm belief in 'natural,' i.e., evolutionary Time. It promoted a scheme in terms of which not only past cultures, but all living societies were placed on a temporal slope, a stream of Time—some upstream, others downstream."[84] Gerald Vizenor declares, "Social science narratives, those unsure reins of final vocabularies and incoherent paracolonialism, overscore the tribal heard as cultural representations. David Carroll argued in *The Subject in Question* that any 'narrative that predetermines all responses or prohibits any counter-narratives puts an end to narrative itself, by making itself its own end and the end of all other narratives.'"

It is not enough, as Albert Memmi reminds, that the colonizer be the master in fact, but in order to satisfy his own need for legitimacy, the colonized must accept his status. Its most important arena of domination is "the mental universe of the colonised, the control, through culture, of how people perceived themselves and their relationship to the world. Economic and political control can never be complete or effective without mental control. To control a people's culture is to control their tools of self-definition in relationship to others." The colonized becomes in a very real sense self-colonizing. In his book, *Missionary Conquest*, George Tinker misconstrues

Robert Thomas's concept of internal colonialism to refer to this psychological internalization of oppression (what M. A. Jaimes-Guerrero terms "autogenocide"), writing "The truth is . . . that Indian people have internalized [the illusion of white superiority] just as deeply as white Americans have, and as a result we discover from time to time just how fully we participate in our own oppression. Implicitly, in both thought and action, we too often concede that the illusion of white superiority is an unquestionable factual reality." Yet despite Tinker's claim, there is always something the dominating system cannot touch. As Jean Raphaël, Montagnais/Mashteuiatsh, maintains, "[T]he Indian will always continue to identify . . . as an Indian." Answering the cant of White superiority, Sioui asserts, "At first both civilizations were sure of their moral superiority. Now, only Amerindian civilization has that certainty." In response to the falsely asserted indigeneity of the Amer-European, Dale Ann Frye Sherman, a California Native, states, "We are of this continent. We were not created elsewhere. We were created here. Our memories are here, and the blood of our ancestors is here. We are made of this continent."[85]

Colonialism succeeds by subverting traditional notions of culture and identity and by imposing social structures and constructs incompatible with traditional society. As a part of the captivity of Indians in the nineteenth century, portrayed as a doomed and vanishing race, scholars of Western social science and literary criticism announced the death of the traditional oral literature (orature) of Native peoples. In her autobiographical text, *Storyteller,* Leslie Silko points out, however, what every Native knows, that the oral traditional is very much alive and imbued with power to create identity and community. She writes, "White ethnologists have reported that the oral tradition among Native American groups has died out because whites have always looked for museum pieces and artifacts when dealing with Native American communities. . . . I grew up at Laguna listening, and I hear the ancient stories, I hear them very clearly in the stories we are telling right now. Most important, I feel the power which the stories still have, to bring us together, especially when there is loss and grief."[86] Yet despite the continued telling, retelling, creation and re-creation of orature among Native peoples, scholars continue to treat it as a dead artifact.

Denise and John Carmody, in their textbook *Native American Religions,* consistently refer to oral tradition in the past tense and depict Natives as having swapped nature for literacy, of "trad[ing] a vast, wrap-around world of wonders for dry, abstract notations on a page."[87] By contrast, Karl Kroeber, in his volume *Traditional Literatures of the American Indian: Texts and Interpretations*, acknowledges that the Native storytelling tradition "is still being carried forward today," but he identifies the medium of that continuance as "new generations of Native American writers"—like Momaday, Silko, and James Welch. In other words, the oral has moved ineluctably to the written. Elsewhere, Kroeber perpetuates the myths of conquest, the metanarrative of dominance, by (re)presenting the Vanishing Indian, writing, "In brief, one is confined to translations, and of a kind which create a confluence of troubling questions. . . . Am I misreading this story because I am ignorant of the *vanished culture* in which it originated and which, to some degree, it reflects?"[88] Similarly, Penny Petrone subtitles her study of Native literature "From the Oral Tradition to the Present." Though she admits, "Oral traditions have not been static" because "[t]heir strength lies in their ability to survive through the power of tribal memory and to renew themselves by incorporating new elements," the presentation and general use of verbs in the past tense posits a linear progression in which orality is left behind in the past.[89] Vizenor states, "The notion in the literature of dominance, that the oral advances to the written, is a colonial reduction of natural sound, heard stories, and the tease of shadows in tribal remembrance."[90]

By treating orature as a dead relic and thus valorizing the written over the oral, one renders the written version normative, a representation of a pure, authentic culture and identity over against current degraded Natives. John Bierhorst, for instance, in his collection *Four Masterworks of American Indian Literature*, rules out the possibility of including any Incan stories because the extant orature is "substantially acculturated."[91] An incident, included by Kroeber in his introduction to *Traditional Literatures*, is illustrative of this tendency to want to fossilize the oral tradition. He tells of, as a child, listening to stories told by Yurok storyteller Robert Spott. When the storyteller deviated from the version Kroeber had "received" from his anthropologist father, the child would "correct" him. He notes that the Indian was "amused by my childish firmness in insisting he adhere exactly to my view of what were 'authentic' versions of his sacred myths."[92] What is amusing and forgivable in a child is far more serious when adopted by an adult scholar. As Vizenor writes, "Native American Indian literatures are tribal discourse, more discourse. The oral and written narratives are language games, comic discourse rather than mere responses to colonial demands or social science theories."[93]

Amer-Europeans have always controlled written literary production through domination of publishing outlets, deciding what will be disseminated and thus read. They have also sought to influence what is read by domination of literary criticism as well. As in other post-colonial situations where the bulk of literary criticism still comes from the *métropole*, the majority of critical studies of American Indian literatures are produced by Amer-European scholars, "'adding value' to the literary 'raw material'" of Native texts. Historian Larzer Ziff, in *Writing in the New Nation*, said that the literary annihilation of Indians would only be checked when they began representing their own cultures. Yet even as Natives begin to produce internal theory and criticism, "most readers and critics influenced by structuralism, modernism, and the dualism of subject, object, or otherness have more confidence in paracolonial discoveries and representations of tribal literatures." Entangled in the metanarrative of Western dominance, this criticism often has more to do with colonial needs and theories than it does with "the wild memories and rich diversities of tribal and postindian literature."[94]

As with George Tinker's discussion of internalized racism, it is amazing how often we are complicitous in this theoretical domination, either by fetishizing our own cultures and thus leaving our scholarship open to summary dismissal by non-Natives or by a preoccupation with questions of identity and authenticity—the very issues most interesting to non-Native critics—in our own criticism. Thus, according to Robert Warrior, "The tendency to find in the work of other American Indian writers something worthy either of unmitigated praise or of unbridled criticism stands in the way of sincere disagreement and engagement. This prevents contentious issues of, for instance, gender, sexual orientation, and economic, social, and political privilege from gaining the attention they deserve. Thus, forums in which complex critical problems of audience, reception, and representation are worked through—rather than pronouncing critical judgment—remain few and far between."[95] Rather than challenging the codes and canons of both theory and praxis of literature and dominant literary criticism, such critical stances leave the field wide open to continued domination by non-Natives.[96]

One particular manifestation of this critical and theoretical domination involves attempts to establish a canon of Native literature, or more often, to subsume it into a national literature and establish its worth within the national canon. Almost always that which is considered for canonization is the traditional orature of the People. Bierhorst, for example, saw his previously mentioned collection of oral literature recorded by non-Natives as a "first step" toward producing a canon of Native American literature, by which he means exclusively oral literature.[97] Similarly, Krupat examines the question of the American canon in *The Voice in the Margin*, hoping to make a case for the inclusion of Native orature, which he considers to be the only genuine Indian literature. In the penultimate chapter of the volume, he states most explicitly what until then he had left only implicit: "So far as the category of an Indian literature—and along with it the general category of local literature—may be useful, it would seem necessary to define it pretty exclusively by reference to the ongoing oral performances of Native peoples."[98]

There is much at work in this discussion of canon and orature. As a starting point, it is worth noting that the academic discipline of English developed in the colonial era, and it should be equally patent that Eurocentric attempts to define a canon since the nineteenth century have been "less a statement of the superiority of the Western tradition than a vital, active instrument of Western hegemony."[99] Limiting consideration or admission to the canon to orature is a way of continuing colonialism. It once again keeps American Indians from entering the twentieth century and denies to Native literary artists who chose other media any legitimate or "authentic" Native identity. In thus limiting Native literature to the oral tradition, non-Native critics and authors may be attempting, as Terry Goldie puts it in his study of Anglocolonial representation of indigenes, *Fear and Temptation*, "to make contact with [an] essential dynamism, a phenomenological presence of life." It is to seek a primitive time when, in Walter Ong's words, language was "a mode of action and not simply a countersign of thought"—when the word was truly performative.[100]

On the other hand, to insist, as Krupat and others do, on a "genuinely heterodox national canon" inclusive of American Indian literature (orature or otherwise) has equally undesirable implications.[101] It becomes equally an instrument of control as Eurocentric standards of judgment are employed to claim into the national canon only those works of which the *métropole* approves, those which best legitimate the existing social order.[102] "Indigenous writing has suffered many of the general historical problems of post-colonial writing, [including] being incorporated into the national literatures of the settler colonies as an 'extension' rather than as a separate discourse."[103] Such incorporation denies Native literature recognition of its distinct existence, specific differences, and independent status as literary production and, as Owens contends, retards consideration of Native works in their own cultural contexts.[104] Natives have never been great respecters of national borders. The very fact that Thomas King, E. Pauline Johnson, Peter Jones, and George Copway—among others—can be, and have been, claimed at various times and for various purposes as part of the national literatures of both the United States and Canada says something more important and complex is occurring in Native literature that merits special recognition as a separate discourse.[105]

Finally, by bringing Native literature into the canon of the United States, Krupat helps establish the indigeneity of Amer-European settler literature as part of a national literature rooted in the new soil of this continent. This quest for indigeneity has been a constant in settler colonies from their inception—from Hector St. John de Crèvecoeur boasting of the "new man" being born as colonists tilled the fields of North America to New Zealand poet Allen Curnow marveling at "something different, something nobody counted on" resulting from living in the new environment to Reinhold Niebuhr observing that in America "all the races of Europe were formed into a new amalgam of races, not quite Anglo-Saxon, but prevailingly European."[106] It validates attempts by Amer-Europeans, such as those of Jerome Rothenberg and the ethnopoetics movement, to incorporate or utilize indigenous forms and aesthetics as part of "an enriching cultural appropriation."[107] Begged, of course, is the question of precisely who is "enriched" and who diminished in the process.

For many non-Native scholars, literature by Indians ceases to be Indian literature when it employs the language of the colonizer and adopts Western literary forms such as the novel, short story, or autobiography. Krupat excludes from Indian literature (which he ultimately defines solely as orature) "writing influenced in very substantial degree by the central forms and genres of Western, or first world literature," thus removing from the category most, if not all, Native authors, including "Momaday, Silko and Forbes." Instead, he labels this "mixed breed literature" "*indigenous literature*."[108] Rather than, as we have argued should be the case, bringing all writings under the rubric of Native literature, the creation of this "in between" category fractures Native literary output. Though Krupat argues against essentialism and brings Natives to task for it, such an approach to literature is highly essentializing, seeing in most writing, what Vizenor terms "a descent from pure racial simulations."[109] James Ruppert, in his recent volume *Mediation in Contemporary Native American Fiction*, shares Krupat's cultural stasis assumption that the oral tradition forms the only pure Native American literature. Refusing to recognize literature by Indians as Native despite its form or genre, Ruppert writes, "The successful contemporary Native writer can create a text that merges delegitimizing influences while continuing oral traditional and culture. The text is *both substantially Native and substantially Western*"[110] David Murray, too, follows a Krupatian analysis. While still looking backward to the forms of the oral tradition, he does, however, ask, "How can the forms of white writing, not just autobiography but novels, poems and plays, be used to express and create Indian subjects (in all senses), and what role does the past play in this use?"[111]

Can one fracture Native literature in such a fashion and segregate orature as a more "pristine" Native literary type? Or isn't there still something "Indian" about it, regardless of its form or the language in which it speaks? Most Native writers and critics would vociferously disagree with the Krupatian formula. So would Goldie, who writes, "[I]s it possible for the [Native] writer to take a European form such as the novel and use it successfully to describe his or her own people? When this question has been addressed to me my usual reaction has been to attempt to deflect it. Regardless of Arnoldian claims for the freedom of the disinterested liberal critic, I question the right of any person to judge another's representation of his or her own culture."[112]

The poet Simon Ortiz argues against those who would see written literature as less than "authentic" Indian literature, maintaining, importantly, that the goal is what makes the difference. He writes, "The ways and methods have been important, but they are important only because of the reason for the struggle. And it is that reason—the struggle against colonialism—which has given substance to what is authentic. . . . This is the crucial item that has to be understood, that it is entirely possible for a people to retain and maintain their lives through the use of any language. There is not a question of authenticity here; rather it is the way that Indian people have creatively responded to forced colonization."[113] Whereas Paula Gunn Allen argues that novels by Indians are not, after all, Western in form but

Native, Ortiz sees no contradiction in being Native and employing Western forms of expression, speaking of "the creative ability of Indian people to gather in many forms of the socio-political colonizing force which beset them and make these forms meaningful in their own terms. . . . They are now Indian because of the creative development that the native people applied to them."[114] In this analysis, Ortiz follows Ngugi, who sees, in the indigenous use of the novel, a way of (re)connecting with the struggles of the people, stating, "The social or even national basis of the origins of an important discovery or invention is not necessarily a determinant of the use to which it can be put. . . . Perhaps the crucial question is not that of the racial, national, and class origins of the novel, but that of its development and the uses to which it is continually being put."[115]

Thomas King sees this "peculiar hybrid of antithetical cultures" (to use Rob Nieuwenhuys' phrase) as positive. As long as literature was oral and in Native languages it was inherently limited, but bilingualism (allophonia) and writing have opened the process and "helped to reinforce many of the beliefs that tribes have held individually, beliefs that tribes are now discovering they share mutually. While this has not, as yet, created what might be called a pan-Indian literature, the advent of written Native literature has provided Native writers with common structures, themes, and characters which can effectively express traditional and contemporary concerns about the world and the condition of living things."[116] Contrary to the critical arrogance of Krupat in his attempts at defining Indian written literature out of existence, King declares, "Whatever definition we decide on (if we ever do), the appearance of Native stories in a written form has opened up new worlds of imagination. . . ."[117]

Just as North American Natives have been no respecters of nation-state boundaries, so have they played with the "rules" of Western literary genre, says Clifford Trafzer. They have "used the written word to extend the boundaries of their own creativity into genres outside Indian oral tradition." According to Petrone, "[N]ative writers have borrowed from Western traditions the forms of autobiography, fiction, drama, and the essay. Their uses, however, judged by Western literary criteria of structure, style, and aesthetics, do not always conform. They are different because form is only the expression of the fabric of experience, and the experience of native writers has been different. Like the archetypal figure, the trickster [celebrated by Vizenor, King, and others], native writers easily adopt a multiplicity of styles and forms to suit their purposes, and in so doing they are giving birth to a new literature. . . ." They easily adopt and adapt the alien forms, and that new literature is still Indian without the essentialized need for beads and feathers.[118]

Murray rightly argues that Leslie Silko, in her novel *Ceremony*, fuses traditional myth with the novelistic form to assert a continuum from oral literature through to novels written in English.[119] Paula Gunn Allen notes that contemporary Native American fiction has two sides: the oral tradition and Western fiction and its antecedents. These "interact, wings of a bird in flight interact. They give shape to our experience. They signify."[120] Tom King labels the product of this interaction "interfusional literature," blending both the oral and the written.[121] But as Warrior cautions, "However much these writers are performing an activity somehow continuous with that of storytellers and singers, they are also doing what poetry [for example] has done in its European forms and in other non-European contexts."[122] In the end, it is a political issue and it may come down to a question of what Vizenor calls the "literature of dominance" versus the "literature of survivance" and which of these two opposing aesthetics Native writers serve.[123]

What may distinguish any people's literature from that of any other group is, as already noted, worldview. Although the rich diversity of Native cultures in the Americas makes it impossible to speak in a general, universalizing way about "things Indian," many believe that one can speak broadly of a worldview common to the indigenous peoples of the hemisphere. Several scholars, both Native and non-Native, have attempted to delineate the components of this worldview and discuss its importance both for Native literature and for Native community in general.

Louis Owens, quoting a 1979 observation of Michael Dorris notes that a requisite for Native literature is a reflection of "'a shared consciousness, an identifiable world-view.' More than a decade later, it seems there is indeed such a thing as Native American literature, and I would argue that it is found most clearly in novels written by Native Americans about the Native American experience. For, in spite of the fact that Indian authors write from very diverse tribal and cultural backgrounds, there is to a remarkable degree a shared consciousness and identifiable worldview reflected in novels by American Indian authors, a consciousness and worldview defined primarily by a quest for identity. . . ."[124] In a similar vein, LaVonne

Ruoff writes, "Divided into numerous cultural and language groups, native North Americans practiced many different religions and customs. However, there are some perspectives on their place in the universe that many native American groups shared and continue to share. . . . Although individual Indians today vary in the extent to which they follow tribal traditions, their worldviews and values continue to reflect those of their ancestors."[125] Thus it follows that the literatures they produce would reflect such worldviews and values.

The differences between this supposed, singular Native worldview and that of the West is often cited as a barrier to crosscultural understanding between Natives and Amer-Europeans. The historian Calvin Martin has cautioned modern-day non-Natives not to assume that the worldview of Natives is the same as that produced by the Enlightenment or that Natives operated (or operate) from the same motivations as Amer-Europeans.[126] Likewise, Rosemary Maxey writes, "Conveying ideas [to Amer-Europeans] in our common language of English is incomplete and misunderstood because of our differing world views, which remain largely unexplored and foreign to one another."[127] In point of fact, as in all colonial societies, the Indian as subaltern knows quite a lot about the mindset and psychological make-up of those in the dominant culture; only the reverse remains untrue.[128] Achiel Peelman agrees with Maxey but attributes the lack of understanding to more than linguistics, observing, "It is interesting to note . . . that a certain number of anthropologists are now convinced that the lack of studies of the Amerindian religious experience . . . is not related to the linguistic incompetency of the anthropologists, but to their inability to enter into the spiritual universe [i.e., worldview] of the Amerindians."[129]

Those who assert such a commonly held worldview differ markedly, however, on the components of it and how precisely it is to be characterized, reflecting more often their own social location and their individual, often highly romantic, perception of Native cultures than any pan-tribal reality. Deloria rests much of it in the spatial versus temporal orientation of Native peoples and in a view of time that is cyclical rather than linear. Owens refers to the "nonanthropocentric and ecologically oriented worldview of the Indian."[130] Sioui describes the "mentality" of Natives as shaped by the attachment to ancestral values and an "awareness that the cultural habits associated with those values have been suppressed in a completely illogical and unjust manner." For him, "this explains both the

Amerindians' singular awareness of their duty to remain, essentially, Amerindian, and the persistence of a particular ideological portrait."[131] James Treat refers to "foundational native values such as holism, equality, respect, harmony, and balance."[132] Ruoff lists "emphasis on the importance of living in harmony with the physical and spiritual universe, the power of thought and word to maintain this balance, a deep reverence for the land, and a strong sense of community."[133] While counseling that it is "difficult to generalize about Native American cultures and religions," Åke Hultkrantz nevertheless asserts: "Four prominent features in North American Indian religions are a similar worldview, a shared notion of cosmic harmony, emphasis on experiencing directly powers and visions, and a common view of the cycle of life and death."[134] The Carmodys suggest "a mythopoeic mentality, great influence from local physical conditions, a keen sensitivity to animals and plants, a rich sense of the spiritual world," and an prediliction for ritual.[135] Blair Schlepp and David Rausch discuss many of the previously named elements and add "respect for family, the preciousness of children, honoring the elderly, pride in craftsmanship, the value of working for a purpose with one's hands, listening to one's neighbor, being discrete [sic] (especially when another's honor and dignity are concerned), taking time to be introspective and contemplative about the mysteries of the universe, and valuing oral traditions that engender humbleness, sharing [sometimes characterized as an ethic of generosity], and laughter."[136] McPherson and Rabb add a belief in the integrity of the person.[137]

Although many Natives would affirm some or all of these components, it is legitimate nonetheless to inquire to what extent they reflect, on the one hand, generalized emotive and psychological factors held in common by many peoples around the world at one time or another and/or an essentialized Indian identity on the other. It is indisputable that worldview continues to be important for Natives as a source of personal and collective energy, identity, and values.[138] Because of the failure of Native cultures to recognize any split between sacred and secular spheres, this worldview remains essentially religious, involving the Native's deepest sense of self and undergirding tribal life, existence, and identity, just as the Creator undergirds all the created order.[139] However, Native religions—these shapers of worldview and identity—often differ from one another as drastically as Christianity differs from Buddhism or Judaism from Hinduism. Thus the worldviews they engender differ as well. It is not so much incorrect to refer to a single Native worldview as it is imprecise. M. A. Jaimes-Guerrero admits this when she states that Indian identity is derived from a sense of place—what Vine Deloria, Jr., and Jaimes-Guerrero term *geomythology*. Worldview and religion are thus "bioregional," varying with the natural environment in which they evolved.[140] McPherson and Rabb also acknowledge this diversity in the title of their pioneering university course, "Native Canadian World Views" (world*views* in the plural).[141] Regardless, these differing Native worldviews are different still from that formed by Western Enlightenment thought and values.

According to McPherson and Rabb, some would argue that it is not in the end "very interesting that different peoples have radically different world views. Such differences may be of interest to the anthropologist who is studying different peoples, but these differences do not cast any light on the nature of ultimate reality. . . ."[142] For McPherson and Rabb, the most virulent form of such an argument also includes a claim that Christianity (or modern Western science) "has given us the true picture of reality and hence that the primitive beliefs of mere savages (or heathens) ought to be discarded, by the savages themselves if they wish to cease being savages." The two authors refer to this argument with "deliberate disrepect" as the "save-the-savages argument."[143]

Christian missionaries did indeed come to save the "savages" from their lives of darkness, idolatry, ignorance, and sin. Louis Hall Karaniaktajeh, Mohawk, responds, "The missionaries say they brought God to America. Helpless God. Can't go anywhere by himself. Needs the missionaries to take him here and there. They say they're still bringing God to the jungles of South America and Africa."[144] Indeed, as Karaniaktajeh alludes, the process is one shared in common by all colonial societies and, in the case of the American Native, continues to this day. If Native cultures are viewed as inherently heathen and can be "mystified still further as some magical essence of the continent, then clearly there can be no meeting ground, no identity, between the social, historical creatures of Europe and the metaphysical alterity of the Calibans and Ariels [of Bermoothes]. If the difference between Europeans and the natives are so vast, then clearly . . . the process of civilizing the natives can continue indefinitely."[145]

Achiel Peelman concedes that non-Natives are mystified by Indians "clinging" to traditional religion while "assimilating" in other ways by borrowing Western technology and other material items. He writes, "They want the Amerindians to be successful in the field of education, politics and commerce, but, at the same time, they spontaneously wish that these 'civilized' Indians would proclaim at the end of the process: 'Now, we have become just like you. Thank you for your civilizing efforts!' But, usually, these 'civilized' Indians don't fall on their knees to thank their western educators."[146] Homer Noley makes clear that genuflection is not an option. Instead, Natives "forcefully express the desire to maintain and to enhance their cultural identity. They claim the right to be Indian *today* as members of the modern world and see the return to their traditional values as the best guarantee for their cultural survival."[147] Although this religious resurgence may be "fascinating and disconcerting" to Euro-Christians, it is "in many ways, a return to the positive content of American Indian identity, the content that makes some sense of the negative discriminatory experience of living as a Native in the U.S. in the late twentieth century." Robert Warrior is not alone in declaring it "one of the most important processes of contemporary American Indian history."[148] In this regard, Peelman again concedes, "Insofar as the suppression of traditional religions was one of the factors that contributed to the social collapse of the exploited and colonized peoples, the revitalization of their traditional religion, in the wake of the growing pressures of secularization and technology, has become an indispensable element in their integral development."[149]

In contrast to the dominant strains of Christianity, the various worldviews of Native cultures and religious tradition do not recognize a radical discontinuity between Creator and creation. As Deloria observes, a primary difference "between Indian tribal religions and Christianity would appear to be in the manner in which deity is popularly conceived. The overwhelming majority of American Indian religions refuse . . . to represent deity anthropomorphically."[150] The biblical witness depicts Yahweh as having inherently human characteristics, even if in the case of the deity these are portrayed as being somehow more than human: thus God is spoken of as not only possessing human emotions such as anger, pleasure, and love but is pictured as the personification of love itself. Many Christians have a felt need for a personal relationship with deity, particularly with the second person of the Trinity. Native religious traditions demonstrate no such interest in an intimacy with ultimate reality. There is also no intimation that the Creator has any different or special regard for human beings than for the rest of the created order. Natives cannot imagine a relationship with ultimate reality separate from all their other relationships that constitute personal and communal life. Nothing can stand apart from ultimate reality, and this reality is experienced in community. This is not, however, to divinize community. As Natives, Peelman correctly contends, "We can truly experience the supreme being once we have found our right place in the universe and once we have developed right relationships"—what in Old English theological language would have been called being *rightwised*.[151] This involves not only right relation between the human self and human others but between self and place.

Any discussion of Native theology must take into account these differences between Western and Native worldviews. It must take seriously these differences in concepts of deity, creation, the spatial orientation of Native peoples, and community. It must be inclusive, as Moises Colop, a Quiché Mayan, contends, not only of Christians but of the majority of Natives who adhere to either traditional or syncretic faiths, thus seeking to encompass—as much as possible—the entirety of Native community.[152]

In seeking such an expansive construct, the definition of theology itself need not be altered. Like philosophical metaphysics, the subject of theology is ultimate reality. It deals with the noumenal in a Kantian sense, asserting "that there is a dimension other than the material one generally recognized as real."[153] It is, as the etymology of the word suggests, "God talk." As McPherson and Rabb ask concerning metaphysics, "Is it really necessary to change the role of philosophy so drastically in order to show that the aboriginal peoples . . . have their own distinctive philosophy? We think not. . . . We see philosophy as the pursuit of truth, and it is in this more traditional sense of philosophy that we believe that [aboriginal people] have their own distinctive philosophy."[154] So it is with theology. The topic of theology is how humanity relates to ultimate reality. Natives define their identity in terms of community and relate to ultimate reality through that community. Thus a profoundly anthropological theology that takes the imperatives of Native community as its utmost goals is nonetheless theology in the strictest sense. Just as Colop can speak of an ecumenical Mayan theology, so one can speak of an evolving Native American theology.

Given the diversity of Indian cultures and worldviews, Native theology is what McPherson and Rabb call "polycentric." They explain this methodological approach as follows:

> This perspective, this polycentrism, recognizes that we finite human beings can never obtain a God's eye view, a non-perspectival view, of reality, of philosophical truth. Every view is a view from somewhere. Hence it follows that no one philosophical perspective can ever provide an entirely adequate metaphysical system. But this does not mean . . . that philosophical systems do not point toward truth, that they have nothing to say about truth. It merely follows that no one perspective can contain the whole truth. Although [Thomas W.] Overholt and [J. Baird] Callicott are on the right track when they say that "no culture's world is privileged in respect to truth," they are wrong to think that this fact leads to relativism. The fact that different cultures can have radically different world views reveals something very interesting not just about cultures, not just about language, but about reality itself and the way in which we can come to know it. Though none is privileged[,] yet each culture's world view, each different metaphysical system, contributes something to the total picture, a picture which is not yet and may ever be wholly complete. Such is the polycentric perspective.[155]

Though there can never be a "supercultural platform to which we might repair,"[156] and though no culture's worldview can be privileged in any universal sense, it can and must be privileged *for that particular culture.*

Ultimate reality, which we see through a looking glass darkly, is like a child's kaleidoscope. How it is perceived depends upon how the cylinder is held, even though the bits of glass forming the picture are unchanging. The task must be to learn as much as one can not only about the given pattern but about the individual bits of glass, so that when the cylinder is shaken we can know something about the new image when it forms. In his essay, "An American Indian Theological Response to Ecojustice," George Tinker alludes to a story that illustrates the polycentric approach. Imagine two Indian communities who live in close proximity to each other, separated by a mountain. A non-Native visitor arrives at the first community. In the course of the stay, she is informed that the tribe's council fire is the center of the universe, and creation myths are told to demonstrate this fact. The following day, the outlander and representatives of the first tribe travel to the other community. The elders of the new tribe declare that their council fire is the center of the universe, and the members of the first nod their assent. Confused, the visitor asks her host, "I thought you said that your fire was the center." The Indian replies, "When we're there, that is the center of the universe. When we are here, this is the center." Tinker concludes, "Sometimes a single truth is not enough to explain the balance of the world around us. . . . Yet we need communal stories that can generate 'functional' mythologies, that will undergird the life of the community (the lives of communities) in new and vibrant ways."[157] We need to examine as many different cultural codes as we can to re-create the structures of human life—self, community, spirit, and the world as we perceive it. Speaking to this point, Goldie quotes Stephen Muecke from *Reading the Country: Introduction to Nomadology*: "Within the issue of Aboriginal sovereignty there is more at stake than the use of lands; there is the right to control the production of [the nation's] mythologies."[158]

Paul Knitter, discussing the work of Sri Lankan thinker Aloysius Pieris, writes, "To *advocates of interreligious dialogue and pluralism*, Pieris voices the 'hermeneutic of suspicion' that perhaps all their conferences, their scholarly and mystico-ritual encounters, might be serving as a holy smoke screen behind which they are avoiding, unconsciously, the harsh realities of poverty, injustice, and exploitation—and perhaps even their own religious complicity in such realities. Is dialogue being practiced on mountaintops by a privileged holy remnant of scholars and mystics, while the masses are left in the valleys to dialogue with malnutrition and disease and lack of land."[159] I would contend that such questions are even more germane to the ongoing colonial situation of American Natives than they are to the situation in Asia. Are we, by our work, merely contributing to the ever-accelerating process of creating a rainforest society in which canopy dwellers live a privileged existence in the treetops while others are left scuttling along and fending for themselves on the floor below?

Five centuries of ongoing colonialism in America, as in other colonial societies, has led to an erosion of self and community due to the dislocation resulting from cultural denigration, enslavement, forced migration, and fostered dependency.[160] This has led to tremendous grief among Native peoples, not unlike the Korean concept of *han*.[161] Speaking of his conversations on the subject with Jake Swamp, the Mohawk leader, Philip Arnold writes, "[G]rief clogs one's throat with a lump so large that genuine speech is obstructed, grief blocks the ears so hearing is impaired, and clouds one's eyes with tears making vision and future sight blurred." Swamp avers that "with the abolition of grief there will come a clearing of the human heart and mind."[162] For Native Americans, as for Koreans, grief can never be finally "abolished." Any Native scholarship or intellectual work must, however, take the ongoing and continual healing of this grief—what Noley and Mary Churchill call a sense of exile and others term a consciousness of removal—as both a goal and a starting point.[163] It must expand the definition of liberation to include survival. Natives engaged in literary production participate in this healing process.

It has been suggested that Native writers are primarily engaged in an act of cultural mediation. Treat writes, "These writings [by Native Christian theologians], like many other types of contemporary native literature, cross cultural boundaries in order to facilitate intercultural understanding and respect and to effect structural change; they are cross-cultural epistles to the cross culture."[164] Greg Sarris, in a similar vein, declares:

> My discussions and stories . . . contribute to current discussions regarding reading of American Indian literatures in particular and cross-cultural literatures in general. . . . What makes written literatures cross-cultural depends as much on their content and production as on their being read by a particular reader or community of readers. Many Americans from marginal cultures with specific languages and mores write in a particular variety of English or integrate their culture-specific language with an English that makes their written works accessible in some measure to a large English-speaking readership. These writers mediate not only different languages and narrative forms, but, in the process, the cultural experiences they are representing, which become the content of their work. Their work represents a dialogue between themselves and different cultural norms and forms and also, within their text, between, say, characters or points of view. This cross-cultural interaction represented by the texts is extended to readers, many of whom are unfamiliar with the writers' particular cultural experiences and who must, in turn, mediate between what they encounter in the texts and what they know from their specific cultural experiences.[165]

This theme of cultural mediation has been taken up by a number of non-Native critics, notably Margaret Connell Szasz, Dorothy R. Parker, James Ruppert, and David Murray.[166] Ruppert, in particular, devotes an entire volume to the topic—*Mediation in Contemporary Native American Fiction*. Defining *mediation* as "an artistic and conceptual standpoint, constantly flexible, which uses the epistemological frameworks of Native American and Western cultural traditions to illuminate and enrich each other," he declares, "Whether by blood or experience, Native Americans today, especially writers, express a mixed heritage." He continues: "As old and isolating world views give rise to new ones, the writer acts out his or her role as mediator-creator."[167] Like Ruppert, Murray focuses on mediation in his book, *Forked Tongues: Speech, Writing, and Representation in North American Indian Texts*, writing: "By paying attention to the mediator . . . rather than what he is pointing to, or in other words by concentrating on the various forms of cultural and linguistic mediation which are always taking place, we reduce the danger of making the space between the two sides into an unbridgeable chasm or turning differences into Otherness."

The concern with getting rid of "old and isolating world views" and "unbridgeable chasm[s]" has always been more of a concern for Amer-Europeans than for Natives, who do not view their own cultural responses as "old and isolating" and who often express scant interest in bridging their worldview with that of the dominant culture. It becomes another way of asserting Western universalism against Native peoples. Ruppert quotes Vizenor:

> Métis earthdivers waver and forbear extinction in two worlds. Métis are the force in the earthdiver metaphor, the tension in the blood and the uncertain word, the imaginative and compassionate trickster on street corners in the cities. When the mixedblood earthdiver summons the white world to dive like the otter and beaver and muskrat in search of earth, and federal funds, he is both animal and trickster, both white and tribal, the uncertain creator in an urban metaphor based on a creation myth that preceded him in two world views and oral traditions.[168]

Ruppert's argument is perhaps strongest with regard to Vizenor, who more so than any other Native writer champions mixed-blood (crossblood/Métis) identity. Even so, he champions these crossblood people *as Indians*.

According to Ruppert, seeing Native literature as "between cultures" is a romantic and victimist perspective. It is better, he contends, to see them as participating in two cultures. Such a stance ignores, again in a universalizing manner, the fact that colonized persons, particularly crossbloods, feel themselves in precisely that unstable location, at once liminal and littoral to two ways of being and knowing. Nieuwenhuys writes of the "emotional confusion" this can engender, describes both himself and others similarly situated as "between two 'homelands,'" and speaks of the "insecurity" shared by those "forced to live between two worlds."[169] Many North American Natives express this same experience. Leonard Crow Dog, a traditional and a peyotist, spoke of the difficulty felt by many Native Christians: "Indian Christians have a very hard time these days as they are caught between two ways of seeing the world."[170] Mourning Dove, writing in the second decade of the twentieth century, describes both herself and her title character in *Cogewea, the Half-Blood* in extreme terms, wondering if there is any place for the "'breed'!—the socially ostracized of two races." "[W]e are between two fires," she writes, "the Red and the White. . . . We are maligned and traduced as no one but we of the despised 'breeds' can know. If permitted, I would prefer living the white man's way to that of the reservation Indian, but he hampers me. I appreciate my meagre education, but I will *never* disown my mother's blood. Why should I do so? Though my skin is of the tawny hue, I am not ashamed."[171] And Owens notes that much Indian fiction reflects a "fragmented sense of self . . . characters who truly find themselves between two realities and wondering which world and life might be theirs."[172] At the same time, however, Owens notes, "Repeatedly in Indian fiction . . . we are shown the possibility of recovering a centered sense of personal identity and significance."[173]

Unquestionably, mediation occurs in Native literatures. The need to appeal and be accessible to a wide readership in order to be published necessitates this. Likewise, it is also true that a knowledge of the cultural codes of the writer leads to a fuller understanding. Ruppert writes as an Amer-European about Native literature, so mediation becomes important to him as an entry point. What, however, about the Native reader? Is there not also something much more intimate going on than cultural mediation? Ruppert is correct that Native authors write for two or three different audiences (local, pan-Indian, metropolitan), but he ignores that in this process such authors most often privilege the Native reader. As David Murray notes, in attempting to categorize and critique Indian literatures, he may be "ignoring the fact that . . . what may be read as derivative Romanticism within a white context may also have stronger and more complex reverberations within relevant Indian cultures."[174] Vizenor's updated trickster stories, by Ruppert's own admission, "place Native American perceptions in a modern framework to delight Native audiences."[175] Simon Ortiz says he writes for "[a]nybody, but maybe Indian people particularly since I always try to focus upon the relationships among us all."[176] And Paula Gunn Allen, who is herself both a critic and a novelist, states that Indian writers often add secondary elements to their intrinsically Native story in order to satisfy a metropolitan audience who will understand and expect them.[177] Thomas King stakes out a more radical position, claiming, "I really don't care about the white audiences. They don't have an understanding of the intricacies of Native life, and I don't think they're much interested in it, quite frankly."[178] Thus the very hybridity of the work, argues Owens, is subversive. The Indian reader becomes the insider, privileged and empowered. The *métropole* is pushed to the periphery, made liminal, at best littoral, in the same way that a non-Native town may exist on the border of a reservation.[179]

The non-Native critic Petrone observes:

> The literature of [North America's] native peoples has always been quintessentially political, addressing their persecutions and betrayals and summoning their resources for resistance. The political dimension is an inherent part of their writing because it is an inherent part of their lives. Debasing experiences reflecting new realities of political and social change created by changing contact situations—suicide, alcoholism, self-destructive behaviour, poverty, family violence, disintegration of the extended family, and the breach between generations—are real problems in the lives and tragedies of Indians today all across the [continent]. The presentation of these lives in poetry, short fiction, novel, drama, and memoir constitutes a political comment. Native writers tell what they see, what they have experienced or are experiencing. They tell what it is like to live as an Indian in today's society, increasingly caught between tradition and mainstream culture.[180]

In this way they are active not only on their own behalf but on that of Native people in general.[181]

A feature that cuts across various Native worldviews is the importance of community. The need for collective survival in diverse, often quite harsh, environments naturally led to such an emphasis. Such an emphasis, as Deloria points out, means that "Indian tribes are communities in fundamental ways that other American communities or organizations are not. Tribal communities are wholly defined by family relationships, whereas non-Indian communities are defined primarily by residence or by agreement with sets of intellectual beliefs."[182] Among the Cherokees, this commitment manifests itself in the *Kituwha* spirit. The historian William McLoughlin summarizes the elements of *Kituwha* as "loyalty to each other, concern for the spiritual power in their way of life, and their insistence upon the importance of tribal unity and harmony."[183] D'Arcy McNickle vividly captured this Native sense of community, in *Wind from an Enemy Sky*, in a single brief sentence: "A man by himself was nothing but a shout in the wind."

Although some, like Reinhold Niebuhr, have questioned whether autochthonous cultures possess community, it is, in fact, the highest value to Native peoples and fidelity to it is a primary responsibility.[184] Although curiously phrased in the past tense—once again relegating Natives to a fast-receding history—Carmody and Carmody are nonetheless correct when they write, "Nothing stood higher in native American conception than the well-being of one's people."[185] Thomas King, himself a Cherokee, declares that the "most important relationship in Native cultures is the relationship which humans share with each other, a relationship that is embodied within the idea of community. Community, in a Native sense, is not simply a place or a group of people." King agrees with novelist Louise Erdrich that it is a place which has been "inhabited for generations," where "the landscape becomes enlivened by a sense of group and family history."[186]

This linkage of land and people within the concept of community, reflecting the spatial orientation of Native peoples, is crucial. Warrior terms *community* and *land* "central critical categories."[187] As Geary Hobson states, "These are the kinds of relationships we must never forget. Our land is our strength, our people the land, one and the same, as it always has been and always will be."[188] When Natives are removed from their traditional lands, they are robbed of more than territory; they are deprived of numinous landscapes that are central to their faith and their identity, lands populated by their blood relations, ancestors, animals, and beings both physical and mythological. A kind of psychic homicide is committed.

Native religious traditions reflect and reinforce this collectivity and remain a primary factor of social integration in Native community. Whereas Christianity is a metareligion, rooted in a fixed sacred written text, the survival of Native religions depend largely "on the willingness of community members to participate in their ongoing realization. The fact that we now find more and more published studies of Amerindian religions does not change this situation."[189] Historically, this lack of a "book" has led non-Natives to view indigenous religious traditions as "inadequate." David Thompson, writing in the 1840s, states: "The sacred Scriptures to the Christian; the Koran to the Mohametan give a steady belief to the mind, which is not the case with the Indian, his idea on what passes in this world is tolerable correct so far as his senses and reason can inform him; but after death all is wandering conjecture taken up on tradition, dreams and hopes."[190] However, as Paula Gunn Allen notes:

> The tribes do not celebrate the individual's ability to feel emotion, for they assume that all people are able to do so. One's emotions are one's own; to suggest that others should imitate them is to impose on the personal integrity of others. The tribes seek—through song, ceremony, legend, sacred stories (myths), and tales—to embody, articulate, and share reality, to bring the isolated, private self into harmony and balance with this reality, to verbalize the sense of majesty and reverent mystery of all things, and to actualize . . . those truths that give to humanity its greatest significance and dignity.[191]

The closest tribal approximation of *sin* in the Christian lexicon is a failure to fulfill one's responsibilities to the community. Conversely, there is generally no concept of *salvation* beyond the continuance of the community. The Sun Dance, practiced by numerous Plains tribes (and increasingly in a pan-Indian context), is illustrative. It is generally said to be performed "that the People might live."

This is not to say that there is no place for individuation in Native society. McPherson and Rabb refer to the "integrity of person" as an element of their generic Native worldview. The self is the locus where tribal values become concrete. The psychoanalyst Erik Erikson developed his theories of stages in psychosocial development of the individual from his work with the Sioux and Yurok.[192] It is simply, as anthropologist Clifford Geertz reminds, that "the Western conception of the person as a bounded, unique, more or less integrated motivational and cognitive universe, a dynamic center of awareness, emotion, judgement, and action organized into a distinctive whole and set contrastively both against other such wholes and against its social and natural background, is . . . a rather peculiar idea within the context of the world's cultures."[193] Native societies are synecdochic (part-to-whole) rather than metonymic (part-to-part), as in the Western world. Donald Fixico notes that Natives tend to see themselves in terms of "self in society" rather than "self and society"[194] It is what Allen refers to as a "greater self" and McPherson calls an "enlarged sense of self."[195] It is in a profound sense a mentality that declares, "I am We."

This oneness "transcends linear time, life, and death."[196] It encompasses what I term the "wider community" that includes all the created order, which is also characterized in kinship terms. No sharp distinction is drawn between the human and non-human persons that make up the community. Thus the Lakota precatory punctuation *mitakuye oyasin*, translated as "all my relations," includes not only one's family nor even all human beings but, as well, "the web of kinship extending to the animals, to the birds, to the fish, to the plants, to all animate and inanimate forms that can be seen or imagined. More than that, 'all my relations' is an encouragement for us to accept the responsibilities we have within this universal family by living in a harmonious and moral manner (a common admonishment is to say of someone that they act as if they have no relations)."[197]

Such an embrace of the universe stands in marked contrast to the dominant streams of Christianity. Carmody and Carmody declare that "it is hard to deny that Christianity lost something precious when it took over the biblical polemic against the fertility gods of the Canaanites and separated God from the cosmos." Peelman, picking up the theme, delineates, "It is also important to note that the radical separation between God and the cosmos in western thinking is also the origin of a series of other dualisms or separations which have profoundly influenced Roman Catholic and Protestant theology: cosmos-history, nature-grace, body-spirit, profane-sacred, world-church, individual-society, man-woman."[198] Native traditions suffer from no such dualistic thinking and thus have "not become the victim of the . . . reduction which characterizes western theology when it moved from its cosmocentric to its anthropocentric vision of reality."[199]

The necessity of community permeates every aspect of Native life, including epistemology. Christopher Ronwanièn:te Jocks argues, "Knowledge without a supportive community to effect it is useless; it is, in some sense, undefined. Until [one] is surrounded by that supportive community, knowledge is not defined because [the knower] is not defined as a human being. Thus knowledge requires a network of knowers, or more accurately, of actors. Knowledge is something you do; not a preexisting tool independent of the person holding it, nor of the uses to which it might be put."[200] Leslie Silko states the same point somewhat differently when she says, "[S]tory makes . . . community" We must have stories, since that is how "you know; that's how you belong; that's how you know you belong."[201]

The importance of story for Natives cannot be overestimated. As Vizenor writes, "Native American Indian identities are created in stories, and the names are essential to a distinctive personal nature, but memories, visions, and the shadows of heard stories are the paramount verities of a tribal presence. . . . Tribal consciousness would be a minimal existence without active choices, the choices that are heard in stories and mediated in names; otherwise, tribal identities might be read as mere simulations of remembrance."[202] Language and narrative have tremendous power to create community. Indeed, it may be that the People may not have life outside of stories, their existence contingent upon the telling and hearing of communal stories. Elsewhere, Vizenor quotes Jean-François Lyotard— "the people do not exist as a subject but as a mass of millions of insignificant and serious little stories that sometimes let themselves be collected together to constitute big stories and sometimes disperse into digressive elements."[203] Two examples testify to this tremendous power of story, at once formative and transformative.

Alister McGrath, in *Evangelicalism and the Future of Christianity*, recalls attending a lecture by a Kiowa Apache from Oklahoma, who learned the story of his people when a young boy. McGrath relates the talk:

> One day, just after dawn, his father woke him and took him to the home of an elderly Kiowa woman. He left him there, promising to return to collect him that afternoon. All that day the woman told this young boy the story of the Kiowa people. She told him of his origins

by the Yellowstone River and how they then migrated southward. She told him of the many hardships they faced—the wars with other Native American nations and the great blizzards on the winter plains. She told him of the glories of the life of the Kiowa nation—the great buffalo hunts, the taming of wild horses and the skill of the braves as riders. Finally she told him of the coming of the white man and the humiliation of their once-proud nation at the hands of the horse soldiers who forced them to move south to Kansas, where they faced starvation and poverty. Her story ended as she told him of their final humiliating confinement within a reservation in Oklahoma. . . . [S]hortly before dark, his father returned to collect him. "When I left that house, I was a Kiowa," he declared. He had learned the story of his people. He knew what his people had been through and what they stood for. Before learning the family history, he had been a Kiowa in name only; now he was a Kiowa in reality.[204]

Barre Toelken similarly relates a conversation he had with Tacheeni Scott, a Navajo, about the "sustaining function" of story: "Why tell the stories? 'If my children hear the stories, they will grow up to be good people; if they don't hear them, they will turn out to be bad.' Why tell them to adults? 'Through the stories everything is made possible.'"[205]

Thus, many contemporary Natives "understand clearly that they are part of today's world but that their tribal traditions, languages, ceremonies, and stories create a relationship to this land that is unmatched by others. Their relationship is with each other as a *community* and with places, plants and animals. Their relationship forms a legacy, and they have a future that is based on past experience. Story is the magic that ties all of these themes and ideas together."[206] As Paula Gunn Allen states, "It becomes clear, therefore, that oral literature must be aproached from the *religious*, social, and literary traditions that influence them."[207]

Contemporary Native writers continue, supplement, and expand the oral tradition, nourishing it while being nourished by it.[208] They help modern-day Natives apprehend and navigate their world just as traditional orature helped their ancestors understand their own. As Clifford Trafzer puts it, "Contemporary Native American writers draw on [the oral] tradition to tell new tales that mirror their survival and continued presence in this country today."[209] They "write out of tribal traditions, and into them."[210]

Thus even as Tom King tells new pan-tribal trickster stories, he acknowledges that he was influenced by traditional storytellers like Harry Robinson.[211] Or as Paula Gunn Allen contends, after its formative period came to a close in 1970, Native fiction "came to resemble traditional Native Narrative more and more while the voice, tone, and style ever more closely replicated a communal voice: multiple, integral, and accretive."[212] Native literatures are dialogic texts that both reflect and shape Native identity and community.[213]

The issue of a communal voice is of vital importance. It is undeniably true, as Larzer Ziff declared, "The process of literary annihilation [a process continuous with, a collaboration conscious or unconscious with, physical extermination] would be checked only when Indian writers began representing their own culture."[214] Narrative is a means that colonized people employ to assert their own existence and identity. The struggle may be over land and sovereignty, but it is often reflected, contested, and decided in narrative.[215] Traditional stories, however, are communal. They belong to the People and define the People—the community—as a whole. In contrast to "the heroes of Western literature who exemplify rugged individualism, the culture heroes in [traditional] Native American literature act to benefit the larger community by bringing power to the people, slaying monsters that have terrorized villages, or bringing a lasting contribution to the people, such as corn, tobacco, or salmon." Reflecting this communal identity-producing role, stories developed communally as well. The notion of a story with a single author, especially one who then has a proprietary right in the act of his or her creation, would have struck pre-Columbian Natives as absurd.[216] As Owens observes, "The privileging of the individual necessary for the conception of the modern novel . . . is a more radical departure for American Indian cultures than for the Western world as a whole, for Foucault's 'moment of individualization' represents an experience forced harshly, and rather unsuccessfully, upon Native Americans."[217]

To be a storyteller in traditional society is to be "one who participates in a traditionally sanctioned manner in *sustaining the community*."[218] Instead, contemporary writers are self-appointed. Paula Gunn Allen recalls being questioned by John Rouillard, a Santee Dakota, about this status and the Western literary forms employed at a seminar on Indian literature. She remembers, "Every Indian in the room who engaged in these activities [writing] had to ask whether we were really Indian. Maybe not, if we were writers. We had to ask ourselves if we were traitors to our Indianness. Maybe we were so assimilated, so un-Indian, that we were doing white folks' work and didn't realize it!"[219] Elizabeth Cook-Lynn also discusses the dilemma for herself as poet, novelist, and scholar, saying:

> The idea that poets can speak for others, the idea that we can speak for the dispossessed, the weak, the voiceless, is indeed one of the great burdens of contemporary American Indian poets today, for it is widely believed that we "speak for our tribes." The frank truth is that I don't know very many poets who say, "I speak for my people." It is not only unwise; it is probably impossible, and it is very surely arrogant, for *We Are Self-Appointed* and the self-appointedness of what we do indicates that the responsibility is ours and ours alone.[220]

To be a writer is to enter a kind of privileged class, educated, separated somehow from the community. Louis Owens contends that Native writers recover authenticity by incorporation and invocation of the oral tradition in their texts.[221] Putting aside the issue of the general truth of this assertion, it nonetheless remains that to put one's authorial signature on a text is to immediately put oneself outside the oral tradition and community.

I would contend that the self-appointed status of the writer is, and must be, one of those things that makes us understand our accountability to Native community. Geary Hobson notes the "deep sense of obligation" Native writers feel toward their communities. Owens states that they write with a "consciousness of responsibility as a member of a living Native American culture" and community. Trafzer considers community "the center of the universe" for Native writers, whose work "reflects the relationship of their community with place."[222] Hobson concludes, "Literature, in all its forms, oral as well as written, is our most durable way of carrying on this continuance [of the People]. By making literature, like the singers and storytellers of earlier times, we serve the people as well as ourselves in an abiding sense of remembrance."[223] Communal, identity-producing potential exists in any contemporary Native text. Gerald Vizenor concurs: "Native American Indian authors have secured the rich memories of tribal generations on this continent; the diverse narratives of these crossblood authors would uncover the creative humor of survivance and tribal counterpoise to the literature of dominance."[224]

It is not an "immemorial . . . and static" character that has been the strength of Native culture and community but, rather, its lability—its "persistence [and] vivacity" as Natives themselves change but remain Native nevertheless.[225] As Warrior claims for Vine Deloria, Jr., and John Joseph Mathews, "Both contend in their work that the success or failure of American Indian communal societies has always been predicated not upon a set of uniform, unchanging beliefs, but rather upon a commitment to the groups and the groups' futures."[226] Not to be committed to Native American community, affirming the tribes, the people, the values, is tantamount to psychic suicide. It is to lose the self in the dominant mass humanity, either ceasing to be or persisting merely as another ethnic minority, drifting with no place, no relations, no real people.[227]

I would contend that the single thing that most defines Indian literatures relates to this sense of community and commitment to it. It is what I term *communitism*. *Communitism*, or its adjectival form *communitist*, is a neologism of my own devising. Its coining is necessary because no other word from the Latin roots *communis* or *communitas*—communitarian, communal, communist, etc.—carries the exact sense necessary. It is formed from a combination of the words *community* and *activism* or *activist*.[228] Literature is communitist to the extent that it has a proactive commitment to Native community, including the wider community. In communities that have too often been fractured and rendered dysfunctional by the effects of more than five hundred years of colonialism, to promote communitist values means to participate in the healing of the grief and sense of exile felt by Native communities and the pained individuals in them. It is, to borrow from Homi K. Bhabha, "community envisaged as a project—at once a vision and a construction—that takes you 'beyond' yourself in order to return, in a spirit of revision and reconstruction, to the political *conditions* of the present."[229]

Linda Hogan testifies to this healing when she titles a volume of her poetry *The Book of Medicines*.[230] Joy Harjo has declared, "To write, the act of writing, of witnessing means taking part in the healing of the people. . . . [A] few hundred years ago, aboriginal peoples were one hundred per cent of the population of this continent. Now we're one-half of one percent of the total population! . . . [W]hy wouldn't Native writers write about disruption and disorientation? And, of course, the resolution is through reassertion of tribal self. . . . The writer has to turn to that which is nourishing, has to make sense of a senseless history."[231] Such healing is both personal and collective. Luci Tapahonso describes writing as a vehicle for reversing the diaspora begun after European invasion: "For many people in my situation, residing away from my homeland, writing is the means for returning, rejuvenation, and for restoring our spirits to the state of 'hohzo,' or beauty, which is the basis of Navajo philosophy."[232] Speaking of the responsibility of Native writers and intellectuals in the process of healing, Robert Warrior writes, "In the concrete materiality of experience, we see both the dysfunctions colonization has created for Indian communities and the ways Indian people have attempted to endure those dysfunctions." He concludes:

> The primary responsibility we face . . . is simply to speak about contemporary Indian lives and understand the ways in which, in the words of Simon Ortiz, "this America has been a burden" to us as human beings. To embrace traditions without taking seriously the path over which we trod toward that embrace is to deny our own selves. In refusing to engage in that kind of denial, we confront both the power of our traditions and the painful stories of Native people who have suffered and continue to suffer, people whose ways of survival present us with the terrible beauty of resistance that rarely finds a voice in Native political processes.[233]

As in Kanafani's resistance literature, writing becomes an essential means of struggle—in the Native case, of celebrating what Warrior calls the "fragile miracle of survival."[234] In seeking to support Native peoples' struggle to be self-defining (for Sioui, the essence of autohistory; for McPherson, the rejection of outside view predicates), and to have representational autonomy, Indian writers are engaged in an act contiguous with the struggle of Other intellectuals around the world. It is one of, in the words of Elizabeth Cook-Lynn, "defiance born of the need to survive," and, as Simon Ortiz says, "it is an act that defies oppression."[235] Gerald Vizenor declares, "The postindian warriors encounter their enemies with the same courage in literature as their ancestors once evinced on horses, and they create their stories with a new sense of survivance."[236] They are engaged in a quest for a liberative perspective in which Natives can see themselves in relationship to each other and to community.[237] What Ruppert observed with regard to modern Native fiction could be said of all

Native literatures: they are "literature with a purpose."[238] Writing prepares the ground for recovery, and even recreation, of Indian identity and culture. Native writers speak to that part of us the colonial power and the dominant culture cannot reach, cannot touch. They help Indians imagine themselves as Indians. Just as there is no practice of Native religions for personal empowerment, they write that the People might live.

In putting forward the concept of communitism, however, I am not suggesting a facile notion of authorial intent. How a given work is received, consumed, appropriated, by Native community is part of the work itself. It helps complete the process. Communitism is, as the word itself implies, communal. It is part of a shared quest for belonging, a search for community. It is the valorization of Native community and values and a commitment to them that may be, in part, politically unconscious.[239] In addition, according to Bhabha, "historical agency is transformed through the signifying process. . . . the historical event is represented in a discourse that is *somehow beyond control*. This is in keeping with Hannah Arendt's suggestion that the author of social action may be the initiator of its unique meaning, but as agent he or she cannot control its outcome. It is not simply what the house of fiction contains or 'controls' *as content*."[240]

In this shared quest, Native writers may not always agree on either the means or meaning of communitism. Community is a primary value, but today we exist in many different kinds of community—reservation, rural village, urban, tribal, pan-Indian, traditional, Christian. Many move back and forth between a variety of these communities.[241] Our different locations—physical, mental, and spiritual—will inevitably lead to different conceptions of what survival, liberation, and communitism require. An examination of different Native writers in different eras shows that this has always been the case since the arrival of Europeans.[242]

Robert Warrior, at the close of his book *Tribal Secrets*, offers his own communitist vision: "Our struggle at the moment is to continue to survive and work toward a time when we can replace the need for being preoccupied with survival with a more responsible and peaceful way of living within communities and with the ever-changing landscape that will ever be our only home."[243] In the meantime, as Deloria proclaims, our work "must certainly involve a heady willingness to struggle for both long and short term goals and at times simply for the joy of getting one's nose bloodied while blackening the other guy's eye. . . . It is the solitary acknowledgement that the question of [human] life and identity is to let the bastards know you've been there and that it is always a good day to die. We are therefore able to live."[244]

CHAPTER TWO

TRICKSTER AMONG THE WORDIES

The Work of Gerald Vizenor

*He looked like a white Indian. . . . He had a slow walk like a som-
nambulist enmeshed in the past and unable to walk into the present.
He was so loaded with memories, cast down by them. . . . He saw
only the madness of the world. . . .*

*This fatalistic man, emerging from the depths of his past with
intolerably open eyes, offered the world first of all an appearance of
legendary elegance. . . . He himself passed invisibly, untouched,
unattainable, giving at no time any proof of reality: no stain, tear,
sign of wear and death coming. It seemed rather as if death had
already passed, that he had died already to all the friction and usage
of life, been pompously buried with all his possessions, dressed in
his finest clothes, and was now walking through the city merely to
warn us.*

ANAÏS NIN,
Under a Glass Bell

It's tough being an Indian in this country. For those on reservations, the
average yearly income is half the poverty level, and infant mortality runs
at three times the national rate. The average life expectancy hovers in the
forties.

For those living in the cities, the difficulties are a little different. The
high unemployment, drug and alcohol abuse, and other problems are still
there. But in urban areas, Native peoples, America's forgotten minority,

are at their most invisible. With only fifteen thousand Indians living in metropolitan New York, for example, it is easy to get swallowed up.

If you live in the city and work in whitestream culture, to folks back home you risk being a White Indian—an Apple (the Indian equivalent of an "oreo," Red on the outside and White on the inside), an Uncle Tomahawk. To non-Natives you are often little more than a muddy-complected White. They look at you strangely if you say that it smells like rain or that green clouds mean hail. And it's best for all that you never teach anyone how to call squirrels.

I made all those mistakes in the more than twenty years that I lived in New York as one of the roughly two-thirds of the nation's Natives who live in cities. They are usually mixed-blood. They are detached from the land and from their tribes. Often they have no tribal status at all. And though to the undiscerning eye, they may be indistinguishable from the population at large, they still go to jail in disproportionate numbers, earn less, and die younger. Gerald Vizenor's work touches these urban Indians' lives in special ways. Two of his recent novels, *Dead Voices* and *Hotline Healers*, demonstrate why.

Vizenor, a mixed-blood Anishinaabe and a professor of American Studies at the University of California, Berkeley, is one of Native America's most prolific and protean authors. He has worked as a journalist, and published seven novels, an autobiography, and numerous volumes of short stories, criticism, and poetry. He is widely considered one of the best writers of haiku in the United States.

Not only does he understand and speak to the modern Native's situation, both on and off the reservation, but he brings to it a fierce Native wit most often absent from the work of contemporaries like N. Scott Momaday, Leslie Marmon Silko, or James Welch. He is also the Native author most drawn to postmodernism. In his novels and short stories, intertextuality and word play abound. For him the postmodern is the tribal, a mirror of oral storytelling. Linear narrative is rejected in favor of stories within stories, digressions within digressions, and abrupt flashbacks. Satire is seen as a perfectly legitimate expression of contemporary existence.

In all his work, he uncompromisingly champions the identity of mixed-blood Indians, whom he calls "crossbloods."

Dead Voices and *Hotline Healers* are Vizenor's antidote to "plastic medicine men." These spiritual hucksters, like the late Sun Bear or SwiftDeer Reagan, peddle a mixture of real and fraudulent spiritual tradition to unsuspecting non-Natives. Sweat lodges for $100! Vision quests only $250!

The "dead voices" are those heard by non-Natives. Divorced from nature, they have lost the stories that liberate the mind and hold the world together. Now they are only "wordies," hearing the dead voices of the printed page and the university lecture. The results are disastrous both for their personal lives and for the environment.

On the other hand, Bagese, the shaman heroine of *Dead Voices*, hears great stories. She and the book's unnamed crossblood narrator (a university lecturer in "tribal philosophies") play the wanaki chance, a meditation game in which the participants actually become animals by entering into their images on tarotlike cards.

Through the wanaki, the pair become bears, fleas, mantises, crows, and beavers. Unlike the urban-dwelling Natives, these animals live tribally. Yet, hunted, exterminated, and captured for study by scientists, they have experiences that mirror those of America's indigenous peoples. As the shape-shifting duo go from transformation to transformation, Bagese's pupil learns to hear the voices, understanding finally that crossbloods (and Natives in general) must survive, simply "go on" in a world where the tribes are gone and the voices are dead.

In *Hotline Healers*, easily his sharpest work since *The Heirs of Columbus* in 1991, Vizenor returns to one of his most familiar characters, Almost Browne (so named because he was born in the back of a car "almost" on his tribe's reservation). Almost travels around selling copies of books by Native authors from a van. Autographed copies of volumes by Louis Owens, Betty Louise Bell, Scott Momaday, and others, commanding premium prices, are snapped up by an eager readership. There are only two problems: the signatures are actually Almost's forgeries, and the neatly bound books are blank. It is a comment not on the quality of the texts mentioned but on the smothering embrace of the dominant culture of things Natives, no matter how spurious. In a loosely connected chapter, Almost, ever the entrepreneur, cashes in on the New Age and the crazed popularity of psychic phone services by creating a hotline where mystic seekers can get in touch with Native healers or find relief by screaming into a telephone receiver held over a "panic hole." He deftly slices through "the primal kitsch and great native insights of Jamake Highwater, Lynn Andrews, and the notable Carlos Casteneda."

Such schemes are only part of the mayhem as Almost is revealed as responsible for the infamous eighteen-minute gap in Nixon's Watergate tapes. His bawdy antics among the Transethnic Situations Department of the University of California throw both students and faculty into turmoil. Pop icons like Claude Lévi-Strauss, Henry Louis Gates, Ishmael Reed, and Gloria Steinem are skewered as they float through Vizenor's *carnage*. Native author Thomas King makes a memorable cameo. Informed readers will also imagine they recognize others in thin disguise.

Central to *Dead Voices* and *Hotline Healers*, as to Vizenor's other work, is the character of the trickster. This comic but compassionate clown undermines people's expectations and punctures the pompous—contradicting and unsettling lives, but, in the very process of disruption, imaginatively keeping the world in balance. By the trickster's actions, the world is defined and recreated.

Both books are ostensibly novels, but as Bagese and her student flow from one transformation to the next, or as Almost bumptiously goes from one venture to another, seemingly extraneous episodes are related. Both books could easily be read as collections of short stories. Conventional narrative has never interested Vizenor, in any case. His words tumble over each other with a poetic ferocity. Neologisms abound. Through deconstruction of narrative and language, he hopes to aid mixed-bloods' efforts at imagining themselves.

The characters in Vizenor's fiction *are* crossbloods. Many of them are city dwellers seeking to recover an identity. In one story, he quotes Anaïs Nin, who refers to an urban Native as being on a "slow walk like a somnambulist enmeshed in the past and unable to walk into the present." He uses the same quote as an epigrammatic excursus at the beginning of his first novel, *Darkness in Saint Louis Bearheart* (reissued in 1990 as *Bearheart: The Heirship Chronicles*). The sad reality for such persons is that the whitestream, not satisfied with controlling the Native's present and future, has rewritten his past as well.

To read Vizenor's fiction is to enter a self-referential, satiric world. Characters recur from book to book, and their stories are retold, becoming in the process new tribal myths. Repetition of events serves as a mnemonic shorthand. Thus, in *Dead Voices*, the story of Martin Bear Charme, who establishes a meditation center on an island landfill in San Francisco Bay, is retold from the author's earlier *Landfill Meditation*. The story of a hunter who watches a squirrel he has shot struggle valiantly but futilely to survive is an incident from his autobiography, *Interior Landscapes*. The Anishinaabe creation myth recurs again and again, reshaped to fit each new circumstance.

Vizenor has always been the literary equivalent of a drive-by shooting. Anyone and anything can become a target of his satiric sensibilities, and being "on his side' is no guarantee of safe conduct through his territory. In *Dead Voices*, for instance, anthropologists are revealed to have been created out of excrement. An urban shaman makes money by using her power to clean up a chemical company's wastes on weekends. In his works, with equal glee, Vizenor takes on tribal officials, Indian activists, identity politics, reservation gambling, and fellow Native academics. He condemns the arrogance of "last lectures" or "terminal creeds," the dogmatic absolutism that people use to define and control the world without ever really engaging it. To take oneself too seriously is the cardinal sin. The problem, in almost every case, is those who seek to define who and what an Indian is and then proclaim that anyone not fitting the invented definition cannot be one.

For Vizenor, satire serves as a magical connection with the oral tradition, a legitimate autobiographical expression of what Natives have become in the world. It is a world of pantribal urban emptiness where "people are severed like dandelions on suburban lawns, separated from living places on the earth." In cities, Natives are forced to become the invented Indians of popular imagination, wearing long hair, beads, plastic ornaments, and imported leather. And not to play the invention game is to become utterly invisible. Yet even in such a place, Vizenor sees possibilities.

In *Dead Voices*, he articulates the choice as being between the chance offered by his urban tricksters and the "drone of cultural pride on reservations." His narrator declares, "I would rather be lost at war in the cities than at peace in a tame wilderness." Perhaps in that penultimate chapter of *Dead Voices* one comes closest to a "real" Gerald Vizenor.

Perhaps, however, it is best not to think that one understands him too easily. He is a contrarian, the crossblood trickster he celebrates in his fiction. His stories are comic acts of survivance, helping crossbloods imagine themselves and negotiate their world the same way their ancestors imaginatively found their way through their own world via story. His works contain truth, but truth that transcends mere fact. And, as a character in one of his stories states, "In a world of lies, the best deception is the truth."

CHAPTER THREE

VENUS ON THE HALF-SHELL?

Why Not?

The optimist proclaims that we live in the best of all possible worlds; and the pessimist fears this is true.

JAMES BRANCH CABELL,
The Silver Stallion

In *Venus on the Half-Shell*, written by Philip José Farmer under the pseudonym Kilgore Trout,[1] Simon Wagstaff roams the universe after Earth's destruction, caroming from one Rabelasian adventure to another as befits his priapic surname. He is a space-age Candide. Unlike Voltaire's naïf, however, who must endlessly endure the assurances of Dr. Pangloss that everything happens for the best in this best of all possible worlds, Simon interrogates those he meets on the issues of hamartiology and theodicy. "Why are we created only to suffer and die?" is for him the "primal question." In the comic novel's final scene, the wayward hero comes face-to-face with Old Bingo, described as resembling a giant cockroach, the last survivor of the first beings, who then themselves demiurgically were responsible for all other life, thanks to failed scientific experiments. Once more, Simon poses his question. The impassive reply? "Why not?"

As in Farmer's masterpiece, issues of dispossession, suffering, and ontological randomness lie at the heart of two recent plays by Native authors working in Canada, *Only Drunks and Children Tell the Truth* and "Drums."[2] In its own ways, each asks and answers the same primal question.

Only Drunks and Children by Drew Hayden Taylor is the second of a projected trilogy of plays dealing with what in Canada is referred to as the "scoop up" phenomenon and in the United States as being "adopted out." The "scoop up" refers to large numbers of Native children, who were removed from their families and cultures and raised by Whites. Though the Indian Child Welfare Act (ICWA), passed in 1978, largely put an end to the practice in the U.S., it continues in some form to this day. Prior to ICWA, it is estimated that roughly one-third of all Native children were being reared in non-Native foster or adoptive homes.

Someday, the first play in the cycle, deals with Janice, an Anishinaabe, who had been adopted as an infant and raised by a wealthy Anglican family in London. Now thirty-five, she is a successful entertainment attorney in Toronto. She returns to Otter Lake Reserve, somewhere in central Ontario, to see her birth mother. The hour-long visit ends disastrously, and Janice flees.

Only Drunks and Children takes up the story five months later. In the interim, Janice, who is known to those on Otter Lake as Grace, has suffered a breakdown, unable to deal with the emotions that have surfaced as a result of her trip to the reserve. Now, following the death of Anne, her mother, Barb, Janice/Grace's sister, goes to Toronto to bring the prodigal back to the reserve to say goodbye. In tow are her boyfriend, Rodney, a science-fiction maven whose brain "needs a good tan," and Tonto, Rodney's brother who serves a trickster function, and true to his role is far wiser than first impressions—or his name—indicate.

If, for Robert Frost, home is that place where when you go there they have to take you in, for Taylor it is a place that actively pursues one with all the deliberate speed of the hounds of hell. Janice refuses to return. After exhausting all arguments, Barb is ready to concede defeat and give up. Tonto, however, suddenly "remembers" Rodney's night blindness, making it impossible for them to drive back that evening and forcing them to spend the night.

The next morning, Tonto goes to work on Janice himself. He explains that he himself was adopted, too, except that his adoption by Rodney's family allowed him to stay on the reserve. Ironically, it was Janice/Grace's "scooping up" that permitted this. After her adoption, Anne "really kicked up a fuss" and persuaded provincial authorities to try a program to foster Native children on the reserve. Tonto was the test case.

Having made a connection, Tonto presses his advantage. When Janice asks *why* he thinks Rodney "thinks like a white person," Tonto pounces:

> There! Boom! You just said the magic word. The whole difference between Native people and White people can be summed up in that one single three letter word. "Why?" White people are so preoccupied with why everything works. Why was the universe created? Why is the sky blue? Why do dogs drool when you ring a bell? "Why" is their altar of worship. Their whole civilization is based on finding out why everything does everything.

Janice remains skeptical, asking the primal question, "And Native people are different? What is your answer to why?" Rodney's response is in complete keeping with Farmer or Vonnegut.[3] He responds:

> "Why not?" That's it. That's the answer. Why was the Universe created? Why not? Why do leopards have spots? Why not? Why do Indians and religious people play bingo? Why not? You keep asking why you should go home to Otter Lake. Instead of asking yourself "why," you should try "why not."

Eventually, almost against her will and much to Barb's amazement, Janice/Grace decides to return to the reserve.

While still in Toronto, Rodney and Tonto casually reveal Otter Lake's greatest secret: Amelia Earhart is living on the reserve. Following her "big belly flop" in July 1937, she retreated to Otter Lake to avoid the spotlight, and has lived there ever since. Living under the name Amy Hart, she has integrated herself fully into the Native community. Rodney tells Janice:

> Yeah, it's not as if it's a secret. Almost every kid from the Reserve has done some essay or project on her in school. After a while the teachers were getting suspicious so we had to make up a story about Indians having a special affinity for her, respecting her because she personifies the feminine presence of the eagle as it flies across Grandmother moon. One guy even equated her with a legend of "the woman who circled Turtle Island" which he made up during lunch hour.[4]

When a still somewhat incredulous Janice wants to alert the media, the trio reins her in:

Barb: Now wait a minute. Don't get carried away.

Janice: But why? This could be. . . .

Barb: . . . Wrong. She doesn't want publicity. Her first husband was a publisher and she got sick of all the publicity. She came to Otter Lake to get away from it all.

Janice: But you said everybody in the village knows.

Rodney: Yeah, in the village. Because we're her family now. It's her secret but it's also ours.

Tonto: Telling other people would be like turning in a friend. No can do.

Janice: Then why are you telling me[?]

Barb: Contrary to what you think, you are still family, whether you care or not.

Janice: Then you're taking one hell of a risk.

Rodney: Not really. So what if you tell somebody else, you'd look cute on the cover of the *National Enquirer*, but then it would just fade away.

Janice: But I'm a respected lawyer. With connections. If I wanted. . . .

Barb: Yeah, if you wanted. But I'm hoping you don't want to. No matter how long you've lived out here, I think you still have some Otter Lake in you.

In fact, when Janice/Grace arrives back at the reserve, Amy's presence stands in stark contrast to her own. The erstwhile aviator has become part of the fabric of life at Otter Lake, even learning Anishinaabe. It is Janice/Grace who is the outsider. It is the play's best trope. Unfortunately, Taylor cannot help squandering it. After Barb and Janice/Grace visit Amy, the latter voices what would better have remained an unspoken conceit, saying, "Barb, think about it. I was born here but I don't feel at home here and Amelia Earhart does. She's family and I'm not because the Children's Aid Society took me away. Doesn't all this seem a little weird to you?"

Despite, however, Earhart's (an outsider's) integration into the Anishinaabe, the potential for essentialism is present in Taylor's work. Barb repeatedly tells her sister that she cannot escape Otter Lake, despite having left at age one: "You're not white. You're Indian, Ojibway. Go look in a mirror." Late in the play, when Janice/Grace tells Tonto that her most recent trip back has left her confused, with no certainty in her life, her fellow-adoptee, referring to Janice/Grace's activities of the previous evening with Barb, responds:

> Tonto: That's an awful lot to forget after one night of drinking. Trust me, you know everything you need to know. People may learn a few facts or stories over the years, but all the real important things in life we know at birth.
>
> Janice: I don't need grave-side therapy right now. You had it easy, you grew up here. You knew everything.
>
> Tonto: That has nothing to do with it. Janice, have you ever heard of a bird called a cowbird? Interesting bird the cowbird. They lay their eggs in other birds' nests then fly off.
>
> Janice: Cuckoos.
>
> Tonto: What?
>
> Janice: Cuckoos. The English have a similar bird called a cuckoo.
>
> Tonto: Whatever. Anyway, the robins or starlings, whichever the nest belongs to, they raise the baby cowbird as a robin or a starling or whatever. But when it grows up, the cowbird is still a cowbird. It lays its eggs in another bird's nest just like any other cowbird. Somewhere, deep inside, it knew it was a cowbird. No matter how it was raised or what it was taught. What are you, robin or cowbird?

Despite, however, the patent essentializing in deployments such as the cowbird metaphor, *Only Drunks and Children* is ultimately more about family and community than racial essence. When Janice/Grace tells Tonto that she does not know whether she is robin or cowbird, he responds that her problem is that she has been trying to figure out the issues of identity in isolation: "2, 3, 4, 8, 10, heads are better than one." And Barb tells her, "This is who we are. Family, friends, we stick together." Those bonds may be frayed by external forces, but they can never be broken by them.

Many of the same issues that drive *Only Drunks and Children*—family, loss, cultural alienation—also motivate Thomas King's "Drums." If a Frostian sense of home lies behind Taylor's play, a Faulknerian idea of history is key to King's finally superior drama. For King, no less than for Faulkner, the past isn't dead and gone; it isn't even past yet.

As the play opens, a woman in traditional dress is seen alone on a darkened stage. As her eyes become more accustomed to the light, she sees she is in the backyard of a typical suburban house, outside of an unnamed city much like Toronto. "Oh, God," she says in dismay, "Not the twentieth century, again." She changes into contemporary clothes and sings the lead of an honor song. She listens for the response to her call, but none is forthcoming.

The yard, it turns out, is that of Eve Steward. She is a fine art photographer married to Adam, a psychologist. Though Eve is Native, she is completely deracinated, out of touch with her culture and even largely unfamiliar with her family history, married to a non-Native and living an existence virtually indistinguishable from that of any White Canadian. Her teenage son, Drum, despite his evocative name, is likewise disconnected—more interested in computers, video games, and borrowing the family car than anything else. About Eve's only connection to her heritage are her neighbors, Harry and Margaret, who try to keep her connected by inviting her to join them at powwows. This placid existence is disrupted when Charm Stillwater walks onto their deck patio.[5]

Charm, the woman from the first scene, introduces herself as Eve's aunt from Alberta. When Eve protests that she has no aunt, the woman responds impassively, "Okay. I'm your great, great, great, great grandmother." The first act depicts Eve's journey from utter disbelief to credulity. As Charm says, in a line reminiscent of Farmer/Trout or Taylor, "You're going to say 'that's impossible,' and I'll explain how the universe actually works, and you'll tell me I'm crazy and call the cops."

As Charm unfolds the story, her youngest daughter, Nona, was said to have died of influenza at residential school. In fact, though, she was raped and murdered by a drunken teacher. The crime was covered up. Nona's body was mutilated and posed to look like a suicide. When told about the event, Charm had gone to the school, seeking revenge. The culprit, however, had already departed, and the administration would not even allow her to claim her daughter's corpse. In her grief, she sliced her arms in imitation of the wounds inflicted upon Nona. Now it seems that she is condemned to pursue Nona's restless spirit through a time beyond time, emerging randomly—or seemingly at random. To Eve's frustration, it becomes evident that Charm won't leave; the woman even tells Margaret the truth of their familial relationship.

The second act begins in a mirror image of the first, except that it is not Charm's but Nona's arrival that opens it. Unlike her mother, though, the teenage girl is pleased by her destination, crying, "The twentieth century!" Eve is no longer so much unbelieving as uncomprehending.

Charm apologizes to Eve, saying that she told Nona "to stay home," to which the latter replies, "So now I have two ghosts in my house instead of one." But in the *kairos* in which Charm and Nona exist, they are not dead. When Eve asks, "Then what are you?" Charm responds, "We're your relations." Nona has not been murdered yet. The past *is not* past yet. Only Margaret understands. She says that her great grandmother, whose shawl she wears, was special to her, but "she's never come to visit me." Charm's reply is telling: "She doesn't have to."

Despite the remoteness in time and space of her upbringing, Nona shows herself to be a typical teenager. Overcoming generational differences that hinder communication, she makes a connection with Drum. They talk about the future. Drum wants to be a computer network administrator. Nona expects to be married and plans on four or five children. Overhearing the young people's conversation, Charm is on the verge of tears. She tells Eve, "Well, it's not going to happen. No children. No stories. Just a drunk with a knife. . . . You live long enough and you realize that everything dies. But no one should die like that." Here, unlike Taylor, King trusts his audience. The unspoken conceit is: although the audience knows—in fact has known all along—that Nona *has* no future, the girl herself does not.

Charm announces that it is time for her and her daughter to go. Now, Eve, who had so protested their advent, equally resists their departure. Gradually, almost imperceptibly, the barriers have melted away. She now wants to know about her family, her relations, the heritage that is rightfully hers. She tells Charm that she's decided to go to the powwow with Harry and Margaret. Nona, still unaware, tells Drum that he and his family should visit them in Alberta. Eve replies, "Maybe we should." Charm sings the call of the honor song again. This time, Drum sings in response, explaining he has been taught by Nona.

Just as Taylor's play is about recovery of place and belonging, so King's details Eve's journey to a similar location. Whereas the former's answers appear to be imbedded purely in genetics—a longing for stories in the blood—the latter's are cultural, knowing who one is through a shared history and learning, however tentatively, one's ties to the culture of one's family. Can such a process be a conscious act of will, if the ties are close enough? Why not?

CHAPTER FOUR

REMNANTS OF THE FIRST EARTH

A Review

The preface to *Remnants of the First Earth*, the first novel by the Mesquakie poet Ray Young Bear, closes with an eschatological prophecy given to the book's narrator by his grandmother. It concerns the People's responsibility and the consequences that will flow from their failure to fulfill them. Their sole obligation, the woman in the narrative instructs the boy, is to continue the Principal Religion of the Earthlodge clans. Young Bear writes:

> It was agreed eons and eons ago that if these ceremonies were not performed, the world would no longer be held together, the elements of wind and ice would whirl together and splinter us apart. Our forgetfulness, in other words, would become a part of a chain of natural and man-made catastrophes—flag wars and ecological suffocation—leading to the end of the earth. And the people who so connivingly and viciously sought to make us forget ourselves by subjugating us, Euro-Americans, would be the root cause.

It is thus ironical that those who seek to save the man by killing the Indian, through a process of assimilation and religious conversion, are killing themselves as well.

This apocalyptic vision lies at the heart of *Remnants*. It speaks of the timelessness of Mesquakie (and by extension Native) existence and tradition and the change and dislocations that have been forced upon them. As Young Bear states in an afterword to his *Black Eagle Child: The Facepaint Narratives*, he has attempted to maintain a delicate equilibrium with my tribal home-land's history and geographic surroundings and the world that changes its face along the borders. Represented in the whirlwind of mystical themes and modern symbols, of characters normal or bizarre and their eventual resolve, the word-collecting process is an admixture of time present and past, of directions found and then lost, of actuality and dream.

Although *Black Eagle Child* was promoted as an autobiography, appear-ing in the University of Iowa Press' series in North American Autobiogra-phy, it was, in reality, a fiction, a blend of "both autobiographical experi-ences and imagination," weaving together poetry and narrative. *Remnants* is a sequel to this earlier volume, continuing the stories of the characters found there. Once again, Edgar Bearchild functions as the author's alter ego, and Black Eagle Child Settlement stands in for the reservation where he is an "enrolled, lifelong resident."

Beginning in the 1950s, when Edgar was a youth, and stretching to 2004, the novel (leavened with Young Bear's distinctive poetry) depicts a changing Black Eagle Child Settlement. Family homesteads built early in the twentieth century are being supplanted by substandard federal housing. Tribal officials are more interested in the daily take from tables at the casino than in preserving the Principal Religion. The reservation school inculcates the values contained in a foreign language, English. The tribe has lost access to the Supernaturals. The process has been working on the People for a long time. As Edgar writes, "When the Corps of Engineers built a dam on the Iowa River in the early 1900s, it only confirmed the realization that we were bound—regardless of what-ever precautions we took—to lose." Grandmother's vision comes closer to fulfillment.

Yet, the settlement remains a place where conventional, linear time means little. A rape and murder that occurred in 1890 still has ramifica-tions as a central reality of Black Eagle Child existence. An ancestor was blackmailed into becoming a federally recognized chief, displacing the traditional hereditary *O ki ma wa ki*, and history was forever changed: "By replacing the window of the Cosmic Earthlodge with aluminum panel-ing, we encouraged a sudden gust of wind to tear us apart, which made us cringe as the other elements gathered around us in force."

For all the dysfunctionality portrayed, *Remnants* remains a novel of hope, one that promotes the power of memory. According to Elizabeth Cook-Lynn, it "will be scrutinized two or three or four generations from now as a brilliant translation of how, against all odds, Indians in America persist in their desire to taste the sweet waters of their origins, yet 'wince at the near catch and busted line.'" The sheer poetic force of Young Bear's prose propels the story of Black Eagle Child settlement along. In ways reminiscent of Leslie Marmon Silko's *Ceremony* and N. Scott Momaday's *House Made of Dawn*—and even Mourning Dove's *Cogewea, the Half-Blood*—he successfully weaves the ceremonial into novelistic form. In *Remnants of the First Earth*, Young Bear brings to mind Lawrence Durrell, a literary stylist of such power that each of his words must be read, chewed, digested, and internalized before they can finally be understood.

CHAPTER FIVE

AN ÜBERMENSCH AMONG THE APACHE

Or, Karl May's Tour of the Grand Teutons

Le Vrai n'est pas toujours le vraisemblable.

SAMUEL JOHNSON, 1759

Four days after Fritz Mandelbaum, a Jewish refugee, arrived in New York in 1939, he stood before a bank of lockers in his new high school. The lockers bore labels, proclaiming their owners' names: J. Edgar Hoover, Babe Ruth, Charles Lindbergh. His teacher, Mr. Saperstein, explained, "Maybe you want to do like the other guys. Don't use your name, but somebody famous, for fun." He writes:

> Ears burning at my ignorance of these Yankee celebrities, I wrote "Old Shatter-Hand" on the . . . card.
> "Where'd you get that name from?" Mr. Saperstein asked. "But—it is from Karl May!" I said. "Who?"
> I still remember how amazed I was and how comforting the amazement. My dummkopf incomprehension of Babe Ruth had been neutralized by Mr. Saperstein's—my teacher's—ignorance of Karl May.[1]

Nearly fifty years later, Mandelbaum, renamed Frederic Morton, notes that when he fled Vienna, he had tucked his copies of Karl May's novels in his suitcase next to his soccer ball and his leather shorts "as keepsakes of a home to which there would be no return." In his *New York Times* essay, "Tales of the Grand Teutons: Karl May among the Indians," Morton states that these volumes were more than mere momentos: "They were also charms. I hoped my trip into strangeness like Old Shatterhand's, would turn into high romance. Never mind that the people I was fleeing were Old Shatterhand's own, whose valor he glorified. The issue of the moment was survival: for me Karl May was talismanic because of his hero's narrow escapes."[2] By writing Old Shatterhand on his locker label he was inscribing himself on the American experience. His reaction to Mr. Saperstein's incomprehension says that, though he may be ignorant of home-run kings and G-men, he knows more about Indians—and hence about the "real" America—than his teacher.

Twenty-three years after Frederic Morton's flight, Chuck Ross, a largely deracinated Dakota was stationed in Mainz-Gonsenheim with the 505th Paratroop Brigade of the United States Army. While there he became aware of the many German Indian clubs. When he finally met one of the hobbyists, "To my surprise I learned that the German knew more about the history of the D/Lakota people than I did! At first I was ashamed of myself for not knowing my own history. Then I decided to learn all I could about D/Lakota history and culture."[3] He continues:

> Because of the German Indian Club experience, I wanted to find out about the history and culture of my tribe, so I started a search for my roots. First, I began looking for my identity in books, reading everything I could get my hands on about the history and culture of the D/Lakota people. I studied the books. Later, I returned home and spoke to my grandparents. They proceeded to tell traditional stories, and I asked them, "How come you never told us this before?"
>
> "Well, no one ever asked us," was their reply.
>
> The elders have a wealth of knowledge. Not only my grandparents, but everybody's grandparents have a wealth of knowledge about the era that they lived in. When I started talking with them, visiting with the older folks, I got a little bit different version than what was in the books. Basically it was the same, but there were still differences.[4]

Ross shared his learnings in a book entitled *Mitakuye Oyasin* in 1989. Among other New Age ruminations, these included harmonic convergence, Edgar Cayce, Atlantis, UFOs from the Pleides, and Jungian psychology. Though he never mentions the name, and though the enthusiast whom Ross met in Germany might deny it, his experience is as much shaped by Karl May as was that of Fritz Mandelbaum/Frederic Morton.

This chapter will examine the work and legacy of May in shaping images of American indigenes. It also will illustrate some of the contemporary work of Native writers as they attempt to address and deconstruct those images. We will have reason, in the course of the chapter, to return to both of these emblematic experiences—those of Morton and Ross. Both testify to the enduring impact of this German popular writer.

It is often fashionable to tar Karl May with the fact that he was Adolf Hitler's favorite writer. It is true that, according to a Berlin newspaper of June 26, 1944, German troops in World War II expressed gratitude to May for providing "the best manuals of anti-partisan warfare" and that, during the same conflict, many Germans felt betrayed in seeing their "allies," the Indians, fight with the American army. Hitler did present his nephew, Heinz, with a set of May's collected works, and, in the aftermath of the Russian debacle, recommended them to his General Staff as morale-boosters.[5] It is equally true, however, that May was Albert Einstein's favorite author—as he was Albert Schweitzer's, Thomas Mann's, and Hermann Hesse's.

He is quite simply every little German boy's—and not a few German girl's—favorite. (According to Bernd Walbert, whose American Ranch Holidays sends May-inspired clients to dude ranches and other "Wild West" vacations in the United States, 90 percent of those visiting dude ranches are "young, single women.")[6] Morton writes, "How peculiar, then, my instinct on reaching America: that I, a Jewish refugee from German conquest, should write 'Old Shatterhand,' a name prototypical of the conquering German, on my high school locker. How ironic that today I still catch myself sneaking to the corner in my library where my five volumes of Karl May are tucked away, where sachems and sheiks ride in gothic typeface down yellowing pages."[7] May wrote seventy-six volumes. He has been translated into thirty-three languages. His books have sold more than 100 million copies, estimated to have been read by 300 million people. He is the best-selling German author of all time. Today, one would be hard-pressed to find a German over the age of twenty who has not read at least one of May's stories or seen one of the films based upon his works.[8] His works are also popular throughout Europe. Yet, as both Morton's and A. C. Ross's experiences point up, his work is almost wholly unknown in the United States, except to a few German émigrés and a handful of Native Americanists and other academics. Though May's works have been continuously in print in Europe, they have been only partially and sporadically available in English.

Karl May wrote popular adventure stories involving Old Shatterhand, a German in the American West after the American Civil War, and Kara-ben-Nemsi, an adventurer in the Middle East. May, labeling his stories *reiseerzahlungen*—travel tales, claimed that they were based upon his own travels and exploits. Old Shatterhand's name was actually Karl, having been given the frontier moniker for his ability to lay out any man with a single punch. Kara-ben-Nemsi means simply Karl, son of the Germans. May did everything to encourage the identity between himself and his heroes. He was photographed in buckskins as Old Shatterhand, and his trusty *Bärentöter*, with studs on its stock (one each for every man he killed), is on display at the Karl-May-Museum in Bamberg.[9] May claimed to speak forty languages, including many Native dialects. In reality, however, the claims were as fictitious as the novels he wrote.

May was born in 1842 near Chemnitz, Saxony, the fifth child in a large family headed by a poor weaver father and a professional midwife mother. He went blind from malnutrition and remained so until he was five. The first thirty years of his life were unremarkable. He attended a teachers' training school but was known primarily for minor scrapes with the law, crimes of petty theft, impersonation, and obtaining money under false pretenses. At twenty-three, he was sentenced to five years in prison for insurance fraud and the fraudulent sale of medicines. Within six months of his release in the winter of 1868, he was back in jail for four years for impersonating a police officer. In 1899, a public inquiry revealed that *Dr.* Karl May had purchased his doctorate from the German University of Chicago, a mail-order organization run by a former barber. It also revealed that 1870–1871, the period of his supposed adventures, had been spent in Zwickau prison. The resulting stress led to May's nervous breakdown.[10] His works are thus "travel lies," conforming to the pattern of earlier such writings as outlined by Percy Adams in his book *Travelers and Travel Liars*. They are the product of a "fireside traveler," who uses his work not to amuse or to instruct but to deceive "for the sake of money, pride, or a point of view."[11] It is the willful sin, the "lie direct" in medieval church English.[12] May journeyed to America only once, in 1908, four years before his death.

While in prison, May began to write. According to Morton, "May, whose background was so wretchedly unheroic, began to write about a knight-errant of nonpareil ethics and muscle. Known as Old Shatterhand in Indian territory, he battles desperadoes. As Kara-ben-Nemsi, he takes on fiendish emirs in the dunes and casbahs of Arabia. May's experience at that point was entirely and provincially Middle European. He had never been west of the Rhine or south of the Alps."[13] Despite the disclosures about the spurious nature of his claims, however, May's popularity never waned. He recovered his reputation. His books continued to sell. And in 1928, sixteen years after his death, Villa Shatterhand, his home in Radebeul, near Dresden, opened as a museum. During the 1960s, a series of immensely successful films was produced, based on May's stories. Those stories also influenced two motion pictures based on the works of James Fenimore Cooper, and a two-part adaptation of Wagner's *Der Ring des Nibelungen*, directed by Harald Reinl (who was responsible for most of these screen versions of May and Cooper), was described as "a De Luxe edition of his Karl May Westerns."

Today, the Karl-May-Museum in Radebeul continues to operate. After the partition of Germany, following World War II, a replica of Villa Shatterhand was built in Bamburg in the Federal Republic, and a new Karl-May-Museum came into being. Open-air festivals of his work held every year in Bad Segeberg, Lennestadt, and Kurort Rathen attract hundreds of thousands of participants. Lex Barker, a minor actor in the United States, the embodiment of Tarzan from 1949 to 1955 in a series of routine pictures, became a major star in Germany, playing both Old Shatterhand and Kara-ben-Nemi and starring in Reinl's production of *The Deerslayer*. French actor Pierre Brice became so identified with May's Winnetou that, years after the last May film, he was appearing as the famed Apache in outdoor pageants. (In much the same way Clayton Moore continued to be the Lone Ranger and Guy Williams lived out his days playing El Zorro in Argentina to the adulation of his Latin American fans.) Thousands of computer web pages are devoted to May and his writings. In addition, there some two hundred Indian clubs in Germany like the one encountered by Ross, attracting as many as 100,000 members.

How does one explain this enduring popularity of Karl May? What are the images of Indians he offered? How do these images continue to influence the great popularity of Indians in Germany and throughout Europe?

The answers to these questions are more complex than they might at first seem, and May's appeal is more intricate than that of, for instance, Louis L'Amour in the United States. Of course, Europe had experience of Indians, both real and imaginary, before May ever picked up a pen. Independent encounters that contributed to European representations of them contemporaneous with May's complicate the task of teasing out the strands of his influence.

Europe probably first saw American indigenes around A.D. 1009, when, according to the Icelandic sagas, *Skræling* were brought to Norway. Inuit captives were probably taken back in about 1420.[14] Later, early German travel writers like Karl Anton Postl and Friedrich Gerstucker were widely read. Balduin Möllhausen wrote 150 potboilers about the American West in the 1860s and 1870s, becoming, in the era before May, the best read author in Germany.[15]

Beyond Germany, numerous other writers were representing American Indians and influencing popular images. Shakespeare's *The Tempest*, written in 1611, is set in Bermoothes (Bermuda), and Caliban, the deformed slave, is an indigene. His name is an anagram for "cannibal" (derived from the name Carib); in the dramatis personae he is described as "a salvage [i.e., savage]" and is the issue of a witch and the devil. In France, François Marie René Chateaubriand helped cement the stereotype of the *bon sauvage*, or noble savage, with works such as *Atala* (1801), which became the first real European bestseller. Later, Gustave Aimard published a "western" a month at times between 1850 and 1870. James Fenimore Cooper was readily available in translation. May modeled his fabrications closely on Cooper and on French author Gabriel Ferry's *Coureur de Bois* (which he helped edit in a German edition). He may also have had access to John Heckewelder's *Account of the History, Manners and Customs of the Indian Nations* (1819), Cooper's principal source of information.

May's westerns revolve around the relationship between Old Shatterhand (Karl) and the Apache warrior Winnetou. Winnetou is the consummate noble savage. Cultured, he carries around a copy of Longfellow's "Hiawatha," which he occasionally reads. In choosing to make this progressive specimen an Apache, May seems to be responding to Ferry. As the French attempted to regain a foothold in the Americas and to establish and shore up Maximillian in Mexico, French literary interest turned from Canada and the Great Lakes region to the Southwest. Ferry's heroes in

Coureur de Bois were Comanche. According to Christian Feest, "If the arch-
enemy of the German people was siding with the Comanche against the
Apache, the latter necessarily had to be the Germans' potential allies. Winnetou, the 'red gentleman' and slightly effeminate Indian chief . . . thus
had to be an Apache."[16] Following the philosophy that the enemy of my
enemy is my friend, this was, Feest notes, recently turned on its head yet
again: "[A] reform-minded member of Austria's Socialist Party published
an appeal for 'more Comanches' in his party—if the Apache were friends
of Karl May, the ultimate petit bourgeois, the Comanches had to be social-
ists."[17] In *Satan and Ischariot*, written in 1894–95, May depicts Winnetou
visiting Old Shatterhand in Dresden. The warrior orders German beer,
which "he likes to drink, but with moderation" and requests a performance of German music. Though the Native does not say anything following the music, May writes "[B]ut as I knew his personality, I knew quite
well how deep an impression the German song had left on his soul."
Again, according to Feest: "Although nothing else is reported about the
chief's reactions, the message is clear enough—an Apache chief who likes
German songs and drinks beer in moderation must be a kindred soul."[18]
He is every bit as much the übermensch as the German narrator.

As with Amer-European representations of their own indigenes, those
of May and other European writers (and their appeal) have more to do
with internal European needs than with any "real" or "authentic" Indians.
According to Schell Halbing, a Norwegian writer who has written over
eighty best-selling westerns under the pen name Louis Masterson, "The
so-called Western Myth is a European myth." Or, as Julian Crandall Hollick observes, "The Wild West for many Europeans has been, always will
be, a mythical place where Europeans can stage their own adventures,
fight their own quarrels, dream their own dreams. If the Wild West had
never existed, then Europe would have had to invent it!"[19]

May's Apaches unfailingly fit the noble savage stereotype. Their enemies, whether Yankees or other Natives, are irredeemably evil. The stories
reflect May's vaguely pacifistic, muscular Christianity and Christian
socialism. His depiction of Apache ritual dispenses with reality completely, and the rites themselves are decidedly Teutonic.

In order to prove his bravery and worthiness before being accepted by
the Apaches, Old Shatterhand must undergo a series of trials. In the final
test, he must swim underwater to a totem pole in the middle of a lake,

while the Mescalero chief Intschu-tschuna, Winnetou's father, throws tomahawks at him. Having triumphed, he is welcomed as a "white Apache." The ensuing description of the "blood brotherhood" ritual is instructive, and worth quoting at length:

> "Old Shatterhand will be blood of our blood and flesh of our flesh. Do the warriors of the Apache give their consent? [They respond with the Siouan, not Apache but nonetheless stereotypically Native, 'Hao.'] Now let Old Shatterhand and Winnetou step up to the coffin and let their blood drip into the water of brotherhood."
>
> So this was to be a blood brotherhood, a real, true blood brotherhood, of which I had so often read. Intschu-tschuna bared his sons lower arm to make a small incision, then took mine and performed the same act. Some blood fell into the two bowls. Winnetou was given mine and I his. Intschu-tschuna solemnly intoned in English, "The soul lives in the blood. The soul of these two young warriors shall pass into each other so that they form one. Forthwith what Old Shatterhand thinks shall also be Winnetou's thought. What Winnetou wants shall also be Old Shatterhand's will. Drink."
>
> I emptied my bowl and Winnetou his. The chief gave me his hand.
>
> "Like Winnetou, you are now the son of my body and a warrior of our people. The glory of your deeds will spread quickly, and no other warrior will surpass you. You join us as chief of the Apaches, and all the tribes of our people will honor you as such.

With its overt Christian and neo-pagan symbology and language, its imagery of Eucharist and of death and resurrection, it resembles the rituals of the "Blood Flag" and the "16 Martyrs" designed by Josef Goebbels for the Nazi Party.

As in much popular literature, there is an element of sexual ambiguity in May's stories (covers of the original Winnetou books designed by Sacha Schneider feature classical, Olympiad-style nudes "disguised" as Indians) and a strong homoerotic undertone in the relationship between Old Shatterhand and Winnetou. The first time Karl sees the Indian he describes him:

> His bronze-colored face bore the imprint of a very special nobility. We seemed to be about the same age. He immediately impressed me as being endowed with an exceptional mind, and an exceptional

character. We looked each other up and down. His eyes shone with a dull fire, and I thought I could detect in them the faint light of sympathy. The others told me that Winnetou has accomplished more, though still in his youth, than ten other warriors could hope to accomplish in a whole lifetime. I believed them. One day, his name would be famous through all the plains, and in all the mountains.

He states that "the cut of his earnest, beautiful face, the cheekbones of which barely stood out at all, was almost Roman." Likewise, Winnetou says of Shatterhand, "I admired his courage and strength. His face seemed sincere. I thought I could love him." He tells the Aryan that "the Great Spirit has endowed you with an extraordinarily robust body."

In *Winnetou I*, the first of the stories chronologically but not the first written, a female love interest is provided for Karl—Nscho-tschi ("Spring Day"), Winnetou's sister who is smitten with the German. Though extraordinarily beautiful, her beauty for Karl seems to lie primarily in her resemblance to her brother: "Her hair reminded me of Winnetou's—and so did her eyes. Her eyes were soft, and velvety, shining through from under thick, black eyelashes. The perfect, delicate shape of her face was not spoiled by the prominent cheekbones which are a common feature among the Indians. Her nose made her profile seem more Greek than Redskin. She must have been about eighteen years old." After Nscho-tschi and her father, Intschu-tschuna, are killed by the evil Yankee, Frederick Santer, Shatterhand and Winnetou are left alone, free to pursue their adventures unencumbered by female restraint. May never introduced another romantic interest in any of the subsequent stories. Interestingly, in Reinl's "Winnetou the Warrior," the first film of the series, based on *Winnetou I*, Nscho-tschi dies but must be resurrected for later entries. After her death, Old Shatterhand allows himself a moment's reflective pause: "I loved her, Winnetou—now I know it, she's gone." To which the *Apache* chief reassures him, "Manetou watches over her."[20]

Christian notions of a universalizing brotherhood and homoerotic subcurrents aside, the root appeal of May's fiction rests in the way it taps into nascent German nationalism and the ideology of European colonialism.

Lisa Bartel-Winkler, an author who, during the Nazi period, would write novels in which the virtuous traits of Indians were explained by their Viking ancestry, wrote in 1924, "In Winnetou Karl May delineates the Indian drama. It is also the German drama. Winnetou is the noble man of his race—he knows about the purity of blood, the longing, and the hope of his brothers, but they have to founder because they are worn down by discord. . . . This is Indian, this is also German. Who has grasped the meaning of the Indian drama has also grasped the meaning of the German drama."[21]

In the valorization of the noble savage, May and his contemporaries were looking back to their own pre-Christian past. In *O Brave New People: The European Invention of the American Indian*, John Moffitt and Santiago Sebastián note, "Of all the Noble Savages of antiquity, all essential textual prototypes for the Renaissance invention of American 'Indians,' other than the geographically very distant Scythians[,] doubtlessly within Europe itself the most discussed group were the Germans (*Germani*). The sylvan-dwelling Teutons first appeared in their ennobled barbarian role in Julius Caesar's *Chronicles of the Gallic Wars* (51 B.C.)."[22] The image was refined and reinforced a century and a half later by Tacitus in *De Origine et situ Germanorum*.[23]

Frederic Morton nuances such an argument and draws out its appeal in May's time, writing, "It's odd, but the country that was to generate so formidable a nationalism in the 20th century had, until the 19th, few heroic figures to call its own. Britain's ran from King Arthur to Lord Nelson; France had a gallery from Roland to Louis XIV. But Germany? The scattered sagas of the Germanic tribes dramatize the end of Rome rather than the dawn of Teutonia."[24] In this mythopoeic nation-building quest, May must be seen as of a piece with composer Richard Wagner, born within a year of each other. Wagner may have given the *Nibelungen* "Teutonic grandeur," but May "made patriotism mythic for the man in the street." In fact, Hans-Jürgen Syberberg, who has made a documentary about May as part of his trilogy (with Wagner and Ludwig of Bavaria) on German cultural mythology sees May as a "poor man's Wagner" retelling the myth of the *Nibelungen*.[25] According to Morton, "Yet both men, on different esthetic levels, helped shape the collective German dream of feats far beyond middle-class bounds—a dream Hitler shaped into a mania."[26]

May gave his readers what they longed for desperately, "an epos of the German conquistador bestriding the world at large."[27] This heroic myth is part of the impulse of German colonialism and much of colonialism in general. According to Schell Halbing, "The so-called Western Myth is a

European myth. When every frontier in Europe was conquered, every wilderness was cultivated, the people still had a need for a dream of something fresh, new, original."²⁸ Or, as Frayling puts it, in May it is as if the Code of the West "has been rewritten by Kaiser Wilhelm."²⁹

Beyond, however, ethnostalgic identification of a glorious Teutonic past with a fast-receding, noble Native American present, there is concrete reason why Europe, in particular Germany and Karl May, should seize upon the image of American indigenes. It is related to the impulse that caused May to make Winnetou an Apache in contradistinction to Ferry's elevation of the Comanche. In "The Germans and the Red Man," Alfred Vagts writes, "The German reader single[d] out the Indian as the one exotic race with which he was and still seems ready to sympathize, and even to identify himself. That the Germans should have this special relationship, stronger than the French or the English, is traceable, most likely, to the fact that Germany was a latecomer to colonialism, and never encountered the Indian as opposing colonization; that her contact with the Red Man was 'only literature.'"³⁰ In the colonial enterprise, there is, as Jonathan Boyarin points out, "the tendency, in the respective imperial contexts of America and Europe, to valorize the other empire's vanquished Other."³¹ Thus, just as the English promoted the Black Legend of Spanish atrocities and the United States created for itself the "tragic mistake" doctrine that gave itself plausible deniability in its own colonialist conquest of the continent, Germans grabbed the image of the dying American Indian, victim of the English, Dutch, French, and Americans, with both hands.³² Central to this vision, however, and to May's ideology, is the myth of the Vanishing Indian.

As I have noted earlier in this volume and in another context, Enrique Dussel, in his *The Invention of the Americas: Eclipse of "the Other" and the Myth of Modernity*, makes clear that "the glorification of Natives as Noble Savages, who are not allowed (alone of all minorities) to enter the 20th century, serves colonial interests, just as did the romanticized world of Orientalism limned by Edward Said. It is no accident that one avatar of imperialism, Karl May, chose as his twin subjects of colonial fantasias the American West of the noble Apache Winnetou and the Arabia of Kara-ben-Nemsi."³³

Robert Berkhofer, in his classic work on representations of American Natives, *The White Man's Indian: Images of the American Indian from Columbus to the Present*, writes, "In May's imaginative ethnography, the Apache were the most peaceful tribe in the trans-Mississippi West, suffering

vicious attacks from the most warlike tribe, the Sioux, their dreaded enemies."[34] They are also avowedly anti-materialist. Though Whites have come
in a recent search for gold in the West, the Apaches have long known of its
sources. They, however, have no use for this "dust of death," employing it
only when necessary for the good of the tribe as a whole in their dealings
with Amer-Europeans. Such a mythic and idealized people cannot, any
more than genuine Natives, be allowed to survive into the modern era.

At the beginning of *Winnetou I*, May writes:

> The Indian Race is dying. The White Man came with sweet words
> on his lips but had a sharp knife in his belt and a loaded rifle in his
> hand. The dying Indian could not be integrated into the White
> world. Was that reason enough to kill him? Could he not have been
> saved?
>
> I came to know the Indians over the course of a number of years,
> and one of them still lives brightly and magnificently in my heart. He,
> the best and most loyal and devoted of all my friends, was a true rep-
> resentative of his race. I loved him as I have loved no other. I would
> gladly have given my life to protect his, as he risked it countless times
> to preserve mine. This was not to be. He died to save his comrades,
> but it is only his body that died, for he will survive in these pages, as
> he lives in my soul. Winnetou, the great chief of the Apaches.

May, the pacificist crypto-colonialist, thus gets to have it both ways. He
can express sentimental regret at the passing of the noble savage, perpetrated by another imperialist power, while being assured that Natives are
kept safely in the stasis box of the past. Nothing more is required of him,
nor does he require any more from his readers. Winnetou—this "true representative of his race"—may live, but it is the noncorporeal existence of
the dead letters of the printed page, his "life" carefully circumscribed by
the non-Native voice of the narrator.

May's frontier may be a place where "civilization" confronts innocence,
but, even as he writes, the outcome of that contest has been decided. It is
a foregone conclusion as the engine of Progress moves inexorably on.
Even his noble savages, in their more prescient mode, recognize it.
Frayling writes, "The more 'cultured' Indians in the 'Winnetou' stories
(the chosen ones) are aware that the Twilight of the Gods is approaching,
that they are 'The Last of the Tribe.' Intschu-tschuna, for example, is

resigned to the fact that 'we cannot stop the white men from coming here and stealing our land. First the scouts and the pioneers. Then, if we resist, the army. It is our destiny'. . . . In May's vision, the myth of the noble savage has less to do with 'back to human nature' than 'forward to European culture' (or, to put it another way, 'away from both primitive and Yankee cultures'). But the noble savage is doomed (and knows it), and there is nothing that the Siegfried of the Sagebrush can do about it."[35] Writing in 1876, May describes

> the site of that desperate fight in which the Indian lets fly his last arrow against the exponent of a bloodthirsty and reckless "civilization". . . . At the beginning of the 19th century the "Redskin" was still master of the vast plains . . . But then came the "Paleface," the White man drove the "Red brother" from his own hunting grounds and through disease, "firewater" and shotguns dealt out death and destruction in the ranks of the strong and trusting sons of the wilderness. . . . What and how the Indian was not supposed to be, that and so he did become through his Christian brother who carried the scripture of love on his lips and the murderous weapon in his fist, depriving mankind and universal history of inestimable potentials for development . . . but traditions will weave their golden gleam around the vanished warrior of the savanna, and the memory of the mortal sin committed against the brother will continue to live in the song of the poet.[36]

At end of *Winnetou III*, Winnetou dies. Before he does so, however, he embraces that final symbol of civilization, the religion of his conquerors, Christianity. His last words are, "I believe in the Savior; Winnetou is a Christian. Farewell." Then to the strains of the "Ave Maria," he crosses over to life eternal.

Once the noble savage is gone, his story is complete, and the conquest can proceed unimpeded. One might feel regret at his passing, but, if it is the work of ineluctable forces, one need not feel any guilt. In fact, according to Jonathan Boyarin, May's colonialist, Christian socialist aesthetic (class harmony, universal brotherhood regardless of race)

> *required* that the noble Red Man be doomed. In a critical essay, Peter Uwe Hohendahl suggests why this may be so. May's anticapitalism

is expressed in his negative portrayal of "Yankee traders." His vision of human solidarity is expressed on the one hand by the ideal group discipline and precise unity of the tribe, the Apaches, and on the other by the depiction of fraternal relations between true pioneer "men of the West"—honest, self-reliant, and tough—and individual Indian men bearing the same qualities. Hence May dreamed of a new order of human solidarity against individual greed and the profit motive. But if this vision were to come about through blood-less revolution, as May insisted, it could perhaps only be sustained by an appeal to the inevitability of progress. And progress means the Indian, with all his potential virtues, must pass on for the sake of the greater human good.[37]

As Boyarin concludes, "Once again the compatibility of the elegiac mode with the smooth history of genocide is reconfirmed."[38]

More than a few Indian enthusiasts maintain that May's stories "some-how . . . really happened."[39] Some German scholars, despite the weight of evidence otherwise, contend that May must have spent some portion of his early life in the United States. They point to his easy familiarity with the American idiom, with argot "as used in the West." Examples pointed to, according to Frayling, include "thounderation," "the deuce," "zounds," "heavens," "hum," "hello," "hang it all," "the devil," "lackaday," "hihihihi," and "the favorite word of the frontiersman—pshaw."[40] In the end, it doesn't really matter. May's works have assumed the mantle of truth that tran-scends the merely factual. His colonialist fairy tales, like those of Cooper, are more authentic to their readers than anything dull reportage of Indi-ans can offer.[41]

For the United States, Frederick Jackson Turner's "frontier" is a myth of creation. This is not so for Europe, however. Its meaning, like that of May's stories, changes over time and space. For Poles in the 1940s and 1950s, the Red Indian (as indigenes are most often called in Europe) is a parable of Poland, abandoned by the Allies at Yalta. During the Cold War, for some in the Eastern Bloc, the struggle of Winnetou and his fellow Natives was the fight *against* American imperialism. For others it was a fantasy escape from the oppressive conditions of life under Communism. In present-day Germany, it is a means to protest and throw off "the stifling conformity of contemporary European society."[42] May's tales provide the illusion of an entrée into a Manichaean realm where clear-cut good and evil battle, an edenic wilderness where the rules of civilized society do not obtain.

Today there are western clubs, like that encountered by Ross, in Belgium, France, Germany, and the Czech Republic, as well as in many other nations. One can find rodeos in Carcassonne, saloons outside Koblenz, and sheriff's offices in Frankfurt. Nowhere, however, are there more Indian clubs than in Germany. Porsches, Audis, and Mercedes stand parked near tipis surrounded by lounging Indians.

Although some of these cultural transvestites embrace May, others attempt to distance themselves from what they recognize as his "naïveté." According to Peter Timmerman, the historian and curator of Munich's Cowboy Club, "We refuse to be identified with the romanticism of Karl May. We're not against Karl May as a writer, but as an ethnologist. May depicted the Indians as all feathers and warpaint. As a result, Europeans received a very distorted image of Indians."[43] Rudolf Conrad, describing a hobbyist encampment in the German Democratic Republic in 1983 at which Archie Fire Lame Deer participated in discussions and led them in a sweat lodge and pipe ceremony, states emphatically, "Karl May is clearly of no importance in such a context."[44] Even some American Natives, albeit often those with a very different agenda from the hobbyists, support the view. Will Tsosie, who runs a "culture camp" near Canyon de Chelly, states, "If you want a generic New Age fantasy experience, I don't want you. *Indianers* do their homework and are here for the real thing. That's what I like."[45] Though many hobbyists claim that their re-creations of Indian life are completely authentic and exacting, in actuality they run a spectrum from "perfectionist" to "creative."[46] Photographs of *Indianer* gatherings bear this out, with those in more recognizable regalia mingling with hobbyists garbed in pan-Indian fantasies of feathers and coonskin caps.

Some scholars and hobbyists even dispute that May is the root source of the continuing fascination with the West and Indians in Germany. It is true that the image shaped by May was reinforced subsequently (even in his own lifetime) by a variety of sources. Visits by Buffalo Bill's Wild West Show from 1887 to 1913 and a homegrown knock-off, founded in 1901 by Hans Stosch-Sarrasani, helped cement May's representations in the popular mind.[47] So did the publication of a disparate variety of books, including the works of Zane Grey; the fictive autobiographies of Grey Owl, Buffalo Child Long Lance (Sylvester Long), and "Big Chief White Horse Eagle";

and the translation of Charles Eastman's *Indian Boyhood* in 1912. Nevertheless, the timing of the manifestations of Indian cultural transvestitism and their continuing connections with May lead to the conclusion that the author's work and its popularity created the phenomenon.

Buffalo Bill's Wild West Show visited Leipzig in 1890. By 1895, Gustav Wustmann reported that the annual Tauchischer Jahrmarkt had become an institutionalized mass expression of *Indianer* enthusiasm, something that would have been unthinkable "thirty years ago." Though Cody's extravaganza may have contributed, it is significant that the other type of costume noted by Wustmann as common was that of the Bedouins. Thus, both Old Shatterhand's America and Kara-ben-Nemsi's Arabia are represented. When Cody's show played Dresden in 1906, May and his wife attended and were invited backstage. Klara May recorded that, when Karl was introduced to the Indians, he immediately began conversing with them in their native tongues. According to Feest, "After a time, the American image-maker, Cody interrupted the conversation: 'You are an idealist, my dear,' he said, patting his German rival's back, 'the only valid law is that of the strong and clever!' To Klara it seemed as if the facial expression of the Indian suddenly changed—'and hate seemed to flash in his beautiful dark eye.'"[48]

Interactions such as this continued. Significantly, Sarrasani chose to build his circus in Dresden. In 1928, at the height of Sarrasani's popularity, the Karl-May-Museum was opened at Villa Shatterhand. Sarrasani visited May's widow to pay his respects, and "his Indians" "consecrate[d] their death songs" to May and laid flowers upon his grave.[49] Following World War II, a man calling himself Silkirtis Nichols, chief of the Cherokee, moved to Germany and became associated with the new Karl-May-Museum and pageants in the west, taking the name Buffalo Child Long Lance![50] Finally, it is significant to note that the first Indian club, the Club Manitou, was founded in Radebeul in 1910, after May had regained his reputation and popularity.[51] Such clubs spread quickly. The Munich Cowboy Club was founded a year after May's death by frustrated would-be emigrants to America.[52] In the end, one must agree with Walther Ilmer of the Karl-May-Gesellschaft: "May created the legend of Winnetou and in so doing raised the sympathy and respect for the American Indians and their way of life. The image the German population has had of the American West and particularly of the American Indian since 1880 has been largely shaped by Karl May."[53] Even Conrad, who seeks to uncover other sources of German interest, concludes that May is the "most lasting" influence: "For the German reader, Karl May's Indian novels established a deeply effective romantic-emotional tie to the American Indian."[54]

Christopher Frayling, describing the decision to make "Der Schatz im Silbersee" ("The Treasure of Silver Lake"), the first film of Karl May's Winnetou stories, writes, "At a time when the popular German cinema relied almost exclusively on Edgar Wallace thrillers, erotic melodramas, fearsome sex education films, and Rider Haggard-type adventure stories for its daily bread, this represented something of a gamble."[55] The tremendous following for Karl May fiction aside, the venture was actually practically risk-free. The African adventures of Haggard and the westerns of May are of a single, colonialist piece, ideologically almost indistinguishable. Ngugi wa Thiong'o has described the sense of inferiority inculcated when Blacks read H. Rider Haggard. How much equally so the Indian child who reads pulp westerns, Fenimore Cooper, or Karl May?[56]

Thomas King notes that Native writers tend to "assiduously avoid" writing historical fiction. The burdens of images and stereotypes such as populate the world of Karl May and Bill Cody (or Louis L'Amour, for that matter) are too great. He elaborates:

> Some of the reasons for this avoidance are obvious. The literary stereotypes and clichés for which the period [the nineteenth century] is famous have been, I think, a deterrent to many of us. Feathered warriors on pinto ponies, laconic chiefs in full regalia, dusky, raven-haired maidens, demonic shamans with eagle-claw rattles and scalping knives are all picturesque and exciting images, but they are, more properly, servants of a non-Native imagination. Rather than try to unravel the complex relationships between nineteenth-century Indians and the white mind, or to craft a new set of images that still reflects the time, but avoids the flat, static depiction of the Native and the two dimensional quality of the culture, most of us have consciously set our literature in the present, a period that is reasonably free of literary monoliths and which allows for greater latitude in the creation of characters and situations, and, more important, allows us the opportunity to create for ourselves and our respective cultures both a present and a future.[57]

Though still tending to eschew historical fiction, an increasing group of Native writers, including King, is beginning to face up to the legacy of image-makers like May, Cooper, and Cody in both their critical/scholarly work and in their fiction in order to deconstruct and dissolve the irony of their lingering influence.

In his novel *Green Grass, Running Water*, King undertakes an ambitious re-imagining of history. It is, however, history of a most postmodern sort, as fictional characters and historical personages collide and interact and mythic and chronological time coexist at all moments. Among other targets of King's humor is James Fenimore Cooper, whose Deerslayer here encounters a figure from Native myth:

> Hello, says Old Woman. I'm Old Woman.
>
> That skinny guy in the leather shirt with fringe stays behind that tree, and all Old Woman can see is a big rifle. A really big rifle.
>
> That's a big rifle, says Old Woman.
>
> You bet, says the skinny man. I'm Nathaniel Bumppo, Post-Colonial Wilderness Guide and Outfitter. You must be Chingachgook.
>
> No, says Old Woman, I'm not Chingachgook.
>
> My friends call me Nasty, says Nathaniel Bumppo. Chingachgook is my friend. He's an Indian. But he is my friend anyway.
>
> But I'm not Chingachgook, says Old Woman.
>
> Nasty Bumppo runs to the next tree and hides behind it. Nonsense, he says. I can tell an Indian when I see one. Chingachgook is an Indian. You're an Indian. Case closed.
>
> I'm sure this is embarrassing for you, says Old Woman.
>
> Indians have Indian gifts, says Nasty Bumppo. And Whites have white gifts.
>
> Gifts? says Old Woman.
>
> That Nasty Bumppo keeps running from tree to tree as he is talking, dragging that really big rifle behind him.
>
> Indians have a keen sense of smell, says Nasty Bumppo. That's an Indian gift.
>
> +++
>
> Whites are compassionate, says Nasty Bumppo. That's a white gift.
>
> +++

Indians can run fast. Indians can endure pain. Indians have quick reflexes. Indians don't talk much. Indians have good eyesight. Indians have agile bodies. These are all Indian gifts, says Nasty Bumppo.

Interesting, says Old Woman.

Whites are patient. Whites are spiritual. Whites are cognitive. Whites are philosophical. Whites are sophisticated. Whites are sensitive. These are all white gifts, says Nasty Bumppo.

So, says Old Woman. Whites are superior, and Indians are inferior.

Exactly right, says Nasty Bumppo. Any questions?

In the interchange between Cooper's White hero and Old Woman, and others like it, King not only deconstructs Cooper's stereotypes but those of May and his disciples as well. The choice of Hawkeye, the persona of the mature Deerslayer, as the name of one of his four old trickster Indians (along with the equally fictive—and colonialist—Ishmael, Lone Ranger, and Robinson Crusoe) further contributes to the process.[58]

In his latest novel, *Truth and Bright Water*,[59] King aims at May more directly. In the first draft of the book, Karl May, a retired schoolmaster and amateur photographer, and his wife rent a car in Montana and set out to drive to Banff for Indian Days. Weeks later the automobile is found in the middle of the prairie, battery dead and out of gas. There are no signs of foul play; windows are rolled up, doors are locked, the Mays are buckled in their seatbelts.

> One of the curious things about the mishap was where the car was discovered. It wasn't found in the mountains where, if you made a wrong turn, you'd end up getting lost in a web of logging roads and trails. And it wasn't found in the foothills where you could take a corner or a curve too fast, skid off the road, and slide down an embankment into a river.
>
> The car was standing in the middle of the prairies. On high ground.
>
> Even if you get yourself lost, you could just look out in any direction, whenever you wanted, and see where you were.

King has simply erased May from the Native landscape, just as Monroe Swimmer, his trickster figure in the work, erases Christian mission presence from the reservation by painting the old church in trompe d'oeil

clouds and sky so that it is almost indistinguable from its natural surroundings.

All the tourist's cameras and exposed film are found in the car. When
the pictures are developed: "All the pictures were panoramas, landscapes,
the sort of thing that you would expect tourists to take, but the neat thing
was that all of the stuff in the distance, the rivers, the mountains, the
clouds, the prairies, was slightly blurry and out of focus, while stuff in the
foreground, the steering wheel, the windshield wipers, the hood of the
car, were crisp and sharp."

King's May does not have the survival skills and wilderness knowledge of Old Shatterhand, and his pictures are those of one uninterested in
the real world. They are reflections of an inward directed gaze. In the subsequent revision of the manuscript, the May story remains, though in
slightly different form. He is now Helmut May, a famous fashion photographer. Otherwise, the incident is essentially unchanged.

Gerald Vizenor attributes the interest of May and others like him to
envy of American indigenes. In his volume of critical essays *Fugitive Poses*
he contends:

> Many artists and authors would be native by the creation of char-
> acters in their novels and other publications. Karl May, the German
> author who created the warrior Winnetou, for instance, and *The Last
> of the Mohicans* by James Fenimore Cooper, *Hiawatha* by the poet and
> romancer Henry Wadsworth Longfellow, *Black Elk Speaks* by John
> Neihardt, *Scarlet Plume* by Frederick Manfred, *Bury My Heart at
> Wounded Knee* by Dee Brown, and *Turtle Island* by Gary Snyder, are
> native creations and connections, a sense of native presence. These
> and many other authors, poets, and artists, such as the painter George
> Catlin and the photographer Edward Curtis, are native in a theater of
> aesthetics, as they created native characters and images that are for-
> ever in the artistic and literary history of the nation.[60]

Similarly, in *Manifest Manners*, he writes:

> Native American Indians have endured the envies of the mis-
> sionaries of manifest manners for five centuries. The Boy Scouts of
> America, the wild simulations of tribal misnomers used by football
> teams, automobiles, and other products, Western movies, and the

heroic adventures in novels by James Fenimore Cooper, Frederick Manfred, Karl May, and others are but a few examples of the manifold envies that have become manifest manners in the literature of dominance. The shamans of the tribes have been envied by urban spiritualists, military men have envied the courage of the tribes, and now, on some reservations, the outrageous riches from casino operations are envied by untold posers in organized crime and politics. ... Frederick Manfred must have envied tribal warriors and the natural lust of the noble savage to create five Western novels in Buckskin Man Tales.[61]

For Vizenor, manifest manners are the moral side of Manifest Destiny—assimilation and all things that would seek to possess, and thus render tame, Native peoples and their imaginations.

In Vizenor's novel *Hotline Healers* Tune Browne is called in to investigate when all the images of Indians disappear from the ethnographic photographs in museums. Attempting to unravel the "vanishing native pose" in pictures by Edward Curtis and others, he labels the arcane escapes "emulsion evanescence" and "postindian transmutation." He notes, "The Karl May Museum near Dresden reported a similar incident on the same night that East German authorities erected the wall in Berlin. . . . The images of natives vanished from snapshots and photographs in the entire museum collection." Noting May's continuation of his earlier impersonations by adopting the pose of Old Shatterhand, Browne concludes, "Karl May vanished with utmost significance in his own stories of the warrior, and the natives, once captured and sold in emulsion, have now vanished in their own creation stories." For Tune Browne, as for Susan Sontag, there is "something predatory" in the act of photography—"it turns people into objects that can be symbolically possessed." For Vizenor, the natives in the photographs are paracolonial simulations, no more genuine than those in Karl May's stories, and, ultimately, Natives cannot be so contained.[62]

In his novel *The Heartsong of Charging Elk*, James Welch also attempts to deconstruct the baggage left by nineteenth- and early twentieth-century image-makers. In an early draft of the work, he posits a university professor, a deracinated, culturally alienated Lakota, not unlike Chuck Ross in Germany. Welch's protagonist visits France where he meets a family of mixed-blood French/Lakotas, the progeny of one of Buffalo Bill's Indians who remained behind when the show moved on. Much to his fascination and shame, like Ross's experience of the Indian hobbyist, the American finds out that these people know more about the Lakota and their history than he does. The difference between Ross's experience and that of Welch's fictional character, however, is significant. Those the latter encounters are actually Lakota, though born and raised in France. The finished novel still accomplishes Welch's critique. The contemporary frame of the university professor has, however, been dropped. The story is now simply that of Buffalo Bill's Indian.

Karl May remains Germany's best-selling author. His work keeps a cottage industry of museums, outdoor dramas, publishing houses, hobby clubs, and scholars busy. His books spawned a series of highly successful films that, in turn, gave birth to the spaghetti westerns in Italy.[63] He continues, long after his death, to shape images of American Natives in Germany, throughout Europe, and, by indirection, in the United States. Those images are complete fabrications. Greg Langley writes,

> But does this really matter? Everybody knows that the West of John Wayne, The Magnificent Seven, and the Marlboro Man is fiction, just as most Germans recognize that May's vision of the West is inaccurate. The fiction of the West, whether it is written by May or Zane Grey, filmed by Sam Peckinpah or Sergio Leone, or personified by Gary Cooper or Pierre Brice, contains a legendary quality that appeals to all of us. And even though much of this image may now have been discredited, the promise of freedom it contains has firmly entered our dreams, whether American or German. Some dreams, it seems, are universal.[64]

Now a growing number of Native voices, claiming the right to representational sovereignty, are saying it does matter. For his part, May, it seems, with his literary model, James Fenimore Cooper, was "fully aware of writing what the world thinks rather than what is true."[65]

"Empor ins Reich des Edelmenschen"

KARL MAY, (1842–1912)

CHAPTER SIX

CLOWNS AND VILLAINS

American Natives and the American Musical

In the 1800s far too many Pocahontases—not to mention pseudo-Pocahontases—tripped across the stage for us to look at them all. Not surprisingly, the superabundant porcelain princesses (like their stuffed-shirt Indian chief counterparts) soon became a glut on the proscenium market.

RAYMOND WILLIAM STEDMAN,
Shadows of the Indian

It is a commonplace that all art tells more about the artist and the era in which he or she lives than about the subject or the period depicted. Nowhere is this more true than in popular entertainment forms. In this chapter, I will examine images of North America's indigenous peoples in American musicals, both stage and motion picture, from their inception to the present. In the process, I will discuss both positive depictions as well as the far more prevalent negative ones, reinforcing stereotypes acceptable to the dominant culture. As will become apparent, on both stage and screen, Indians have been portrayed largely as either clowns for comic relief or as savage villains. All too often they have been erased completely from stories and settings in which they would logically appear. Though these phenomena are hardly unique to musicals, being reflected also in other forms of popular culture, it is in musicals that they perhaps come into sharpest focus.

In his book *Mass Media/Mass Culture*, Stan Le Roy Wilson defines "popular culture" as "the culture of everyone in a society."[1] He goes on to state,

"It can be so pervasive that we seldom notice it. In order for us to notice it, we must step back and consciously observe it."[2] If one accepts this as a working definition of popular culture, are musicals part of that popular culture? If popular culture is that which we all, in a given society, share, can we consider musicals "popular?"

At first glance, this might seem to be a questionable proposition. With ticket prices from Broadway musicals regularly fetching $75 for a top seat, they would hardly seem an art form for the masses. Closer examination, however, reveals that musicals are indeed part of popular culture as defined by Wilson. Musicals are a peculiarly American invention, growing out of a melding of light opera with English music hall traditions. The exact date of the birth of the musical remains in dispute among scholars. Some consider the first musical to be *The Black Crook* in 1866. Others maintain that it was not until 1881, with the staging of *Patience*, that the musical theatre was born. For our purposes, this debate need not be resolved. Music and drama have always been linked, and from the earliest days of musical stage productions in the United States, these musical plays were considered popular entertainment, a bastard child of the high-culture form of opera. Further, with the advent of motion pictures and television, musicals were brought at low cost to mass audiences. They have both shaped and reflected popular attitudes in the United States, particularly in the twentieth century.

Accepting, then, that musicals are an element of popular culture, how does this popular medium intersect with reflection concerning representations of American Indians? The depiction of race and ethnicity in popular entertainment deserves careful scrutiny. How the "other" is portrayed says much about cultural attitudes and raises important questions for theological anthropology (i.e., who is considered human) and values (i.e., what value is ascribed to the culture of that other). As already indicated, popular entertainment both reflects and shapes attitudes. Although, in some circumstances, it can perform a subversive function, it can also reinforce prevailing ideology and aid in the indoctrination of the mass populace in that ideology. This has certainly been the case with American Indians.

In discussing depictions of Natives in movies, Vine Deloria, Jr., states, "Underneath all the conflicting images of the Indian, one fundamental truth emerges: the white man knows that he is alien and he knows that North America is Indian—and he will never let go of the Indian image because he thinks by some clever manipulation he can achieve an authenticity that can never be his."[3] As a result, in the popular imagination, real Indians cannot be permitted to survive into the twentieth century. Their very real, continued existence serves as a painful reminder of the illegitimacy of whitestream claims to North America. Indians must therefore be represented by the images described by Daniel Francis in his book, *The Imaginary Indian*, or by Robert Berkhofer in his *White Man's Indian*. They must be stereotyped, relegated to a fabulous nineteenth century, seen as an extinct breed. This is necessary if the myth of the frontier, upon which so much of American self-image is based, is to survive intact. In the musical, this condition is often reflected in a form of homestyle ethnic cleansing, wherein Natives are either erased entirely from the landscape depicted or pushed to the periphery as stereotypical representatives of a vanishing race.

In the collective American psyche, Amer-Europeans conquered a vast, unsettled, primeval wilderness. They bent it to their plow and to their will. The reality, however, was starkly different. These stalwart souls discovered a land already inhabited.

Berkhofer limns two distinct stereotypes of American Indians. Both of these are inextricably bound up with White self-evaluations, describing Natives in terms of what they were not or what they lacked in Amer-European terms. First is the "noble savage" or, for Berkhofer, the "good Indian." These Indians lived in harmony with nature in a state of "liberty, simplicity, and innocence." They were physically beautiful and dignified and regal in demeanor. Brave in combat, they were tender and loyal in familial and personal relationships. Juxtaposed with this image is that of the bloodthirsty or "bad Indian." Upon these Natives are heaped all the negative qualities of whitestream society, many of them associated with sex. They are naked, leacherous debauchers. They are lazy, deceitful, and treacherous.[4]

To Berkhofer's categories must be added a third, the stereotype of the "half-breed." An extension of the "bad Indian" image, half-breeds have no redeeming virtues. They are neither White nor Indian. As such, they are the degenerate products of miscegenation, distrusted by both cultures and fitting in nowhere.

These myths have pervaded the American imagination and are widely reflected in popular culture, including the musical theatre. They have persisted from colonial times to the present. As Jan Elliott states, "Indians are the only minority group that Indian lovers won't let out of the 19th century. They love Indians as long as they can see them riding around on ponies wearing beads and feathers, living in picturesque tee-pee villages and making long profound speeches."[5] Whites still expect, even now, to see Indians as they once were, living in forests or performing in Wild West shows rather than working on farms or living in urban areas. In fact, today most Native persons are of mixed blood. Roughly two-thirds now live in cities. Many are indistinguishable to the uncritical whitestream eye from their White or Black neighbors. In the dominant culture, however, Natives who resist assimilation often are judged by Whites in light of the half-breed stereotype. Reservation Indians are viewed as indolent, drunken, and degraded—and with the advent of casino gaming, greedy. According to Berkhofer, "Degenerate and poverty-stricken, these unfortunates were presumed to be outcasts from their own race, who exhibited the worst qualities of Indian character with none of its redeeming features."[6]

Understanding these myths is vital if one is to understand treatment of Natives in the American musical. At the risk of oversimplification, they are the operative attitudes that drive the portrayals of Indians (or lack thereof) in the musical. As a popular art form, it reflects the hopes, fears, and desires of the wider culture. In the process, myths of the dominant culture are refined, recast, and reinforced. Indian characters are either stereotyped or ethnically cleansed, purged entirely from a White-dominated environment.

The first known effort to deal with Indians on the musical stage appears to have been *Tammany; or, the Indian Chief,* which debuted at the John Street Theater on March 3, 1794. It marked the beginning of exploitation of Native themes to serve purely White ends. By glorifying Tammany, an actual Native leader "whom tradition credited with great wisdom and respect for white people"[7] (and actually often referred to as "Saint Tammany"[8]), the play, by indirection, promoted the Tammany Society (which like the present-day men's movement, appropriated Native structures and names) and its anti-Federalist agenda. It also advanced the stereotype of the noble savage.

Owing much to tragic opera, the plot revolves around the eponymous chief, who is in love with Manana. When the woman is abducted by Spaniards, Tammany rescues her. The Spanish, however retaliate and burn the lovers to death in a cabin. Through it all, Tammany is the very embodiment of the "good Indian," dignified and loyal. Defiant of the invaders, he is a true "son of the forest." He sings, "The sun sets in night and stars shun the day / But unfading glory can never decay / You white men deceivers, your smiles are in vain / The son of Alkmoonac shall ne'er wear your chain." Another Indian, Weegaw, provided comic relief. The authors noted that the duet between Manana and Tammany was "altered from an old Indian song."⁹

Tammany also marked the beginning of a new piece of ideology concerning America's indigenous peoples. The villains of the piece were Spanish. America's Anglo-Saxon power structure was already divorcing itself from the genocide being perpetrated against the Native population. Others committed atrocities but not Americans. And when such things did occur at their hands, it was an aberration, the act of a crazed individual acting beyond the bounds of propriety and authority. It was a tragic mistake not to be replicated. The critic Ward Churchill has pointed out, in fact, that this "tragic mistake" doctrine persists in seemingly affirmative works like those of Tony Hillerman or the popular—and elegiac—*Dances With Wolves*.¹⁰ Whitestream culture always manages to separate itself from culpability.

The evening of December 15, 1829, saw the premiere of a straight play, *Metamora; or, the Last of the Wampanoags*, at the Park Theater in New York. Based on the events of King Philip's War ("Metamora" being a poetic rendering of King Philip's Indian name, Metacomet), and written by John Augustus Stone, the play debuted just a week after President Andrew Jackson delivered his first annual address to Congress, in which he called for removal of Indians to the trans-Mississippi West. It presents Metacomet as a noble figure, fighting for his homelands. As he dies, he utters, "My curses on you, white men!" According to historian Jill Lepore, this is "THE END. The end of the play and the end of the race. The audience rises in rapturous applause. . . . A tragic death, yes, but a necessary one. *Metamora* mourned the passing of Philip and the disappearance of New England's Indians but it mourned those losses as inevitable and right."¹¹

Metamora helped prepare whitestream audiences for Indian removal. It spawned a number of imitators, as Native-themed plays became the rage. It became itself one of the most performed plays of the nineteenth century and was staged as late as 1887. It was, however, more than half a century after *Tammany* and well after support for removal waned that Indians again became a subject for the musical stage.

On November 29, 1847, *Metamora; or the Last of the Pollywogs* bowed in at the Adelphi Theater in Boston. Written by the Irish-born actor and showman, John Brougham, it parodied Stone's 1829 play. According to Lepore, "This time Philip would not stay dead."[12] Three English colonists ("Badenough," "Worser," and "Vaughan") repeatedly shoot the Native leader, who staggers and dies, crying, "I feel it's almost time for me to slope/ The red man's fading out, and in his place/ There comes a bigger, not a better race/ Just as you've seen the squirming Pollywog/ In the course of time become a bloated frog." The chorus intones, "We're dying, die, die, dying/ We're all dying like a flock of sheep." But Metamora responds, "You're lying, lie, lie, lying/ You're all lying; I wouldn't die so cheap." He rises to declare, "Confound your skins, I will not die to please you."[13]

According to Lepore:

> In *The Last of the Pollywogs*, John Brougham parodied more than a few elements of the stage Indian, and, perhaps most powerfully, he resisted the vanishing-Indian theme prevalent in the nineteenth-century Indian drama by simply refusing to kill off his protagonist. In its final lines ("I will not die to please you") Brougham's parody acknowledged the cultural importance of the dead stage Indian in placating whites' fears of real-life Indians. But while *The Last of the Pollywogs* mocked the conventions of early Indian dramas, it also expressed bitter scorn for Indian peoples, an attitude that was becoming increasingly widespread at midcentury.[14]

Real Wampanoags had, after all, become "Pollywogs," and Metamora's wife was "Tapiokee." Support for removal as a policy may have faded but disdain for Natives was on the rise.

In 1855, Brougham mounted another musical production with a Native theme. Turning again to actual history, he premiered *Pocahontas; or, The Gentle Savage* on Christmas Eve. Retelling the story of John Smith and Pocahontas, the entertainment, as the title suggests, depicted the noble savage, as represented by the Indian maiden. Underlying White hostility was betrayed, however, once again by the names Brougham gave to his unhistorical characters. Names like "Cod-Livr-Oyl," "Ip-Pah-Kak," "Kal-O-Mel," "Kross-As-Kan-Be," "Lump-A-Sugah," and "Poo-Ti-Pet" not only demonstrate White attitudes of superiority but do so by showing that, to White ears, Native languages were little but gibberish.

The success of *Pocahontas* led its star, Charles M. Walcot, to write a Native-based production of his own. *Hiawatha; or, Ardent Spirits and Laughing Water* was a horrible pastiche of the Hiawatha legend. According to the *New York Times*, "He [Walcot] has interpolated jokes and puns of the most agonizing kind, and utter regardless of historical truth makes 'Hiawatha' a critic, a censor, a satirist, a singer of comic songs, and a dancer of absurd jigs."[15] Taking a leaf from Brougham's songbook, Walcot created characters like "Pooh-Pooh-Mammi" and "No-Go-Miss." The relationship of racism against Natives to racism against African Americans and Asians in such names cannot go unnoticed.

In 1879, W. S. Gilbert (of Gilbert and Sullivan fame) collaborated with Frederic Clay on *Princess Toto*. Although the plot, centering on a fairy-tale princess who has no memory, did not deal with Native themes, according to Gerald Bordman, "Gilbert was droll as ever, and even managed to include some twitting of popular American Indian stories."[16] Exactly what is meant by this odd, and potentially offensive, phrase is uncertain. At any rate, "Without superior music the piece failed."[17]

It was replaced, however, at the same theatre, by another reworking of the Hiawatha story. This burlesque, like the earlier version, bore little relation to historical reality. Although the work did portray Whites having "penn-etrated the forest not for-rest but for plunder," it also contained numerous numbers like "Indians Never Lie," which place it firmly in the noble savage tradition.[18]

A bit of irony accompanied the next attempt at an Indian musical nine years later. *Dovetta* opened in New York on April 22, 1889—either accidentally or by design, on the day of the first White "land run" into what was to become Oklahoma, signaling the end of Indian Territory and, with it, hopes for Native territorial sovereignty. The play told the story of an Indian woman torn between her love for a fellow Native, Rainbow, and U.S. Army Lt. Robert Brambleton. When Dovetta learns, however, that she is actually White, captured by the tribe's chief and adopted after a raid, the choice is made: she goes with Brambleton.[19] Fears of miscegenation are played upon. Each race must stick to its own kind.

The threat of miscegenation is also present in *Ogallallas*, opening in New York on February 19, 1894. It claimed to be "the first major musical to center on the American Indian." Earlier efforts, cited above, were forgotten. The play debuted a little more than three years after approximately three hundred Oglalas were massacred at Wounded Knee.[20]

The carnage of Wounded Knee impinged not at all, however, upon *Ogallallas*. A simple love story, the play involves an army contingent escorting a group of women across the plains. The band is captured by Indians. When Capt. Deadshot atempts to rescue them, he is trapped too. After this, Deadshot, a Mexican named Cardenas, and the Indian War Cloud (again, an actual Native chief) all vie for the affections of one of the abducted women. No doubt much to the audience's relief, she decides upon Deadshot just as the cavalry arrives to save them.[21]

With one other minor example (*The Maid of Plymouth* in 1894), thus ended the depiction of Natives on the musical stage in the nineteenth century. It is important to note, in keeping with Anglo-Saxon denial of culpability for atrocities against Natives, that the worst years of the Indian Wars, from the end of the American Civil War until the late 1870s, produced no works dealing with Indians. The years 1879 and 1880 produced a flurry of interest. And a decorous interval of three years passed after Wounded Knee before Indians again became fodder for popular entertainment rather than army Hotchkiss guns.

As Oklahoma approached statehood, the year 1907 saw a sudden upturn of interest in musicals concerning Natives. On August 12, *The Alaskan* bowed in at the Knickerbocker Theatre. This twenty-nine-performance flop had a chorus of Eskimos and featured a song entitled "The Totem Pole" ("My father's father was an eagle") led by Totem Pole Pete while the chorus line, dressed as totem poles, cavorted.[22]

The previous month had witnessed the opening of *The Follies of 1907*. This first edition of the famous show by impresario Florenz Ziegfeld parodied figures of the day from Enrico Caruso to Andrew Carnegie. Its titular plot, however, concerned the introduction of John Smith and Pocahontas to "modern life."[23]

Later in the year, *Miss Pocahontas* revisited the same, now familiar tale. Once again playing fast and loose with history, the show made Smith out to be a braggart warrior condemned to marry an old crone or be executed. Choosing death, he is rescued by the Native princess even though she really loves John Rolfe. In its revisionism, it even made Chief Pow-Ha-

Tan a mixed blood with an Irish father—thus fulfilling the need for a traditional musical clown.[24]

In 1919, even the great Cole Porter associated himself with an "Indian show," writing the music for *Hitchy-Koo, 1919*, one of a series of popular reviews. The bill featured Chief Eagle Horse and Princess White Deer, two Natives, singing and dancing as a novelty. According to Bordman, "The show's limited success discouraged Porter, and it was another five years before a new Cole Porter score was heard on a Broadway stage." Porter would return, however, to a thumping, tom-tom, pseudo-Indian style for the song "If You Like Les Belles Poitrines," cut from a later show. The style is so wildly inappropriate for a song about the breasts of Parisian women, one is forced to ask if the urbane Porter thought his audience would associate the "primitive" rhythm with elemental sexuality.[25]

By far the most successful spectacle with an Indian influence came five years later, in 1924, with the premiere of *Rose-Marie* by Otto Harbach, Oscar Hammerstein II, and Rudolf Friml. Not only was the show the biggest grosser of its decade, but not until *Oklahoma* in the 1940s would its multi-million-dollar box office gate be surpassed. Its phenomenal success can be traced in large part to its "exotic" setting and its ability to tap into the dominating ideology of the time, reflecting Native assimilation in the person of its heroine and the vanishing Indian in other elements.

In the operetta, Rose-Marie La Flamme, a mixed-blood singer, works at a small hotel in the Canadian Rockies. She is in love with Jim Kenyon. Ed Hawley, however, desires her as well. In order to get the girl all to himself, Hawley casts suspicion on Jim for the murder of an Indian named Black Eagle, who had previously accused Jim of claim jumping. In fact, Black Eagle is stabbed by his wife, Wanda, after he discovers her and Hawley (whom she loves) in an embrace. When accused, Jim flees into the woods. Convinced that her lover is a killer, Rose-Marie agrees to marry Hawley. Thanks, however, to Sgt. Malone of the Mounties, the truth comes out, Jim is cleared, and the couple is reunited.[26]

In its treatment of Natives and Native themes, *Rose-Marie* left much to be desired. The half-breed stereotype does not operate with regard to Rose-Marie. It may be that this depiction runs to only one gender, the male. She is nonetheless portrayed as speaking broken, inferior English: her first line of the play, written in bad dialect, is "I am take sleigh ride with Jeem." There is no worry, however, expressed about her marrying Jim. It is a mark of patriarchy that miscegenation fears run only to White women. It is perfectly acceptable, even historically common, for White men to have sex with and/or marry Indian women.

Musically, Rose-Marie and Jim's "Indian Love Call," supposed to be a Native song, was nowhere near Native in its chromatics. The same can be said about the "Totem Tom Tom," a number reminiscent of the totem pole dance in *The Alaskan*. Bordman is probably correct, however, that they "undoubtedly conveyed red-skin images to the audience."[27]

Rose-Marie also became the earliest Broadway musical with Native imagery to make the transition from stage to screen, being filmed in 1936 by W. S. Van Dyke II as a vehicle for Nelson Eddy and Jeanette McDonald.[28] The film's screenplay bore little resemblance to the book of the original show. The blonde McDonald's Rose-Marie is now a White, a Broadway star surnamed de Flor, in search of her brother accused of a crime. Mountie Eddy becomes the love interest. Despite such changes, Native representations remained an integral part of the drama, beginning with a credit crawl over an imposing totem pole.

If Rose-Marie herself is no longer of mixed ancestry, a new character, conforming to the half-breed stereotype, is introduced. McDonald's guide into the wilderness in search of her brother is Boniface, a shifty-eyed, sinister Indian. When Boniface robs and deserts her, Rose-Marie is told, "That's the trouble with those half-breeds; you can't trust them." Later she catches up to Boniface, whom she discovers drinking; he is the epitome of the degraded, drunken Indian. Threatening to turn him in for having alcohol on the reserve, she coerces him into helping her. At the first opportunity, however, he again sneaks away, leaving her stranded.

Other Indians are stereotypical noble savages. When Eddy convinces Rose-Marie to attend the Natives' annual Corn Dance, an event described as "like our Thanksgiving and Mardi Gras" rolled into one, the audience is treated to stock documentary footage of large numbers of Indians in great, carved canoes. Rose-Marie remarks, "There are so many of them. I never dreamed things like this were still going on." Once more, Indians are trapped in the nineteenth century.

At the ceremony itself, the "Totem Tom Tom" of the stage version is replaced by "The Tom Tom Dance," a mishmash of different traditions from a variety of regions. A giant drum is rolled out and a Native dancer performs a stylized dance on it. From there, the festival degenerates totally into a Busby Berkeley-like production number, complete with Indian maidens as chorus girls.

With assimilation again the dominating ideology and termination and relocation the government policy, *Rose-Marie* was remade for the screen in 1954. Filmed in Cinemascope by Mervyn LeRoy, and starring Ann Blyth and Howard Keel, it was more faithful to the original operetta. The treatment of Natives, however, still left much to be desired.

"Rose-Marie" became the subject of parody in 1999 in the "mini-musical" *Dudley Do-Right*, written and directed by Hugh Wilson and based on the cartoon created by Jay Ward. When first encountered, the stalwart Mountie (Brendan Fraser) and his girlfriend, the luminous Nell Fenwick (Sarah Jessica Parker), are even reprising Eddy and MacDonald's famous duet, "Indian Love Call."

After the musical interlude, Nell says, "I hear they're having an authentic Corn Festival Dance at the Reservation—complete with fireworks and everything!" As the pair approach by canoe, it is a scene directly out of the 1936 film. Twitting McDonald's nineteenth-century stereotypes and the wider culture's longing for authenticity, generally, Parker's Nell exclaims, "Dudley, this is totally authentic!" To which Do-Right replies, "This is Canada, Nell. Things are real up here."

When they put ashore, they are at the reserve of that tribe of "South Brooklyn Indians, the Canarsie Kumquats." The chief, played by Alex Rocco, greets them wearing large, heavy-rimmed eyeglasses and asks how they are. Nell replies, "Me do well." To which the Indian replies, "Good for you, sugar."

The Corn Dance itself is a copy of "The Tom Tom Dance" from the 1936 *Rose-Marie*, complete with dancing on an oversized drum. Then, though the thumping rhythm never changes, the Natives break into Irish step-dancing. The chief says to Dudley, "This 'River Dance' stuff is really hot, lately." The number ends with a crescendo as a female dancer slides across the stage in a splits; sporting an ear-to-ear smile, she raises one arm and says, "Hao!" In reality, the "Corn Festival Dance" is a nightly show. Later in the film, a giant ear of corn unfolds to reveal a beautiful "Corn Maiden" inside. As the chief's right-hand man, Standing Room Only, explains, it's "basically a dinner theater we're running here."

All of this is played strictly for laughs, operating, as did the original cartoon, on dual levels, one for children and the other for adults. Its depiction of Natives can be viewed as affirmative. The Indians speak perfect English and display scant patience when Whites expect otherwise. They tread a fine line between savvy marketing and self-exploitation as they run their spectacle for Whites desiring "authenticity."

When the bad guys with villain Snidely Whiplash invade the village, history is subtly critiqued. Whiplash says, "Torch it. Burn everything." But then he stops and declares, "Have the photographers take pictures of the boys straightening up the place. Learn from history or repeat it."

Only at the end does this affirmative portrayal falter. As the villain's forces approach the village, the narrator intones, "Kumquats never walked away from a fight. They preferred to run." As the Indians run headlong, like those fleeing for the Stronghold at Wounded Knee, the chief collapses, winded. Nell says to him, "I thought Native Americans could run all day." Rocco replies, "Yeah, like we're really Indians." Ultimately, it seems these are the "casino Indians" of latter-day stereotype, merely greedy frauds making a fast dollar by staging pseudo-cultural (retro)spectacles.

Sigmund Romberg turned to Native topics and borrowed from *Rose-Marie* for his operetta *The Love Call* in 1927. Based on Augustus Thomas's straight play *Arizona*, it dealt with the efforts of Lt. Denton and his Rangers to rescue trapped ranchers from an Indian massacre. Indians receive a slightly fairer shake than usual, in that the "massacre" was precipitated by a villainous White (perhaps, again, the "tragic mistake" at work). The play flopped.[29]

Hoping for a hit like *Rose-Marie*, Rudolf Friml returned to a story with an Indian heroine that same year. The day after Christmas, *The White Eagle* opened. Based on Edward Milton Royle's straight play, *The Squaw Man*, which had produced a well-known early movie, *The White Eagle* featured music by Friml and a book by Brian Hooker and W. H. Post.

The plot concerned the younger brother of a British nobleman forced to flee to America under threat of arrest for a crime he did not commit. Here he becomes a successful rancher and marries an Indian girl named Silverwing. When his brother dies, the Englishman inherits the title. Feeling that her presence will hinder her husband, Silverwing, ever the noble savage, kills herself so as to not stand in his way. The "good Indian" sacrifices herself rather than interfere with White aspirations. Although some reviewers criticized the bright colors of the sets and costumes "as not correct for Indian motifs," the rousing "War Dance" finale, probably no more authentic, received general approbation.[30]

The next year, Florenz Ziegfeld mounted *Whoopee*, starring Eddie Cantor. Based on Owen Davis's play *The Nervous Wreck*, it featured a score by Walter Donaldson, one of Tin Pan Alley's most successful tunesmiths. In the show, Cantor is induced to elope with Sally Morgan so that she can avoid a forced marriage to the local sheriff. In reality, Sally loves an Indian named Wanenis. The sheriff pursues the eloping couple to the reservation. There it is revealed that Wanenis has no Indian blood at all but was adopted. Freed once again from the specter of miscegenation, Sally is able to marry her true love.

Producer Ziegfeld loved the western setting. He "bedecked his beauties in feathers luxurious beyond an Indian's most colorful fantasies."[31] When financial setbacks struck Ziegfeld, he sold the show to Samuel Goldwyn, who brought it to the screen virtually unaltered in 1930.

The year 1930 also witnessed the birth of one of the most enduring shows with Indian components, George and Ira Gershwin's *Girl Crazy*. A New York playboy is sent by his father to Custerville, Arizona, a town where he can get into no trouble at all. Accompanied by Gieber Goldfarb, the cabby who drove him all the way there, he quickly transforms a moribund dude ranch into a swank club with gambling and women. Goldfarb even becomes sheriff of Custerville and finds that he can talk to local Indians in Yiddish.

This throwaway detail is more than comic invention and deserves comment. It is, in fact, a subtle perpetuation of one of the oldest slurs against Natives. As early as Columbus's return from his first voyage, the Catholic hierarchy found Native languages riddled with Hebrew words. This led, of course, to the widely held belief that Indians were the Lost Tribes of Israel. By having Gieber speak to Natives in Yiddish, this ancient bit of racism is recast.

Similar problems afflict other parts of the book of *Girl Crazy*. When Gieber (called Louie in the straight-play adaptation) first arrives in Arizona and is asked if he doesn't like the West, he replies, "You oughta give it back to the Indians." The austere landscape is thought worthless and uninhabitable. Being without value, it is fit only for Indians. Likewise, when women arrive from "Chicago and points East," they query whether or not Indians don't still scalp people.[32]

The only on-stage Native character in the show is Eaglerock, described in the dramatis personae as "a real Indian." This character does cut against stereotype. He speaks English as well as anyone and is normally attired in Western-style dress. At one point, asked why he is wearing more traditional Indian garb, he twits the stereotype, saying, "You know it wouldn't be fair for a real Indian to come to a dude ranch without looking like one." And when the Gieber character shows up in full regalia, announcing himself, "Me Big Chief Push-In-the-Face," Eaglerock has fun with him by speaking Chinese and German.[33] Nonetheless, the character and his reactions say much about White expectations for Indians as colorful relics of the last century.

Girl Crazy was filmed in 1932 as a vehicle for the comedy duo of Bert Wheeler and Robert Woolsey. In 1943, it was brought to the screen again by Busby Berkeley and Norman Taurog. This version featured a radically rewritten book and starred Mickey Rooney and Judy Garland. Custerville has been changed to the only slightly less offensive Codyville. Ethnic cleansing, however, is complete as the frontier is stripped of its remaining Natives. The only Indians are poseurs, Whites dressed up as Natives for a rodeo parade. The only remaining mention of Indians is when Garland tells Rooney of an old, local Indian legend of two star-crossed lovers. Indians themselves may be gone, but their quaint stories remain, forever attached to a landscape that is now fully in the possession of Whites. In the 1990s, *Girl Crazy* once more resurfaced as *Crazy for You*. The newly rewritten book once again is ethnically cleansed, featuring no Indians.

In 1935, director Edward Sutherland shot an original Rodgers and Hart musical called *Mississippi*. A thinly disguised clone of *Showboat* set in the years prior to the American Civil War, it starred Bing Crosby as a reluctant riverboat singer and Joan Bennett as his love interest. W. C. Fields, in the Cap'n Andy role, provided comic relief as the Commodore.

The Commodore is a swaggering teller of self-aggrandizing tales. He claims he has been plying the river "ever since I took it away from the Indians." He calls Indians "redskins" and says his last encounter with them was thirty-five years previous when, armed only with a Bowie knife, he cut a path through the "wall of human flesh" that was the "Shug" Indians. His graphic telling makes women swoon.

To expose the Commodore as a pompous windbag, the other characters "haunt" him, using a cigar store wooden Indian. Terrified and repentant, he says, "Why I would no more think now of harming a hair on a red man's head than I would of sticking a fork in my mother's back." He declares, "Some of my best friends are Indians." While it might seem that this outcome is affirmative of Natives, a closer examination reveals otherwise. The characters gaslight the Commodore not to vindicate Indians but merely to prove him a fraud. Further, the very fact that the genocidal annihilation of Natives (even in the guise of the fictional "Shugs") was viewed as a suitable topic for comic relief calls into question much of the period's prevailing attitudes about Indians.

On March 31, 1943, the curtain rang up for the first time on the box office champion successor to *Rose-Marie*. Like the show it displaced, *Oklahoma!* had Indian roots. Written by Rodgers (*Mississippi*) and Hammerstein (*Rose-Marie*), the musical represents the height of the frontier myth. The landscape has been thoroughly cleansed until it becomes the vacant wilderness of White historical imagination. Once it is emptied, Whites are free to occupy it without molestation. There are no African Americans in *Oklahoma!* There are no Indians. That one could write a musical about Oklahoma, whose very name means "land of the red people," without any Natives is remarkable. Then, as now, it had the highest Indian population of any area of the country.

Further, the source material for *Oklahoma!* was a straight play by Lynn Riggs called *Green Grow the Lilacs*. The playwright, born in the year the play is set, was the son of a prominent White cattleman and a Cherokee mother. And though it is easy to talk about a Cherokee mixed-blood like Riggs being so culturally alienated that he wrote a play about Oklahoma with no Indian characters, a close reading of his work leads to a suggestion that something far more subtle is at work in the ethnic cleansing of *Oklahoma!*

Riggs's play is an affectionate depiction of the land of his childhood. Set just outside Claremore, Riggs's hometown, both the play and the musical take place in Indian Territory—not Oklahoma Territory. Claremore is in the heart of the Cherokee Nation. What I am driving at is the suggestion that *Green Grow the Lilacs* is not devoid of Indian characters at all but is in some sense a play *about* them.[34]

It is entirely possible that the hero, Curly McClain, is an Indian. McClain (or McLain) is a fairly prominent Indian surname. The nickname "Curly" could have come about because Curly, as a mixed-blood like

Riggs himself, had curly hair, an uncommon trait among Natives. Further, it is somewhat more likely that Indians would have been the cattlemen and Whites the farmers during the period depicted. This adds a different spin on lines in the musical, lifted in part from the Riggs text, like "Territory folk must stick together" and "The farmer and the cowboy must be friends."

The argument is bolstered by the presence of other Natives in Riggs's play. When, for instance, the posse comes to get Curly at Aunt Eller's, she chides them for taking the side of the U.S. marshal and calls them "furriners," a perfectly sound response for any territorial citizen, White or Native. They, however, defend themselves along explicitly racial lines. One claims, "My pappy and mammy was *both* born in Indian Territory! Why, I'm jist full of Indian blood myself." To which another responds, "Me, too! And I c'n prove it!"

This line of thought opens important points—most notably the traditional fear of intermarriage. Laurey is clearly White. Did Rodgers and Hammerstein, not knowing the historical context, read the text too superficially? Or in 1943 was miscegenation more than they thought whitestream Broadway audiences would tolerate? After all, Curly actually marries Laurey in both the straight play and the musical, and there is no eleventh-hour revelation that he is White rather than Indian. In this regard, it is interesting to note the characterization of the other man vying for Laurey's affections. In both the play and the musical, when Curly is told that Jud Fry (known as Jeeter in the Riggs play) has designs on the girl, he explodes, "What! That bullet-colored growly man 'th bushy eyebrows. . . ." Bushy eyebrows were thought by Cherokees to be a distinguishing trait of Whites, and "bullet-colored" (i.e., grey) would be a perfectly logical way for the browner Indian to describe a White man.[35]

Three years after *Oklahoma!* Indians played a role in another historically based western musical. Mounted by Rodgers and Hammerstein with songs by Irving Berlin and a book by Herbert and Dorothy Fields, *Annie Get Your Gun* was the fictionalized story of sharp-shooting star Annie Oakley, who thrilled audiences at Buffalo Bill's Wild West Show.

Annie is shown being "initiated" into the Sioux Nation. This causes her to sing, "I'm an Indian, Too" ("Just like Battle-Ax/Hatchet-Face, Eagle-Nose/Like those Indians/I'm an Indian, too."), demonstrating the perverse attraction of Whites to the cultures they attempted to destroy. Later, unable to attract the attention of Frank Butler, with whom she is in constant competition, she receives the advice of the great Sioux leader Sitting Bull, who tells her that perhaps she should deliberately lose a shooting match to Butler in order to stroke his male ego.

It is true, of course, that Buffalo Bill traveled with Natives as part of his extravaganza. It is also true that Sitting Bull toured for one season with him as a "prisoner of war." During that time, he was alternately booed as the "killer of Custer" and mobbed by a fascinated public seeking autographs. Such is America's simultaneous attraction and repulsion toward its indigenes. During his tenure, Sitting Bull knew Oakley and, in fact, once remarked to her that he could not understand how Whites could be so unmindful of the poor among them.[36] It, however, stretches credulity to the breaking point to believe that he cared, or even knew, about her love life.

A critical and popular success, *Annie Get Your Gun* ran 1,147 performances. It was turned into an equally successful film by George Sidney in 1950, starring Betty Hutton. Neither the play nor the film were seen for years, largely because of Irving Berlin's concern that its portrayal of Natives would be judged offensive. Footage of "I'm an Indian, Too," performed by Judy Garland, appeared, however, in the compilation *That's Entertainment III* in 1994.

Though the Hutton movie became available only in late 2000, the moribund state of Broadway musicals led to a stage revival of *Annie Get Your Gun*, beginning with previews in February 1999. The solution for a show long "considered unrevivable, in large part because of its hopelessly outdated portrayal of Indians," was, as with *Girl Crazy*, to drastically rewrite it. According to Peter Marks in the *New York Times* on January 24, 1999, the fix "is one that has become increasingly common in musical theater: wholesale renovation; treating the original as a shabby apartment with unnecessary clutter and a lot of potential. . . . Annie, get your makeover."[37] "I'm an Indian, Too" was deleted entirely. And Sitting Bull, who in the 1946 original spoke in a broken English, saying things like "Sitting Bull go to see Great White Father about Indian Territory," now was deliberately putting people on when he "sound 'em like this."[38]

An original musical with Native representation made it to the screen in 1946: *The Harvey Girls*, also directed by George Sidney. Set in Sandrock, New Mexico, the film purports to tell the story of the Harvey Girls, frontier waitresses who, at the beginning of the film, are described as "the first civilizing force" in the wilderness. They "conquered the West as surely as the Davy Crocketts and Kit Carsons."

In its actual depiction of Natives, the movie is neither inaccurate nor unsympathetic. They are seen as existing on the periphery of the society Whites built. They are present but marginalized, mere spectators at the show being staged by Amer-Europeans. They are silent, not taking part. Yet, in other elements, the film advances the frontier myth in an aggressive, sure-handed manner. The landscape of *The Harvey Girls* has been as thoroughly ethnically cleansed as that of *Oklahoma!*

The female lead (once again, Judy Garland) has been lured to Sandrock by the beautiful letters of a suitor, who tells her that "there is a dream in this great land that not everyone sees, waiting for a man and a woman with a little vision." This is an empty wilderness awaiting the civilizing ministrations of White colonizers. This verbal impression is reinforced visually by camera shots through the window of the train transporting her to her new life that show a vast, vacant land just beyond the ribbon of civilization that is the railroad. Garland arrives in Sandrock, described as "2000 miles from everywhere." An aerial shot at night makes the town appear as a well of light—and hence a beacon of civilization—amidst endless darkness threatening to engulf it. In the Harvey Girls' limited interaction with Natives, there are hints of fear of racial impurity with sexual overtones. Finally, in the song "The Wild, Wild West," detailing the colorful characters to be found in the area, desperadoes, cowboys, gamblers—even cattle—are mentioned, but Indians are not. In short, although Indians are physically present on-screen, *The Harvey Girls* presents an ethnically cleansed country.

Similar western musicals underwent such a cleansing. In fact, the late 1940s and 1950s saw an upsurge in these entertainments. As the federal government began to reassess the Indian New Deal, musicals reflected the deteriorating attitudes and policies that would culminate in termination and relocation. Broadway shows and original movie musicals like *Ticket to Tomahawk* (1950), *Paint Your Wagon* (staged, 1951; filmed, 1969), and *Calamity Jane* (1953) either present an ethnically scrubbed landscape or use Natives as comic devices. Without exception, when Natives are depicted, their history and culture are casually distorted with no regard for accuracy.

The most bizarre of these musicals deserves to be singled out for discussion. *Red Garters* (1954) billed itself as "a new kind of 'western.'" Filmed on surreal, minimalist sets to resemble a Broadway play, the movie follows the efforts of a wandering cowboy to avenge the death of his brother in Limbo County, California. In town, Indians are shown mixing easily with Whites, even bellying up to the bar together in the local saloon. Together the two groups celebrate the "Battle of July 13th," the only fight ever to occur between Indians and Whites in Limbo County. When asked about the encounter, Minnie Redwing announces that the Indians won and that her grandmother has a "trunkful of scalps to prove it." She proudly proclaims that it "set the palefaces back 10 years." A sign at the celebration confirms her boast: "Don't let it spoil your appetite because the palefaces lost the fight."

Despite such silliness, the superficial viewer might think that, in the matter-of-fact interaction between Natives and Whites, *Red Garters* presents an affirmative image of Indians. In reality, however, the film is so intent on subverting the cliches of the western genre that the opposite is true. Audiences are warned at the movie's outset not to take it "too seriously" because it "takes place in a land that never existed." The less than subtle name "Limbo County" reinforces this impression. For the makers of *Red Garters*, as for those of more conventional westerns, Natives in the "real" West remain savages.

The year 1954 also represented the beginning of another enduring musical tradition involving Natives with the mounting of Jerome Robbins's *Peter Pan*. Based on a straight play and novel by J. M. Barrie, the musical uses the Indians of popular imagination as pure comic relief. Tiger Lily, the leader of the Native band, is blonde! Her people speak in the stereotypical "um" construction (e.g., "Where I leadum, you follow."). Their musical number, to pseudo-Native rhythms, is entitled "Ugh-a-wugga." They are portrayed as inherent cowards, afraid of the sounds of the forest in which they live. At one point, scared to death, Tiger Lily cites a "famous Indian proverb: When in doubt—run!"

The production, filmed for showing on the new medium of television, periodically still appears on NBC. The stage show has also been revived numerous times. A recent 1990s revival underwent a makeover similar to that of *Annie Get Your Gun*. Director Glenn Casale found the Indian dialogue objectionable and cut "Ugh-a-wugga." Tiger Lily is no longer blonde. According to Peter Marks, "Mr. Casale, in an interview, also said he was put off by the idea of Tiger Lily and her followers traversing Neverland in search of Lost Boys' scalps. Instead, he decided to emphasize the agrarian culture of the Indians; in his production, they could be seen traveling this way and that on the stage, bearing fruits of the harvest."[39]

Part of the problem with *Peter Pan* is the Barrie source material, where Indians are viewed as interesting primitives, a remote race whose very mention acts as a talisman that can make children fly. Not all the depredations can be so traced, though.[40] *Peter Pan* actually had been adapted for the screen a year earlier in an animated musical version by Walt Disney. Although in some respects more faithful to the Barrie text, it treats Natives no better.

Disney's Captain Hook may sound like the rapacious conquerors of the continent when he calls Indians "redskins," proclaims his intent to "use them" to get at Peter, and kidnaps and tortures Tiger Lily. Unfortunately, the Lost Boys are equally despicable. When they are bored and in search of entertainment, "hunting" is decided upon. Tigers and bears are ruled out as game when John Darling suggests "aborigines." Peter orders them to "capture a few Indians." Off they go, singing the cheery ditty "Following the Leader," which declares, "We're out to fight the Injuns, the Injuns." During the hunt, they come upon a footprint. One of the boys identifies it as belonging to a Blackfoot, a tribe claimed to be "quite savage." He says, however, that it will be easy to sneak up on the Natives, since Indians are "cunning but not intelligent."

Meanwhile, Peter is coming to the aid of Tiger Lily. He outsmarts the pirates and rescues her, but in all his boyish enthusiasm, while having fun playing with Hook, he momentarily forgets her and she nearly drowns. She is expendable, secondary to interaction among Whites.

When Tiger Lily is returned to her father's village, the chief uses sign language even though proficient in English. He announces that he is "heap glad" to have his daughter back. As in the live musical, Indians speak in the "um" construction. A question raised as to the first time an Indian ever said "Ugh" leads to a song, "Why Does He Ask You How" (named for the stereotypical Indian greeting). Indians sing about themselves in the third person and refer to themselves as "Injuns." When a beautiful Indian girl kisses one of the males and he blushes, the question is answered, "Why is the red man red?" One of the Indians dances on an oversized drum in a deliberate borrowing from the 1936 version of *Rose-Marie.*

In Disney's *Peter Pan*, Natives are repeatedly referred to as "savages." Though they exhibit some redeeming qualities, such as familial love, they are fundamentally the "bad Indians" of stereotype. Although *Peter Pan* may be casually dismissed as a child-eyed fantasy view of "Natives," it was written by adults and teaches children the traditional stereotypes held widely by grownup Amer-Europeans. In 1995, Disney Studios again plumbed Native themes for *Pocahontas.* A review for Blockbuster Video called the production a "[v]isually stunning Disney animated feature loosely based on the true story of the Indian princess saving the life of English colonist John Smith. Superb family entertainment, with many beautiful songs (Alan Menken and Steven Schwartz) . . . and a powerful message to both kids and adults."[41] The feature included, as the voice of Powhatan, the Indian activist Russell Means, who declared the film to be the best Hollywood depiction of Indians ever. It turned the real, adolescent Pocahontas into a gorgeous, nubile young woman, modeled on Native actress Irene Bedard.

Back in 1958, producers Cy Feuer and Ernest Martin turned to a Native-based musical with *Whoop-Up*, based on the novel *Stay Away, Joe.* Set on a modern-day reservation, it finally allowed Indians out of the nineteenth century. As such, the stage production, and its images of Indians, merits extended discussion. Unfortunately, the representation is of the degraded, drunken reservation stereotype.

In the show, Glenda runs a bar, half of which sits on the reservation. She loves Joe, but he prefers Billie Mae Littlehorse. Fortunately for Glenda, Joe prefers his drink more. He trades her parts from his automobile in exchange for liquor. According to Bordman, "By the end of the evening she not only has Joe's car, she has Joe."[42]

Whoop-Up ran only fifty-six performances, but the same material was filmed ten years later as *Stay Away, Joe*, starring Elvis Presley. The songs of the Broadway show were scrapped in favor of ones better suited to Presley, and though there are some affirmative elements, it basically serves only to reinforce the same tired stereotypes as the play.

Joe Light Cloud (Elvis) has left the reservation to seek his fortune in the dominant culture. He becomes a well-known champion rodeo rider.

As the credits roll, he sings a haunting ballad to his homeland as the camera cranes over the beautiful, stark southwestern landscape. Even a thousand miles away, he can hear "The Call of the Hills of Home." The canyon walls "echo, 'How can you stay away?'" He acknowledges that his "dreams are where the eagles fly." He sings, "For far too long have I stayed away from this land I love and denied my heart. Now I know that I must go where the hills say, 'Don't stay away.'" The song bespeaks of a spiritual connection to the land and of the importance of home.

The scene then shifts to the home of Joe's family, a shack on the reservation. A member of Congress and a local banker have arrived with a proposition for Joe's father, Charley Light Cloud. Joe has persuaded them to provide Charley with a herd of cattle. If this pilot program works, the government will implement it on the whole reservation. Charley, who boastfully claims to be "a direct descendant of great chiefs and mighty warriors," accepts "in order to prove an Indian can be an honest, hardworking American citizen and not a lazy bum like some White people think."

In reality, the congressman is using Charley, hoping that if the cattle program succeeds he can use it as a stepping stone to the governorship. It is merely another example of Whites exploiting Natives for their own purposes. He asks the Indian to keep the deal a secret but is warned by the banker that as soon as they leave the "moccasin telegraph" will begin to work. The banker declares, "By tonight there'll be more Indians here than at the Little Big Horn." Unfortunately for all concerned, Charley really *is* a lazy bum. The family dwelling is a shack not so much out of poverty as out of Charley's failure to make repairs.

Smoke signals over the hill announce the return of Joe. When Charley asks his father what the "smoke talk" says, the elder Light Cloud rebukes, "A lot of good it did to send you to school. Can't even read your own language." Although wrapped in a racial slur, it is also a subtle comment on assimilation and cultural alienation.

Joe does get back, bringing the herd with him. It is the occasion for a wild party. A drunken Joe sings, "Stay Away, Joe," which it seems is his nickname among the tribe. The song is about fealty to family and friends, as he states that if ever anyone is in trouble, "a whoop and holler, and I'll be there." Unfortunately, it is also about the sexually predatory Indian male: "Love and leave 'em, screamin' and a kickin', Stay Away, Joe."

After the song, Joe's sister, Mary, approaches. She lives in town and works at the bank. She too is alienated from her people, who say of her, "She's city-folk now." She even has a WASP boyfriend, who, whenever she questions whether their relationship can work, invokes the names of John Smith and Pocahontas. When she asks Joe why he has come home, he replies that he just needs to know that it is still there.

Immediately after these expressions of almost covenantal loyalty to family and land, however, Joe reverts to type as sexual aggressor. During the next musical number, he steals the girlfriend of one of his friends and sneaks away from the party to have sex with her. The woman is provocatively named Billie Jo Hump.

The treatment of Native women in *Stay Away, Joe* is informative. All the young (and uniformly attractive) Indian women are oversexed. All of them must have Joe. The song "Dominick," in which Joe attempts to get a lethargic bull to do his stud duty, is choreographed into a naked sex romp between Joe and not one but two young Indian women.[43] The only strong Native female character is Joe's stepmother. She is, however, only half Indian (and half Mexican) and is ridiculed by the males as a "scorpion squaw." Further, her strong matriarchal presence is undercut by macho, comic business such as showing her at the party smoking a cigar.

With the festivities well underway, Joe instructs one of his friends to slaughter one of the cows for a barbecue. After all, just one cow won't be missed. The friend is so drunk, however, that he kills the herd's *one* bull by mistake. Joe spends the rest of the picture trying to get another bull, get the replacement to procreate, and otherwise set things right.

On his way to get the new stud, slow-witted Joe is beguiled by a fast-talking sales pitch from a car salesman and buys a flashy red convertible he can't afford, evoking Jack and the beanstalk. Unlike the stage version, in which he cannibalizes the car for drinks, here he sells the car piecemeal in order to get cash to try to save the herd, which Charley and his wife have begun to sell off one at a time to get funds to renovate their shack.

Joe goes to the bar owner, Glenda, for help. As in the stage musical, Glenda has designs on him. In the movie, however, it is not an Indian girl but Glenda's daughter Mamie, a naïve, Lolita-ish virgin, that Joe prefers. The threat of miscegenation looms large as all the White women are eager to sleep with something vaguely brown. Joe leeringly sings a song to himself, a bowdlerized version of "Alouette": "Mamie, Mamie, Lovely Little

Mamie." The point here cannot be missed: the Indian, ever the sexual predator, treacherous and lascivious, views White women as helpless prey ready to be plucked to satisfy his base appetites. Once again it can be seen that inter-racial dating and marriage are acceptable if the male is White—as in the relationship of Mary and her beau Loren. Later, however, Glenda, who once wanted Joe herself, will take up arms to defend her daughter—her *White* daughter—from the Indian.

Joe cons Glenda into meeting him in Flagstaff with the promise of sex. His real agenda is to be alone with the daughter. As soon as the mother is gone, Joe calls his friends to the bar for a party. While they drink in the front room, Joe is in back, making time with the virgin White woman. Their tryst is interrupted by the return of Glenda, who arrives at the scene with a shotgun, having caught on to the ruse. She chases Joe off, shooting up what's left of his car.

In a striking scene, that night Joe is seen sleeping with the family dog in his stripped automobile out by what is left of the herd. He is the prodigal son reduced to low estate. He sings, "Hello, Misfortune," telling the evil fates, "I been away so long, I bet you thought you'd seen the last of me." He acknowledges "drinkin' all my money." He has relied on his own values and wits rather than the covenant with land and family that began the film. This has led him to the brink of disaster.

The scene shifts to Joe's family. They have been making changes in their home in anticipation of a visit from Mary and her fiancé Loren's family. They have made the shack into a model of suburban propriety with carpeting, an indoor toilet, and new furniture. But it is an ignorant person's version of such an abode; it is the view from the outside, looking in. For example, they install a toilet but have no water hook-up, and rather than fixing holes in the floor, they simply carpet over them. When the Whites arrive with Mary, they express the frontier mentality, seeing not Indian country but a landscape already ethnically cleansed. The mother says, "It is striking to find such a lovely home in the midst of all this wild country." Mary's fiancé proclaims it "an oasis in the desert." It is, however, held together with glue and spit. It quickly falls apart, and the fraud is exposed. The Whites leave, but Mary stays "where I belong." Once again, the limits of assimilation are laid bare.

Eventually, a happy ending is manufactured to fit the genre. This, however, is secondary. The Indians of *Whoop-Up* and *Stay Away, Joe* are the degraded phonies of the White imagination, resisting assimilation. They look forward only to their next party or their next drink. Sexually promiscuous and aggressive, the men must be fended off from assaults on White womanhood.

Since the failure of *Whoop-Up*, Broadway has not attempted a musical with all-Native themes. In fact, aside from revivals, only two new shows in the intervening years have touched significantly on Indian imagery, *The Fantasticks* and *The Will Rogers Follies*.

The Fantasticks began life as a production at the University of New Mexico in 1956. Set in the West, it was, in its original incarnation, entitled *Joy Comes to Deadhorse* and sported a villain who was a "half-breed Apache."[44] This stereotypical, treacherous half-breed was lost as the show was revamped for its New York premiere, as *The Fantasticks*, at Barnard College in 1959. Negative Native imagery, however, remained. Mortimer, whom the script makes clear is "not really an Indian, you know,"[45] nevertheless plays one in the "Rape Ballet."

The authors, in notes to the published script, have tried to disavow the "Rape Ballet" as culturally dated and intended in the sense of abduction rather than rape as nonconsensual sex—even going so far as to write a replacement number, "Abductions (And So Forth)," for a 1990 tour.[46] It remains, however, in the text. And associations of Indians with rape, or even abduction and pillaging, merely serve to reinforce the stereotype of the bad, marauding savage. The entire number is, in fact, set in motion by the cry, "Indians, ready? Indians—Rape!"[47] In 2000, *The Fantasticks* finally was filmed for the screen, after forty-one years.

In 1991, *The Will Rogers Follies* came to Broadway. Taking the form of a revived Ziegfeld Follies, the musical is a romanticized account of Ziegfeld star Will Rogers. It is both accurate and positive in its portrayal of Rogers as an Indian.

Around one-fourth Cherokee from both sides of his family, Rogers, as the show points out, experienced racism growing up, was raised to appreciate his heritage, and never considered himself anything other than that oxymoron to White ears: "an Indian cowboy." He even began his career with Texas Jack's Wild West show, billed as "The Cherokee Kid." Near the end of the production, reflecting on his life, Rogers muses, "Not bad for a half-breed Cherokee ropesmith." It goes a long way toward dispelling notions of mixed-bloods as illiterate, degraded specimens who cannot be trusted.

Unfortunately, other Native representations in the show are less affirmative. The first image of the play, for instance, is the "Indian Sun Goddess," a *topless* Ziegfeld Girl in Indian regalia, descending a staircase. This is followed by a male "Indian of the Dawn" doing a dance, directly out of the 1936 *Rose-Marie*, on a giant drum, one of the most enduring Native tropes in musicals, it seems. Then a chorus line of beauteous chorines in various states of Plains Indian dishabille exhibits itself for audience approbation. The musical's authors clearly use the license granted by the Ziegfeld Follies conceit to play fast and loose with history. In the process, they reinforce ethnic stereotypes of homogenized nineteenth-century Indians and of Indian women as beautiful, desirable, and acceptable objects of White lust.

This lengthy, though by no means exhaustive, review of Native representations in the popular culture venue of the musical is necessary to demonstrate just how deeply ingrained in the American psyche are myths of Indians and the frontier. Historical accuracy is discarded. In its place are the stereotypes limned above—even when the intent is supposedly sympathetic. Often a homegrown ethnic cleansing occurs in which Natives are erased totally from the environment depicted. It says much about theological anthropology, Whites' views of the humanity of Indians. It also demonstrates the consistency of racism, as parallels between treatment of Indians and that of Blacks and other racial/ethnic minorities are seen.

In the final analysis, Natives, as a conquered, colonial people, become the total possession of the Amer-European colonizer. Their image is manipulated to create the illusion of Amer-European legitimacy on the continent. Everything they have and everything they are may be appropriated and used to serve the ends of the whitestream culture.

CHAPTER SEVEN

INNOCENTS ABROAD

Or, Smilla Has a Sense of Snow,
but Our Kanawakes Are in Egypt

*The destruction of the Inuit is our own, both our own fault and our
own death. The mirror cracks as we look into it and read our own
demise. . . . It is here that we learn that history is not remote but ever-
present, and that it is at once both a mythology and one of the brutal
facts of our own existence.*

CARLTON SMITH,
Coyote Kills John Wayne

During the late nineteenth century and the first decades of the twentieth,
Native Americans came to Europe as performers in Wild West shows, as
tourists, and as soldiers in the Great War. Of course, even before these
arrivals, Europeans had clear images of North American Indians from the
works of local authors like Gustave Aimard, Gabriel Ferry, Balduin Möllhausen, and Karl May, and through translations of James Fenimore
Cooper. That these writings were made up largely out of whole cloth and
bore little or no resemblance to the lives and histories of real Indians was
of little importance. Yet, even as popular images of the indigenes of the
Western Hemisphere were being cemented through performance and literature, actual, living and breathing indigenes were present in the "Old
World" as more than (retro)spectacle. In this chapter, we shall examine two
works, one authored by a non-Native in the late twentieth century and the
other by an Indian in the nineteenth, for what they can tell us about the
nature of that Old World's encounters with Natives. Each at least hints

that the imbrications of colonialism and capitalism create a different story than that commonly imagined. Together, they challenge our presuppositions about "Native Americans" and stretch the boundaries of the North American experience.

Peter Høeg's novel *Smilla's Sense of Snow* might seem, at first blush, a peculiar choice in any discussion of Old World encounters with Natives. Set largely in Copenhagen, Denmark, it is a mystery about one woman's refusal to accept official explanations concerning the death of a small boy whom she had befriended. Published in Danish in 1992 and in English translation the following year, the book met with both critical and commercial success. The *Los Angeles Daily News* compared it to the work of Scott Turow and Martin Cruz Smith, "full of fascinating detail, thick with life, peopled with characters in whom the reader may believe absolutely. . . . One of the best novels to come out of continental Europe in quite a while."[1] Høeg writes in heady prose, chewy and mouth-filling like "pink, slightly frothy whale blubber eaten from a communal platter."[2]

The comparison with Cruz Smith is perhaps more apt than the reviewer knew. Certainly the book resembles his *Gorky Park* in its texture. Beyond that stylistic similarity, however, Martin Cruz Smith, who writes about KGB investigations of murders in Moscow, is, as noted earlier, American Indian. His choice discomfits easy designations of what constitutes Native American literature. Is Native American literature simply any creation by a Native American (whatever that means)? Likewise, *Smilla's Sense of Snow*, though written by a White male and about persons who eschew the designation *Native American*, indisputably deals with indigenes of the Western Hemisphere. Such is the authority of Høeg's voice that the reader is left marveling at how he can narrate so convincingly the life of a Native woman. The book's failing is that, though Høeg is expert at creating a believable and atmospheric thriller, he is incapable of working it out in anything but the conventional terms of the action genre.[3]

The novel describes the dogged search of Smilla Qaavigaaq Jaspersen, the daughter of a Greenlander Inuit mother and a wealthy Danish father, for the truth in the death of an Inuit boy who lived in her apartment house. Born in 1956 in Greenland, she began grammar school there but was raised in Denmark. The book's title refers to the heroine's Inuit ability to "read" snow like music, a skill that unlocks the mystery. Though it is always dangerous to read a novel as ethnography,[4] *Smilla's Sense of Snow* contains a great deal of verifiable information about contemporary Inuits and their ethnography.

The Inuit, one of the groups often lumped together under the collective title of Eskimo, are a circumpolar people, inhabiting a vast territory stretching from Greenland, across northern Canada and Alaska, to Siberia. First reports of them in Europe date to c. 985, when the Vikings found evidence of abandoned Dorset culture habitation in southern Greenland. A Norse account of the early thirteenth century describes them as "a very small people." By the fourteenth century, the Norse were engaged in sporadic military conflict with them that continued for over a century. Skin boats were displayed in both Nidaros Cathedral in Denmark and Trondheim Cathedral in Norway. Inuit captives were probably taken to Norway around 1420.[5] Official "state colonialism" of Greenland began in 1721.[6] As noted by Høeg, the "first large shipments" of Greenlander Inuits began arriving in Denmark in the 1930s.[7] Today perhaps as much as 10 percent of the Greenlandic population of 46,000 live there.[8] They come to the *métropole* for education and employment. This ongoing colonial encounter lies at the core of Høeg's novel.

Though fiction, *Smilla's Sense of Snow* is carefully researched. Høeg draws his historic ethnographic material from Knud Rasmussen and, to a lesser extent, Jean Malaurie's *The Last Kings of Thule*.[9] His information about contemporary Inuit existence is consistent with that readily available from a variety of sources, including official Danish governmental statistics.

Rasmussen, like the fictional Smilla, was the Greenland-born offspring of an Inuit mother and a Danish father. As a child, he learned to drive dogs and spoke *Kalaallisut*, Greenlandic Inuit, before he spoke Danish. Even after being taken to Denmark, he continued to cherish his Greenlander heritage, later writing, "When I was a child I used often to hear an old Greenlandic woman tell how, far away north at the end of the world, there lived a people who dressed in bearskins and ate raw flesh. . . . Even before I knew what travel meant, I determined that one day I would go and find these people."[10] He joined his first arctic expedition in 1902. In 1909, he founded Thule (present-day Nuuk), the world's northernmost trading post, named for the mythical end of the earth. From there, between 1912 and 1924, he mounted five expeditions. The best-known of these, the so-called Fifth Thule Expedition from 1921 to 1924 was an ambitious twenty-thousand-mile trek across Inuit territory from Greenland to

Siberia. His ten-volume account of the expedition and its findings remains a primary source of ethnographic information about the Inuits.[11]

Yet, while drawing upon these sources, Høeg acknowledges the limits of ethnography. Narrating Smilla's voice, he writes, "The ethnographers have cast a dream of innocence over North Greenland. A dream that the Inuit will continue to be the bowlegged, drum-dancing, legend-telling, widely smiling exhibition images that the first explorers thought they were meeting south of Qaanaaq at the turn of the century."[12] These assumptions of cultural stasis, coupled with an innate Eurocentric sense of superiority, come up again when Malaurie is discussed:

> In *The Last Kings of Thule*, Jean Malauri [*sic*] writes that a significant argument for studying the interesting Polar Eskimos is that you can thus learn something about human progression from the Neanderthal stage to the people of the Stone Age.
>
> It's written with a certain amount of affection. But it's a study in unconscious prejudices.
>
> Any race of people that allows itself to be graded on a scale designed by European science will appear to be a culture of higher primates.
>
> Any grading system is meaningless. Every attempt to compare cultures with the intention of determining which is the most developed will never be anything other than one more bullshit projection of Western culture's hatred of its own shadows.[13]

Even Rasmussen, himself part Inuit, envisioned Thule performing a dual function. Writing to Vilhjalmur Stefansson, he stated that the outpost would be both "bigger and cheaper than a common tradesplace, meant to be like a gentle preparer for civilization and the white man," a place where "cultural purposes" would come before profit.[14] Such cultural purposes being avowedly assimilationist.

Though it is not common to think of Denmark as a colonial power, its relationship to Greenland is unquestionably colonial in character, and the Inuits remain a colonized people. In discussing the multiple effects of colonialism, Høeg relates the story of an aged Inuit informant, speaking in the 1930s:

In the thirties, when they asked Ittussaarsuaq—who as a child had wandered with her tribe and kinfolk across Ellesmere Island to Greenland during the migration when Canadian Inuit had their first contact in seven hundred years with the Inuit of North Greenland—when they asked her, an eighty-five-year-old woman who had experienced the entire modern colonization process, moving from the Stone Age to the radio, how life was now, compared to the past, she said without hesitation, "Better—the Inuit very rarely die of hunger nowadays."

Emotions must flow purely if they're not to become confused. The problem with trying to hate the colonization of Greenland with a pure hated is that, no matter what you may detest about it, the colonization irrefutably improved the material needs of an existence that was one of the most difficult in the world.[15]

According to a 1987 profile, the "Greenland Inuit today enjoy such benefits as education, modern transportation and medical care; yet their traditional culture and belief system have eroded, leading the Inuit to be engulfed by alcoholism, disease, and poverty. The result is a high suicide rate."[16] Denmark's presence may have brought opportunities, but at a price. Reminiscent of Navajo and Laguna men being used to mine uranium, Greenlander Inuits found employment in cryolite extraction but only as *kivfaks*, doing the dirty work of cleanup.[17]

Pressures to assimilate are unrelenting. Høeg notes, "In Nuuk the waiting list for housing is eleven years. Then you get a closet, a shed, a shack. All money in Greenland is attached to the Danish language and culture. Those who master Danish get the lucrative positions. The others can languish in the filet factories or in unemployment lines. In a culture that has a murder rate comparable to a war zone."[18] Similarly, Smilla describes her experience in school: "When we moved from the village school to Qaanaaq, we had teachers who didn't know one word of Greenlandic, nor did they have any plans to learn it. They told us that, for those who excelled, there would be an admission ticket to Denmark and a degree and a way out of the Arctic misery. This golden assent would take place in Danish."[19] In the 1950s and 1960s, the Danish government abandoned the more blatantly coercive aspects of its colonial policies. A modicum of Home Rule was granted in 1953, when Denmark passed a new constitution. In the ultimate assimilative rhetorical move, the Danish government officially proclaimed Greenland the nation's northernmost county. The people were no longer Greenlanders or Inuits but "Northern Danes," to "be educated to the same rights as all other Danes."[20] According to Inuit scholar Robert Petersen, professor emeritus at Gronlands Universitet in Nuuk:

> This resolution was not mentioned in the constitution itself, but it was made clear in the previous debate and in a referendum in Denmark—not in Greenland—that the colonial status of Greenland had formally ended. In fact, no real change occurred, as Denmark for a long time administered the common human rights or civil rights in Greenland and continued to govern Greenland with the same civil servants and the same administrative body as before.[21]

The period of "Danization" had begun.[22] It was in large part merely a colonial codification and "justification of Danish privileges."[23]

The Høeg novel, however, exposes the limits of assimilation and the persistence of cultural codings. Though some have become total Northern Danes, others cannot.[24] Smilla says of herself, "I usually tell myself that I've lost my cultural identity for good. After I've said this enough times, I wake up one morning, like today, with a solid sense of identity. Smilla Jaspersen—pampered Greenlander." Yet, as she herself indicates, Smilla's scientific credentials and her father's wealth make her an exception. The majority of urban Inuits in the Copenhagen of Høeg's book exist as a ghettoized, dysfunctional population, the poor in a country where virtually everyone is middle class. Even so, Smilla considers herself "in exile," a "desert plant" out of place in Denmark where she has felt colder than she ever felt at home in Greenland.[25]

Cultural misunderstandings and incompatibilities lie at the root of these problems for Høeg. Danes used calipers to measure Inuit crania in an effort to prove they were somehow subhuman. The Inuit arrivals in the 1930s wrote to their relatives that the Danes were pigs because they kept dogs in the house. Smilla declares, "Not one day of my life has passed that I haven't been amazed at how poorly Danes and Greenlanders understand each other. It's worse for Greenlanders, of course. It's not healthy for the tightrope walker to be misunderstood by the person who's holding the rope. And in this century the Inuit's life has been a tightrope dance on a cord fastened on one hand to the world's least hospitable land with the world's most severe and fluctuating climate, and fastened on the other end to the Danish colonial administration."[26]

Here Høeg may betray his own ethnocentrism. Though there is undoubtedly some validity to what he says, in the normal colonial situation, inevitable cultural misapprehensions aside, the colonized knows quite a lot about the colonizer out of necessity. Only the reverse remains untrue. As Johannes Olivier states, "There is as it were a veil between the natives and their European masters on account of which the essential character of the former remains almost entirely unknown to the latter."[27] Smilla says, "I no longer make an effort to keep Europe or Denmark at a distance. Neither do I plead with them to stay. In some way they are part of my destiny. They come and go in my life. I have given up doing anything about it."[28] In the end, it is Smilla's ability to exist in both cultures that enables her to solve the mystery of the Inuit boy Isaiah's death. Significantly, however, it is an indigenous trait, her sense of snow, a cultural skill shared with other Greenlanders, that provides the key that Danish authorities cannot see. It is at once a connection to home and heritage and a metaphor for the ultimate incommensurability of differing worldviews—Inuit and European. As Smilla remarks, "Maybe it's just the usual problem: ice is incomprehensible to those who were not born to it."[29]

Just as Smilla was born to snow and ice, the Mohawks of Kanawake were born to fast water. At first glance, *Our Caughnawagas in Egypt* might seem to have little in common with *Smilla's Sense of Snow*. Louis Jackson's prose is as spare, almost flat-footedly direct, as Høeg's can be stylish. The true account of a British military expedition in 1884–85 would seem to have little in common with a novel of contemporary life in Denmark. Yet the two share more than is readily apparent. Each gives the reader a story of Western Hemisphere indigenes out of place, having to cope with a culture and an environment that is not their natural location. Though brief, *Our Caughnawagas* is as rich in detail as Høeg's book. And both, perhaps unintentionally, shed light into the darker corners of the colonial experience.

Kanawake (Caughnawaga is an older rendering of the name) is a small Mohawk reserve in Québec just over the American border. *Our Caughnawagas* tells the story of an incident today almost unknown outside the Kanawake community.

In September 1884, the British prepared to mount an expedition to relieve Khartoum, the capital of Anglo-Egyptian Sudan. The city was threatened

by Mar Mullah. Proclaimed the *Mahdi*, the "guided one" or messiah foretold by Mohammed, he had launched an insurrection in the Sudan the
previous year. General Charles George "Chinese" Gordon had been dispatched to assist the Khedive in evacuating garrisons from the country.
Now Gordon and his men were themselves trapped and in need of rescue.
General Garnet Joseph Wolseley was ordered to undertake the relief.

General Lord Wolseley was, at fifty, a venerable presence in Her
Majesty's army, the veteran of colonial wars in far-flung corners of the
empire. Born in County Dublin, Ireland, in 1833, he entered the army in
1852 and first saw action in Burma. He subsequently fought in the Crimean
War and the Sepoy Rebellion in India and commanded British forces in the
Chinese War of 1860. In 1861, he was sent to Canada as assistant quarter-
master-general, rising to deputy quartermaster in 1865.

A "typical British imperialist," Wolseley considered anyone with
Native blood a "savage."[30] He saw his role in British North America as
one of pacifying the Indians and keeping American annexationists at bay.
In 1870, he commanded the force sent to put down the Red River Resistance of Louis Riel. He wrote in his diary, "Hope Riel will have bolted, for
although I should like to hang him from the highest tree in the place, I
have such horror of rebels and vermin of his kidney that my treatment of
him might not be approved by the civil powers."[31] Three years later, he
led the campaign against the Ashanti in Africa. And in 1882, he defeated
and captured Arabi Pasha in Egypt and was raised to the peerage as Baron
Wolseley as a result.

Now, with Gordon threatened in Khartoum, Wolseley suddenly recognized the worth of Natives. Realizing that if Khartoum, which lies on
the Blue Nile near its confluence with the White Nile, were to be relieved,
the expedition would need boatmen experienced at shooting rapids in
order to negotiate the cataracts of the Nile, he personally directed that
Mohawks from Kanawake form part of the Canadian contingent expressly
to perform this function.

Thus it was that "in spite of discouraging talk and groundless fears,"
a contingent of fifty-six Mohawk volunteers, commanded by Captain
Louis Jackson, one of their own, found themselves aboard the *Ocean King*
bound for Alexandria, being bidden farewell by the Governor General
himself.[32] Once in Egypt, they worked with Egyptian boatmen and conveyed men and materiel up the Nile, performing their jobs in exemplary

fashion, with the loss of only two men. On February 6, 1885, the Natives departed from Alexandria for the voyage home. Upon his return, Jackson wrote *Our Caughnawagas*. His subtitle is both descriptive of content and a clever rhetorical device to establish not just the importance of the Mohawks to the campaign but their primacy: "A Narrative of what was seen and accomplished by the Contingent of North American Indian Voyageurs who led the British Boat Expedition for the Relief of Khartoum up the Cataracts of the Nile."

In an introductory preface, T. S. Brown reflects what Robert Warrior has called the rhetoric of novelty, the impulse to always see any act or creative production by a Native American as the first of its kind. Commending the book, Brown writes, "There is something unique in the idea of the aborigines of the New World being sent for to teach the Egyptians how to pass the Cataracts of the Nile, which has been navigated in some way by them for thousands of years, that should make this little book attractive to all readers."[33] Herman Melville implicitly makes a similar claim in his narrative poem *Clarel*, based upon his travels in Egypt and Palestine. In it, American travelers are shocked to discover Ungar, a Cherokee Confederate veteran, "[d]rilling some tawny infantry" on the banks of the Nile and conversing with Turkish naval officers in Jaffa as a mercenary for the sultan.

Yet, as Hilton Obenzinger points out in his book *American Palestine*, such sights were "altogether plausible" and far from unique. He writes:

> In 1868, the khedive of Egypt, eager to modernize his country, particularly his military, against the pressures of the Ottoman sultan's dominance and European penetration, engaged Thaddeus Mott to employ American advisors. Mott, employing William Tecumseh Sherman as advisor, recruited Charles P. Stone, veteran of the Mexican War and survivor of McClellan's intrigues, as the Egyptian chief of staff; and as a brigadier general Stone selected William W. Loring, who had fought Indians, Mexicans, and Mormons, as well as Union troops, to join scores of other veterans from both Union and Confederate armies. Many of the American mercenaries considered their service a contribution to the independence of an emerging nation against the tyranny of the sultan, while the Egyptians, finding the United States' lack of geopolitical interest in the region particularly

appealing, valued American experience in the exploration of Western territories and the conquest of indigenous tribes for their own quest for expansion and modernization.[34]

The Mohawks of the Khartoum expedition may have been volunteers, but their recruitment reflects a consistent pattern of employing one colonized Other against another. Jackson's "boys" may have been no less savages to Wolseley than Louis Riel's Métis, but they had a valuable skill to be exploited in adventuring in the Sudan.

Another ground on which Brown recommends Jackson's account is explicitly ethnographic. He writes that the book will interest "especially as it is written by one born and bred in Caughnawaga, who, with the quick eye of an Indian, has noticed many things unnoticed by ordinary tourists and travellers." Then, attesting to the authenticity of the Native's voice in the text, he states, "It is written off-hand and goes forth to the public as it came from the pen of the writer, to be judged in its style and the matter contained, by no standard but its own."[35] The addition of eight attractive engravings, depicting, among other subjects, Egyptian boats, irrigation techniques, the Sphinx, and the pyramids at Giza heightened its appeal. The book is part professional account of the military expedition, part "fish-out-of-water" story of what it was like to be a North American Indian in Egypt, and part ethnographic travelogue.

Jackson notes at the outset the "groundless fears" the Indians held while still in Canada. These apprehensions continue after they disembark in Egypt. The contingent departs the wharf in Alexandria by train on October 8. Jackson writes, "After leaving Alexandria I was surprised to see people standing up to their necks in the swamps, cutting some kind of grass. I saw also cattle lying perfectly still in the water with just their heads out. This sight scared my boys as to what the heat would be further south."[36] The different natural environment made the Mohawks, so fearless at home on the St. Lawrence, uneasy.

Crocodiles apparently were a special concern, alluded to no fewer than three times in the brief text. On October 26, the flotilla arrived at Wady Halfa. Jackson relates, "One of the voyageurs while wading must have stepped into some seam, he jumped quickly back into his boat, leaving behind his moccasin and said he was bitten by a crocodile, which all of us were kind enough to believe and we advised him not to wade any more."[37] In fact, one of the few virtues Jackson found in the 175 Dongolese whom he had under his command was their familiarity with the landscape. He wrote, "It proved lucky for these men that the Nile does not scare them, for they had to swim for it on more than one occasion."[38] Finally late in the navigation of the river, the water has fallen, exposing hundreds of rocks upon which "crocodiles could be seen by the dozen, sunning themselves." Jackson notes that one "brute" was twenty-five feet long.[39]

The North American indigenes are on a military mission, but they are also eager tourists. Jackson is shown a "sacred tree" by a Christian Egyptian: the dozens of nails driven into the trunk attest to the many healings it has wrought. He notes the regret of himself and his men at having to "pass such famous places as Thebes and Luxor," even though they camped "quite close to Thebes and there were guides waiting with candles to show us over the place but we had no time to spare and so were not permitted to wander about."[40] And when they reach Abu-Simbel, "the boys" form an "exploring party" for sightseeing; Jackson is prevented from accompanying them, though, since he must remain in camp and deal with supplies. It is at the end of their service, however, that the Mohawks prove their mettle as tourists and not soldiers. Arriving in Cairo on February 5, 1885, and scheduled to depart the following day, the group undertakes what could only have been a whirlwind tour. Jackson writes that "an opportunity was given to us to visit the following places of interest: Kass el-Nil Bridge, Kass el-Nil Barracks, Abdin Square and Palace, The [sic] Mosque Sultan-Hassan, the Citadel, the Mosque Mohamet-Ali, the Native Bazaar, the Esbediah Gardens, and finally Gizeh and the Pyramids."[41] In fact, the entire nature of tourism in Egypt is changing. Once the opportunity of a determined elite, it is becoming increasingly accessible. Upon reaching Assiout, some 240 miles from Alexandria, Jackson observed that "Messrs. Cook and Son the great tourist agents had just commenced to build a large hotel, which when returning home I found already finished. I noticed a sign over a mud house door 'Egyptian Bank.'"[42]

Jackson *is* a keen observer of the Egyptian landscape and its inhabitants. He provides good descriptions of houses, boats, customs, agricultural details, and of a local funeral. Often he compares what he sees to what he and his men know back at Kanawake. Brown writes that the volume "is written with a most excellent spirit that might wisely be imitated by other travellers. The writer finds no faults, blames nobody. . . ."[43] Yet, despite such encomia, Jackson is not without his ethnocentric biases when it comes to his observations (though they are biases that doubtless would be shared by his Anglo-Canadian readership). In reaching the first Egyptian settlement where the expedition camps after departing Alexandria, he notes, "I saw more rats at a glance than I had ever seen before in all my life." At Assiout, when the Mohawks see a group of "Nubian prisoners," Jackson describes them as "black, ugly and desperate looking fellows chained together with large rusty chains round their necks." And at the same locale, he sees that "there were flies in the children's faces and eyes beyond description."[44] In the end, Jackson states, "I have not seen the place yet where I would care to settle down."[45] Likewise, he finds difficulties with the locals. He notes, "It was a pity that we could not get the slightest information from the Egyptian crew with us, who seemed very adverse to us so much so, that I could not even learn their names far less any of their language."[46] About the "Dongolese" under him, he writes, "To give an idea of the trouble we had. I need only say that these Dongolese generally understood just the contrary of what they were ordered to do. They would pull hard when asked to stop or stop pulling at some critical place when hard pulling was required."[47] Later he observes of them, "Scolding was of no use, they neither understood nor cared. I may mention another peculiarity of theirs. I had noticed many scars on their bodies, but could not account for it, until one of them fell sick when the other cut his skin to bleed him, and filled the cut with sand."[48]

The job of "our Caughnawagas" ended at the Dal cataract. Their orders became to assist in "passing boats up the . . . cataract, until the last boat passed."[49] That final vessel passed the rapid on January 14, and the following day Jackson received orders to return to Wady Halfa, bringing the Mohawks' active service to a close. Brown in his preface declares that Jackson was "generous in his acknowledgements for every act of kindness and proper consideration shown to him and his party, by Her Majesty's Officers of all ranks in command of the expedition."[50] Indeed he was. In the third to last paragraph of his book, he writes, "I cannot conclude without expressing my satisfaction at the handsome treatment accorded us by the British Government, and should our services be of assistance in the proposed Fall campaign in Egypt, they will be freely given. We were allowed just double the amount of clothing stipulated in the contract, the overcoats being given to us at Malta on our way home."[51]

So, clothed in their new overcoats, compliments of Her Majesty, the Mohawks arrived home, "well pleased with what we had seen in the land of the Pharos [sic] and proud to have shown the world that the dwellers on the banks of the Nile, after navigating it for centuries, could still learn something of the craft from the Iroquois Indians of North America and the Canadian voyageurs of many races."[52] The main British force reached Khartoum two days too late to save Gordon and his men. Upon his return to England, Lord General Wolseley was created Viscount Wolseley and made commander-in-chief of the British army. New overcoats versus a promotion for leading a failed operation. And so it goes.

CHAPTER EIGHT

HELL AND HIGHWATER

The subject can never reconcile the split between itself and its mirror imago, the eye which sees and the eye which is seen, the I who speaks and I who is spoken, the subject of desire and the subject of demand, who must pass through the defiles of the others as signifier. It is this alienation, this gap between being and meaning, subject and signifier, self and other, which the classical realist system of representation would suture.

CAROLE-ANN TYLER,
"Passing: Narcissism, Identity, and Difference"

The quincentenary of the "Columbus event" in 1992 provoked protests and teach-ins by Natives and increased interest in the history of North America's indigenes by Amer-Europeans. Unfortunately, this heightened whitestream interest in Natives as history did not translate generally into *awareness* of contemporary Natives, their cultures, and their struggles for, in Gerald Vizenor's terms, survivance—"more than survival, more than endurance or mere response; the stories of survivance are an active presence."[1] Instead, the year saw a boom in publication of books on Native topics and an upsurge in what Vizenor calls "varionative" literature, trends that continued unabated at the end of the decade.

According to Vizenor, "The *varionative* is an uncertain curve of antecedence; obscure notions of native sovenance and presence. The *varionative* traces of ancestors are scriptural, episodic, and ironic in narratives.

The *penenative* is the *autoposer*, the autobiographical poseur, or the almost native by associations and institutive connections."[2] In sum, the variationative stands in counterpoint to communitism. In place of ties to family and Native community are the anti-communitist "plastic medicine men" who peddle Native traditions—real and fictive—for material gain and recognition, those who write revenge fantasies about their lack of acceptance by tribal peoples, who must distort the chronology of Native histories to fit their genealogies, who essentialize Natives and blame their Indian blood for their own alcoholism, who write "autobiographies" in which it is impossible to tell from what tribal tradition they come. They are White lies and Redskin reveries.[3] As Vizenor would state, such simulations "would bear minimal honor in tribal memories."[4]

The variationative comes easily to mind, in different ways, when reading four texts that came out in the wake created by the *Nina*, the *Pinta*, and the *Santa Maria* five hundred years after they first sailed into this hemisphere and into Amer-European mythology: *Touching the Fire, Earthmaker, Star Warrior,* and *Kill Hole*. All four raise questions about the appropriation and display of Native culture and heritage.

In his introduction to *Touching the Fire*, Roger Welsch asks readers to "imagine Golgotha in the hands of a group of radical Muslims who close it to Christian pilgrims and erect a mocking parody of the Crucifixion at its crest. Imagine the Wailing Wall held by a Christian fundamentalist sect that decides to dismantle it and scatter its blocks irretrievably. What if Israeli guerillas occupied the Kaaba in Mecca and set to rebuilding its shelter into a temple?"[5] Although these desecrations are not wholly unthinkable, they would, one hopes, at least provoke an outcry among humane people. Such things, however, are commonplace for America's indigenous peoples whose holy sites are defiled, whose sacred objects are imprisoned in museums and private collections, whose very remains have been seen as relics suitable for public display.

Such disrespect angers Welsch, who was adopted by the Omahas in 1967 and who has since tried to observe the responsibilities that come from such an act. In *Touching the Fire*, he tells the story of Natives' spiritual objects and of attempts to reclaim them from museums, anthropologists, and collectors. He cautions, "There is no factual history of such things. Such things are spared factual history by virtue of their own power. Such things live best and strongest within the heart, within the imagination of those who love them."[6] And so he gives readers the story of the Sky Bundle, the most sacred and powerful object of the fictional Turtle Creek Band of Nehawkas.

Although ostensibly a collection of short stories, *Touching the Fire* is best read as an inverted novel, told in reverse chronological order. It begins in 2001 as the Nehawkas attempt to gain repatriation of the Sky Bundle from a museum in Boston, and then the bundle is traced back to its very creation sometime in the distant past.

As the book opens, the Nehawkas are seeking sufficient funds to repatriate the bundle. In order to get the money, the tribe must go before an arts and historical society which opposes return of Native artifacts. All seems lost until the most oafish and comical member of the team working on the case, Moose Man Elk, gets an idea. Appearing before the committee, the tribe proposes to build the Turtle Creek Plains White Folks Museum, a living museum-cum-theme park along the lines of Colonial Williamsburg, where Indians can visit a suburban tract house and see how Amer-Europeans really live. The committee is so shocked that it gratefully hands over the funds for the bundle in return for tribal agreement to drop the other project.

In another story, the tribe secures a Jefferson Peace Medal (once an item in the Sky Bundle) for reburial by making so many exact replicas that no one can find the real one in what turns into a sort of Native version of button-button or three-card monte, a moccasin game.

The hand of the trickster is, in fact, never far away in these stories. Those familiar with Native literature will perceive more than a passing similarity to Vizenor or Thomas King in Welsch's style and satiric wit. Welsch's tricksters, like their counterparts in Native traditions, are at times prophetic, at times parodic, but they are always contrarians who act to subvert expectations.

The stories reflect authentic traditions. Throughout, Welsch makes a fine effort at reflecting a Native sensibility. In his acknowledgments, he thanks a lengthy list of Native friends and collaborators, including Frank La Flesche and Reaves Nahwooks and Clydia Nahwooksi. He does not totally escape, however, the pull of romanticism. He repeats the tired saw that the Mandans may have been the descendants of Europeans and terms them extinct. He writes:

The Mandan tribe of the Upper Missouri Valley offers a dramatic example of lost information and wisdom. . . . What could the Mandan have taught us?

We'll never know, because war and disease crushed the Mandan during the nineteenth century. As a people, as a culture, they are gone. Aside from a few drawings and the brief accounts of travelers, we know little of them. Are their songs and stories dead, too? . . . No, the Mandan's stories are still alive in *our* spirits. Are the visions and dreams of the Mandan dead simply because we do not know the complete historical and geographical facts of the Mandan? Of course not.[7]

Though the Mandans were decimated by smallpox in 1837 and suffered depredations from other tribes subsequently, today they are part of the Three Affiliated Tribes (along with the Arikaras and Gros Ventres) on the Fort Berthold reservation in North Dakota, where they maintain their separate tribal identity.

The saga of the Sky Bundle is reminiscent of the Omaha's Sacred Pole, but the story is far from unique. Less than a mile from where I write this essay, there is a tobacco shop. Until a recent change of ownership, there was a display case of antique smoking implements in the rear of the store. Amid ancient meerschaums and opium pipes were several Native pipes. The pipes were assembled, their stems attached to their carved bowls. They were sold by John Collier's Bureau of Indian Affairs in 1936 for prices ranging from six dollars to fifteen dollars. A framed letter from the Blackfoot agency in Montana gave their histories and provenance. Most striking among these objects was a black pipe. It was identified as Blackfoot and as having come out of a beaver medicine bundle, the most powerful bundle for the Blackfoot. The letter of conveyance stated that the agency despaired of ever obtaining such an object for sale because of its rarity.

Other elements in *Touching the Fire* reflect different tribal traditions. The tale of the Jefferson Peace Medal, for instance, recalls a similar medallion (currently in the collection of the Oklahoma Historical Society and one of many such tokens bestowed by Washington) given to the Cherokee chief Thomas Chisholm and found in a grave in 1903. Welsch thus universalizes his story until it is no longer the story of a single tribe or a single object but of all Native peoples and their struggle to recover their patrimony.

Welsch chooses fiction as the medium for his message out of respect for those who honored him enough to adopt him and for the power he believes resides in their sacred objects and stories. He quotes Buddy Gilpin, an Omaha: "They are like fire. If I put your hand in fire, on purpose or accidentally, no matter how good your heart or how quick your mind, no matter, your hand will be burned. Fire is fire and cannot be otherwise. Fire is good and fire is the heart of our home, but fire must be fire. The ways of the Powers are like touching the fire."[8] The things that are right about the choices Welsch makes are wrong about *Earthmaker*.

Jay Miller, the assistant director of the D'Arcy McNickle Center at Chicago's Newberry Library, purports in his subtitle to *Earthmaker* to relate "tribal stories" from Native North America. His collection is "intended to tell of the old time, before Europeans and Africans came in huge numbers and before changes were forced on the Americas."[9] By sampling a range of traditions, Miller hopes, it will be possible to sense the commonalties between them. Unfortunately, he fulfills little of the promise.

The problem derives from Miller's peculiar choice to blend tribal traditions and myths. Thus the aetiological story of clan origins about an Indian girl who marries a bear combines Tsimshian and Tlingit myths. Miller's version of the Windigo is an amalgam of Cree and Ojibway tellings. And the myth of the Sun's warlike twins and their life on earth with an elderly couple melds Zuñi and Acoma beliefs. The Cherokee story of Corn Mother is described as a "generalized" account.[10] The pertinent question Miller should be asking is why certain shared traditions are told differently by different peoples—even those living in close proximity and of the same language family—rather than whether it is possible to blend them into a single coherent narrative.[11]

This homogenizing of traditions renders the volume useless to the serious student and will only confuse interested casual readers, who will believe they are getting "legitimate" tribal stories. Told here in a stilted style, intended by the book's author to approximate oral performance, all the myths presented are available in better renditions elsewhere.

Miller clearly wants to be sensitive to Native peoples and would like to tell their stories. His introduction to *Earthmaker* is a fair discussion of the Natives of different regions and their lives before European contact. Once again, however, a broad-brush, generalizing approach undercuts his intentions. In his drive to find commonalties, he passes over rich and subtle diversity in favor of a kind of meat-grinder approach in which everything that comes out of the grinder looks and tastes pretty much the same.

Mythopoeia of a different sort is at work in *Star Warrior: The Story of SwiftDeer*. Authored by Bill Wahlberg, a psychotherapist, it purports to tell the story of Harley SwiftDeer Reagan. In the preface, Wahlberg describes going on a "medicine journey" to southern Mexico, sponsored by the Ojai Foundation, in 1983. The teacher on the trip was Reagan, described as "a half-breed Native American shaman with a Ph.D. in psychology."[12] According to Wahlberg, "SwiftDeer taught from what he called 'one of the twelve shields of knowledge of the ancient elders, the Twisted Hairs of Turtle Island.' He explained that in the ancient legends of the early people of Mexico, a Twisted Hair was one who wandered, seeking knowledge from many cultures. Twisted Hairs then integrated the truths of many cultures to record what were called the twelve shields of knowledge of the ancient ones."[13] With SwiftDeer's guidance, writes the psychotherapist, "I have sundanced, vision quested, fasted, and been buried in the earth overnight. I have learned the blessings of sweet grass. I have prayed in hundreds of sweatlodge ceremonies. I have begun to comprehend the power of the Sacred Pipe."[14] Ten years after their initial meeting, Wahlberg becomes Reagan's Boswell.

The text itself is a remarkable document. Although written by Wahlberg, it is told in the first person in Reagan's voice, with only occasional interpolations. The text is so tragicomically transparent that it needs almost no comment. In the preface, Wahlberg notes, "SwiftDeer is not a guru. His ability to be himself is one of his greatest strengths; he does not pretend to be other than he is. While he is a light for others, he makes no claims of personal enlightenment."[15]

Star Warrior tells the story of Harley SwiftDeer Reagan, a decorated Marine veteran of Vietnam who spent eight months at Bethesda Naval Hospital after receiving a crippling wound at Khe Sahn, a martial arts expert, and a self-proclaimed Cherokee "shaman" and "sorcerer." He relates his early training by his maternal grandmother, Spotted Fawn Raper, a full-blood Cherokee whose father survived the Trail of Tears and who probably learned Cherokee medicine from the Pin Society (i.e., the Keetoowahs). Under Spotted Fawn's tutelage, he was initiated into the secret Cherokee sexual practices at thirteen by a traditional "phoenix firewoman," Martha Spins Fire Eagle.

Apparently in order to fit this genealogy, Reagan changes the dates of the Trail of Tears—and the administration of Andrew Jackson. In his introduction to the volume, he writes, "Like nearly all the Cherokee, my relatives were forced west during the devastating and tragic purge of Indian people by President Andrew Jackson in the 1850s. They went mainly to Oklahoma but the records show that one group came to Texas and was befriended by the president of the Republic of Texas, Sam Houston, who was married to a Cherokee woman. Later this group was also expelled from Texas. . . . My relatives returned to Texas in the twenties and settled near Lubbock, where I was born."[16] The Texas Cherokee presence dated from 1819 or 1820. They were expelled in 1839, around the time of the completion of the Trail of Tears.

Born during a violent, but cleansing, thunderstorm, he is announced by Spotted Fawn as Unhua Oskenonton Anikawi, the Deer that Runs Swiftly Through the Forest Carrying the Magic.

After Vietnam, SwiftDeer continued his apprenticeship with Tom "Grandfather Two Bears" Wilson, a Navajo medicine man and a Twisted Hair, who appears in Carlos Casteneda's books as "don Gernaro." Two Bears purifies SwiftDeer's blood with an otter spirit, using a nagual stone placed over his third chakra, and teaches him to shapeshift into a crow. Later, SwiftDeer "bonds" (marries) two women, Mary ShyDeer and Dianne NightBird. He founds the Deer Tribe Métis Medicine Society ("a Shamanic Lodge for Ceremonial Medicine"), based in Scottsdale, and is the "eighteenth nagual and spiritual leader of the Feathered Winged Serpent Wheel."

SwiftDeer's story is filled with events both marvelous and painful. According to Reagan, "Grandfather told me a time might come when I would take my stand publicly as a guardian of children."[17] That time came in 1970 in a café outside of Flagstaff. Four Navajo children sat at the counter, asking for ice cream but being refused service. Four rowdy Whites go over and pour ice cream, syrup, and nuts over them as they scream. Using his skills as a karate master, SwiftDeer makes short work of the racist bullies. It is a scene directly out of Tom Laughlin's 1971 film *Billy Jack*.

There are other remarkable aspects to the text. Despite the monological nature of its attempted discourse, dialogized speech manages to break through. In one of his insertions, Wahlberg quotes Jeff Gray, a former resident of Lubbock: "The Reagans were notorious in Lubbock as storytellers.

Local residents consider them among the best liars Lubbock has ever produced, which in itself is no small feat!"[18] Other autoposers and plastic medicine men pass easily through the text. Reagan quotes Sun Bear and Carlos Casteneda and interacts with Lynn Andrews and Hymemeyosts Storm (both of whom "guided" his bonding to ShyDeer), Rolling Thunder, Humbatz Men, and Wallace Black Elk. The open paths to the horizon of the New Age apparently lead to a contained, completely self-validating world. The last of these, Wallace Black Elk, confronts SwiftDeer: "I do not understand what you are doing. By everything I've heard, you don't follow the sacred teachings of my people. It is said you ignore old and proven ways, basic to what we believe in. I acknowledge that what you do works for you. That you have strong medicine is apparent. However, I cannot support you, because in your medicine you turn away from the traditional ways of my people."[19] SwiftDeer's anti-communitist response is instructive: "Traditionalists insist we should covet the dogmas of the past. They suppress and shun new knowledge primarily to protect the old ways. I am convinced that one of the reasons my teachings are ignored by traditionalists is because acknowledging them means change for some of the old ways. Old dogma would have to die. In this sense, I bring death. I am the Death Bringer. Understandably, I am a threat."[20] SwiftDeer, it seems, is not only Billy Jack; he is also Šiva the Destroyer.

It is easy to dismiss this curious admixture of spiritual traditions, psychobabble, sexual libertinism, and hucksterism as harmless nonsense. It is part, however, of a larger appropriation and abuse of Native cultures that has gained momentum through the New Age movement. It takes in well-meaning White seekers who are searching for meaning and healing in their lives and believe that they are getting "authentic" Native teachings and practices. It excludes Natives and their contemporary issues entirely in favor of feel-good self-actualization and empowerment. In the process, it makes having serious discussions of Native cultures and values impossible.

Perhaps the most bizarre aspect of *Star Warrior* is that anthropologist Francis Huxley was somehow persuaded to provide the foreword. Huxley notes the criticisms that people such as SwiftDeer and Casteneda have received from scholars, "which challenge the source of the teachings and raise questions about . . . credibility." He relates having gone to SwiftDeer, asking him to abandon "difficult claims" and admit to those he taught "that certain things he claimed were part of Cherokee tradition in fact came from other traditions." According to Huxley, "So, he shot back, what did I know about the things that took place in Cherokee kivas?"[21]

Tradition and personal identity are also the issues raised by *Kill Hole*. In his dedication, author Jamake Highwater writes, "At the close of the twentieth century there are many voices that echo in our blood memory: writers, composers, and poets whose creations resonate in our lives and in our imaginations. *Kill Hole* is imbued with traces of that blood memory."[22] Like Roger Welsch, Highwater turns to fiction to make his points, though he does so for different reasons.

At one time Jamake Highwater was among the best known Native American writers. He produced not only fiction but historio-philosophical works such as *The Primal Mind* and *Ritual of the Wind*. Describing his family, he wrote, "Though my mother could neither read nor write she spun her recollections in Blackfeet and French. . . . My father was not a traditional Indian . . . and he knew very little about his Eastern Cherokee heritage despite his intense pride in being Indian."[23] As Vizenor writes, however, "The *indians*, of course, are simulations, the absence of natives, and the reminiscer turned out to be the absence of the *real* in his own varionative poses and stories."[24] According to Highwater, "I am an Indian only because I say I am an Indian. I am not enrolled on the reservations of my mother or father. I came by my heritage through the legacy of my mother and my own long efforts to reclaim an obscure identity."[25]

Highwater was, however, not an Indian. In 1984, syndicated columnist Jack Anderson revealed that "one of the country's most celebrated Indians has fabricated much of the background that made him famous." He wrote that Highwater "lied about many details of his life. Asked why someone of such genuine and extraordinary talent felt he had to concoct a spurious background, Highwater said he felt that doors would not have opened for him if he had relied on his talent alone."[26] In a 1987 review of *Ceremony of Innocence*, Doris Seale wrote:

> One might be tempted to cite the author for his helpless and ineffectual women, were it not for the fact that none of his characters seem competent to cope with life on any level. The reader unfamiliar with true Native history will be at a loss to understand from his book how the People managed to survive at all.

Recently, Jamake Highwater's identity as a Native person has been called into question by a noted political columnist, and by *Akwesasne Notes*, a highly regarded and widely distributed Native newspaper. On the basis of this book, it seems likely that they may be right.[27]

These events form the backdrop to *Kill Hole*.

The novel, a 1992 installment in Highwater's Ghost Horse Cycle (*Legend Days, Ceremony of Innocence*), finds artist Sitko Ghost Horse living in an unnamed city where an AIDS-like plague is ravaging the population. Just before a major showing of his erotic paintings, he breaks down in conversation with his gallery owner, "'God,' Sitko moaned, 'what am I doing here? They'll destroy me. I've known it all along . . . they want to destroy me.'" A few days after the exhibition, his fears are realized. A reporter contacts the gallery owner, claiming that Sitko is not an Indian but someone named Seymour Miller who has been "appropriating somebody else's culture and degrading it" with his art. No longer able to sell his paintings, he faces professional ruin. When his lover dies of the mysterious disease, he flees the city into the desert.

Sitko comes upon a remote, seemingly timeless Indian community. Unfortunately, he has arrived during their most sacred religious rite. Since the presence of outsiders is forbidden, unless he can prove he is Native, he will be put to death. All he can do is pathetically repeat the genealogy he recites by rote: "My grandmother was called Amana! Her husband was Far Away Son! But he died. She had a child. With a stranger. That child was my mother, Jemina Bonneville! And my foster father was named Alexander Milas-Miller. And when I was adopted I was called Seymour Miller. They called me Sy Miller. But I am Sitko Ghost Horse! That is who I am!"

At the Indian village, Sitko's only allies are a dwarf and a hermaphrodite or two-spirit (the writing makes her exact nature unclear) named Patu. With Patu's help, he escapes. As the novel ends, he is fleeing into the desert, pursued through the darkness by one of the tribal priests. It is Highwater's private view of hell. It is not so much a revenge fantasy as a paranoid one. There is, however, an upside to paranoia: at least you think someone's paying attention to you.

Robert Service wrote that there are strange things done in the midnight sun. Apparently also in the remote deserts and in Cherokee kivas.

CHAPTER NINE

ORIGINAL SIMPLICITIES AND PRESENT COMPLEXITIES

Reinhold Niebuhr, Ethnocentrism, and the Myth of American Exceptionalism

The Deity cannot alter the past, but historians can and do; perhaps that is why He allows them to exist.

SAMUEL BUTLER

History is always written wrong, and so always needs to be rewritten.

GEORGE SANTANAYANA

There can be no justice, no simile of truth or good faith, argues Derrida, without seeking a voice or space for the absent. And because the absent—by their very nature—are not present, they are denied hegemonic representation. The result is that history is haunted: the ineffable, the unrepresentable, the unknowable howl at the borders of consciousness and undermine narrative. "Hegemony still organizes the repression, and thus the confirmation of a haunting," argues Derrida, and thus, "haunting belongs to the structure of every hegemony." History, the very record of this hegemony, is problematized and deconstructed by these specters.

CARLTON SMITH
Coyote Kills John Wayne

As the American Civil War ended, Captain William Fetterman, sent West to the Dakota Territory to enforce the United States' Manifest Destiny, boasted, "Give me 80 men, and I'll ride roughshod through the whole Sioux nation." This, he thought, would settle "the whole Indian business," conclusively. On December 21, 1866, he had his chance. With eighty men in his command, he was dispatched to protect a work detail outside the grounds of Fort Phil Kearny from a Sioux raiding party. Pursuing the small band of Indians over a ridge, he encountered a force of some two thousand warriors. No American soldiers survived. A substantial portion of the Sioux nation had ridden roughshod over Captain Fetterman.[1]

More than a hundred years later, when the country's greater Manifest Destiny had wrecked on the shoals of the Vietnam War, Kingman Brewster, president of Yale University, reportedly observed that what America needed was a renewal of national pride and self-confidence—"a spiritually heads-up way of walking briskly about the world as a people." He declared that what was required was that peculiarly American virtue—hope.

Both these men, Fetterman in his arrogant and contemptuous assumptions about his own abilities and the righteousness of his cause and Brewster in his felt need for a revitalized American self-image, expressed a belief in American exceptionalism. Each gave voice to a long-held myth that this nation had a divine calling. Fetterman lived at a time when the myth was living and vibrant, the faith of a new nation not yet a century old. Brewster called for investing the old myth with new vigor and meaning, looking back nostalgically on a transmitted past when the myth was supposedly real.

Between the expressions of Fetterman and Brewster lived Reinhold Niebuhr. Although he pointed out the fallacy of this providential theory of empire, in the final analysis, I believe, he was seduced by the myth. He ended up merely rehearsing it in a new key. This chapter will reflect upon Niebuhr's views on American history in the hope of shedding light on their strengths and weaknesses. In the process, we shall see how Niebuhr's particular telling of that history affects historiography relating to Native Americans.

Before turning, however, to the Niebuhrian analysis, it is necessary to turn to the mid-1970s to see how the nostalgic longing for an American past operated. The time is not chosen at random. The war in Vietnam, in many ways, represented the end of American innocence. It represented the end of the America about which Niebuhr had written through most of his career.[2] Yet the myth was not finally a casualty of an Asian war. It remained alive in the popular imagination to be resuscitated by Ronald Reagan and George Bush only a few years later.

Americans in 1975 had suffered, according to one school of thought, their first defeat in war.[3] They longed for the America of Charles Ives and Aaron Copeland tone poems—a brash, young nation of limitless possibilities. Many "remembered" America as a Gary Cooper kind of a country, too big for its youth and too gentle for its size. That America was slow to anger but mighty when aroused. It never started a war, but if some decadent, corrupt European power did, it would finish it for them. Beginning, somewhat tentatively, in *The Nature and Destiny of Man*[4] and *The Children of Light and the Children of Darkness*,[5] Reinhold Niebuhr critiqued this view of America and its history. His critique gained force with the publication of *The Irony of American History* in 1952. His most rigorous analysis came, I believe, as the Vietnam War began to escalate, with *A Nation So Conceived* (coauthored with historian Alan Heimert). He would return to this theme of American history throughout the remainder of his life, and his views of it are foundational to his understanding of the United States as an actor on the world stage.[6]

In *The Irony of American History*, Niebuhr limns three different types of history: the pathetic, the tragic, and the ironic. Pathos is that element of history that inspires pity but deserves neither admiration nor contrition. Suffering resulting from purely natural causes, such as earthquakes and floods, is the clearest example of pathos. Tragedy is the conscious choice of evil for the sake of the good. For Niebuhr, that the United States had to have and threaten to use nuclear weapons in order to preserve itself and its allies was tragic. As will be seen, irony "consists of apparently fortuitous incongruities of life which are discovered, upon closer examination, to be not merely fortuitous."[7] It elicits laughter. It is distinguished from the pathetic in that humans bear responsibility for it. It is distinguished from the tragic in that the responsibility rests on unconscious weakness rather than conscious choice.[8] Irony, unlike pathos or tragedy, must dissolve when it is brought to light. These three, then, are the categories Niebuhr will pursue in his discussion of American history.

American history for Niebuhr is ironic. There is a gap between the ideal of America's self-image and the reality of its history and existence. From the beginning America saw itself as special. It possessed a strong sense of messianism.

Niebuhr is ambiguous and contradictory in both *The Irony of American History* and *A Nation So Conceived* as to when America's sense of its providential role began. He most often speaks of it beginning with the founding of the nation. He and Heimert write, for instance: "Most of the nations, in Western culture at least, have acquired a sense of national mission at some time in their history. Our nation was born with it. . . . Like Israel of old, we were a messianic nation from our birth. The Declaration of Independence and our Constitution defined the mission. We were born to exemplify the virtues of democracy and to extend the frontiers of the principles of self-government throughout the world."[9] Yet, at other times, he cites evidence that this messianism was taking shape in the earliest colonial period. For example, he quotes William Stoughton, a seventeenth-century figure: "If any people have been lifted up to advantages, we are the people. . . . We have had the eye of God working everywhere for our good. Our adversaries have had their rebukes and we have had our encouragements and a wall of fire round about us."[10]

In reality, many of the colonists who first came to North America did so already possessing a sense of divine mission. This was particularly true of the British.[11] Both Alfred A. Cave, in his paper titled "Canaanites in a Promised Land: The American Indian and the Providential Theory of Empire," and Djelal Kadir, in his book *Columbus and the Ends of the Earth: Europe's Prophetic Rhetoric as Conquering Ideology,* have demonstrated this fact. They show that biblical language was used to spawn and spur colonial ideology. Cave points out that the English looked upon the Native population as Canaanites inhibiting conquest of the promised land; they would either be exterminated or, like the Gibeonites, submit "as drudges to hewe wood and curie water."[12] Indians were spoken of as the sons of Ham, a justification also used, of course, for the subjugation and enslavement of Africans.[13] Kadir shows convincingly that the colonizers crossing the Atlantic did so with the conviction that they were exercising their God-given right to lands held in escrow for them from the foundation of the world.[14]

Regardless of the exact timing of the development of American messianism, Niebuhr is correct in claiming that by the founding of the Republic it was firmly entrenched. He writes, "[W]e came into existence with a sense of being a 'separated' nation, which God was using to make a new beginning for mankind. We had renounced the evils of European feudalism. We had escaped from the evils of European religious bigotry. We had found broad spaces for the satisfaction of human desires in place of the crowded Europe. . . . [Our forebears] believed . . . that we had been called out to create a new humanity. We were God's 'American Israel.'"[15] This belief quickly became official ideology of the new nation. By 1850, Herman Melville, one of the first truly American authors,[16] would write, "We Americans are the peculiar, chosen people—the Israel of our time. . . . The political messiah has come in us."[17]

The United States, then, was a messianic nation. As such, according to Niebuhr, it suffered from the two weaknesses of messianism—moral pretension and political parochialism. It also was victim to two hazards. The moral hazard was that it would equate its sense of mission with actual virtue. The political hazard was that it would fashion its policies too slavishly to its original sense of mission even as conditions changed.[18]

America's self-image is of a humble, agrarian nation. Yet it is an urban, industrial power. In its mind, it is the most moral nation on earth. Yet it is a hegemonic superpower forced to maintain the nuclear balance of terror. In its mind, it is still youthful little America. Yet it is the most powerful nation the world has ever known. According to Niebuhr, writing in 1952, "This has given our national life a unique color, which is not without some moral advantages. No powerful nation in history has ever been more reluctant to acknowledge the position it has achieved in the world than we. The moral advantage lies in the fact that we do not have a strong lust for power, though we are quickly acquiring the pride of power which always accompanies its possession. . . . On the other hand, we have been so deluded by the concept of our innocency [sic] that we are ill-prepared to deal with the temptations of power which now assail us."[19] In speaking thus, I would argue, Niebuhr shows that he, too, falls victim to the myth of American exceptionalism. In attempting to justify and encourage America's assumption of responsibility in world affairs, he denies that the United States acts from the same motivations of self-interest and will-to-power as other nations. A similar flaw can be seen in his discussion of the origins of American power and self-image, even as he recognizes the disingenuous nature of many expressions of that image.[20]

Both America's power and its self-image derive largely from what Niebuhr and Heimert term its "original endowments." John Smith, upon first seeing the North American continent, stated that he had never seen a land more suited for human habitation. These "broad spaces for the satisfaction of human desires," a vast continent teeming with resources, were America's original endowments. These endowments made democracy possible.[21] At some point, however, the view of these "uncovenanted and unmerited mercies" changed to a Deuteronomistic belief that they were deserved because of America's virtue.[22] "Prosperity," writes Niebuhr, "which had been sought in the service of God was now sought for its own sake."[23] And once achieved, it was looked upon as evidence of God's favor.

Even, however, as he speaks of unmerited mercies, Niebuhr endorses the foundational myth, aggressively advancing the "frontier" mentality and the assimilationist push of the dominant culture. According to him, European colonists found a "vast virgin continent, populated sparsely by Indians in a primitive state of culture."[24] The reality was, of course, starkly different. Though pre-Contact population numbers vary widely and are vigorously debated, it seems clear that the area now making up the United States was home to between ten and twenty-five million Natives at the time colonization began. Ultimately, Niebuhr and his coauthor of *A Nation So Conceived* err in the same way as did Henry Nash Smith in his seminal *Virgin Land: The American West as Symbol and Myth*. The critique of Smith by Richard Slotkin (who has chronicled the evolution of the frontier myth in three important volumes) is equally applicable to Niebuhr. Slotkin writes, "[He] was right when he said that the frontier was a key myth in shaping the American culture, but he also got things wrong. He marginalized the matter of race. He didn't appreciate the full significance of the violence used in the conquest of the West. Ignoring the pursuit of white supremacy allows Americans to feel more democratic than they are."[25]

Although Niebuhr is aware of slavery and racism, he ignores the indigenous population of the continent almost entirely. The only mention of it, in either *The Irony of American History* or *A Nation So Conceived*, is on the first page of the latter. He and Heimert, in fact, employ the term "native American" in nativist fashion to refer to those Whites who were born here, as opposed to immigrants. They refer to Manifest Destiny, that process by which the United States spread over an entire continent, as a means of "replenish[ing] America's stock of available opportunity."[26] In this sense, it becomes a sort of nineteenth-century Lebensraum.

In this regard it is significant to note that Alan Heimert, Niebuhr's coauthor, was a student of (and successor to) Perry Miller, noted Harvard intellectual historian. Miller, in his well-known *Errand into the Wilderness*, also was able to write an entire volume on the colonization of America with only scant mention of its original inhabitants, much of that being given over to a rehearsal of the Pocahontas story.[27] Yet Indians are ignored in Niebuhr's other writings as well.

In *The Irony of American History*, Niebuhr speaks of America's illusion of its own "innocency," claiming that the United States lived for a century "not only in the illusion but in the reality of innocency."[28] He goes on to state, "We were, of course, never as innocent as we pretended to be, even as a child is not as innocent as is implied in the use of the child as the symbol of innocency. The surge of our infant strength over a continent, which claimed Oregon, California, Florida and Texas against any sovereignty which may have stood in our way, was not innocent. It was the expression of a will-to-power of a new community in which the land-hunger of hardy pioneers and settlers furnished the force of imperial expansion."[29] Richard Reinitz, in his study *Irony and Consciousness: American Historiography and Reinhold Niebuhr's Vision*, contends, "This judgment is dubious and does not make sense in terms of Niebuhr's ironic framework. For example, it is difficult to see how the treatment of the Indians can be described as innocent in any but an entirely illusory sense without grossly distorting the moral reality of their destruction."[30] Reinitz concludes that Niebuhr "reinforces rather than exposes irony-inducing illusion of innocence."[31] Further, in his *Pius* [sic] *and Secular America* Niebuhr notes that in its ideals of "liberty and equality" the United States has "failed catastrophically only on one point—in our relation to the Negro race"[32] Later in the same volume, he writes, "In a nation that prided itself on being a melting pot for all the races of men, or rather of Europe, the Negro was prevented by law or by custom from participating in the process."[33]

Niebuhr's acceptance of the assimilationist push of American culture, about which he still manages to voice a mild critique, is understandable given his recent immigrant roots. In some sense, he suffered from what might be called "Whitaker Chambers syndrome."[34] He endorses the "melting pot" with its "implied conformity to some 'American' social pattern"[35] as a process by "which all the races of Europe were formed into a new amalgam of races, not quite Anglo-Saxon, but prevailingly European."[36] He fails to recognize assimilationism as the moral and social aspect of Manifest Destiny, what Native writer Gerald Vizenor terms "manifest manners."[37] While acknowledging that past wrongs against African Americans, whom they term "the least decently treated of the nation's minorities" (again ignoring indigenes), have led to occasional notions of "black supremacy," he and Heimert aver that, since the New Deal, America has accepted that all people are equal "no matter what degree of diversity divides them."[38]

With Manifest Destiny fulfilled and the Civil War behind them, Americans turned to imperialist endeavors to be assured that the youthful vigor and vitality of the nation were not waning.[39] With the so-called Spanish-American War, the United States became a world power. According to author John Lukacs, it did so "not because of some kind of geopolitical constellation, not because of the size of its armed forces, but because that was what the American government and the majority of the American people wanted."[40] Lukacs goes on to say, "Before 1898 the United States was the greatest power in the Western Hemisphere. Twenty years later the United States chose to enter the greatest of European wars. . . . In 1918 it decided the outcome of the war. By Armistice Day the United States was more than a World Power; it was the greatest power in the world."[41]

Reinhold Niebuhr recognized the importance of the First World War for the emergence of United States power and responsibility in the world. He failed, however, to understand its importance in shaping his own thought and his view of America and its history.

As he makes clear, America had for a very long time regarded itself as different from Europe, although it tended to overstate the uniqueness of its character and achievements. It had always viewed itself not primarily as a steward of resources, or even of its own power, but of an ideal. Beginning in 1898, and culminating in 1918, this self-perception began to shift subtly. As John Lukacs writes,

> "Many Americans were now inclined to believe that it was the destiny of the United States to provide a model for the Old World. For a while these two essentially contradictory beliefs resided together in many American minds. In 1918 the second belief had temporarily overcome the first. This was the result of a revolution of American attitudes. . . . In 1914 not one American in a thousand thought that the United States would, or should intervene in the great European war. In less than three years that changed. By 1917 most

> Americans were willing—and many were eager to go Over There,
> to decide and win a war through the employment of American mus-
> cle, American practices, American ideals."[42]

America, in short, was no longer just a "shining city on a hill," whose rai-
son d'être was to keep the democratic ideal. The nation now had a revised
messianic purpose to extend that ideal over the entire earth. The "War to
Make the World Safe for Democracy" transformed America's mission, and
the disastrous Treaty of Versailles endorsed that new mission.

For Niebuhr, who supported American intervention, the war became
"identified with the cause of democracy in the world."[43] He came to view
the extension of democracy as the American mission from its inception
despite his own historical evidence to the contrary. Further, this mission
was, for Niebuhr, "more valid than other forms of national messianism"
because democracy was normative in that no better form of government
had yet been found.[44] Although the United States retreated from global
involvement in the years following World War I, the war itself demonstrated what the nation's historical destiny was to be. World War II reinforced this in Niebuhr's mind, and, writing in 1952 and 1963, he was
determined that America not retreat into isolationism once again, shrink-
ing from its destiny and failing to live up to its responsibility. In sum, World
War I bequeathed a philosophy of moralistic internationalism to the American people, and Reinhold Niebuhr espoused it even while critiquing it.

Such a philosophy creates other blind spots for Niebuhr. He admits
that America is not immune from the temptation of believing that the
"universal validity" of the ideal it holds in trust justifies "our use of power
to establish it."[45] Yet he points out the "moral ambiguity of the imperial
enterprise, of the mixture of creative and exploitative purposes and consequences in the impingement of strong nations on weak ones."[46] To claim
the "moral ambiguity" of such imposition is to permit it in the service of
that universally valid ideal. Force, either covert (i.e., economic) or overt
(i.e., military), becomes permissible to advance the ideal.

In addition, although Niebuhr and Heimert caution that it is parochial
to consider American republicanism superior to European parliamentar-
ianism,[47] their own Eurocentrism leads to a different parochialism. They
write, "[W]e [the United States] are the most assiduous propagators of the
idea that the whole world wants our political freedom. The sober fact is

that the peoples of the world desire national freedom, but have no knowledge of, or desire for, individual freedom except as it has validated itself
as a servant of justice and community."[48] Despite this acknowledgment
of other possibilities for communitist values, liberal democracy is still considered normative (in itself an acceptance of much of the American myth).
On two occasions, however, the authors question whether non-European
peoples are capable of realizing that norm. Critiquing the Wilsonian vision
of self-determination and democracy, they note that it had the "defect that
it did not clearly state in what sense the democratic ideal was universally
valid, and in what sense it was an achievement of European culture,
requiring political skills and resources which may be beyond the reach of
primitive or traditional cultures." Later, they return to the same theme,
stating,

> "The lesser evil of this parochialism is to regard our institutions as
> purer exemplifications of a common democratic cause. The greater
> evil is that we may aggravate a common inclination of the whole
> European democratic world to regard democratic self-government
> as a simple option for all peoples and all cultures, whether primitive
> or traditional, without calculating in what degree they have acquired
> the skills, which have put political freedom in the service of justice
> in the West; or whether they possess the elementary preconditions
> of community, the cohesion of a common language and race, for
> instance, which European nations possessed at least two centuries
> before the rise of free institutions."[49]

Though the point merits discussion and, no doubt, contains elements of
truth, to question whether indigenous or traditional (far less Eurocentric
terms than *primitive*) cultures possess community—when in most such
cultures adherence and loyalty to community is held as a paramount
value—seems little short of absurd. As the coauthors contend, it is parochial to believe that liberal democracy is for everyone. The far greater
parochialism, however, is to assume that "Western civilization" has a corner on the conditions requisite for its attainment.

The myth of American exceptionalism was reinforced by victory in
World War II and its aftermath. The United States, alone of all nations,
had been able to fight a two-front war and bring it to a successful conclusion. In addition, because it escaped the devastation of its industrial

capacity suffered by other nations, it emerged as the preeminent economic power following the war.[50] Its military deterrent stood in the way of perceived Soviet expansionism. America did not withdraw from the world as it had following the Great War.

Niebuhr spoke of the historical moment in almost eschatological terms. America had reached the climax of its history.[51] It had moved from isolationism and continental security, with their concomitant irresponsibility, to global responsibility with all its insecurities. It had been forced to give up simplicity for complexity. America might be only "one little community" among many communities of the world, but it alone had "tasted all the bitter and sweet fruits of mature vitality which is the portion of mankind as a whole."[52] Niebuhr and Heimert wrote, "In every aspect of our national life we have been forced to re-enact in a specific drama the old pattern of humanity, for we have been driven from the Garden of Eden [of isolationism and irresponsibility] and an angel with a flaming sword has barred our return."[53]

Eventually, the myth of American exceptionalism and the internationalism it fostered (and which Niebuhr so fervently endorsed) led to involvement in Southeast Asia. There the United States looked less like a mature, responsible world power than like a giant, deranged postal employee, who, having shot everyone in sight, turned the gun on himself as well. As had Wilson's "War to End all Wars," this Indochinese adventure too wrought a major change in Reinhold Niebuhr's thinking.

Niebuhr's demonizing of Communism had prevented him, in either *The Irony of American History* or *A Nation So Conceived*, from applying his critique of the ironic character of American history with complete intellectual rigor. In this, as Richard Reinitz points out, he was hardly alone: "Most liberal intellectuals ... tended to see America's virtues more clearly than America's faults in the atmosphere of intensive Cold War, but Niebuhr's irony by its own logic should have been a device for exposing the pretensions involved in those virtues."[54] However, "during the Cold War Niebuhr seemed to be incapable of maintaining enough distance on the United States."[55] Although, of the two books, *A Nation So Conceived* is the more critical—and, as previously pointed out, the more rigorously Niebuhrian—"its view of the United States remains extremely favorable."[56] Ultimately, it was America's deepening involvement in Vietnam "that led Niebuhr to apply his ironic concept in a deeply critical way to the

United States and to imply an ironic history markedly different from that which he had outlined in his original book[s] on the subject."[57]

In a 1967 article, entitled "The Social Myths of the 'Cold War,'" Niebuhr moves away from sharp distinctions between the behavior of the United States and the Soviet Union, coming closer to equating their actions and motives in foreign affairs. Most importantly, he clearly recognizes American imperialism. He had begun a critique of Wilson's World War I policy in *A Nation So Conceived* but saw the president's maneuvering of the country into war as a creative achievement; now he declared, "The Wilsonian doctrine was an ideal moral fig leaf for a messianic nation in its first encounter with the problems of a nascent imperial dimension of power."[58] The same year, in "Vietnam: Studies in Ironies," he became even more critical of American motives and war aims. He was also able to admit that Ho was, at once, "a national patriot *and* a communist."[59] His disaffection would continue to deepen over the next few years.

By 1969 Niebuhr could write, "I must admit that our wealth makes our religious anticommunism particularly odious. Perhaps there is not much to choose between communist and anti-communist fanaticism, particularly when the latter, combined with our wealth, has caused us to stumble into the most pointless, costly and bloody war in our history."[60] And, in "The Presidency and the Irony of American History," he termed the conflict a consequence of America's pride of power, pride of virtue, and pride of riches.[61] Finally, in a 1970 op-ed piece in the *New York Times*, "Redeemer Nation to Super-Power," he related the war to "pretensions that can be found throughout American history,"[62] especially "the tradition of our self-righteous estimate of our own motives amidst the moral ambiguities of international power politics."[63] According to Reinitz, "This short piece suggests how Niebuhr's ironic vision of American history can be turned into a critical tool while offering the hope of some resolution of national problems through a bitter acknowledgment of how our illusions have led us to contribute to our own problems."[64] For Niebuhr, Vietnam was no longer an expression of American responsibility but of the illusion of its own omnipotence.[65]

Reinhold Niebuhr died on June 1, 1971. The war in Vietnam was still almost four years away from final resolution. That America's illusions did not die with that conflict's conclusion is testified to by the statement of Kingman Brewster cited at the outset of this essay. Edward Said has pointed out that the old myths still can be seen in operation in American involvement in the Gulf War. He writes that "in the American view of the past, the United States was not a classic imperial power, but a righter of wrongs around the world, in pursuit of tyranny, in defense of freedom no matter the place or cost."[66]

Yet never again after Vietnam would the myth of American exceptionalism be accepted so uncritically by so many. Reinhold Niebuhr could only have written *The Irony of American History* and *A Nation So Conceived* at the precise historical moments when they were written, at the zenith of the American Century. Perhaps only then could he be seduced by the very myths he sought to expose. In 1943, as the United States still waged World War II, Niebuhr said that it awaited the judgment of history whether the messianic pretensions of Anglo-Saxon imperialism were the swan song of a decadent and dying world view or the naive and egoistic corruption of an emerging world community.[67] Sixty years later, perhaps that question has been finally answered.

Niebuhr's acceptance of key components of the myth of American exceptionalism, and the "Manifest Destiny" ideology it engendered, led him to accept, and hence ignore, the nation's treatment of Native peoples. This ethnocentric blindness toward the indigenes reflects "our blithe national habit of trying to get on with a future unencumbered by a past" (what Donald Shriver refers to as "American pragmatic forgetfulness").[68] It highlights the danger that ensnares too much of the scholarship on American history. The history of the continent is seen as commencing in 1492, and it is written only as the interaction of Amer-Europeans. Indians figure in the story only as they are impediments to non-Native designs.[69]

Vine Deloria points out, "Writing history is too often the privilege of the winners. It is the luxury in which they indulge themselves in order to cover up their shortcomings and prevent further discussion of actual events and personalities. American history in particular has been a victim of this syndrome. Americans cling tenaciously to their myths. . . . History . . . may, in fact, be simply a collection of articles of secular faith, which cannot be disturbed without peril."[70] He maintains that manipulations of history are necessary to prove Amer-European legitimacy on this continent because "the white man knows that he is alien and he knows that North America is Indian. . . ."[71] In this, he echoes Luther Standing Bear, almost half a century earlier. In 1933, Standing Bear declared:

The white man does not understand the Indian for the reason that he does not understand America. He is far too removed from its formative processes. The roots of the tree of his life have not yet grasped the rock and soil. The white man is still troubled with primitive fears; he still has in his consciousness the perils of this frontier continent, some of its fastnesses not yet having yielded to his questing footsteps and inquiring eyes. He shudders still with the memory of the loss of his forefathers upon its scorching deserts and forbidding mountain-tops. The man from Europe is still a foreigner and an alien. And he still hates the man who questioned his path across the continent.[72]

In the end, American Indians remain a colonized people, and, as Tunisian postcolonialist Albert Memmi has alluded, it is not enough for the colonizer to control the present and future of the colonized, he must rewrite the past as well.

PART TWO

Law

CHAPTER TEN

INDIAN PRESENCE WITH
NO INDIANS PRESENT

NAGPRA and Its Discontents

Although wrongs have been done me, I live in hopes. I have not got two hearts. These young men, when I call them into the lodge and talk with them, they listen to me and mind what I say. Now we are again together to make peace. My shame is as big as the earth, although I will do what my friends advise me to do. I once thought that I was the only man that persevered to be the friend of the white man, but since they have come and cleaned out our lodges, horses, and everything else, it is hard for me to believe white men any more.

BLACK KETTLE, 1865

I never met Black Kettle, the great Cheyenne peace chief. He died almost ninety years before I was born, but I saw him once—or rather, I saw part of him once.

When I was about six years old, my mother and grandmother took me to the site of the Washita Massacre, where, on November 27, 1868, George Armstrong Custer and his Seventh Cavalry launched an unprovoked attack on Black Kettle's camp. One hundred and three Cheyennes, including Motavato (as his own people knew Black Kettle) and his wife, were slain. Of that number, only eleven were warriors. As a child, roaming the killing field, I was too interested in looking for relics to feel the overwhelming sense of grief I have felt there on subsequent visits.

After visiting the massacre site, they took me to a small museum in nearby Cheyenne. I raced around amid army uniforms, rifles, and other artifacts. Then I came upon a glass museum case containing human remains, a skull, and a few other bones. There, surrounded by other exhibits, were the bones of Motavato. Horrified by the gruesome display, I quickly called the visit to an end. Upon arriving home, I told my elder brother what I had seen. He replied, "I think it's a great step forward. When I was your age [nine years earlier], they were in the window of the local newspaper office."

White men not only "cleaned out" (stole) the lodges, lands, and possessions of Indians but robbed Indians of their persons as well—selling them into slavery, forcing assimilation and cultural genocide upon them, and, in the most bizarre turn, looting their graves as well. For decades, thousands of skeletons were gathered systematically and shipped away to be displayed and warehoused in museums. By the early twentieth century, it was grimly joked that the Smithsonian Institution in Washington had more dead Indians than there were live Indians. Amateur archaeologists and "pothunters," seeking artifacts for sale, completed the process. In the late 1980s, it was estimated that "museums, federal agencies, other institutions, and private collectors retain[ed] between 300,000 and 2.5 million dead bodies taken from Indian graves, battlefields, and POW camps by soldiers, museum collectors, scientists, and pothunters."[1] The Smithsonian alone was estimated to contain approximately 19,000 sets of remains. According to Walter R. And Roger C. Echo-Hawk, "Motives for Indian body snatching range from interests in race biology, to museum competition for anthropological 'collections,' to commercial exploitation, to just 'carrying out orders.'"[2] In addition to the human remains themselves, millions of funerary, ceremonial, and cultural objects were taken.

This massive theft was spawned in part by a belief that Native nations were rapidly dying out. Spurred by the myth of the Vanishing Indian, anthropologists fanned out across Indian country to document Native cultures.[3] These expeditions reflected not only Amer-Europeans' stasis assumptions about Native cultures, but betray anthropology as, to again use Claude Levi-Strauss's phrase, "the handmaiden of colonialism."[4] The impulse is no different from that of geneticists today who, in the Human Genome Diversity Project, rush to record indigenous DNA patterns and coding with scant regard for native peoples themselves.

At the same time anthropologists rushed to record Native culture, archaeologists collected Indian remains for what they might tell scientists and future generations. However, as Walter and Roger Echo-Hawk report, "All tribes throughout Indian ... country ... have been victimized by what has become the most grisly and frightening problem confronting Native Americans today. The impact upon Native people, regardless of the motive, is always the same: emotional trauma and spiritual distress."[5] A Department of the Interior report acknowledged this in 1979, stating, "The prevalent view in the society of applicable disciplines is that Native American human remains are public property and artifacts for study, display, and cultural investment. It is understandable that this view is in conflict with and repugnant to those Native people whose ancestors and near relatives are considered the property at issue."[6] Granted, human remains, from any period, can tell us much about lifeways, diet, diseases, and many other things. Yet we do not see archaeologists hurrying to excavate colonial cemeteries in New England churchyards for what they can say about early colonists. As the Echo-Hawks conclude:

> Systematic disturbances of non-Indian graves, on the one hand, are abhorred and avoided at all costs, while Indian people are actively searched out, dug up, and placed in museum storage. Criminal statutes in all fifty states very strictly prohibit grave desecration, grave robbing, and mutilation of the dead—yet they are not applied to protect Indian dead. Instead, the laws and social policy, to the extent that they affect Native dead, do not treat this class of decedents as human, but rather define them as "non-renewable archaeological resources" to be treated like dinosaurs or snails, "federal property" to be used as chattels in the academic marketplace, "pathological specimens" to be studied by those interested in racial biology, or simple "trophies or booty" to enrich private collectors. The huge collections of dead Indians are compelling testimony that Indians have been singled out for markedly disparate treatment.[7]

Recognizing the problem and answering the protests of tribal elders and other Natives, the United States Congress passed a series of laws designed to protect Natives from further theft and desecration. The first of these enactments was the Archaeological Resources Protection Act of 1979 (ARPA). Designed to preserve sites on federal lands, it provided for fines and incarceration for removing "archaeological resources" from federal property without a prior permit pursuant to the Antiquities Act of

1906. The law was amended in 1988, strengthening provisions concerning looting of "federal property."[8] Designed to halt commercial vandalism on federal lands, the act did nothing to protect remains on private property.

In 1990, Congress enacted the National Museum of the American Indian Act, creating a museum for Native culture and history within the Smithsonian. As part of the legislation, the Smithsonian was required to catalogue and identify the origin of Native human remains in its holdings "in consultation and cooperation with traditional Indian religious leaders and government officials of Indian tribes." If the inventoried remains could be identified as a specific individual or associated with a particular tribe, the museum was required, upon request of the descendants or the tribe, to return the remains and any funerary objects associated with them.[9] The act was the first law to require repatriation and reburial of human remains. A short while later, Congress also passed the Native American Graves Protection and Repatriation Act (NAGPRA).[10] The act

> prohibits trade, transport, or sale of Native American human remains and directs federal agencies and museums to take inventory of any Native American . . . remains and, if identifiable, the agency or museum is to return them to the tribal descendants. The Act mandates the Secretary of Interior to establish a committee to monitor the return of remains and objects and authorizes the Secretary to make grants for assisting museums with compliance. The Act prohibits remains and objects from being considered archaeological resources, prohibits disturbing sites without tribal consent, and imposes penalties for unauthorized excavation, removal, damage or destruction.[11]

In addition to human remains and funerary objects, it also mandated the return of sacred objects and other cultural patrimony. NAGPRA, drafted in consultation with archaeologists, "represents a broad national reburial [and] repatriation policy."[12] Any institution receiving federal funds is covered by its requirements.

From the beginning NAGPRA has presented challenges to archaeologists, museums, and tribes alike. Museums and universities often have dragged their heels at compliance, and some have sought to impose conditions upon tribes before repatriating objects. Archaeologists have decried requests for return of remains and objects as unfairly inhibiting scientific inquiry. Walter and Roger Echo-Hawk respond:

> When non-Indian institutions possess Indian sacred objects and living gods and when they control disposition of the dead, they become little more than quasi-church facilities imposed upon Indian communities, regulating the "free" exercise of religion for dispossessed Indian worshipers. First Amendment religious freedoms are clearly controlled from the pulpit of science when museums elevate scientific curiosity over Indian religious belief in the treatment of the dead. Should Indians protest, some scientists are quick to raise the specter of research censorship, comparing such protesters to "book-burners" and referring to Indian plans for the disposition of their deceased ancestors as the "destruction of data."[13]

One of the more interesting disputes involved hair recovered by archaeologist Robson Bonnichsen at a ten-thousand-year-old site in Montana. Realizing that human hair does not decay like other genetic material, Dr. Bonnichsen developed a sophisticated system of filters and recovered a bundle of hairs that he planned to subject to DNA testing. Before any tests could take place, however, the Confederated Salish-Kootenai and the Shoshone-Bannock demanded the return of the hair pursuant to NAGPRA; the Bureau of Land Management, which controlled the site, acting on behalf of the tribes, barred the Bonnichsen team from the site and prohibited the proposed tests. Bonnichsen protested that the hairs he had recovered were not "remains" within the definition of the act, since they were not associated with any burial site but were rather of the type that humans normally lose daily. He has declared, "Two years of work were totally disrupted. Repatriation has taken on a life of its own and is about to put us out of business as a profession."[14] After two years of dispute, regulations under NAGPRA were amended to exclude naturally shed hair from the workings of the act.

Controversy over NAGPRA came to a head with the discovery of a largely intact skeleton on the banks of the Columbia River at Kennewick, Washington, in July 1996. James Chatters, a private consultant in archaeology and paleoecology, examined the skeleton at the request of the local sheriff. Upon initial review, based upon its physical characteristics, Dr.

Chatters concluded that it was the remains of a Caucasian male about fifty years old. Sent to the University of California at Riverside for radiocarbon dating, bone samples were determined to be between 9,100 and 9,400 years old. Two other anthropologists who also examined the skeleton, Catherine J. MacMillan of Central Washington University and Grover S. Krantz of Washington State University, agreed that it had Caucasian features.

As with the Bonnichsen hair samples, the scientists proposed DNA tests. Once the find was made public, however, and before any such testing could be performed, the Umatilla Confederated Tribe, whose reservation is across the Columbia in Oregon, laid claim to it under NAGPRA, demanding the study of the skeleton cease. They were quickly joined by four other tribes with common ancestral ties to the region, the Colville Confederated Tribes, the Nez Perces, the Wanapum Band of Walla Walla Tribes, and the Yakama Nation. Because NAGPRA requires that tribal affiliation be determined as prerequisite to repatriation, and because the extreme age of the paleo-Indian remains makes specificity difficult if not impossible, the cooperation of the five claimants became crucial. Responding to the requirement of specific tribal affiliation, Bill Yallup of the Yakama tribal council stated, "We are no different one from another, we are all Indian."[15]

When the U.S. Army Corps of Engineers—which assumed jurisdiction over what was now called the Kennewick Man by scientists and simply the Ancient One by Natives (out of respect for their ancestor, they refuse to use the nickname)—announced that it would turn the remains over to the tribes, scientists protested. Douglas Owsley, a forensic anthropologist at the Smithsonian, stated, "They need to reconsider this decision. Skeletons from this period are extremely rare. We know very little about them. If there is no further opportunity to examine these remains, we will be losing information that is important to every American." James Chatters, who first viewed the Ancient One, declared, "It's been like a gold mine where normal people all of a sudden go goofy. My thinking was, here was an opportunity to look at us as less separate."[16]

Two lawsuits were brought in the United States District Court in Portland, seeking to prevent repatriation and reburial. One was filed by a group of eight scientists, desiring to make further tests. A second was pursued by the Asatru Folk Assembly, a new religious movement of approximately five hundred persons who claim to follow pre-Christian Norse traditions. Both complaints relied on Chatters's initial description that the

Ancient One was Caucasian, contending that therefore ARPA rather than NAGPRA applied. Asatru president Stephen McNallen stated, "We don't want to offend Native Americans, because, really, we have a lot in common with them."[17] Most scientists, however, remained skeptical, claiming that from a single skeleton it was impossible to conclude that Caucasians resided in North America more than 450 generations ago. Even Chatters himself admitted that his initial characterization was based on modern forensic standards, "When it [the Ancient One] turns out to be old, the whole equation changes. We're not sure what people looked like back then."[18]

Nevertheless, the "brief viewings" of Chatters and others and their "initial impression" were seized upon by proponents (including the Asatru Folk Assembly) of a variant of the Bering Strait theory known as the Euro-Bering migration. As described by the *New York Times*, "It [the discovery of the Ancient One] adds credence to theories that some early inhabitants of North America came from European stock, perhaps migrating across northern Asia and into the Western Hemisphere over a land bridge exposed in the Bering Sea about 12,000 years ago, or earlier, near the end of the last Ice Age."[19] Robson Bonnichsen once again lambasted the operation of NAGPRA, saying, "This is a battle over who controls America's past. We have already used the term paleo-Indian to describe remains of this area. But this may be the wrong term. Maybe some of these guys were really just paleo-American."[20] Having used the Bering Strait theory to make Indians immigrants not fundamentally different from those who disembarked at Ellis Island, it is now used to make them European as well, the populating of the hemisphere no different than Columbus's (or Vikings') "discovery" centuries later.

At least some of the scientists party to the suit disputed the contention. Gentry Steele, a physical anthropologist at Texas A&M University, pointed out that paleo-Indians "appear Caucasoid or Asian to the untrained eye," but that traits actually fall somewhere between the two groups. He stated, "That's not to say that southern Asians populated the area. It could mean that North American Indians looked more like South Asians than they do today." He concluded, "What we're trying to say is that the individual could be the model to the ancestors of all North American and South American Indians." Dr. Steele expressed his belief that NAGPRA did apply to the discovery and that the Ancient One should be repatriated, *but* only after further study.[21]

As the controversy continued, and while litigants awaited a hearing on a preliminary injunction against the Corps of Engineers on October 23, the *New York Times*, which previously had reported the debate, decided to enter the dispute more actively. On October 22, it ran a front-page story (continued in its "Science Times" section) entitled "Indian Tribes' Creationists Thwart Archeologists." The article, heavily slanted in favor of the scientists, likened Natives seeking return of ancestral remains pursuant to the provisions of NAGPRA to Christian fundamentalists. It declared, "Since the repatriation act was passed in 1990, American Indian creationism, which rejects the theory of evolution and other scientific explanations of human origins in favor of the Indians' own religious beliefs, has been steadily gaining in political momentum. Adhering to their own creation accounts as adamantly as biblical creationists adhere to the book of Genesis, Indian tribes have stopped important archeological research on hundreds of prehistoric remains."[22]

The article rehearsed the disputes over both the Bonnichsen hair find and the Ancient One. It stated that similar cases throughout the West had "given some archeologists the feeling that their field is in a state of siege" and cited four other instances in which studies of Indian or paleo-Indian remains were halted because of NAGPRA demands. The clear message of the piece was that important, legitimate inquiry was being stymied by dogmatic Native "creationists." It quoted Vine Deloria, "a history professor at the University of Colorado and a prominent Indian advocate and legal scholar," concerning material in his recent book, *Red Earth, White Lies: Native Americans and the Myth of Scientific Fact.* According to the *Times*, "In his book, Mr. Deloria dismisses as 'scientific folklore' the theory, embraced by virtually all archeologists, that America's native peoples came from Asia across the Bering Strait 10,000 or more years ago. . . . Using some of the same arguments embraced by fundamentalist Christians, Mr. Deloria also dismisses the theory of evolution as more unsubstantiated dogma."[23]

Minimizing the comments of archaeologists sympathetic to Natives, the article focused on those who saw NAGPRA demands as anti-intellectualism. Quoting Steve Lekson, as archaeological research associate at Deloria's own institution, it read, "Some people who are not sympathetic to fundamentalist Christian beliefs are extraordinarily sympathetic to Native American beliefs. I'm not sure I see the difference."[24]

Three days later the *Times* printed two letters to the editor critical of the newspaper's reporting.[25] On November 2, however, it ran an op-ed piece by Pulitzer Prize–winning writer N. Scott Momaday. Momaday, long a believer in the Bering Strait theory and in the benefits of Western science, repeated the fundamentalist characterization. Referring to the long history of poor relations between scientists and Natives, he labeled Native actions in situations like that involving the Ancient One as "vengeance" for past depredations.[26] In the context of the ongoing imbroglio concerning the Ancient One, the *New York Times* reporting and the enlistment of Momaday are troubling for many reasons.

The newspaper clearly contended that Native "religious fundamentalists" are the primary force demanding the return of human remains and opposing scientific testing. Their fear, it is claimed, is that analysis of remains will "disprove" traditional tribal protologies, which often state that the tribe in question has been on its ancestral lands since creation. Although traditional creation myths are an important part of tribal identity and are often deeply held, they are not the prime factor in NAGPRA repatriation requests.

Native traditions prescribe respect for the remains of ancestors. The fear among many Natives about scientific testing is not that it will contradict or disprove sacred accounts concerning tribal origins but that it will further desecrate the remains. Native leaders have stated as much in the tug-of-war over the Ancient One. Armand Minthorn, a spokesman for the Umatillas, ruled out DNA testing, saying, "That goes against all our beliefs [on how to treat the dead]."[27] Walla Walla chief Carl Sampson, at a conference with the Corps of Engineers, echoed Minthorn: "We're tired of the desecration of our ancestors. You don't understand us, you that aren't Indian here today. We're going to put that body back into the ground no matter what your supreme law says."[28]

Many Natives feel that any study of human remains is disrespectful. For others, however, testing is permissible provided it is nondestructive. Among the Colvilles (one of the NAGPRA claimants of the Ancient One), for instance, nondestructive study of remains, including measurement and bone scraping, is a common practice.[29] DNA testing is opposed because such analysis consumes the sample it tests. Though naturally shed human hair may not be human remains within the intended scope of NAGPRA, the objection is simply that the testing will destroy the hairs. If the real fear was that human origins in the Americas would prove to be the product of relatively recent migrations from Asia and thus cast doubt on the literal truth of tribal protologies, why would tribes, as noted by the *Times*, allow radiocarbon dating of human remains, which also could tend to lend credence to the same theory?

Reportage in the *Times*, as in most of the whitestream media, assumes the scientific fact of the Bering Strait theory.[30] Beringia, the presumed land bridge between Asia and North America, is thought to have existed three or four separate times, beginning 70,000 years ago. If ancestors of present-day Natives migrated across such a bridge (and in his work Deloria raises serious objections to such a proposition), they certainly did so much earlier than 10,000 to 12,000 years ago and were active in the Americas at a much earlier date.

The question of the origin of humans in this hemisphere has troubled Europeans and Amer-Europeans at least since Columbus returned to Spain in March 1493. Accompanying him were captive indigenes, beings who appeared to be human. Their existence posed a threat to the prevailing biblical exegesis of the day, which assumed the literal historical truth of the story of Noah and his ark. Such a "fundamentalist" or "creationist" reading of Hebrew scripture led to a belief that there were only three continents, each peopled by the offsprings of a different son of the ark builder after the biblical flood. Many concluded that the people erroneously labeled Indians were the ten lost tribes of Israel.[31]

When early Russian explorers discovered that Alaska and the Aleutian Islands stretched out to almost touch Asia, it was imagined that the indigenous peoples of the Western Hemisphere must have originated on that continent. The Bering Strait theory in its modern form stems only from 1739. In that year, a portrait painter named Smibert arrived in Boston to paint the colonial aristocracy. Seeing Indians, he noticed the similarity to Siberians he had glimpsed in the Russian court and pronounced them Mongolians. According to anthropologist Clark Wissler, "From that day to this, notwithstanding the intensive research of specialists, everything points to a Mongoloid ancestry for the Indian."[32] More precisely, one might say that everything has been made to point to such an origin.

For many years, Vine Deloria points out, it was contended that Indians were relative newcomers to the hemisphere, "latecomers who had barely unpacked before Columbus came knocking on the door."[33] The political/ideological value of such an assumption is clear. According to Deloria, "If Indians had arrived only a few centuries earlier, they had no real claim to land that could not be swept away by European discovery. Aleš Hrdlicka of the Smithsonian devoted his life to the discrediting of any early occupancy of North America, and a whole generation of scholars, fearfully following the master, rejected the claims of their peers rather than offend this powerful scholar."[34] Coincidentally, Hrdlicka was responsible for the largest collection of skeletal remains repatriated pursuant to NAGPRA—756 specimens excavated by him on Kodiak Island between 1932 and 1936.[35]

In 1926 a site was uncovered near Folsom, New Mexico, that revealed much earlier signs of human habitation than any previously known. Radiocarbon dating of a Folsom culture dig outside Lubbock, Texas, disclosed an age of 9883, plus or minus 350 years. In the 1930s, a few years after the Folsom discovery, road builders near Clovis, New Mexico, found a deposit of fossilized bones of mammoths and an extinct type of bison. Associated with the find was a previously unknown type of projectile point. These "Clovis points" were about four inches long and distinguished by their concave appearance and their fluted edges. Subsequently, such points have been found in all of the forty-eight contiguous United States and into Mexico. According to Peter Farb, "So uniform was the culture across the continent, particularly east of the Rockies, that a site in Massachusetts is scarcely distinguishable from another Llano [Clovis] site in, say, Colorado." The Clovis site was dated to 11–12,000 years ago. Testing of any other archaeological site could yield a date no earlier than 12,000 years. Initially an unwelcomed and embarrassing discovery, Clovis ultimately was embraced, and the "Clovis barrier" of 12,000 years for human habitation in the Americas became the new scientific orthodoxy. Such a date fit neatly with the Bering Strait theory.[36]

In *Red Earth, White Lies*, Deloria details the cases of a number of scientists, many of them eminent, whose careers and reputations suffered as a result of challenging this established orthodoxy. Several archaeologists, including Louis Leakey, found or evaluated sites that they believed broke the Clovis barrier. All of these, however, were discredited. Then, in 1976, local lumbermen accidentally discovered a site near Puerto Montt in south-central Chile. When an interdisciplinary team headed by anthropologist Thomas Dillehay began excavating the site, known as Monte Verde, they realized that it was extraordinary. Radiocarbon dating led to a conclusion that the most impressive remains dated to 12,500 years ago—and at the deepest level nearly 32,000 years. Proponents of the Clovis barrier, including the acknowledged dean of paleo-Indian archaeology, Junius Bird of the American Museum of Natural History, joined in dismissing the discovery and attacking Dillehay. According to Dillehay:

> Much of the debate about the existence of pre-Clovis people in the Americas hinges on standards of archaeological evidence. Clovis advocates maintain, with some justification, that most pre-Clovis sites are nothing more than jumbled deposits of old soil and much younger artifacts and plant remains. Pre-Clovis advocates counter that their opponents are isolationists and chauvinists, that they too often reject sites without proper evidence of disproof. If the same standards were applied to Clovis sites, they go on to say, many of those sites would not be accepted either.[37]

Dillehay concludes:

> Although I was braced for some criticism when we first began excavating Monte Verde, I was taken aback by how quickly our work was cast into the middle of the pre-Clovis controversy. Every few months, it seems a new instant analysis of Monte Verde and other pre-Clovis sites appeared, all without a site visit or a review of all the evidence. . . . Instant-opinion-hurling has become something of a sport in the study of the first Americans—a sport that reveals our arbitrary understanding of . . . the peopling of the Americas.[38]

In January 1997, a multidisciplinary team including some of Dillehay's staunchest critics gathered at the University of Kentucky to review evidence, followed by a three-day site visit. All agreed that the Clovis barrier had been broken, dating one stratum at Monte Verde to 12,500 years. Unspoken in reporting of the event was any discussion of the much older layers claimed by Dillehay.

The verification of a site of such antiquity, populated by a sophisticated and sedentary people, ten thousand miles from the Bering Strait raises important questions. According to a report of the January visit in the *New York Times*:

In the depths of the most recent ice age, two vast ice sheets converged about 20,000 years ago over what is now Canada and the United States and apparently closed off human traffic there until sometime after 13,000 years ago. Either people migrated through a corridor between the ice sheets and spread remarkably fast to the southern end of America or they came by a different route, perhaps along the western coast, by foot and sometimes on small vessels. Otherwise they must have entered the Americas before 20,000 years ago.[39]

Hearing such speculation and the words of Dillehay above, one can sympathize with Deloria's plea that in all honesty, therefore, "'science' should drop the pretense of absolute authority with regard to human origins and begin looking for some other kind of explanation that would include the traditions and memories of non-Western peoples."[40] Larry Zimmerman, anthropologist at the University of Iowa, echoes Deloria when he states the need for "a different kind of science, between the boundaries of Western ways of knowing and Indian ways of knowing."[41]

New discoveries are made regularly, in diverse areas and branches of science, that cast doubt on the received story of the peopling of the Americas. In July 1996, the same month the Ancient One was found in Washington, paleo-Indian skeletal remains, dated at 9,700 years, were discovered on Prince of Wales Island in southern Alaska, leading to consideration that the area was occupied 30,000 or more years ago.[42] The linguistic analysis of Johanna Nichols of the University of California at Berkeley suggests humans were in the New World 35,000 to 40,000 years ago.[43] Spears have been found in a mine in Germany, suggesting Stone Age people systematically hunted big game 400,000 years ago—as opposed to the 40,000 years previously assumed. Evidence has been found that humans lived in the harsh cold of Siberia as early as 300,000 years ago; before the find, it had been assumed that human habitation before the advent of fully modern Homo sapiens, perhaps 40,000 years ago, was impossible.[44] Most intriguing of all is the discovery of a Clovis point in Siberia by Russia archaeologist Sergei B. Slobodin and American doctoral candidate Maureen L. King. Radiocarbon dating of material associated with the point indicates that it is 8,300 years old—more than 2,000 years younger than those at Clovis itself.[45] The find, if confirmed, would indicate that if there was travel between Asia and the Americas it was hardly the one-way street usually put forth. All of this research, though not necessarily either "proving" tribal protologies or "disproving" the Bering Strait theory, should demonstrate that knowledge of human origins and the populating of the Americas is neither as definitive nor as absolute as scientists sometimes suggest. It is a common joke in Indian country that the only physical evidence for a Bering Strait migration is a single fossil footprint, and scientists cannot tell in which direction it is heading.

The Bering Strait theory is simply that—a theory. Alternative theories, ranging from continental drift, to polygenesis, to human genesis in the Americas, have been put forth. Such theories, while seeming outlandish to some, are vitally important in freeing the imagination and opening the seams of what has been largely a closed discussion conducted without the participation of traditional Natives. According to historian Homer Noley, "Unfortunately, today's public schools teach one of the theories as if it were fact, namely the Bering Strait land bridge theory. It is a theory not supported by adequate evidence, but it is held by those who need convenient answers to their questions. The truth is nobody knows the origins of the Native tribes on this continent."[46] Philosopher Paul Feyerabend states that science as a way of knowing the world is "inherently superior only for those who have already decided in favor of a certain ideology. . . . Science took over by force, not by argument."[47] Noley notes, "Neither anthropology nor history rests on principles or methods that are absolute, as mathematics does. The choice of a point of reference too often becomes merely the judgment of the scientist or historian. [Determinations of fact often depend] on the judgment call of the person or group making the first diagnosis. Events that follow that judgment are justified by the diagnosis."[48]

Certain evidence, in fact, militates against the Bering Strait theory. For example, Native tribes record the purest type-A and type-O blood groups in the world, plus the only groups entirely lacking type-A. Moreover, aside from those in the Arctic and sub-Arctic, there is among most groups an absence of type-B blood, the overwhelmingly predominant blood group in east Asia. How are these facts to be reconciled with an Asian migration at a relatively recent date? If such a migration did occur, how did the immigrants so quickly populate the entirety of the Americas and so rapidly adapt to widely diverse environments from frozen tundra to South American rainforest? If it occurred, how did an obviously highly mobile people manage to change so quickly into sedentary inhabitants like those of Monte Verde? Once again, one can understand Deloria's conclusion:

> Not only does the more recent interpretation of human evolution militate against American Indians being latecomers to the Western Hemisphere, an examination of the Bering Strait doctrine suggests that such a journey would have been impossible even if there had been hordes of Paleo-Indians trying to get across the hypothetical land bridge. It appears that not even animals or plants really crossed this mythical connection between Asia and North America. The Bering Strait [crossing] exists and existed only in the minds of scientists.[49]

It is sometimes argued that the absence of any credible scientific evidence for any alternative theory leaves only the Bering Strait theory. But it is always dangerous to draw conclusions on the basis of the absence of evidence.

> It is a reasonable and well documented principle that the frequency of archaeological finds falls sharply with their age; Karl Butzer has estimated that 11,000 year old sites [for the sake of argument, roughly the date of the Clovis barrier] will be found 10–15 times more often than 30,000 year old sites, and over 100 times more often than a 75,000 year old site. Even given all the clever techniques which archaeologists have developed to locate artifacts, it is no surprise that few finds have been made in Siberia and Alaska, where sparse resources and a bitter climate probably limited the human population to small, widely separated communities, further reducing man's already vanishing fingerprint.[50]

Who knows what finds yet await discovery in the Orinoco or the Amazon? Might certain previously discredited pre-Clovis sites need to be reevaluated in light of the confirmation of Monte Verde? As Thomas Dillehay states, "Archaeologists will probably never find the remains of the very first Americans. Even if they do, they may not recognize those remains for what they are."[51]

In the October 22 article in the *New York Times* concerning the supposed travesties wrought by NAGPRA, the author writes that "according to many Indian creation accounts, natives have always lived in the Americas after emerging onto the surface of the earth from a subterranean world of spirits." This is true. Native nations, however, as already noted, are possessed of a tremendous variety of creation accounts and religious traditions that vary widely. To homogenize them and then to juxtapose them with Western science is only to conflate them and ultimately to do a disservice to all concerned. In fact, some tribes—notably the Cherokee and the Delaware—preserve myths about a migration from lands across the water.[52] Still others, such as the Hopi and the Colville, as noted by Deloria, speak of transoceanic moves by boat.[53]

Reading accounts of the controversy over the Ancient One, a reader might get the impression that NAGPRA has been an unmitigated disaster— "that the relationship between archaeologists and Native Americans is a negative one, with little in common on either side."[54] In reality, a number of tribes have cultural heritage programs or historic preservation offices that include archaeological work. William Tall Bull and Ted Rising Sun, among others, have shown that history and archaeology, though they have been too often employed for domination, can be tools of resistance as well, "capable of allowing [dominated] groups to free themselves from participation in the dominant ideology."[55] Though presenting challenges, NAGPRA has functioned reasonably well and has led to the repatriation of thousands of remains and important ritual objects. Rather than fighting tribes in the name of science and denouncing their legitimate demands as "religious fundamentalism," the lesson for archaeologists to draw from NAGPRA is the need to cultivate good relations with the Natives whom they study and on whose ancestral lands they work. This is the sensible suggestion of William D. Lipe, president of the Society for American Archaeology, in a letter he wrote in response to the dispute over the Ancient One.[56] Such an approach could benefit not only scientists but the tribes as well.

A few years ago I returned to that museum in Cheyenne, Oklahoma. I was no longer able to see Motavato. He had been buried. As I recall, an American flag flew above his grave. It was like the one that he had been given on a trip to Washington, where he met with President Lincoln. The army colonel who presented it promised him that, as long as that flag flew above him, no soldier would fire upon him. That flag fluttered above his lodge at Sand Creek on the day in November 1864 when soldiers did attack. This flag was the same. Only now sixteen stars, representing further theft of Native lands, had been added. I never knew Motavato, but somehow I don't think he would approve.

◆ ◆ ◆

Note: The problem with writing timely, topical essays is that time does not cooperate by standing still. The lag time between finished manuscript and publication, in either journals or books, is generally ten to twelve months. Events continue to unfold during that hiatus, with the result that a piece, while still relevant, may not be quite as to-the-moment when it sees the light of day as it was when illuminated only by the flicker of a computer screen. In the case of the Ancient One, however, nothing has proceeded rapidly.

With the suits by the eight scientists and the Asatru Folk Assembly pending, the Army Corps of Engineers rescinded its original decision to turn the Ancient One over to the tribes. On June 2, 1997, John Jelderks, the federal magistrate hearing motions in the case, denied the scientists' request for immediate access to the skeleton. He did, however, order the Corps to reconsider its decision.

In a written opinion in July, the judge elaborated on the June 2 decision. While making it clear that he was not deciding the ultimate disposition of the remains, he did term the decision-making process followed by the Corps flawed, finding that it had chosen "to suppress [its doubts about the applicability of NAGPRA] in the interests of fostering a climate of cooperation with the tribes." He concluded by ordering all parties to report back to the court on a quarterly basis, beginning October 1, 1997.

James Chatters created a reconstruction of the Ancient One's head, based on his study of the bones. It looked uncannily like Patrick Stewart's. The forensic anthropologist himself admitted that it came to him in a sort of epiphanic moment as he molded the clay, "Jean-Luc Picard!" referring to the British actor's most familiar role in *Star Trek: The Next Generation*. Subsequent analysis has, once again, questioned Chatter's view. Others feel that the Ancient One may more closely resemble the Ainu, the indigenous people of Japan. Still others see a link to Pacific Islanders.

The Asatru Folk Assembly has withdrawn its suit. The Corps had at least until the autumn of 2000 to notify Jelderks whether it would allow the scientists to examine the Ancient One. According to the *New York Times*,

"If the government refuses, [he] may well open the case for trial. He has indicated in court papers that he would like the parties to argue before him what 'indigenous' means, since that is apparently, in his opinion, key to applying Nagpra [sic]. It is a different way of phrasing the question, 'What is an Indian?'"[57] Secretary of the Interior Bruce Babbit has gone on record as recommending repatriation, supporting the tribe's position.

Preliminary studies by Francis McManamon, chief archaeologist for the National Park Service, for the Department of the Interior, "seem to lean toward the possibility that there is a plausible affiliation between the dead man and one or more modern tribes."[58] Ironically, and to the consternation of Natives involved, the final answer may be DNA analysis. In early 2000, Judge Jelderks gave the government six months to perform such testing. Not only would this represent the desecration the tribes had sought to avoid, but it might also mean having to extract other samples from other Native skeletons for comparison purposes.

In August 1999, hunters in the Yukon discovered a body exposed by melting glacial ice. The remarkably preserved remains, which include soft tissue, were tentatively dated at five thousand years old, although subsequent analysis indicated a much younger age. At the time of discovery, Diane Strand, heritage resource officer for the Champagne and Aishihik First Nations, stated that they believed the remains to be a tribal ancestor. Unlike the tribes involved in the Kennewick controversy, however, the tribe in Canada did not oppose further testing. They believed that such analysis would only confirm their claim to the land they know as theirs. Strand states, "According to stories recorded by our elders, we have been here since time immemorial, since when animals could speak to people."[59]

In the meantime, the controversy over the Ancient One and the search for human origins in North America continues to swirl in the media.[60] Motavoto must be rolling in his grave. Now, at least, he, unlike the Ancient One, has a grave in which to spin.

CHAPTER ELEVEN

LOSING MY RELIGION

Native American Religious Traditions and American Religious Freedom

Despite desires and assurances to the contrary, Indians did not vanish. In spite of the efforts of both Church and State, through coercive evangelization and promulgation of regulations like the Religious Crimes Codes that sought to ban indigenous religious traditions, suppression could not be complete. The gods of Native North America have never left themselves without witnesses.

JACE WEAVER,
Native American Religious Identity: Unforgotten Gods

The summer of 1993 was a particularly hopeful one for those of us interested in Native American religious freedom. In Congress, amendments were introduced to the American Indian Religious Freedom Act of 1978 that would reverse the negative positions taken by the United States Supreme Court regarding sacred sites in *Lyng v. Northwest Indian Cemetery Protective Association* and ceremonial use of peyote in *Employment Division v. Smith.*[1] Provisions were included restoring the "compelling state interest" test as the standard in religious freedom cases, permitting free exercise of Native religious traditions by prisoners, ensuring access to sacred sites and the availability of eagle feathers for religious practice, and providing enforcement mechanisms. These amendments, known variously as the Religious Freedom Restoration Act (RFRA), the Native American Free Exercise of Religion Act (NAFERA), and the American Indian Religious Freedom Act of 1993, were endorsed by every major religious organization in the country, in addition to legal, human rights, environmental, and Native groups. Easy passage was predicted.

In June of that same year, the Supreme Court decided *Church of Lukumi Babalu Aye v. Hialeah*.[2] The unanimous decision, in action brought by practitioners of Santeria, struck down a ban by Hialeah, Florida, on animal sacrifice. Although the Court's opinion did not retreat from the *Smith* case's virtual abolition of the compelling state interest test as the standard in free exercise cases under the First Amendment, it did find unconstitutional a prohibition that the dominant culture had sought to impose upon a minority religion. In addition, two justices, Harry Blackmun and Sandra Day O'Connor, who dissented (at least in part) in *Smith*, took the opportunity to reaffirm their opposition to its principle. And David Souter, who had not been a member of the Court at the time of *Smith*, authored a separate, carefully crafted opinion in which he called upon his colleagues to reconsider the decision in that case.

The summer of 1993 was a hopeful time. Yet as autumn came, hopes began to fall like the leaves from deciduous trees. RFRA was passed (thus restoring the compelling state interest test), as was the provision relating to peyote, but other necessary provisions, including that related to sacred sites, remained mired in Congress. With the sweep of the "Republican Revolution" in 1994, Native issues dropped from the public agenda, and it is doubtful that they will receive much attention for some time to come.[3]

Further, in the ensuing years, there were 288 cases under RFRA, and even many supporters admitted that the law had been abused. No fewer than six constitutional challenges to RFRA found their way into the courts by 1997. The Supreme Court agreed to hear one of these, involving whether the landmark status of a Catholic church in Boerne, Texas, represented a "substantial burden" on its ability to carry out its mission. In the *Boerne* case, a brief on behalf of the church by Douglas Laycock, a law professor at the University of Texas, contended that if RFRA were overturned "the entire body of law on congressional enforcement power" would be "called into question, and much of it would have to be overturned." Other legal scholars, such as Ira Lupu of George Washington University, argued that the law was unconstitutional inasmuch as it went "way beyond what the Supreme Court has said the Constitution requires of the states."[4]

Writing in 1997, I noted that, as for the High Court itself, four of those who took part in the *Smith* decision, including Justice Blackmun, had left the Court. The views of their successors on these matters remained an uncertainty, and, even if they were so disposed, their presence probably did not create a majority for a strong position in favor of free exercise of religion.

A few months later, I wrote:

> Prognostication is more properly the province of pundits rather than professors. It may be true that those who do not know history are condemned to relive it, but history remains an unreliable forecaster of future events. The common law, however, is based on the principle of *stare decisis*. Cases are decided in accordance with precedent. Therefore an examination of past judicial decisions should allow the legal scholar to predict with at least some accuracy how a court will rule in a given instance. This is, of course, a gross oversimplification. There is space for creativity, personal philosophy, and change in any ruling.[5]

Sadly, many of my fears about the future of First Amendment litigation voiced in the original version of this essay, published in 1998, have been realized in subsequent events. On September 25, 1997, the Supreme Court handed down its decision in *City of Boerne v. Flores*. The 6-to-3 decision struck down RFRA as unconstitutional. In so doing, the High Court reaffirmed the *Smith* rule and once again consigned the compelling state interest test to the judicial recycling bin. Justices O'Connor and Souter, who previously had made clear their opposition to *Smith*, joined by Justice Stephen Breyer (who was not on the Court at the time of either *Smith* or *Lukumi Babalu Aye*), dissented and called again for a reexamination of *Smith*. Ruth Bader Ginsburg, perhaps the most liberal of the justices, voted with the majority.

The compelling state interest test in free exercise cases dates from 1963. In *Sherbert v. Verner*, the Court said that for the government to infringe upon the practice of religion, it had to demonstrate a compelling interest.[6] In disposing of RFRA and reaffirming Justice Antonin Scalia's majority opinion in *Smith*, the Court virtually discarded *Sherbert v. Verner*. It did not, however, take the law back to *Cantwell v. Connecticut* ("clear and present danger"), the predecessor of *Sherbert* in 1939.[7] Instead, it marched confidently back to *Reynolds v. U.S.*, the case outlawing Mormon polygamy in 1879, which gives government almost unbridled power to act.[8]

Though phrased in terms of separation of powers between Congress and the courts rather than in freedom of religion, the majority opinion in *Boerne* nonetheless has serious implications for First Amendment jurisprudence. Its logic would appear to apply equally to NAFERA, which now seems open to challenge.[9] On September 22, 2000, President Clinton signed the Religious Land Use and Institutionalized Persons Act. Passed with broad bipartisan support, the law sought to undo *Boerne* in some instances. It restored the compelling state interest test in the case of zoning and land-marking regulations and in the case of persons confined in state institutions. Unfortunately, under the logic of *Boerne*, this legislation would also be unconstitutional.

The most troubling aspect of *Boerne* is that none of the nine justices, including the dissenters, questioned the major premise underlying the decision. For years it had been settled that in cases of constitutional rights, the Court could set a base level of protection, but Congress could raise the bar. Conservatives rejected this "one-way ratchet," and now they have been vindicated by the majority opinion in *Boerne*.

The *Boerne* decision offered me a joyless opportunity to say, "I told you so." From my location as one involved in both religious and Native American studies and as a lawyer and teacher of constitutional law, my central point is that, as vital and correct as I believe passage of RFRA and NAFERA to have been, I do not for a moment believe them to be a panacea in Native land and religious freedom claims. There will continue to arise conflicts between the dominant whitestream culture and Native religious traditions, and these will continue to be decided against Native interests. From the inception of the American Republic, there has been a tension between the obligation of the United States to protect Native rights and its policy of forcing their relinquishment. As Justice Thurgood Marshall declared in *Choctaw Nation v. Oklahoma*, at least since the Indian Removal Act of 1830, it has been apparent that policy, not obligation, would prevail.[10] Yet this is not simply a story of naked power, of a state's ability to impose its will upon the less powerful.

My colleague at Yale Law School, Stephen Carter, in *The Culture of Disbelief*, writes of both *Lyng* and *Smith*:

> Religions that most need protection seem to receive it least. . . . Native Americans, having once been hounded from their lands, are

now hounded from their religions, with the complicity of a Supreme Court untroubled when sacred lands are taken for road building or when Native Americans under a bona fide compulsion to use peyote in their rituals are punished under state antidrug regulations. (Imagine the brouhaha if New York City were to try to take St. Patrick's Cathedral by eminent domain or if Kansas, a dry state, were to outlaw religious use of wine.)[11]

Carter attributes this to a trivializing of religion in American culture and an attempt to ban religion from public discourse in response to the Christian Right's attempt to reshape society along lines it favors. In fact, neither *Lyng* nor *Smith* nor their progeny, as repugnant and offensive as they are, are incomprehensible and (with the exception of the elimination of the compelling state interest test) would have been highly unlikely to come out otherwise, because American jurisprudence, as currently contoured, is incapable of understanding, let alone taking cognizance of, Native land and religious freedom claims in their full scope.

Native religious traditions are very different in character from Christianity and other Western religions. First, they are not primarily religions of ethics, or dogma, or theology. Rather, they are religions (if one may even use the term with regard to Native traditions) of ritual practice. Further, they are not only religions of ritual observance but they also permeate every aspect of daily life and existence. Natives, as is commonly said, draw no distinction between everyday life and their spirituality. There is not, as there is in Western religion, a sharp bifurcation between sacred and secular or profane spheres. Finally, Native religious traditions are intimately and inexorably tied to the land and often cannot be practiced merely anywhere, as Christianity can. For this reason, Native land claims, whether or not they are advanced in this manner, carry in themselves an explicitly religious claim.

The First Amendment guarantees that "Congress shall make no law respecting an establishment of religion, or prohibiting the free exercise thereof." Though it speaks in absolute terms ("make *no* law") and refers to "exercise" of religion, a word that on its face would seem to refer to practices, it in some sense does not mean what it says. The legislative history and subsequent interpretation both make clear that the concept of religion it embodies is a very Western, Enlightenment ideal. It is the flip-side or, if you will, the perfect corollary to freedom of speech and freedom of the press, also protected by the First Amendment. One is free, within certain defined parameters, to say or print whatever one wishes. Likewise, one is free to *believe* whatever one wishes. One is not free, however, to *do* whatever one wishes, *wherever* one wishes, even if one feels compelled by religious belief to do so. As Vine Deloria and Clifford Lytle put it in *American Indians, American Justice*, "Beliefs are beyond the reach of government no matter how unorthodox, but religious practices can be regulated by the state."[12] What Stephen Carter fails to say is that Kansas has always had the power to prohibit sacramental use of wine if it can demonstrate a compelling state interest in the subject matter and relate the ban to a valid secular purpose, such as Prohibition or the protection of alcoholics. Similarly, perhaps with slightly more difficulty, the City of New York could exercise its eminent domain power over St. Patrick's Cathedral, just as it landmarks churches, such as the one in Boerne, Texas, and requires them to maintain edifices that may have outlived their usefulness and for which churches, as non-taxpayers, receive no tax breaks, the usual compensation for such interference. The only thing that makes the sacramental wine or condemnation of St. Patrick's examples so inconceivable is that they deal with a majority religion rather than a minority one or a new religious movement, making it unthinkable that a legislative body would ever attempt such a thing.

Thus, the First Amendment and the concept of religion it embodies can never afford full protection to Native religious traditions. It cannot encompass religions of ritual practice, or those that cannot be separated from other aspects of life into their own distinct sphere, or those that depend upon a particular place for their performance. It cannot do so, I argue, because, as intimated by the late historian James Washington in his article "The Crisis of Sanctity of Conscience in American Jurisprudence," although it has a particular conception of religion, it lacks a concept of the sacred or holy.[13]

Early on, law in North America absorbed into itself the doctrines of discovery and conquest to justify colonial claims. It also sought to impose upon the land English concepts of land tenure and ownership, concepts totally foreign to the indigenous population. In 1828, Chancellor James Kent, the so-called father of American jurisprudence, wrote in his seminal work, *Commentaries on American Law*:

When the country, now within the dominion of the United States, was first discovered by the Europeans, it was found to be, in a great degree, a wilderness, sparsely inhabited by tribes of Indians, whose occupation was war, and whose subsistence was drawn chiefly from the forest. Their possession was good and perfect to the extent requisite for subsistence and reasonable accommodation, but beyond that degree their title to the country was imperfect. Title by occupancy is limited to occupancy in point of fact. Erratic tribes of savage hunters and fishermen, who have no fixed abode, or sense of property, and are engaged constantly in the chase or in war, have no sound or exclusive title either to an indefinite extent of country, or to seas and lakes, merely because they are accustomed, in search of prey, to roam over the one or coast the shores of the other. Vattel [Swiss legal theorist Emerich Vattel] had just notions of these aboriginal rights of savages, and of the true principles of natural law in relation to them. He observed, that the cultivation of the soil was an obligation imposed by nature upon mankind, and that the human race could not well subsist, or greatly multiply, if rude tribes, which had not advanced from the hunter state, were entitled to claim and retain all the boundless forests through which they might wander. If such people usurp more territory than they can subdue and cultivate, they have no right to complain, if a nation of cultivators puts in a claim for a part.[14]

So the concept of "aboriginal rights" entered the law in North America. While initially it took a treaty to create legally cognizable title in the courts, a concept of "aboriginal title" evolved. It was refined in *Otoe and Missouria Tribe of Indians v. United States*. Begun in 1939, this was the first case to deal with the question of compensability for aboriginal title. To establish such title, the Otoe and Missouria had to prove that they had lived in their ancestral homeland to the exclusion of all other Indians, and that neighboring tribes recognized their claim to the ownership of their land.[15] Though the Otoe and Missourias prevailed in their claim almost thirty years later, the fact that they were required to meet such a standard at all displays scant understanding of Native cultures and the centrality and sacrality of land to them.

This standard would receive perhaps its harshest application in Canada in the case of *Delgam Uukw v. the Queen*, decided in 1991, in which Chief

Justice Allan McEachern of the Supreme Court of British Columbia dismissed the land claims of the Gitksan and Wet'suwet'en peoples. McEachern rejected Native claims that the Creator had given them the specific land in question at the beginning of time. ("While I have every respect for their beliefs, there is no evidence to support such a theory and much good reason to doubt it.") Echoing Chancellor Kent, he went on to state, "Aboriginal life, in my view, was far from stable and it stretches credulity to believe remote ancestors considered themselves bound to specific lands."[16]

The clash of cultures with radically different epistemologies was evident as McEachern delivered his decision. He stated that "the Gitksan and Wet'suwet'en civilizations, if they qualify for that description, fall within a much lower, even primitive order." With regard to the Native claim that they had possessed the territory in question since the time of Creation, he wrote, "I am satisfied that the . . . witnesses honestly believe everything they said was true and accurate. It was obvious to me, however, that they were recounting matters of faith which have become fact to them. If I do not accept their evidence it will seldom be because I think they are untruthful, but because I have a different view of what is fact and what is belief."[17] Then, having ruled their oral traditions inadmissible as evidence, he found that the Natives could not prove that they had occupied the land from "time immemorial," which is, "as everyone knows, . . . a legal expression referring to the year 1189 (the beginning of the reign of Richard II), as specified in the the Statute of Westminster, 1275."[18]

In so speaking, McEachern betrayed an extreme colonialist, ethnocentric bias. "He treats them [Natives] like wolves. . . . The analogy would be closer to a wolf society than a human society," anthropologist Michael Asch declared.[19] McEachern also revealed a shaky grasp of British history and legal precedent. The year 1189 represents the beginning of the reign of Richard I, not Richard II. Further, he confuses "time immemorial," which simply means a "time when the memory of a human is not to the contrary" with the phrase "time of memory," a term used by both Blackstone and Lord Coke meaning "when no man alive hath any proof to the contrary, nor hath conusance to the contrary."

For their part, Natives believed they had met the burden of proof set by McEachern. Miluulak (Alice Jeffrey), hereditary chief of the Gitksan, declares:

Our people have been asked over and over: "How can you substantiate who you are? Who are you to say you have ownership of the territories?" The answer is clear. We have ownership by what we call *Ayook Niiye'e*. It is the law of our grandfathers, and the first law that our people have is called, *Ayook'm Simoquit Gimlahax*, which we call our relationship with the Almighty, who is the grandfather of the heavens. He is the one who breathes life into each and every one of us.

The laws of our grandfathers go so far back in time that you cannot discount them. The song that we sing when a new chief takes his title is called *Limx ooii*. It means for thousands of years our people have existed. When you talk to any of us, and you look at all the symbols that we have, that dates us, telling us how long we have occupied and held our territories. When we count time, it is from the flood onward, which is well over ten thousand years of existence. This more than substantiates our claim above that any other people would have in regard to to our territories. It substantiates our right to rule our lives as we see fit.

When they ask what we feel our basis is in regard to title, I don't think there is any question. The title is very clear. The ownership has never changed. It is only the definition in the law in regard to ownership that has changed.[20]

John Petoskey, in his essay "Indians and the First Amendment," writes:

Although the First Amendment prevents governmental interference with the free exercise of religion, this protection has been substantially denied by the United States government in regard to Indian religions based on specific sites. This denial is based not so much on any improper application of Supreme Court First Amendment principles and analysis, although it is that; rather, the denial is rooted in religious ethnocentrism that permeates the relationship between the United States and Indian societies whereby the courts are judging Indian religious claims by standards developed for Judeo-Christian religions.[21]

He is unquestionably correct concerning the ethnocentrism of the judicial system. After all, there have been more than fifty cases adjudicated in the federal courts involving sacred sites and religious freedom claims; Natives have lost every one of them. Petoskey errs, however, when he speaks of a "misapplication" of "First Amendment principles and analysis," in that he does not take into account the history and purpose of the free exercise clause. He does not take into account the absence of a concept of the holy or sacred.

Seen in this light, the decisions in *Lyng* and *Smith* and their progeny, however lamentable and objectionable, come into focus and become comprehensible. To state briefly the facts of each case: In *Lyng*, the Supreme Court refused to block construction of a timbering road that would have a devastating impact on land considered sacred to the Yurok, Karok, and Tolowa tribes in northwest California; in *Smith*, the High Court upheld denial of unemployment benefits to members of the Native American Church who had been dismissed from their jobs as a result of ritual use of peyote.

In *Lyng*, the Court refused to prohibit the road despite the undisputed fact that it "would cause serious and irreparable damage to the sacred areas which are an integral and necessary part of the belief systems and life-ways of Northwest California Indian peoples."[22] The Court seemed to infer, though it did not affirmatively say so, a compelling state interest in building the road for economic purposes and in the state's ability to control lands it owned. The Court stated flatly, "The Constitution simply does not provide a principle that could justify upholding [the Indians'] legal claims."[23] The majority opinion, authored by Justice O'Connor, is shot through with language demonstrating the lack of a concept of the holy.

Even the strong dissent by Justice Brennan, joined by Justices Marshall and Blackmun, which struggled to uphold the Natives' claim, admitted that is not enough simply to allege that the land in question is sacred. Although the United States Court of Appeals for the Ninth Circuit had enjoined construction of the road, it acknowledged the same thing. The dissenting opinion at that lower level accurately presages the Supreme Court decision and squarely addresses the absence of the holy. In considering a report on the proposed road, commissioned by the U.S. Forest Service, a report that recommended against construction, the dissent declared that the report had applied an "inappropriate definition" of religion. It reads in part:

> The report states, "Because of the particular nature of Indian perceptual experience, as opposed to the particular nature of predominant

non-Indian, Western perceptual experience, any division into 'religious' or 'sacred' is in reality an exercise that forces Indian concepts into non-Indian categories, and distorts the original conceptualization in the process." The report then suggests that hunting and fishing are religious activities for Indians. While that may be true in an anthropological sense, the federal Constitution does not recognize such a broad concept of "religion."[24]

The *Smith* case can be viewed in a similar light, dealing with ritual observance and containing, as it does, language that points up the absence of the holy. The major flaw of the *Smith* decision—and it is indeed a major flaw—is the virtual repeal in religious freedom cases of the compelling state interest test. Under the *Smith* rule, laws that are neutral and of general applicability need not be subjected to heightened scrutiny even if they have significant adverse effects upon religion. As envisioned by the Court in *Smith*, the government would have to demonstrate a compelling interest in a legislative enactment only when it failed to meet the twin tests of neutrality and general applicability. Thus only laws enacted deliberately to suppress or discriminate against a religion would come under this more rigorous test. Such was the test in *Lukumi Babalu Aye*.

The *Smith* rule was all the more startling in that it was gratuitous. As Justice O'Connor said in her concurrence, the same result could be reached by positing a compelling state interest in preventing drug use or, one supposes, by finding such an interest in keeping drug-free at least those who work in drug rehabilitation centers (as the persons involved in the case did). Even those, like myself, who considered it essential to restore the compelling state interest test via RFRA, have to admit that generally only poorly drawn laws will be struck down, since a compelling interest can be found in almost any instance.

What, then, must be done? Naming and delineating this lacuna in the jurisprudential system—the absence of the holy—is one thing. To propose a corrective is quite another. Judges fear that if a concept of sacredness was imported into the law it would be impossible to regulate any conduct no matter how destructive, and that every individual would become a law unto herself or himself.[25] And the freedom to act, unlike the freedom to believe, cannot be absolute.

Prior to *Lyng* and *Smith*, some courts applied a test by which they were called upon to determine whether a given practice or site was "central" to a particular Native religious system. This "centrality" approach, however, proved largely unworkable because of the difficulty of factual determination and because it set so high a standard before legal protection would attach. The anthropologist Deward Walker notes:

> As interpreted by the courts . . . "central" has a meaning best described as indispensable, essential, or requisite. The courts have, therefore, introduced a very high standard that must be met for First Amendment protection of American Indian sacred geography. Under this interpretation of "central," preservation of a specific sacred site can be achieved only if is deemed to be essential, indispensable, or requisite for the practice of a particular tribal religion. In its applications, this standard goes well beyond the meaning of "infringement" and borders on "extinction." In other words, to receive First Amendment protection, American Indians must demonstrate that a change will not merely infringe but virtually destroy a religious practice or belief. Judgments by courts as to centrality, therefore, are being made in terms of a standard of survival/extinction.[26]

As an alternative to centrality, Walker suggests *integrity* as a standard. *Integrity* means "an unimpaired condition" or "the quality or state of being complete or undivided," "completeness." According to Walker, "Infringement then can be understood as a forced or undesired change in the customary practice of a religion." This test has the virtue of being "more open to factual investigation than a standard of centrality. Determination of whether the integrity of a religious practice has been violated would rest on the answers to factual questions." Among the inquiries upon which such a determination might be made, Walker suggests three:

1. Is the affected practice (or site) held by members of the group to be an essential part of their religion? or,
2. Are there alternatives to the affected practice (or site) acceptable to members of the group? or,
3. Would removal or alteration of the affected practice (or site) impair or prevent other essential practices of the religion?[27]

In 1996, the Supreme Court of Canada applied something like Walker's test in *Van der Peet v. the Queen*.[28] Dorothy Van der Peet, a Sto:lo Indian, was convicted of selling salmon to a neighbor. Before the Supreme Court, the issue was whether there was a constitutionally protected aboriginal right to engage in commercial fishing. The High Court found against such a right in *Van der Peet*: "While he court didn't rule out the native commercial fishing right, it has put the onus on natives to clearly prove that the practice previously existed."[29]

Opponents of aboriginal rights quickly heralded *Van der Peet* as placing a limit on the "expansive interpretation" given such rights by the Canadian government and courts.[30] Though the case was undeniably a loss, Native leaders, in contrast, stated that the Court "had finally set a clear test for defining Indian rights that many Indian nations can easily meet."[31] Accounting for these divergent reactions was the failure of non-Native critics to understand the new test articulated by the court and its potential implications. The decision stated that courts must look at both Natives' relationship to the land and the "practices, customs [and] traditions" of a given Native culture. Aboriginal rights are those "practices, customs or traditions" that are "integral to a distinctive culture" and that existed at the time of non-Native settlement. Though reflecting in this latter requirement whitestream stasis assumption about Native cultures, the real hope of *Van der Peet* nevertheless lies in this language that opponents see as a limit—that practices, customs, or traditions integral (that is, "essential to completeness," "constituent") to a distinctive culture will be protected. The approach in *Van der Peet* is essentially that advocated by Walker. Though admittedly far from perfect, it should nonetheless make it easier to protect cultural and religious traditions and sacred sites that until now have been extremely difficult to vindicate in the courts. While it remains to be seen if courts in the United States will adopt the *Van der Peet* rule, Indian laws in Canada and the United States tend to parallel each other broadly, and the case should give Natives new legal arguments.[32] Had integrity been the test in *Lyng*, the outcome would have been different.[33] And I successfully argued for Walker's approach in my letter brief in an administrative procedure before the Bureau of Land Management and Advisory Committee on Historic Preservation in a case involving Quechan sacred lands in California.[34]

Vine Deloria has suggested that it is a mistake to focus exclusively on First Amendment analysis and issues. He believes federal/Indian treaties should be enough to protect Native religious traditions through the application of the principle of tribal sovereignty. His advice merits hearing. As resistant as courts may be to them, treaty and sovereignty claims are, like the aboriginal title of the *Otoe and Missouria* case, at least categories the law can apprehend.

I myself believe that ultimately we will be forced always to seek redress from Congress and through the legislative process in curative bills such as RFRA and NAFERA. Elizabeth Cook-Lynn illustrates why this should be so when, citing scholars such as Deloria and Felix Cohen, she states that, for Native Americans, "America's legal theory often violates the basic principles of justice."[35] It should be noted that some of the most significant Native victories, such as the return of Blue Lake to the Taos people, have been accomplished through work in the corridors of Washington rather than in the courts.

The best that can be hoped for is a restoration of the compelling state interest test by a future Supreme Court more concerned than the current one with the religious liberties of all Americans—perhaps coupled with the integrity test of *Van der Peet* or possible tests suggested by Justices Brennan, Blackmun, and Souter, who, while affirming traditional First Amendment interpretation, extended their reach to grasp, I believe, some concept of the holy. In their dissents in both *Lyng* and *Smith*, Brennan and Blackmun argued for a centrality test by which courts would be called upon to balance the centrality or indispensability of a practice or site to a Native religious tradition, as interpreted by the Natives themselves, against the claimed state interest opposing it. As noted above, this, broadly speaking, was the approach of RFRA, in itself not free from problems. For his part, David Souter, in his concurrence in *Lukumi Babalu Aye*, called for courts "to preserve a right to engage in activities necessary to fulfill one's duty to one's God, unless those activities [threaten] the rights of others or the serious needs of the State."[36]

Lacking a concept of the holy, our legal system is finally incapable of comprehending Native land and religious freedom claims. As the cold winds of autumn prepare to blow for yet another year, it continues an open question whether freedom of religion for America's indigenous people's will remain, as Justice Blackmun said in his dissent in *Smith*, "merely an unfulfilled and hollow promise."[37]

CHAPTER TWELVE

TRIANGULATED POWER AND
THE ENVIRONMENT

Tribes, the Federal Government, and the States

*Finally the ecologists arrived with predictions so chilling as to
frighten the strongest heart. At the present rate of deterioration, they
told us mankind could expect only a generation before the species
would finally be extinguished. How had this situation come about?
Some ecologists told us that it was the old Christian idea of nature:
the rejection of creation as a living ecosystem and the concept of
nature as depraved, an object of exploitation and nothing more.*

VINE DELORIA, JR.,
God Is Red (2d ed.)

In 1631 John Winthrop, the recently arrived governor of Massachusetts,
wrote, concerning the indigenous inhabitants of the "new England": "This
savage people ruleth over many lands without title or property; for they
inclose no ground, neither have they cattel to maintayne it, but remove
their dwellings as they have occasion, or as they can prevail against their
neighbors. And why may not Christians have liberty to go and dwell
amongst them in their waste lands and woods (leaving such places as they
have manured for their corne) as lawfully as Abraham did among the
Sodomites?"[1] He went on to justify the conquest with a detailed exegesis
of the Hebrew scriptures, envisioning the Europeans as the ancient
Israelites and the Natives as the Canaanites driven from the Promised
Land. What makes this bit of articulated conquering ideology noteworthy
is that Winthrop preached it almost verbatim in 1629 in England, before

he ever set eyes upon the North American continent, and later repeated it aboard the *Arbella*, the ship bringing him to his new appointment.[2]

In 1823 Chief Justice John Marshall incorporated the doctrines of discovery and conquest into the law of the youthful United States. In *Johnson v. McIntosh* he wrote: "We will not enter into the controversy, whether agriculturists, merchants, and manufacturers, have a right, on abstract principles, to expel hunters from territory they possess, or to contract their limits. Conquest gives a title which the Courts of the conqueror cannot deny, whatever the private and speculative opinions of individuals may be, respecting the original justice of the claim which has been successfully asserted."[3] Five years later, however, Chancellor James Kent, the father of American jurisprudence, codified the principle that Marshall refused to entertain.[4] As noted in the previous chapter, citing the work of Swiss jurist Emerich Vattel, Kent pronounced that "cultivators of the soil" had priority over hunters in terms of rights to property. He adopted fully Winthrop's vision of the continent as "a wilderness, sparsely inhabited" by Indians who merely roamed over the land with "no fixed abode."[5]

Kent's view, and not that of Marshall, ultimately was to prevail. In 1985, in one of the leading cases in environmental law, the Ninth Circuit Court of Appeals observed, "Indian reservations may be considered as potential locations for hazardous waste disposal sites . . . because they are often remote from heavily populated areas."[6] To those in the whitestream, Indian country is still sparsely inhabited by rude hunters. The environment of Native lands can be sacrificed to the greater good of society because both they and their inhabitants are of lesser value than more densely "settled" areas.

Indian lands have suffered from the polluting effects of heavy industry, toxic dumping, contamination of air and drinking water from off-reservation sources, and from fallout from nuclear testing and arms production. Most particularly, they have been damaged by the impact of mining operations on reservations and adjacent to them. To some extent, all mining degrades the environment. In situ mining (traditional deep mining) is the least harmful in this respect, but traditionally it has the potential for considerable damage due to mine wastes and geological subsidence. New techniques of exploitation, however, can reduce this risk.[7]

By contrast, surface mining, a common technique of coal exploitation on western reservations, has a severe environmental impact because a great deal of earth must be moved in order to extract the resources. Surface mining takes one of three basic forms: strip mining, open-pit mining, or terrace mining. Although these techniques are safer and easier than in situ mining, "gas, dust and noxious odors can be expected near the mines. Both the overburden and the tailings from the processing plant . . . present substantial disposal problems."[8] Strip mining is capable of extracting minerals to a depth of approximately 180 feet in relatively flat terrain. Reclamation normally consists of flattening the piles of overburden, replacing topsoil, and replanting. Open-pit mining is feasible for deeper deposits and irregular terrain. Overburden and minerals are removed together and carted out of the pit by means of a series of haulage roads or conveyor belts. The minerals are taken to processing plants, while the overburden is normally dumped distant from the pit. It is generally considered impractical to backfill the pit with overburden. Terrace mining is a variant of open-pit mining employed when deposits cover an extended area but are relatively shallow. Overburden is trucked away and stored, at least temporarily, rather than being dumped directly back into the pit. The process results in a large worked-out area, which must be reclaimed.[9]

The impact of mining in western states has placed a severe burden on the environment. The associated problems, perceived need for development and resources, and a myriad of other environmental issues have created tensions among Native nations and the federal and state governments. Historically, western states have pressured the federal government and the tribes to permit a sharing of responsibility with regard to Indian lands. They have done so under the banner of proper balance between environmental protection and development. With the onset of the energy crisis in the 1970s, states became determined "to acquire additional control over developmental activities within their borders regardless of whether such development occurs on private, state [,tribal], or federal lands."[10] In the absence of federal or tribal authorization to regulate Indian lands within their borders, states unilaterally sought jurisdiction over such lands.[11]

Dialogue among the three levels of government (tribal, federal, state) has revolved principally around three interrelated issues. The first is the question of federal plenary power over, and trust responsibility to, Indians. The second is the question of federal preemption and the right of states to pass reasonable regulations relating to lands within their borders pursuant to their police power when such regulations do not conflict with federal legislation. Third is the inherent sovereign power of tribes recognized by treaty and the United States Constitution. Each of these three strands must be kept in mind when discussing environmental regulation on Indian lands.

The Articles of Confederation gave Congress "sole and exclusive power . . . managing all affairs with the Indians, not in any of the states, provided that the legislative right of any state within its own limits not be infringed or violated."[12] Article I, section 8 of the Constitution dropped the states' rights proviso, granting to Congress exclusive authority "to regulate commerce . . . with the Indian tribes."[13] With this power came a concomitant responsibility. In *Cherokee Nation v. Georgia*, Chief Justice Marshall determined that Indian tribes were "domestic dependent nations."[14] The federal government stood in a protective relationship toward the tribes, similar to a "guardian" over a "ward." From this grew the trust relationship between the federal government and Natives. "Later courts stretched the notion of a protective duty to tribal governments into almost unbridled power over them."[15] The doctrine of Congress' "plenary power" over Indians evolved.[16]

Such plenary power has been interpreted as giving the federal government authority concerning Indian lands equal to that exercised by it over federally owned lands in the public domain pursuant to the Property Clause.[17] The United States Court of Appeals for the Eighth Circuit declared in *Griffin v. United States*: "The power of Congress over the lands of the United States wherever situated is exclusive. When that power has been exercised with reference to land within the borders of a state neither the state nor any of its agencies has the power to interfere."[18] While the power of the federal government may not be restricted by state regulation, the states may prescribe reasonable police regulations insofar as those regulations do not conflict with congressional action and are thus preempted.[19] Once Congress has acted, however, such action overrides conflicting state laws. As the Supreme Court noted, "A different rule would place the public domain of the United States completely at the mercy of state regulation."[20]

The third leg of this triangle of relationships is that of the sovereignty of tribes themselves. According to Felix Cohen, "Perhaps the most basic principle of all Indian law, supported by a host of decisions. . . , is the principle that *those powers which are lawfully vested in an Indian tribe are not, in general, delegated powers granted by express acts of Congress, but rather inherent powers of a limited sovereignty which has never been extinguished.*"[21] For Cohen, treaties were not grants of power to tribes but to the federal government. "What is not expressly limited remains within the domain of tribal sovereignty."[22] Tribal governments thus exercise over Indian lands what is commonly referred to in the law as a "clipped sovereignty."[23] The precise extent of such inherent sovereignty is a much debated point. According to Getches, Wilkinson, and Williams, "In challenges to state assertions of authority over Indians, the existence of congressional plenary power has proved to be a formidable shield guarding the reservations as enclaves for the exercise of tribal governing authority. A tension persists between the federal trusteeship obligation, with its preemptive exclusions of state intrusions that impede tribal sovereignty, and exercises of congressional powers that often remove or denigrate Indian rights and tribal sovereignty."[24]

For many years states largely acquiesced in the exercise of federal and tribal power over Indian lands within their borders; when conflicts did arise, they were resolved by cooperation rather than conflict.[25] Beginning in the 1920s, however, energy-producing states enacted measures for the conservation and orderly production of petroleum and natural gas.[26] These enactments provided for prorationing,[27] spacing of wells, and the pooling and unitization of land overlaying a single reservoir.[28] Conflict arose when a common source of supply underlay both private or state land and federal or Indian lands.[29] Spokesman for the states felt that the conservation laws of the state in which the wells lay should govern, particularly in cases where state lands overlay the same pool.[30] Otherwise, state attempts at regulation largely would be rendered ineffective. The situation was resolved by federal and tribal deference to the states.

During the early days of drastic prorationing in Oklahoma, the Osage, the richest energy-producing tribe in the state, frequently appeared before hearings of the Oklahoma Corporation Commission concerning allowable production on controlled lands.[31] Although they steadfastly maintained their jurisdictional immunity, the Osage always abided by orders of the commission in the interest of conservation.[32] Similarly, the federal government acquiesced in the conduct of lengthy spacing hearings, under the laws of Utah, concerning the Aneth Field, which underlay controlled lands in that state.[33]

In the early 1970s, with a growing awareness of degradation of the environment and the need for inexpensive, seemingly limitless resources, good will and cooperation among the three levels of government disintegrated. In response to increasing pressure for both land and natural resource development, western states began to enact comprehensive land-use legislation.[34] Contending that any effective land-use system must include federal and Indian lands within their borders, the states undertook to legislate controls for such lands, drawing little or no distinction between them and private or state-held property. The question quickly became whether state governments would be permitted to effectuate their plans and impose environmental requirements on controlled lands.[35]

The answer was a series of court challenges in Idaho, Oregon, and California.[36] In *Andrus v. Click*, involving state regulation in a national forest, the Idaho Supreme Court ruled that standards more stringent than set by the federal government were not preempted. It stated that "the mere fact that federal legislation sets low standards of compliance does not imply that the federal legislation grants a right to an absence of further regulation."[37] Facing a nearly identical issue, the Oregon Court of Appeals, following the logic of *Click*, found "the preservation of the environmental quality of its lands is a subject particularly suited to administration by the states."[38] When a federal court finally addressed the issue, however, it found the broader view of federal power over controlled lands to be dispositive.[39] Since that time, western states have continued to assert aggressively the right of states to regulate the environment on Indian lands.[40] The result has been ever-increasing conflict between the states, on one hand, and the federal government and tribes, on the other.

There is little dispute that tribes have the authority to regulate conduct affecting the environment when it occurs on trust lands within the boundary of a reservation, subject to the plenary power of the federal government. Such conduct can be regulated even when it involves nonmembers of the tribe in question. States sometimes have attempted, however, to assert jurisdiction over conduct of both Indians and non-Indians on trust lands. When such an assertion takes place, courts are called upon to undertake a careful balancing of tribal, state, and federal interests in order to determine the appropriate regulatory power.[41]

Because of the General Allotment Act of 1887[42] and similar laws, which allocated reservations into individual parcels and opened "surplus" lands for settlement, significant portions of land within the exterior boundaries of many reservations are held by non-Indians. The result is a "checkerboard," in which adjacent parcels may be owned by Indians and non-Indians. Controversies arise as to which level of government has the power to impose environmental regulation upon these fee lands in non-Native hands. The issue is especially critical because of the migratory nature of resources such as air, water, and wildlife. Activities on non-Native property can have substantial effects on Indian lands.

Recognizing the potential for environmental damage to tribal trust lands from activities on adjacent lands held by non-Indians on reservations, the United States Supreme Court found that tribes had the right to regulate such conduct under certain circumstances. While the High Court overturned a ruling by the Ninth Circuit Court of Appeals that took a broad, traditional view of tribal sovereignty, it nonetheless recognized the inherent sovereign power retained by tribes. In delivering the opinion of the Court, Justice Potter Stewart stated that a "tribe may . . . retain inherent power to exercise civil authority over the conduct of non-Indians on fee lands within its reservation when that conduct threatens or has some direct effect on the political integrity, the economic security, or the health and welfare of the tribe."[43] In the ensuing years, lower courts have utilized this "*Montana* exception" to recognize tribal regulatory authority over non-Indian conduct affecting natural resources within reservations because of the potential effect on "the health and welfare of the tribe."[44]

In 1989, however, the Supreme Court's decision in *Brendale v. Confederated Tribes and Bands of Yakima* created a controversy concerning the continued vitality of the exception. *Brendale* involved the attempt of the Yakima Nation to impose zoning restrictions on two parcels of land owned by nonmembers on its reservation. The first property was located in a part of the reservation that was 97 percent tribal land. The other was in a heavily checkerboarded area. While the Court ultimately decided that the tribe could regulate the first lot but not the second, it was badly divided, with none of the three separate opinions speaking for a majority. In his opinion, speaking for four justices, Byron White raised questions about the *Montana* exception permitting tribal exercise of authority over non-Indians.[45]

Most commentators agree that "considerable care is necessary to divine rules" from *Brendale*. Lower courts have struggled as to its meaning.[46] The Environmental Protection Agency (EPA) does not recognize it as controlling authority, instead continuing to rely on the clearer *Montana* decision, with which it finds *Brendale* "fully consistent."[47] Western states, however, have been quick to seize upon the latter case as a means to attempt to gain control over reservation lands. The Conference of Western Attorneys General points to Justice White's opinion and repeatedly overstates the scope and reach of the case, writing that "*Brendale* effectively replaced the *Montana* criteria and limited tribal jurisdiction over nonmember fee lands to circumstances where such lands constitute a small percentage of distinct reservation units maintained in a natural state."[48] The attorneys general contend that the EPA's stance with regard to the decision "diverges from Supreme Court requirements and raises questions whether determinations controlled by [its] regulations will accurately reflect the relative limits of state and tribal authority within Indian reservations."[49] Such a disingenuous reading of *Brendale* only serves to confirm Joseph Singer's statements concerning the assumptions underlying power and property in America. In analyzing *Brendale* and other recent cases, Singer writes:

> The Supreme Court has assumed in recent years that although non-Indians have the right to be free from political control by Indian nations, American Indians can and should be subject to the political sovereignty of non-Indians. This disparate treatment of both property and political rights is not the result of neutral rules being applied in a manner that has a disparate impact. Rather, it is the result of *formally unequal* rules. Moreover, it can be explained only by reference to perhaps unconscious assumptions about the nature and distribution of both property and power. This fact implies an uncomfortable truth: both property rights and political power in the United States are associated with a system of racial caste.[50]

The EPA refusal to recognize *Brendale* is, in fact, totally consistent with its longstanding policy of encouraging tribes to assume regulatory control and management responsibilities for environmental programs.[51] In the absence of such an assumption, EPA will tend to assume direct implementation and enforcement within reservation boundaries. State regulation is strongly disfavored. Though the EPA gained considerable support for its position in the mid-1980s, when amendments to various federal environmental protection laws were enacted, its position took shape as early as 1982 when the EPA Administrator commissioned a study of environmental programs on reservations that would take into consideration "the unique political status of Indian tribes."[52] Six months later, President Reagan issued an "American Indian Policy Statement," which affirmed that "tribal governments had the primary responsibility for meeting the needs of tribal members," and the agency responded with its own policy, declaring that tribes were "the primary parties for setting standards, making environmental policy decisions and managing programs for reservations."[53] With its policy in place, EPA began to limit state authority over reservations and act on the opinion that "tribal governments retain civil-regulatory authority over all reservation lands, regardless of ownership."[54] Pursuant to standards of federal regulatory law, courts have been willing to give extreme deference to EPA determinations denying state jurisdiction within reservations.[55]

The federal leg of the triangle of power is clearly implicated in decisions involving Indian lands. They have responsibility for controlled lands. Moreover, the U.S. Supreme Court in *New Mexico v. Mescalero Apache Tribe* stated that the federal policy of promoting sovereignty includes fostering economic development.[56] According to the Conference of Western Attorneys General, "Thus, federal interests are implicated where a tribe attracts an industry onto its reservation to broaden the tribe's economic base, and may be recognized as a factor against allowing states to impose strict regulations that would restrict or prohibit the industry's operations."[57]

Since 1963 with the passage of the Clean Air Act, Congress has enacted a series of laws that evidence a broad public commitment "favoring preservation of resources and protection of fragile and life-supporting ecosystems."[58] In general, these laws permit the EPA or, in the case of the Surface Mining Control and Reclamation Act, the Office of Surface Mining to delegate to states the authority to enforce minimum federal standards or, in some cases, stricter state requirements. As these enactments came up for renewal in the early 1990s, they were usually amended to permit tribes to assume jurisdiction as "states" in lieu of direct federal administration.

Such a delegation, however, is probably unnecessary. Inherent tribal sovereignty should be sufficient to support tribal authority over both trust and fee lands within the confines of a reservation.[59] For instance, in *Nance v. EPA*, the Supreme Court let stand a determination by the Ninth Circuit Court of Appeals that the Northern Cheyenne had sufficient independent authority to regulate its reservation in order to prevent significant deterioration of air quality.[60] Likewise, the Resources Conservation and Recovery Act (RCRA) contains no provisions permitting tribal assumption in lieu of the federal government. Yet the Ninth Circuit affirmed the EPA's decision allowing tribes in Washington state to administer hazardous-waste programs despite the absence of specific legislative grants.[61] Further, the EPA itself does not view environmental legislation as delegating federal power to the tribes. As recently as July 1991, it affirmed its position that tribal governments are "the appropriate non-federal parties for making decisions and carrying out environmental program responsibilities" on reservations.[62]

The Clean Water Act (CWA) has been a particular point of contention in the struggles among federal, state, and tribal governments. Section 518 of the CWA provides for tribal assumption of responsibility for protection of water resources held by the tribe, held by the United States in trust for them, held by a tribal member if it would be subject to trust restrictions upon a change in ownership, "or otherwise within the borders of an Indian reservation."[63] Tribes and the EPA have interpreted the section as permitting tribal exercise of power within the exterior boundaries of reservations.[64] States, however, argue that the statute cannot be read in such a manner. To do so, they contend, renders the first three clauses of the sentence, which apparently set limits on tribal authority, meaningless.[65]

In the debate, the EPA and the tribes clearly have the better case. Other federal environmental statutes have similar language and have been interpreted in like fashion. The agency maintains that Congress made a legislative determination that conduct affecting water quality would have a serious and detrimental impact on tribes within the meaning of the *Montana* exception. Therefore, it concludes that "any impairment [of water quality] that occurs on, or as a result of, activities on non-Indian fee lands are [*sic*] very likely to impair the water and actual habitat quality of the tribal lands."[66]

The migratory nature of water makes it imperative that tribes be permitted to regulate its quality throughout the borders of reservations. Any other rule would have the potential to frustrate their regulatory schemes entirely. Checkerboarded authority over migratory resources (air, water, wildlife), mirroring the checkerboard in ownership patterns, is a recipe for disaster. In making such an argument, one must be aware that it is a double-edged sword. It could easily be used to justify state regulation over reservations within their borders. Such a rule, however, would be contrary to the inherent sovereignty of Native nations and must therefore be dismissed. "Spillover" effects from activities on reservations have been used by states to argue for on-reservation regulation by them. Those who advance such an argument must be equally aware that "spillovers spill over both ways." Thus off-reservation pollution affecting the health and welfare on reservations should provide a basis for assertion of tribal jurisdiction beyond the boundaries of their territory. The Conference of Western Attorneys General contends, however, "Tribal sovereignty . . . is more limited [than that of states], and the mere allegation of on-reservation effects would not be sufficient to restore authority divested from the tribe as a matter of federal law."[67] In early 1993 Isleta Pueblo in New Mexico set water quality standards for the Rio Grande, requiring that the water be clean enough for ceremonial and recreational purposes, and the EPA approved such standards. The city of Albuquerque, located five miles upstream of Isleta, routinely discharges sewage into the river and, in order to meet the tribally determined standards, would have to spend an estimated $250 million over the next decade. Consequently, the city sued to overturn the EPA action.[68]

Other aspects of EPA policy have been equally contentious. The western attorneys general argue that the administrative agency errs when it labels all property within reservations as "Indian lands," thus permitting tribal jurisdiction. The EPA definition is, they aver, in actuality that used for "Indian country," a term which includes fee lands. Federal courts have tended to define "Indian lands" as those in which Indians have a property interest.[69] In the *Washington* case, however, the Ninth Circuit accepted the EPA's synonymous definition as "a reasonable marker of the geographic boundary between state authority and federal authority."[70] Similarly, the attorneys general question whether the EPA can act as a neutral mediator in disputes over the proper reach of tribal jurisdiction because of federal trust responsibilities to tribes. They fear that the agency "may be pressured to err in favor of tribes."[71] Judicial review, however, should provide an adequate check upon erroneous or capricious exercises of administrative power as a result of such "pressure."

The triangulation of powers over Indian lands is virtually certain to become increasingly conflictual. No federal or state program is likely to take adequate account of Native cultural and spiritual considerations.

Meanwhile, states will continue to grasp for regulatory control over Indian lands, contrary to inherent tribal sovereignty.[72] According to a study commissioned in 1986 as part of amendments to Superfund legislation, there were twelve hundred hazardous waste sites located on or near twenty-five reservations studied.[73] Natives continue to fear that reservations will become dumping grounds for off-reservation wastes if states are permitted to control land use and environmental regulations on reservations—thus evoking the specter of disparate treatment spoken of by Singer and perpetuated by the attitude, evinced by Winthrop and Kent, that Indians sparsely inhabit the land and have no real sense of modern concepts of lands use or tenure.[74]

Currently, the entire system of environmental protection in the United States remains under assault at both the federal and state levels. Despite the fact that polls show that Americans want more—not less—environmental legislation if it will lead to a cleaner environment, Congress has attempted in recent years to roll back protections provided by a number of laws, including the Endangered Species Act, the Clean Air Act, the CWA, the Safe Drinking Water Act, and Superfund. It also introduced a "takings bill," which would require compensation to landholders for any loss in value as a result of environmental controls. Known as the Private Property Protection Act, the bill would have a chilling effect on any future regulations as the "cost" required to be paid by the federal government becomes prohibitive. A similar provision was passed by the Washington state legislature. Montana and Idaho have enacted legislation that provides for higher levels of pollution in the watersheds of streams and lakes. Wyoming placed a bounty on wolves reintroduced into Yellowstone National Park.[75] High oil prices made energy and the environment hotly contested issues during the 2000 presidential race, with Republican candidate George W. Bush recommending oil drilling in the Arctic National Wildlife Refuge, a move that could have devastating consequences on the environment, for the calving grounds of the Porcupine Caribou herd, and thus for the Native peoples who depend on the caribou. The move is one supported by the Alaskan legislative delegation in Washington.

Both federal and state governments often appear intent on abandoning any pretense of national stewardship over natural resources. It seems the only ones that will speak out for the earth in Indian country are the Indians themselves.

CHAPTER THIRTEEN

SCALING RÍOS MONTT

Indigenous Peoples, International Human Rights, and the Pinochet Case

We invited the subversives to lay down their arms. We had military encounters, there was a war. . . . Later, we legalized a concept of special powers because the violence did not permit us to impart justice. And we gathered up the assassins and criminals, we judged them and we shot them, but in accordance with the law.

GEN. EFRAÍN RÍOS MONTT,
President of Guatemala

First we kill all the subversives, then we kill their collaborators, then their sympathizers, then those who remain indifferent, and finally the indecisive.

GEN. IBÉRICO SAINT JEAN,
Controller of Buenos Aires

First they came for the Jews, and I did not speak out, because I was not a Jew. Then they came for the communists, and I did not speak out, because I was not a communist. Then they came for the trade unionists, and I did not speak out, because I was not a trade unionist. Then they came for me, and by then there was no one left to speak out for me.

MARTIN NIEMÖLLER

Charles Evans Hughes, a legal realist, once expressed the height of legal realism when he declared that the law meant whatever judges said it meant at any given moment. "The only question for lawyers," he wrote, "is how will the judges act."[1] Recently, in the area of human rights and indigenous peoples, Hughes's question has received renewed attention as a result, as is often true, of a case that did not involve indigenous peoples at all—the proceedings in Spain against former Chilean dictator and senator-for-life Augusto Pinochet Ugarte. That case, familiar only because of procedural wranglings in Great Britain over jurisdiction, has a complicated procedural history virtually unknown outside of Spain. And it stands in a line of cases since the Second World War that seek to bring international human rights violators to account.

THE PINOCHET CASE

In 1996, the Union of Progressive Prosecutors in Spain decided to file criminal complaints against persons in the Argentine and Chilean militaries for the deaths and disappearances of Spanish citizens in those countries. This was quickly followed by private actions by groups and individuals, employing a Spanish procedure that permits private citizens to initiate criminal proceedings before instructing courts. A private action, charging a number of Argentine soldiers with genocide and terrorism in connection with that country's "Dirty War" during the 1970s, was accepted by Judge Baltasar Garzón Real on July 10, 1996.

The Union also filed a complaint against Pinochet and others in the Chilean military, alleging genocide, terrorism, and crimes against humanity. Again a private action followed, this one filed by the Salvador Allende Foundation and Izquierda Unida on behalf of thousands of Chilean citizens. Judge Manuel García Castellon accepted the case.

In March 1998, the Office of Public Prosecutor asked the courts to close their investigations, arguing that they lacked jurisdiction. The central issue was whether Spanish courts could investigate and try foreign military for crimes committed on foreign soil. In three separate and far-reaching opinions, both Garzón and García Castellon found that jurisdiction did, in fact, lie. The cases were consolidated before Garzón in October 1998.

Upon hearing that Pinochet was present in Britain, Izquierda Unida asked the court to interrogate the former dictator concerning the crimes for which he was being investigated and asked that he be charged in the disappearance and kidnapping of a number of named individuals. Simultaneously, the Chilean Association of Relatives of the Detained and Disappeared (Asociacíon de Familiares de Detenidos y Desaparecidos) requested that he and others be formally charged with murder, genocide, terrorism, and torture.

Acceding to Izquierda Unida's plea, on October 14, Garzón sent a request to British authorities through Interpol, asking that Pinochet's statement be taken and that they guarantee that he would remain on British soil until he could be questioned.[2] Two days later, the magistrate issued an international arrest warrant for the general for the crimes of genocide and terrorism. Specifically, the warrant alleged that under Pinochet "an armed organization was created, taking advantage of the military structures and the usurpation of power in order, with impunity, to institutionalize a terrorist regime." By its nature, the regime "subverted the constitutional order in order to efficiently carry out the plan of systematically disappearing and eliminating members of national groups, imposing on them forced displacements, kidnappings, tortures, assassinations and disappearances, taking advantage of the aid and coordination of other countries, particularly Argentina." It did so through the joint counterinsurgency program of "Operation Condor."[3]

It was at this point that the case grabbed international headlines. Though the case would drag on for over a year, events in this early stage began to unfold with sometimes confusing rapidity in both Britain and Spain. The same day Garzón transmitted his warrant, Metropolitan Magistrate Nicholas Evans issued a warrant for Pinochet's arrest, alleging that he murdered Spanish citizens in Chile between 1973 and 1983. On October 17, London Metropolitan Police arrested the eighty-two-year-old former dictator at the hospital where he was recovering from back surgery. The following day, Garzón transmitted a second international warrant. Five days later, on October 22, Metropolitan Magistrate Ronald Bartle issued another British warrant for the crimes of torture, conspiracy to torture, taking of hostages, conspiracy to take hostages, and conspiracy to commit murder. On October 23, Pinochet, already in custody, was arrested on the second warrant.[4]

The day the second British warrant was issued, attorneys for Pinochet applied for a writ of habeas corpus, claiming that their client was being held illegally. They asked for judicial review to quash the first warrant. They contended that Pinochet was not a Spanish national and that the Spanish court therefore lacked any jurisdiction over him. Beyond that, they stated that he was entitled to immunity from prosecution as a former head of state. On October 26, they made the same application with regard to the second warrant. After two days of hearings, the Divisional Court of the Queen's Bench threw out both arrest warrants, but stayed its order on the second warrant pending an appeal to the House of Lords.[5]

Meanwhile in Spain, the public prosecutor appealed García Castellon's October 1 ruling on jurisdiction. The Criminal Chamber of the Audiencia Nacional, sitting en banc, heard the appeal on October 29, voting the next morning. No decision was announced, however, until November 4. Armed with the court's ruling affirming jurisdiction in Spain for the crimes alleged, the Spanish government submitted a formal request for Pinochet's extradition to Britain. The request greatly expanded the crimes alleged against the former dictator, charging him with conspiracy to take over the Chilean government by coup and thereafter committing murder, genocide, torture, and hostage-taking. The next day, Carlos Cezón González, writing for the court, published his opinion.[6]

Even as González was issuing his opinion, the case came before the Law Lords, a committee of the House of Lords and Britain's highest court. Amnesty International and others representing alleged victims were granted leave to intervene. Human Rights Watch also made a written submission. On November 25, the committee hearing the appeal, by a vote of three to two, ruled that Pinochet was not immune from prosecution as a former head of state. They also held that persons accused of human rights abuses in violation of international treaty could be tried in any nation that was a signatory to the treaty. Pinochet was being charged pursuant to the United Nations Convention against Torture and Other Cruel, Inhuman or Degrading Treatment or Punishment; the Convention against Taking Hostages; the Convention on Genocide; the Covenant on Civil and Political Rights; and the Geneva Convention.

In reliance on the Law Lords' decision, British Home Secretary Jack Straw gave permission to move forward with Pinochet's extradition on December 9, 1998, but he excluded the crime of genocide from the proceedings. Two days later, a Spanish indictment was preferred in Madrid, and on December 24, further particulars were supplied in accordance with the European Convention on Extradition. On January 15, 1999, however, the Lords' judgment was set aside on the grounds that the committee had not been "properly constituted," because one of the judges had an undisclosed tie to Amnesty International, one of the intervenors.[7]

On January 18, the case was reheard by the House of Lords. Their decision on March 24 was even stronger than the November 25 opinion. By a vote of six to one, they stated that extradition could proceed. They did, however, drastically narrow the charges against the Chilean dictator.[8]

Though Britain's highest court had ruled that extradition could move forward, legal proceedings continued for months, as Pinochet sought to avoid being sent to Spain. On January 11, 2000, Home Secretary Straw, cognizant of the fact that the affair had become an albatross around the neck of Britain's Labour government, announced that he was "minded" to release the now eighty-four-year-old former dictator because of health concerns. Over the objections of six international human rights organizations and the requests of Belgium, France, and Switzerland, who had joined with Spain in seeking the general's extradition, an English court on January 31 upheld Straw's right to set him free based on his deteriorating physical and mental health. The judicial process continued.[9] On March 2, while Garzón contemplated a further appeal, Pinochet was released, based on "humanitarian" considerations, a finding that he was too ill to aid in his own defense. He was immediately flown back to Chile on a waiting Chilean Air Force transport.

INTERNATIONAL LAW AND UNIVERSAL JURISDICTION

Garzón and García Castellon were not the first, since World War II and the precedent set by the International Military Tribunal (the "Nuremberg Tribunal"), to attempt to hold foreign officials accountable for crimes committed abroad. In 1995, a federal district court in Boston awarded ten plaintiffs $47,000,000 in damages against former Guatemalan Defense Minister Héctor Gramajo Morales in the deaths, disappearances, and arbitrary detention of Guatemalans and in the rape and torture of American nun Diana Ortiz during the 1980s.[10] And, in a suit by six Haitian refugees, a Miami, Florida, court held former Haitian dictator Prosper Avril liable for $41,000,000 for torture and imprisonment.[11] Actions have also been brought in the United States against Salvadorans, a Chilean, a Uruguayan, and an Ethiopian for alleged human rights abuses.[12] In September 2000, 15 Asian women filed a class-action lawsuit against Japan in the United

States District Court for the District of Columbia; the plaintiffs were survivors of World War II who had been forced to serve as "comfort women" for the Japanese armed forces during the conflict.[13] These, however, were all civil actions.

In 1961, following his abduction from Argentina by Israeli agents, Adolf Eichmann was tried by Israel for crimes against humanity. His conviction was upheld by the Supreme Court of Israel the following year.[14] In 1985, United States courts authorized the extradition to Israel of a death camp guard, who was subsequently acquitted.[15] After capture during a U.S. military intervention, a federal district court convicted former Panamanian strongman Jorge Noriega of drug trafficking.[16] In 1983, the Italian League for the Rights and Liberation of People initiated criminal charges against members of the Argentine military accused in the disappearance of Italian citizens.[17] Convictions were subsequently obtained. On December 6, 2000, a court in Rome sentenced two retired Argentine generals to life in prison; five other officers received sentences of 24 years. Though, as of this writing, all those convicted remain in Argentina, the Italian government has stated it will seek extradition.[18] France tried Alfredo Astiz, a captain in the Argentine navy, in absentia for the murder of two French nuns; he was convicted and sentenced to jail.[19] It also tried and convicted the international terrorist known as "Carlos," whose crimes took place in multiple countries. On August 24, 2000, Ricardo Miguel Cavallo was arrested in Cancún, Mexico as he attempted to flee to Argentina. Cavallo was accused of being a former Argentine military officer who participated in torture for the junta. His arrest was pursuant to a warrant by Judge Garzón as part of his ongoing investigation of Argentine crimes during the "Dirty War."[20] Such cases, as problematic as some of them may be, reflect a growing consensus among nations that crimes against international law may be tried in countries other than those in which the alleged offenses took place.

Though such a consensus may be evolving, it is hardly a novel concept. Piracy has been long recognized as a violation of the law of nations that may be tried anywhere.[21] In resisting extradition to Spain, Pinochet claimed that the acts for which he stood accused were performed in his official capacity as head of the Chilean state and that he was thus immune from prosecution. The doctrine of state immunity, on which he relied and with which the Law Lords struggled, stems from a time when rulers and their domains were considered synonymous (*l'Etat c'est moi*) and the sovereign definitionally could do no wrong. Yet, as Lord Millett stated in his opinion in the *Pinochet* case, it is debatable whether even before the Nuremberg Tribunal the doctrine "accorded protection in respect of conduct which was prohibited by international law."[22] He pointed out that as early as 1841 commentators held that "the Government's authority could not confer immunity upon its agents for acts beyond its powers under international law."[23] Chief Justice John Marshall acknowledged as much in 1812 in his seminal opinion in *Schooner Exchange v. McFaddon*.[24]

Commenting on *Schooner Exchange* in 1946, before the Nuremberg Tribunal delivered its judgment, Sheldon Glueck wrote, "As Marshall implied, even in an age when the doctrine of sovereignty had a strong hold, the non-liability of agents of a state for 'acts of state' must rationally be based on the assumption that no member of the Family of Nations will order its agents to commit flagrant violations of international and criminal law."[25] He continued, "In modern times a state is . . . incapable of ordering or ratifying acts which are not only criminal according to generally accepted principles of domestic penal law but also contrary to that international law to which all states are perforce subject. Its agents, in performing such acts, are therefore acting outside their legitimate scope; and must, in consequence[,] be held personally liable for their wrongful conduct."[26] In agreement with Glueck, Lord Millett concluded that the concept of state immunity was of relatively recent origin and that it had been "mistakenly raised" to the "status of some holy fetish," as some of his fellow Law Lords did.[27]

There is no disputing that the tribunals in Nuremberg and Tokyo following World War II changed forever any conception of the absolute immunity of states and their agents for crimes against international legal norms. In announcing its decision, the Nuremberg court put the matter bluntly: "The principle of international law, which under certain circumstances protects the representatives of a state, cannot be applied to acts which are condemned as criminal by international law. The authors of these acts cannot shelter themselves behind their official position in order to be freed from punishment. . . ." Though the tribunals represented a victor's justice, the principles behind them were unanimously affirmed by the United Nations on December 11, 1946. The General Assembly also charged a committee "to treat as a matter of primary importance plans for the formulation, in the general context of a general codification of offenses against peace and the security of mankind, or an international criminal code, of the principles recognized in the Charter of the Nuremberg Tribunal and in the judgment of the Tribunal."[28]

According to Lord Millett, the Israeli Supreme Court's decision in the *Eichmann* case was a "landmark . . . of great significance." Although many legal scholars have expressed concern about the means by which Eichmann was brought to Israel for trial, "Israel's right to asset jurisdiction over the offenses has never been questioned." Millett cites the case as authority for three propositions:

> (1) There is no rule of international law which prohibits a state from exercising extraterritorial jurisdiction in respect of crimes committed by foreign nationals abroad.
> (2) War crimes and atrocities of the scale and international character of the Holocaust are crimes of universal jurisdiction under customary international law.
> (3) The fact that the accused committed the crimes in question in the course of his official duties as a responsible officer of the state and in exercise of his authority as an organ of the state is no bar to the exercise of the jurisdiction of a national court.[29]

The United States district court in *Demanjanjuk v. Petrovsky* followed *Eichmann*, declaring that "certain offenses may be punished by any state because the offenders are common enemies of all mankind and all nations have an equal interest in their apprehension and punishment."[30]

In the half-century since the Nuremberg Tribunal, the international community has taken major steps in its condemnation of human rights violations. Beginning with the Universal Declaration of Human Rights, several international agreements have been signed, making clear that certain acts, even if committed by nations themselves, are violations of international law and cannot be tolerated under any circumstance. These include the Convention on Genocide (1948), the Covenant on Civil and Political Rights (1966), the Convention against Taking Hostages (1979), the Convention against Torture (1984). A Convention on Crimes against the Peace and Security of Mankind has been drafted (provisionally adopted, 1988). International tribunals have been established to try war criminals in the former Yugoslavia and Rwanda. And in July 1998, a UN diplomatic conference, meeting in Rome, adopted a statute to create an International Criminal Court.

Thus, since World War II, "there has been a clear recognition by the international community that certain crimes are so grave and so inhuman that they constitute crimes against international law and that the international community is under a duty to bring a person to justice who commits such crimes."[31] In short, they are crimes of universal jurisdiction, and persons accused of them will neither be sheltered by national sovereignty nor escape jurisdiction by fleeing from one country to another. Put simply: you can run, but you can't hide. Today, joining piracy on such a list would be war crimes, crimes against peace, genocide, slave trade, hijacking, terrorism, hostage-taking, and torture.[32]

The last of these, torture, presented the greatest problem before the Law Lords. The Convention against Torture was not signed until 1984 and did not enter into force in Britain until 1988 with the passage of the Criminal Justice Act, well after most of the crimes of which Pinochet was accused had been committed. Counsel for Pinochet relied on the decision of the United States Ninth Circuit Court of Appeals in *Siderman de Blake v. Republic of Argentina* in 1992. In that case, an Argentine family brought a civil action against Argentina for acts of torture committed by its military. In finding that Argentina was immune from suit, the appellate court wrote:

> The Sidermans argue that since sovereign immunity itself is a principle of international law, it is trumped by jus cogens [i.e., preemptory norms]. In short, they argue that when a state violates jus cogens, the cloak of immunity provided by international law falls away, leaving the state amenable to suit.
>
> As a matter of international law, the Sidermans' argument carries much force. . . .
>
> Unfortunately, we do not write on a clean slate. We deal not only with customary international law, but with an affirmative Act of Congress, the [Foreign Sovereignty Immunity Act]. . . . [W]e conclude that if violations of jus cogens committed outside the United States are to be exceptions to immunity, Congress must make it so.[33]

Siderman, however, was a civil action for damages and not a criminal case, in which rules of immunity may be viewed differently.[33]

In the end the Law Lords limited charges of torture against Pinochet to those alleged to have been committed after 1988. Such a limitation, however, was neither patently manifest nor necessary. The Geneva Convention, the Universal Declaration of Human Rights, and the Covenant on Civil and Political Rights all forbade torture prior to the Convention against Torture and prior to 1973, the date of the coup that brought Pinochet to power in Chile and the earliest offense with which he was charged. The United Nations passed a further resolution regarding torture on December 9, 1975. The preamble to the Convention against Torture states that the signatories act "desiring to make *more effective* the struggle against torture and other cruel, inhuman or degrading treatment or punishment throughout the world. . . ."[35] In fact, the *Handbook on the Convention against Torture and Other Cruel, Inhuman or Degrading Treatment or Punishment*, coauthored by Jan Herman Burgers, Chairman/Rapporteur to the Convention, states:

> It is expedient to redress at the outset a widespread misunderstanding as to the objective of the Convention. . . . Many people assume that the Convention's principal aim is to outlaw torture and other cruel, inhuman or degrading treatment or punishment. This assumption is not correct insofar as it would imply that the prohibition of these practices is established under international law by the Convention only and this prohibition will be binding as a rule of international law only for those states which have become parties to the Convention. On the contrary, the Convention is based upon the recognition that the above-mentioned practices are *already* outlawed under international law. The principal aim of the convention is to strengthen the existing prohibition of such practices by a number of support measures.[36]

Spain, for instance, ratified the Convention against Torture in 1987. Torture, however, had been a crime against the interior security of the Spanish state since 1978, when it was added to the penal code after Spain ratified the Covenant on Civil and Political Rights.[37] In *Xuncax v. Gramajo*, the U.S. District Court for the District of Massachusetts, relying on *Filartiga v. Pena-Irala*, found that the "universal condemnation of the use of torture was fully established" prior to 1982, when most of the crimes alleged took place. The *Gramajo* court even applied the Torture Victim Protection

Act, passed in 1991, retroactively to reach conduct in 1989.[38] It would therefore seem, as Lord Millett averred, that, whatever date torture (at least "systematic use of torture on a large scale and as an instrument of state policy") assumed the status of jus cogens, violations of which are subject to universal jurisdiction, it had done so well before 1988 and probably by 1973.[39]

Despite this evolution and the various instances cited above (as well as others like them), the decisions of the Law Lords and the Spanish magistrates represent a new internationalizing of human rights law, upholding the principle of universal jurisdiction in cases of human rights violations. Though Pinochet remains at liberty, he is under investigation in Chile, and an arrest order has been issued. The Spanish and British precedents remain and have implications far beyond the case of the Chilean dictator.

III. GUATEMALA PROSECUTIONS

Just a month after Pinochet's arrest, the Guatemalan Mutual Support Group (Grupo de Apoyo Mutuo) filed charges in Belgium against Efraín Ríos Montt, former president of Guatemala, for actions stemming from his seventeen months in power in 1982 and 1983.[40] Then on March 27, 2000, following the Pinochet precedent, Judge Guillermo Ruíz Polanco opened an investigation of eight Guatemalans on charges of genocide, terrorism, and torture. Accusations being investigated were lodged by Nobel laureate Rigoberta Menchú Tum in December 1999 and refer to three specific cases, the assault by Guatemalan security forces on the Spanish embassy in 1980, the murder of four Spanish priests, and the torture and killing of members of her family, including her mother (her father had died in the embassy attack).[41] Among those named are three former presidents, Ríos Montt, Fernando Romeo Lucas García, and Oscar Humberto Mejía Víctores, and five of their aides, including two former defense ministers and chiefs of staff of the army, Benedicto Lucas García and Héctor Gramajo Morales (who has already been adjudged culpable for a variety of acts during the period from 1982 to 1989), and an interior minister, Donaldo Alvarez Ruíz.[42] The magistrate again relies on the Convention against Torture, the Covenant on Civil and Political Rights, and the Convention on Genocide. Guatemala is a party to all three. Believing that Menchú's complaint was neither "capricious" nor "frivolous," Ruíz said that failing to move forward with the case would be "nothing more than an unpardonable cover-up and pervert the cause of justice."[43] As in the *Pinochet* case, it can be expected that charges, spanning the eight-year combined rule of the three former dictators, may be expanded. The case against them may be even stronger than that against Pinochet.

Guatemala in the 1970s and 1980s was the Platonic form of a counterinsurgency state. In 1954, with the backing of the U.S. Central Intelligence Agency, a self-styled *liberacionista* army, led by rogue colonel Carlos Castillo Armas, had overthrown the democratically elected government of President Jacobo Arbenz. Thereafter, the Guatemalan army was increasingly politically ascendant. A failed coup by a group of disgruntled leftist junior officers on November 13, 1960, began what became a thirty-six-year-long civil war. By 1970, any pretense of civilian government had been abandoned.[44] In 1978, Lucas García, defense minister in the administration of his predecessor General Kjell Eugenio Laugerud García, became president after an election the *Washington Post* described as marked by "fraud . . . so transparent that nobody could expect to get away with it."[45]

Upon assuming the presidency, Lucas García created a death squad run directly out of the national palace, the Secret Anti-Communist Army (Ejercito Secreto Anticomunista, or ESA), which launched a campaign against all perceived opponents, trade unionists, universities, opposition politicians.[46] His project was "an attempt to strengthen the authority of the state through sheer terrorism."[47] Repression became "increasingly blind, random, and massive" directed by Minister of the Interior Donaldo Alvarez Ruíz and head of the police Colonel Germán Chupina Barahona.[48] Such actions were, however, counterproductive.

The Lucas regime was ineffective both politically and militarily. Unable to govern, it fell back upon force, able only to repress the unarmed population of the cities. It was incapable, however, of either controlling the countryside or stemming the growth of the revolutionary movement. Military morale sank and the ranks of insurgents swelled during the "arbitrary slaughter," hastened by "paramilitary activity, summary executions, kidnappings, and forced disappearances, leaving eight hundred bodies a month on the streets."[49]

In May 1978, almost immediately after Lucas took office, seven hundred Kekchí Mayans gathered at Panzós in the Alta Verapaz province to protest their eviction from land they had been working in the so-called

"Zone of the Generals" (land appropriated by military officers and developers, where Lucas himself had 78,000 acres). According to Suzanne Jonas, in *The Battle for Guatemala*, "In response to peaceful protest by the Indian community, army troops (literally hand in hand with the landowners/evictors) opened fire on the unarmed crowd, killing over 100, wounding 300, and subsequently dumping their bodies into mass graves (which, according to observers, had already been dug, indicating a premeditated slaughter)."[50]

The Panzós massacre marked a turning point in three distinct ways. First, it marked a departure from traditional security force methods of disappearance, torture, and murder and signaled that massacre was to be a counterinsurgency tactic in the future. Second, it said to the government and security forces that the indigenous population was part of the insurgency and "subversive" by definition. Finally, and ironically, it, and the subsequent increased military presence in the highlands, drove into the rebel camp many of the *indigena* population, who, though not in favor of military rule, were indifferent and neutral toward the insurgency. Thus, the army's view of the *indigenas* became a self-fulfilling analysis—if not prophecy. The military considered them subversive by definition and the army's actions made them so, because they had nowhere else to go. This would prove critical in the assaults upon the Mayan population in the years to come.

A second catalyzing event occurred in early 1980. On January 31, thirty-one Quiché Mayans, accompanied by university students, entered the Spanish embassy in Guatemala City at the invitation of the Spanish ambassador, who had been investigating the murders of the Spanish priests referenced in Menchú's present complaint. Their purpose was to present a list of grievances at a press conference. Instead, security forces stormed and firebombed the building. Thirty-nine persons, including Menchú's father and the former vice-president of Guatemala, Eduardo Cáceres Lehnhoff, burned to death. Only the ambassador and one of the Mayans, Gregorio Yujá Xona, survived. Yujá Xona, taken to a hospital for treatment of burns, was kidnapped that night; his badly beaten and tortured corpse was found the next day. The army further responded by invading Nebaj, from which the peasants had come, carrying out depredations against the female population. Again, according to Jonas, "this contributed to the subsequent incorporation of entire Indian villages into the revolutionary movement."[51]

The year 1981 saw yet another escalation by the Lucas regime against the Guatemalan populace, with nine thousand civilian casualties that year alone. In June, General Benedicto Lucas García, the president's brother, chief of staff of the army, and defense minister in the waning days of President Lucas's government, launched a new counterinsurgency campaign against the guerillas.[52] In September, he ordered the formation of the first Civil Patrol (Patrulla de Autodefensa Civil), supposed self-defense units composed of forcibly recruited peasants to serve as an army auxiliary. By early 1982, however, the failure of the offensive was undeniable. Resources had been drained, and little or nothing had been done to halt the rise of the insurgency movement. On March 23, 1982, a coup of mid-level officers, led by Ríos Montt, deposed Lucas García. Jennifer Schirmer notes, in her study *The Guatemalan Military Project*: "Nevertheless, the Lucas regime managed to kill an estimated 35,000 on both sides as a result of the . . . operations in the highlands as well as in Guatemala City—the majority of the victims unarmed civilians."[53] He also "virtually destroyed the democratic opposition," eliminating "an entire generation of political and grassroots leaders."[54]

It was not, however, Lucas García's repression or his death toll that led to his overthrow. International isolation and a cutoff of United States aid because of the country's human rights record contributed to the military's discontent. The primary motivation behind the coup d'etat, however, was a belief that the government was losing the counterinsurgency war and that drastic changes were necessary to reverse the process. According to Jonas, "[W]hat is most striking is the unity and single-minded determination of all those involved in the campaign against *la subversión*. Inherent within this vision was the assumption that the planned genocide that left 100–150,000 civilian casualties was necessary to establish 'social peace'; the human rights crimes were simply beside the point, because the Indian population was 'subversive' by definition."[55] Under Ríos Montt, the repression took on dimensions new and horrifying in both scope and intensity.

The day after the coup, Héctor Gramajo was named deputy chief of staff of the army, serving as "coordinator and supervisor" of operations in the western highlands. Together with others on the Army General Staff, Gramajo planned a campaign he continues to refer to as his "baby."[56] On April 5, 1982, a confidential Plan Nacional de Seguridad y Desarrollo (National Plan for Security and Development) Directive Number 0002 was presented to the ruling junta. It was approved on April 10, and the campaign commenced ten days later.[57]

The program was essentially that designed by General Benedicto Lucas and already well underway before the coup. Drawing upon his training at St. Cyr, "General Benny," as Lucas was known, followed French counter-insurgency strategies from Indochina and Algeria. As a way of combating the guerillas and pacifying the countryside, the rural population was to be relocated into fortified towns, essentially strategic hamlets. In order to accomplish the plan, entire villages were burned, and many of the inhabitants were massacred. By the army's own admission, 440 villages were razed.[58] Gramajo refers to these villages as *pueblos fantasmas* (ghost towns).[59] Although the campaign also struck at the "urban infrastructure" of the guerillas, the key component was this scorched-earth policy in rural areas.[60]

Ríos Montt described the campaign, initially called "Operation Ashes," as one designed to "surgically excise evil from Guatemala," and "dry up the human sea in which the guerilla fish swim."[61] As Schirmer points out, however, "The searing contradiction of scorched-earth warfare . . . is that in order to accomplish this 'separation,' certain areas are targeted for massive killings: that is, the military must treat the civilians they are to 'rescue' *as though they are combatants*, killing and burning all living things within the 'secured area.' No distinction is made between combatant and noncombatant; separation is purely rhetorical. Nor are killings accidental 'abuses' or 'excesses'; rather, they represent a scientifically precise, sustained orchestration of a systematic, intentional massive campaign of extermination."[62] Though the security forces blamed the guerillas for using the campesinos as shields and making the killings necessary, nonetheless, after 1982, everyone was considered a guerilla.[63]

The major departure from Lucas's plan was the 30/70 policy designed by Gramajo. Whereas, according to Gramajo, *luquista* (Lucas) forces targeted 100 percent for extermination, the new campaign was to expend only 30 percent of its energy in killing. The remaining 70 percent was to be an effort to provide shelter and food for the survivors.[64] Ríos Montt called the program *frijoles y fusiles.* Preserving the alliteration, it is sometimes called "beans and bullets" in English. Later he referred to it as *techo, trabajo, y tortilla* (shelter, work, food).

Following the coup, Ríos Montt declared a state of siege, prorogued Congress, and suspended all constitutional guarantees, ruling by "law-decree."

At his explicit instruction, clandestine courts known as the Tribunals of Special Jurisdiction (Tribunales de Fuero Especial, or TFE) were established. As the Guatemalan leader said, "If [justice] is not rapid, then it loses its effectiveness, and confidence in the law is lost. Normally, the legal process just goes on and on and on."[65] The TFE met in secret and meted out swift and rough justice. No effective right to counsel existed. In 1982, twenty-nine persons were convicted; fifteen were executed and fourteen sentenced to prison. Later, when 400 cases were transferred to the Supreme Court, 112 accused were released. When Schirmer asked Ríos Montt what happened to those set free, he admitted, "They were later assassinated [by the army] on the street, in their homes, in the countryside, because they were dangerous."[66]

It is a positivist legal theory that separates law and morality. It is rule *by* law, rather than a rule *under* law. As Schirmer observes, "Non-securitized and inherent rights not subject to the power of the State do not exist within the military's definition of the term in Guatemala."[67]

The Guatemalan population is composed of approximately 60 percent Maya, 30 percent ladino (those of mixed ancestry that identify themselves as primarily Hispanic), and 5 percent Castillano (those whose identity is strictly Hispanic).[68] During the Ríos Montt regime, the counterinsurgency campaign assumed an explicitly ethnocidal character. *Matazonas* (killing zones)—in essence, free-fire zones—were established in Mayan areas. Post-massacre survivors report that troops "took special care to kill the *costumbristas* [bearers of custom] and other local transmittors of indigenous tradition with their strong ties to the local habitat."[69] Torture, to obtain information and secure collaboration and obedience, grew. Large numbers of Mayans were driven from their homes. In Quiché, 80 percent of the population was displaced.[70] Towns dominated by ladinos were spared destruction and retaliation.

The thirty-six-year Guatemalan civil war claimed as many as 200,000 victims. Ninety percent of these were civilians. Though it lasted only seventeen months, at least 50,000, and perhaps as many as 75,000, deaths and disappearances can be attributed to the Guatemalan military and Civil Patrols during the Ríos Montt regime. In a newspaper interview, which he later repudiated, Ríos Montt himself claimed the figure at 150,000.[71] Two hundred thousand refugees fled to Mexico. And anywhere from 300,000 to 1,000,000—10 percent of the Guatemalan population—went into hiding

or swelled the urban homeless population of Guatemala City.[72] The overwhelming majority of these victims were Maya.

In his attempt to avoid extradition, Pinochet contended that the "acts
of torture were carried out for the purposes of protecting the state and
advancing its interests, as [he] saw them, and were therefore governmental functions and were accordingly performed as functions of the
head of state."[73] The Guatemalan military offered a similar rationale—
"the idea that unjustifiable violence occurs only outside State structures;
violence by the State to defend itself is mandated, and thus justifiable."[74]
In Guatemala, however, officials also offer a version of the "tragic mistake" doctrine.[75] The massacres and torture were the acts of individuals in
the field beyond the control of the central government. Schirmer, however, makes the salient point:

> [T]o boast, on the one hand, of one's calculated Task Force *strategy*
> of pacification (compared to the failure of *luquista* "tactics") and the
> reestablishment of hierarchy, discipline, and the command structure
> while shrugging off, on the other hand, one's helplessness to stop
> the "excesses" and "abuses" of commanders who caused 440 villages
> to be razed and, by the army's own estimates, thirty thousand to be
> killed within less than eight months, does not follow. How massive
> and excessive does the killing have to be before it is recognized as
> intentional policy?[76]

On August 8, 1983, Ríos Montt was toppled by his defense minister,
General Oscar Humberto Mejía. As with Ríos Montt's seizure of power,
"the basic change was not in the project but in who would direct it. The
1983 coup was basically a cosmetic adjustment to shed the dysfunctional
elements while continuing the same basic policies."[77] Though the bulk of
massacres had occurred under Ríos Montt, they continued under his
successor.[78] Relocation into "model villages," known as "poles of development," intensified as a means of creating enforced dependency, "a form
of instrumentalized military control over minimum daily needs (food,
drinking water, housing, electricity, credit, and fertilizers), with a denial
of sufficient access to land and wage-earning jobs."[79]

Mejía ordered the abolition of the TFE as a political embarrassment,
but use of the Civil Patrols grew.[80] The Civil Patrols, created by Benedicto
Lucas, grew to 300,000 members by the end of 1982 under Ríos Montt.

Under Mejía, they burgeoned. By November 1983, members numbered 500,000. And by the end of 1984, 1,300,000 men were patrolling, representing 10 percent of the total Guatemalan population and one-quarter all adults.[81] Ninety-five percent of those in the Civil Patrol were, once again, Maya. *Indigenas* were used against *indigenas* in an attempt to destroy growing ethnic unity. The wearing of *traje*, traditional Mayan dress, was essentially forbidden. Any man found wearing traje was subject to impressment into the Civil Patrol, and refusal meant execution.[82]

The Mejía regime represented, then, "the military's forceful social, economic, and physical reordering of indigenous life," an intentional restructuring of "socio-cultural, economic, and settlement patterns" in the highlands.[83] The objective was to "fracture the very bases of the communal structure and of ethnic unity, destroying the factors of reproduction of culture and affecting the values on which it rests."[84] Schirmer concludes, "What is clear is that the extraordinary brutality dealt these Indian communities, together with economic and political forces, have dramatically and inexorably transformed the internal dynamics of indigenous communities vis-à-vis ethnic and class divisions and leadership."[85]

Mejía handed over the government to civilian control in 1986. Just days before the inauguration of the new president, Vinicio Cerezo, a law decree was issued, granting amnesty for all "political and related common crimes" from March 23, 1982 to January 14, 1986.

IV. GUATEMALA AND THE *PINOCHET* CASE

A number of key points in the rulings of Garzón and García Castellon and in the opinions of the Law Lords support the case against Ríos Montt and others.

Spain's Organic Law of Judicial Power (OLJP, Ley Orgánica del Poder Judicial) establishes that Spanish courts have jurisdiction over crimes committed outside Spain when such crimes can be found to be genocide or terrorism under Spanish law, as well "any other offense which according to international treaties or conventions should be prosecuted in Spain."[86] Following the French court in the Klaus Barbie case, Garzón found that genocide belongs to "an international repressive order to which the notion of borders is fundamentally foreign." He ruled that "genocide is such a fundamental threat to the international community, it must be pursued in any country, [independent] of where it was committed, and that the fact that genocide is included as a crime against the exterior security of the state [under Spanish law] shows the recognition of this principle by . . . Spanish legislators."[87] In the first hearing before the Law Lords, Lord Lloyd of Berwick, though ultimately deciding against extradition based on claims of immunity, admitted that "the common law incorporates the rules of customary international law."[88]

In finding that Pinochet could be charged with genocide, Garzón gave what at first blush would appear to be a stretched and questionable reading to its definition under Spanish law. According to the Spanish Criminal Code in effect at the time the crimes were alleged to have been committed, genocide is defined in terms of acts undertaken "for the purposes of destroying, in whole or in part, a national ethnic, social, or religious group."[89] Because Pinochet's actions in Chile had not been taken against or had not affected a particular ethnic group, the public prosecutor argued that they did not meet the definition of genocide. Garzón, however, interpolated a comma between the words *national* and *ethnic* in the statutory language where there was none. Thus crimes against a national group (in this case, Chileans) would suffice. On appeal, the Criminal Chamber of the Audiencia Nacional affirmed Garzón's interpretation. The appellate court pointed out that, in the Convention on Genocide itself, the comma was, in fact, present and that it had been added in the Criminal Code in 1995, bringing the national law in line with the convention. It stated that "the lack of a comma between 'national' and 'ethnic' cannot lead us to conclusions that limit the scope of genocide as understood in our domestic law . . . in relation to the international definition."[90]

In the case of Guatemala, there is no need to worry about the possibly disingenuous nature of this interpretation. Resolution 96 of the UN General Assembly in 1946 characterized genocide as an attack upon a group for racial, religious, political, or other reasons. In addition to killing, the acts that have been discussed as genocidal include causing physical or mental harm, inflicting living conditions designed to bring about destruction, and forced displacement.[91] There can be little disputing that the actions of the Guatemalan government and military against the indigenous majority during the regimes in question constitute genocide as defined by both the 1948 convention and Spanish law in effect at the time. Further, though magnitude alone cannot be an index of genocide, it should be noted that Pinochet stood accused in the deaths and disappearances of four thousand individuals. Those under investigation in the Guatemala case may be responsible for well over 100,000 fatalities. Finally, the hundreds of thousands of refugees in Mexico (in addition to those who fled to the United States and elsewhere) demonstrate that genocide is unquestionably a threat to the international order, justifying universal jurisdiction.

Importantly, Garzón stated that "the definition of national group . . . does not exclude the cases in which the victims belong to the same group as the transgressor, that is to say, the alleged cases of 'autogenocide,' as is the case of the mass murders in Cambodia."[92] Illustrating the permeable nature of lines of racial/ethnic identification in Guatemala, Ríos Montt was considered Mayan until he began to rise in the military hierarchy and "became" ladino. In addition, Ríos Montt's aggressive attempts to foster his own brand of evangelical Protestantism and concomitant suppression of Catholicism and traditional Mayan practice can arguably be considered part of the genocidal campaign in Guatemala as an attack upon religious groups.[93]

With regard to terrorism, it is defined under Spanish law as applying to those who "acting in service or collaboration with armed bands, organizations or groups whose purpose be to subvert the constitutional order or gravely alter public peace," commit one of a number of enumerated offense, including kidnapping, murder, and assault.[94] In seeking a dismissal of the investigation in the Argentine and Chilean cases, the public prosecutor argued that "public order" and "public peace" referred to Spanish public order and peace. Garzón, however, rejected the contention, finding that this would thwart prosecution of all crimes committed outside of Spain, in clear contravention of the universal jurisdiction granted under the OLJP. As a second objection, the prosecutor maintained that "armed band" could not include the entirety of a state and its armed forces. In response, Garzón noted that the state as such was not alleged to have committed terrorism, "but rather those who were the highest authorities in the State, used the Armed Forces, its members and economic and paramilitary group[s], to form a terrorist organization that undertook systematic terrorist actions."[95] On appeal, the Criminal Chamber once again supported Garzón's reading, finding that there must only be an intent to subvert the legal or social order of the country where the terrorist act is committed. It further held that in the Chilean case, the crimes alleged could be terrorism even though conducted under color of authority. The court stated unequivocally, "It is, no doubt, the most vile form of terrorism, as it eliminates risk and avails itself of the apparatus of authority to perpetrate its crimes under the guise of authority and even patriotism."[96] As in the case of genocide, the use of the Guatemalan armed forces and the Civil Patrols would fit with this definition of state terrorism propounded by Garzón and the appellate panel.

The charge of torture presented Garzón with the most jurisdictional difficulties. While torture is prohibited by international law, it was not incorporated into the Spanish Criminal Code until 1978, well after most of the crimes alleged in Argentina. He avoided the problem created by consideration of an ex post facto law by finding torture to be an element of the crime of genocide rather than an independent crime. García Castellon, however, did rely on torture in the Chilean case, finding that the 1978 incorporation applied only to crimes committed within Spain itself. He found that international law establishes "that every state will do whatever is necessary to establish its jurisdiction."[97] He left open, however, whether the court claimed jurisdiction based only on crimes committed against Spanish citizens and/or after 1978. In its opinion of November 5, 1998, the Criminal Chamber adopted Garzón's formulation, saying that if Spain had jurisdiction to prosecute genocide abroad, it would necessarily have to reach "crimes of torture in the context of genocide." It also said that such reach extended to *all* victims and not just Spaniards.[98]

Once again, these jurisdictional problems disappear in the Guatemalan case. All crimes under investigation are alleged to have been committed after 1978, when Lucas García came to power, and thus after the incorporation of torture into the penal code. This, however, would still leave the issue debated by the Law Lords, concerning acts of torture prior to the Convention against Torture in 1984 (and its still later codification by signatories). It seems clear that even before the Convention, however, and probably not later than December 9, 1975, when the UN General Assembly adopted its Declaration on the Protection of All Persons from Being Subject to Torture and Other Cruel, Inhuman or Degrading Treatment or Punishment, torture had assumed the character of *jus cogens* under international law. This is particularly true if the torture is widespread, systematic, and part of a larger campaign against a civilian population. The distinctive addition of the Convention was the international criminalization of even single acts of torture.[99] The acts alleged in both the Chilean and Guatemalan cases were not isolated acts of torture. Rather, they were part of an ongoing conspiracy which remained alive throughout the period. In Chile, that period is the span of Pinochet's rule from 1973 until 1990. In Guatemala, it is from the time of Lucas García's assumption of power in 1978 until the restoration of civilian government in 1986. The dimensions of the crimes alleged in Guatemala are on "such a scale that they can justly be regarded as an attack upon the international legal order" and rise to the level of crimes against humanity.[100]

This ongoing conspiracy is also relevant for Spanish jurisdiction. Even if one rejects claims to universal jurisdiction (and its principle that persons who commit crimes of sufficient gravity against the international order should be safe nowhere), if it could be shown that an act were committed in Spain or against a Spanish national in furtherance of the conspiracy, arguably a Spanish court could take jurisdiction over the entire conspiracy.

Finally, as already noted, in attempting to avoid extradition to Spain, Pinochet contended that any acts he undertook were within his capacity as head of state. His attorneys submitted that "acts by police, intelligence officers and personnel are paradigm official acts."[101] He would thus, he maintained, be immune from prosecution. Those accused in Guatemala have made similar claims. Though the Law Lords argued over the matter, it seems clear that crimes such as torture, hostage-taking, and genocide, outlawed as they are by international law, can never be functions of the state or its agents. As Lord Nicholls of Birkenhead stated in the first *Pinochet* decision, "International law recognises . . . that the functions of a head of state may include activities which are wrongful, even illegal, by the law of his own state or by the laws of other states. But international law has made plain that certain types of conduct, including torture and hostage-taking, are not acceptable on the part of anyone. This applies as much to heads of state, or even more so, as it does to everyone else; the contrary conclusion would make a mockery of international law."[102] To say otherwise would fly in the face of the principles of the Nuremberg Tribunal and allow even the most egregious offender—a Hitler, a Pol Pot, a Milosevic—to shelter himself behind his official position and thus escape justice. Lord Steyn concluded, "I do not believe that it is correct to attempt to analyze individual elements of [the] campaign and to identify some as being criminal under international law and others as not constituting international crimes. If Senator Pinochet behaved as Spain alleged, then the entirety of his conduct was a violation of the norms of international law. He can have no immunity against prosecution for any crime that formed part of that campaign."[103]

One final point in Garzón's rulings deserves notice. In seeking dismissal, the public prosecutor argued that Argentine laws preventing prosecution constituted *res judicata* in the criminal proceedings in Spain, making it impossible for them to proceed. The same could have been said about Pinochet in Chile. Among other technical jurisdictional findings, the judge ruled that amnesty laws could not bind Spanish courts in such circumstances, where the laws in question violated international agreements that Argentina had ratified.[104] As with the Argentineans and Pinochet, Ríos Montt and the other Guatemalans being investigated enjoy immunity at home. While the Guatemalan peace accords of 1996 do not guarantee amnesty for crimes against humanity, those being investigated have an earlier amnesty under the 1986 decree-law. Garzón's ruling is thus important as the Guatemalan investigations move forward.

V. CONCLUSION

Though the election of a socialist president has changed the political landscape in Chile considerably since Garzón first ordered Pinochet's arrest, the former dictator remains loved among certain segments of the Chilean population. Despite his scorched-earth counterinsurgency campaign and policies, Ríos Montt enjoys similar esteem in Guatemala. He is the leader of the Frente Republicano Guatamalteca (FRG, Guatemalan Republican Front), a leading political party. In the 1999 elections, the FRG captured 63 of 113 seats in Congress, and Ríos Montt was elected president of the legislature.

The former dictator, however, is no Cincinnatus, turning his hand from his plow to return to the aid of a Guatemala in need. Barred from seeking the presidency by a constitutional prohibition that bans anyone involved in a coup, Ríos Montt has sought power by other means. In 1995, he forged an alliance with Alfonso Portillo, an economist, lawyer, professor, and former leftist, who had returned from fifteen years of exile in Mexico for supporting the guerillas. The slogan for Portillo's presidential bid that

year on the FRG ticket—"Portillo, the presidency; Ríos Montt, the power"—
was spread across billboards showing a broadly smiling Ríos Montt
embracing Portillo and his vice presidential candidate. On January 14, 2000,
the same day he was elected president of the Congress, Ríos Montt swore
Portillo in as Guatemala's new president, representing the first defeat for
a CACIF-backed candidate since democracy was restored in 1986.[105] Attorneys for those under investigation have already asked the Guatemalan
government to charge Rigoberta Menchú with treason for bringing the
case and have sought her detention.[106] On the other hand, the Guatemalan
prosecutor for human rights, Julio Arango, has promised to provide information and cooperate in any way possible with the Spanish court.[107]

Ríos Montt cannot and will not be tried in Guatemala. Trial abroad is
thus the only way to bring him and other offenders to account. As Lord
Phillips of Worth Matravers said in his opinion in the second *Pinochet*
hearing, "The nature of these crimes is such that they are likely to involve
the concerted conduct of many and liable to involve the complicity of officials of the state in which they occur, if not the state itself. In these circumstances it is desirable that jurisdiction should exist to prosecute individuals for such conduct outside the territory in which such conduct
occurs."[108]

Arrest remains a problem. Fear of arrest in the Belgian cause of action
led Ríos Montt to cancel a trip to Belgium in 1998, where he was to attend
a meeting of donor nations that have promised aid to help Guatemala
rebuild from the civil war.[109] Carlos Vila, prosecutor in the Spanish probe,
has threatened to issue international arrest warrants for him and the
others.[110] On March 27, a defiant Ríos Montt announced, "I am only afraid
of God. They can do whatever they want." Three weeks later, however, he
cancelled a planned trip to France, where he was to celebrate Easter, saying only, "Guatemala is more beautiful."[111]

There are obviously those who oppose the internationalizing of human
rights law represented by the Spanish court investigations. The Office of
Public Prosecutor in Spain has sought a termination of the investigations
into the alleged Guatemalan abuses, claiming the courts lack jurisdiction.
Similar contentions failed, however in the *Pinochet* case.[112] Some object,
saying that public servants will be compelled to curtail travel for fear of
arrest abroad.[113] Yet as Robert Jackson, speaking for the United States at
the opening of the Nuremberg Tribunal, declared, "While this law is first

applied against German aggressors, if it is to serve any useful purpose it must condemn aggression by any other nations, including those which sit here now in judgment."[114] In September 2000, pursuant to a suggestion by United Nations Secretary General Kofi Annan, Canadian Foreign Minister Lloyd Axworthy announced that his country was establishing an international panel to study and draft guidelines for determining the relative boundaries between nation-state sovereignty and international human rights.[115]

Lord Millett observed, "[W]e have come . . . a long way in a relatively short time"[116] in our concepts of international law and human rights. As the British Privy Council noted in *In re Piracy Jure Gentium*, international law has never become a crystallized code at any time for all time but is, rather, a living and expanding part of the law, which courts must interpret in contemporaneous fashion.[117] Sheldon Glueck expanded upon that notion, saying that "unless we are prepared to abandon every principle of growth for international law, we cannot deny that our own day has its right to institute customs."[118] The *Pinochet* case and related cases in Britain and Spain should give indigenous groups and their advocates, who want to see Ríos Montt and others like him brought to justice, new arrows in their legal quivers, as human rights law becomes ever more internationalized. As Tenzing Norgay and Edmund Hillary did to Everest (or, if you prefer, as Izaak Walton did to a fish), Ríos Montt may yet be scaled.

PART THREE

Culture

CHAPTER FOURTEEN

IT CAME FROM OUTER SPACE

Of Museums, Meteorites, and Messengers of the Gods

*I am getting ready to speak at length about ghosts, inheritance, gen-
erations of ghosts, which is to say about certain others who are not
present, not presently living, either to us or in us or outside us, it is
in the name of justice. Of justice where it is not yet, not yet there. . . .
It is necessary to speak of the ghosts, indeed to the ghost and with it.
. . . To be just: beyond the living present in general. . . . A spectral
moment, a moment that no longer belongs to time. . . . This justice
carries life beyond present life or its actual being-there, its empirical
or ontological actuality. . . . There is then some spirit, Spirits. And
one must reckon with them. One cannot not have to . . . and the thing
is even more difficult for a reader, a professor, an interpreter, in short
. . . a "scholar" . . . a traditional scholar doesn't believe in ghosts—
nor in all that which could be called the virtual space of spectrality.*

JACQUES DERRIDA,
Specters of Marx

Ellis G. Hughes was a discoverer. His name may not ring with the historical
immediacy of Columbus, da Gama, or Coronado, but he deserves to be
remembered in their fraternity. In November 1902, the one-time miner
was walking near the present-day intersection of Grapevine and Sweet-
briar Roads in the hills above West Linn, Oregon, when he found a fif-
teen-and-a-half-ton meteorite, still the largest known in the United States.
This traveler from outer space was not imbedded in the soil, as would be

expected after it endured a supersonic collision with the Earth. Instead, it rested lightly (as lightly as 15 1/2 tons can rest) upon a prominence, its smaller end on the surface of the knoll as though it had been placed there. Granite boulders surrounded it in proximity. Like the hearty European explorers of earlier times, Hughes captured his discovery, appropriating it to his own use. Shortly after making his find, he dragged the aerolite to his barn, where for the next three years he charged visitors twenty-five cents to have a look at it.[1] And in common with those bold men of yore, Ellis Hughes discovered what was neither lost nor unclaimed. It had been used by Native Americans for thousands of years as part of their cultural and ceremonial life.

Perhaps Hughes thought he was transporting the meteorite from prehistory to history, in the common Amer-European understanding of those terms. Alternatively, perhaps he was simply beguiled by the imaginary jingle of all those quarters from the unwashed masses that had been unable to get to Chicago and see the elephant. Whatever his thinking, he was dragging the Willamette Meteorite, as it came to be known, into a controversy, one that would continue into the next century.

The land where Huges found the stone was owned by Oregon Iron Company. When Oregon Iron Company learned that its meteorite had been stolen (in reality, when it learned it *had* a meteorite), it demanded the rock's return. When Hughes refused, the company brought an action against him in the state courts of Oregon. On July 17, 1905, the Oregon Supreme Court ruled that the meteorite rightfully belonged to the corporation. A year later, the company sold it to Mrs. William Dodge for $20,600, and she donated it to the American Museum of Natural History in New York. From 1935 onward, it sat comfortably (as comfortably as 15 1/2 tons away from home can sit) as the centerpiece of the museum's Hayden Planetarium. The meteorite is so large—seven by ten feet across at the top and four and one-half feet thick—that when the museum began construction of a new Rose Center for Earth and Space, it had to build the wing around it. It has been seen and touched by an estimated forty to fifty million visitors (at far more than twenty-five cents a head). It has been a favorite chair for children to sit upon while having their pictures taken.[2]

This New York love affair with a space rock seemed threatened in late 1999, when the Confederated Tribes of the Grande Ronde Community of Oregon (Grande Ronde), an amalgam of a number of tribes from the

Willamette Valley, made a demand for its return under the provisions of the Native American Graves Protection and Repatriation Act.[3] Specifically, the tribe claimed that the object was sacred to the Clackamas, members of which formed part of the modern-day tribe. Though the Grande Ronde request only grabbed the attention of the New York (and hence national) media as the new museum complex was set to open in February 2000, it had actually been made in November of the previous year. Museum officials stressed the size of the object and that to return it would mean dismantling part of their $210 million facility. When Grande Ronde refused to negotiate (that is to say, to agree to leave it in the planetarium), the museum filed suit in federal district court for the Southern District of New York on February 28.[4] The museum contended that the meteorite is not the type of object covered by NAGPRA. It also claimed that the Grande Ronde request "potentially impairs the museum's ability to share this exceptional scientific specimen with the public." Neil deGrasse Tyson, the planetarium's director, stated that "untold numbers of visitors . . . were turned on to science because of their encounter with this meteorite. It's not simply an artifact on display."[5] (It was, after all, also a backdrop for children's photography.)

NAGPRA protection for human remains and funerary objects has already been discussed in Chapter 10, "Indian Presence with No Indians Present." As noted there, however, these are not the only classes of objects covered by the law. The act also provides for repatriation of "sacred objects" and "cultural patrimony." It is worth examining the Grand Ronde claim in light of these categories, against the backdrop of both Clackamas history and the 1905 *Oregon Iron* decision.

NAGPRA defines sacred objects as those "specific ceremonial objects which are needed by traditional Native American religious leaders for the practice of traditional Native American religions by their present day adherents." Regulations promulgated pursuant to the act make it clear that this includes objects needed for the renewal of ceremonies prevented or discontinued because of the absence of the object in question.[6]

In arguing his case before the Oregon Supreme Court, Ellis Hughes maintained that the Indians had severed the meteorite from the land for use in their rituals, making it personal property. He further contended that they had abandoned the object by ceding the lands upon which it was found by treaty in 1855. The Oregon court, however, found that "the mass is one of nature's deposits, and presumptively it was primarily part of the soil or the realty upon which it was discovered." The justices quoted the appellate court, which also found for Oregon Iron Company, that it possessed "none of the characteristics of personalty, [and] it became, by falling on the earth through the course of nature, a part of the soil."[7]

In treating the peculiar attitude of aerolite when found by Hughes, as if arranged by human design, the Court went through tortured "conjecture" that it could have deposited by "an ice floe," or "thrown out by the force of an eruption, or uncovered by the decomposition or erosion of the natural deposits about it."[8] It dismissed the equally plausible scenario that it had been erected as part of a staged ritual environment by the Indians, finding "there could be no rational inference that the Indians dug it from beneath the surface of the earth and removed and erected it in the position . . . considering its great weight" and the "primitive tools and implements with which they had to do their work."[9]

Even conceding that the local tribes may have "worshiped and utilized" the meteorite, the Oregon court noted that "tradition tells us they worshiped Mt. Hood and other immovable objects as they existed in a state of nature, and there could have been no severance or appropriation by such use."[10] The museum, following the logic of *Oregon Iron*, contended that the Willamette Meteorite was "a natural feature of the landscape, rather than a specific ceremonial object."[11]

Despite the museum's contention, however, this should not be dispositive for purposes of NAGPRA. The position of the Oregon court in finding that the meteorite was not an "Indian relic" and, equally, the museum's position in the litigation reflected a Eurocentric bias that to be of worth the rock must be tooled, it must be the product of human creation and instrumentality. Such a view is completely contrary to traditional Native American practice and tradition. Mt. Hood may have been worshiped, untooled, and immovable, but it has not wound up in a New York museum, either. Tim McKeown of the National Park Service notes that, if the Willamette Meteorite were repatriated, it would not be the first such object returned: in 1996, Portland, Oregon returned the ten-ton basalt boulder known as the Wallula Stone to the Umatillas. Though the Wallala Stone may have petroglyphs on its surface, this is not necessarily a germane difference in evaluating the relative merits of the two claims.[12]

In its request, Grande Ronde averred that the meteorite was seen as a messenger of the gods and was known as "tomanowos," or "sky person." Ryan Heavy Head, a Blackfoot acting as a consultant to the tribe on repatriation issues, states that it represented all three elements in the Natives' worldview—air, water, and earth. Medicine men believed it came from the moon (air); it was made of earth; and water collected in the pockmarks in its surface. The site became a place for the conduct of vision quests by the Natives to seek messages from the spirit world. They also washed their faces in the water collected in the rock's natural bowls (which was considered holy) and dipped their arrows into it in time of war and before hunting.[13]

Evidence at trial in the *Oregon Iron* case supports the contention. Testimony elicited from Susap, a seventy-year-old Klickitat described as "about the last of his tribe," was that he had, as a young boy, gone hunting with Wachino, a Clackamas chief who showed him the meteorite, described its religious uses to him, and told him it was called "Tomanowos." Sol Clark, a forty-seven-year-old Wasco, also testified that his mother had told him of a "kind of magic or medicine rock" known as Tomanowos that fit the description of the meteorite where "they used to send their young people out there—generally made them go on dark nights. . . ."[14] These Native accounts are also supported by contemporaneous Amer-European statements. Writing in 1854, in *Sketches of Mission Life among the Indians of Oregon*, Zachariah Atwell Mudge reported, "When a young man wishes to become distinguished, he goes out at night—perhaps some night when the clouds overhang the sky—and an awful mystery seems to enshroud the object of his adventure. He claims to meet either Talipaz [the Creator] or his spirit. Sometimes he says, 'Tamanawas,' that is, a moving spirit of power, 'came upon me.' He now knows what is to befall him, or he vainly thinks, in his superstition, he knows more than common mortals. He claims to be a great 'medicine man'; and, strange enough, his people allow his claim!"[15] Mudge goes on to state that medicine men believe they receive their power from Tamanawas: "So powerfully does ignorance keep the red man a slave to imposition."[16] Such claims are also consistent with ethnographic accounts of tribes in the Pacific Northwest.[17]

In short, there seems to be ample proof that the meteorite was a sacred object used in specific ceremonies by the Clackamas and related tribes. NAGPRA protection should attach regardless of the extraterrestrial—or

terrestrial—origins of the object. Some supporters of the museum's claim
to the aerolite contended, however, that the Clackamas today are all Christians and that they abandoned their traditional ceremonies. The implica-
tion here seems to be that the tribe did not want the object back to renew
ceremonies but rather to attract the public to a museum of its own. This
would be a question for the trier of fact.

It is clear that the assimilationist policies of the federal government
"hounded" (Stephen Carter's word) Natives from their traditional religious practices to Christian conversion.[18] Traditional ceremonies were
banned for decades pursuant to the so-called Religious Crimes Codes. Yet
NAGPRA says that to meet the standards for repatriation the object must be
used in a ceremony currently conducted by traditional practitioners or be
necessary in renewing rituals that are part of a traditional religion. In order
to meet the test, it seems patent that there must be an extant "traditional
religion" carried on by "traditional Native American religious leaders."

Grande Ronde and the Clackamas maintained, however, that they
needed the meteorite to perform the ceremonies for which it was traditionally employed. June Olson, cultural resource manager for the tribe,
says, "It's a link from our tribal people today to our ancestors in traditional beliefs. It's a connection we're all kind of looking for, and there isn't
a lot of them left." She said that Grande Ronde wanted to make the meteorite available for traditional religious people to use in ceremony. According to Heavy Head, the knowledge of how to take care of Tomanowos has
been kept alive until the present by tribal elders. He states, "If it wasn't
really important to the religion and to the people, then with the 100 years
that have gone by, we still wouldn't be talking about it, songs wouldn't be
remembered about it, people wouldn't be trained to take care of it in case
it came back."[19] This would seem to satisfy the requirements of NAGPRA.
As Jack Trope writes, "The definition recognizes that the ultimate determination of continuing sacredness must be made by the Native American religious leaders themselves since they must determine the current
ceremonial need for the object."[20]

Even if, for some reason, it were to be decided that the Willamette
Meteorite was not a sacred object, within the meaning of NAGPRA, Grande
Ronde and the Clackamas would still have grounds to request repatriation of the aerolite as "cultural patrimony." NAGPRA defines "cultural patrimony" as "an object having ongoing historical, traditional, or cultural

importance central to the Native American group or culture itself," such that it is considered the property of the group and not any individual. The definition has the virtue of being more encompassing than the ritually-rooted definition of "sacred object." Based upon the history of the Willamette Meteorite, it seems clear that it falls within the definition of cultural patrimony.

The problem here is one of "right of possession" under the terms of the act. Once a tribe has proven it has a valid claim to an object (either a sacred object or cultural patrimony), it must present "at least some evidence" that the museum does not have the "right of possession." Thus Grande Ronde would have to make some showing that the American Museum of Natural History did not obtain the Willamette Meteorite "with the voluntary consent of an individual or group that had the right to sell or transfer the object."[21] If Grande Ronde could meet this requirement, however, the burden of proof would shift to the museum, and if it could not prove a right of possession, it would be required to return the meteorite.[22]

A preliminary showing that the museum did not have the right of possession to the Willamette Meteorite might be difficult but not by any means impossible. The Clackamas were party to a treaty, signed on January 22, 1855, and ratified on March 3 of that same year, that ceded the land where Hughes found the meteorite almost fifty years later.[23] The land passed into the hands of Oregon Iron Company. The Oregon Supreme Court ruled that the company owned the meteorite, and the company subsequently sold it to Mrs. Dodge, who, in turn, donated it to the museum.

Native cultures are complex systems in which no element stands in isolation. Hunting involves more than the act of stalking and killing the animal itself. It also involves preparation, the making of arrows and rituals for success prior to the hunt. It involves rituals performed after the kill to show respect for the sacrifice of the prey and to ensure future game. If hunting rights were retained by the Clackamas, it could be shown that the use of the meteorite in hunting rituals was incident to hunting itself.[24] Grande Ronde was terminated in 1954. When it regained recognition in 1983 pursuant to the Grande Ronde Restoration Act, Congress did not restore hunting, fishing, and trapping rights.[25] The relevant date for purposes of Grande Ronde's NAGPRA claim, however, would be that of Hughes's appropriation in 1902, years before their rights were terminated.

Under NAGPRA, tribal custom probably would be looked to in determining "whether the initial transfer of the item out of tribal control was consensual."[26] The treaty would seem to fit this requirement. In *Oregon Iron*, however, Sol Clark testified that "Tomanowos" "belonged to the medicine men of the tribe."[27] If it could be adduced that those signing the treaty could not alienate the meteorite without the approval of the medicine men, it might be enough to shift the burden of proof to the museum. Alternatively, it might be shown that the Clackamas did not believe that they were ceding access to the object when they ceded the land itself. Continued visits to the meteorite after 1855 and its use in rituals could indicate this. Under canons of construction that have been developed by the courts, treaties must be liberally construed in favor of the Indians and interpreted as the Indians themselves would have interpreted them at the time of making. Ambiguities must also be resolved in favor of the Indians.[28]

The tribe had a strong case for the meteorite as both sacred object and cultural patrimony. Tracy Dugan, speaking for the tribe, declared, "This is a sacred object to the people of the Willamette Valley. It was used by our ancestors. We want to bring it back here to our reservation and make it available for people to use in the traditional way."[29] It would be properly cared for. The tribe also said it would provide access to the public, as well. Regardless, the question was rendered moot in mid-June 2000, when, faced with possibly years of litigation, Grande Ronde and the museum reached an agreement. Under the accord, the meteorite will remain at the museum. In turn, the museum will allow the tribe access to it for ceremonies. Should the museum ever remove the Willamette Meteorite from display, other than for cleaning or maintenance, ownership will revert to the tribe.

Tomanowos traveled a long path from somewhere between Mars and Jupiter to its home on Earth. That journey was prolonged by Ellis Hughes, Oregon Iron Company, and Mrs. William Dodge. The American Museum of Natural History is just making it longer.

CHAPTER FIFTEEN

NATIVE REFORMATION IN INDIAN COUNTRY?

Forging a Relevant Spiritual Identity among Indian Christians

Christian, n. One who believes that the New Testament is a divinely inspired book admirably suited to the spritual needs of his neighbor.

AMBROSE BIERCE,
The Devil's Dictionary

I guess [it] is a big struggle for Native Americans who have forsaken, sometimes not of their own accord, their traditional teachings.

BARBARA GRAY-KANATIYOSH,
Turtle Island

Religion today, or at least Christianity, does not provide the understanding with which society makes sense. Nor does it provide any means by which the life of the individual has value. Christianity fights unreal crises which it creates by its fascination with its own abstractions.

VINE DELORIA, JR.,
Custer Died for Your Sins

The survival of Christianity among America's indigenous peoples is an open question. Native American lawyer-theologian-scholar Vine Deloria sounded the alarm thirty years ago in his now famous manifesto, *Custer Died for Your Sins*. The "impotence and irrelevancy of the Christian message," Deloria said, was causing a widespread resurgence of indigenous religious traditions among Indians.[1] Today only 10 to 25 percent of the nation's approximately two million Natives identify themselves as Christians.

Such statements and statistics are startling to many whitestream Christians. After all, both the Roman Catholics and Episcopalians, together representing more than 320,000 Indian Christians, have multiple Indian bishops. In August 1992, Stanley McKay, a reserve-born Cree, was elected moderator of the United Church of Canada, that country's largest denomination. And Native voices are beginning to assert themselves at the tables of theological discourse throughout mainline Christianity.

These accomplishments, however, belie a continued decline in church membership. The attachment of many Natives to "the faith" remains nominal. In most denominations, they are underrepresented in the ranks of clergy. Few Native professors teach at seminaries. And the same month that McKay was chosen to lead the Church of Canada, the annual meeting of the Tekakwitha Conference, representing Indian Roman Catholics, ended amid acrimonious charges that its leaders were denying Indian culture and selling out to a church hierarchy closely associated with the conquest and cultural genocide of America's indigenes.

THE TERRIBLE IRONY

At the heart of these contradictory images is what Marie-Therese Archambault, a Franciscan nun, described as "the terrible irony" of being both Indian and Christian.[2]

The Europeans who invaded this continent over five hundred years ago came, it is said, with the sword in one hand and the Bible in the other. From early on, the church was an active agent in the colonial enterprise, preaching not only assimilation into the dominant culture but also an acceptance by Natives of the crimes being perpetrated against them. George Tinker, an Osage teaching at the Iliff School Theology in Denver, has gone so far as to call the colonization of the Americas, a "missionary conquest" in his book of the same title.[3]

Most Americans probably know at least a part of this past. It's present-day missionary activities that shock them. William Baldridge, a Cherokee and former professor at Central Baptist Theological Seminary, continues to be surprised by the number of well-meaning Whites who say they thought "we stopped doing missions like that a hundred years ago." Today, for many Natives, to become Christian still means to stop being Indian.

Baldridge joined with Kim Mammedaty, an ordained Native clergyperson, at the 1991 Biennial Meeting of the American Baptist Church in calling for the end to continued "spiritual oppression."[4] Challenging the church to recognize its "complicity in evil," the pair called for missionaries among Indians to be brought home. The resolution was soundly defeated in a contentious session. Both Baldridge and Mammedaty have since left the church.

The roots of the current mission system go back to the early 1870s when President Ulysses S. Grant, as part of his "Peace Policy," put much of the decision making for reservations in the hands of churches. Thirteen denominations, including Catholics, mainline Protestants, and Quakers (who first urged the plan), were given exclusive control over seventy-three Indian agencies. The denominations, moreover, were prohibited from interfering with matters on each other's reservations. Churches also exerted control over procurement and disbursement. For Natives, the system meant lack of any choice in Christian association. Attendance at religious services became compulsory, and traditional practice was forbidden. The avowed goal was assimilation.

When this ecclesiastical serfdom ended in the early 1930s, a number of other Christian denominations, primarily fundamentalist and Pentecostal, began Indian missions. Ironically, inroads by these sects led mainline Native congregations to move to a less expressive, more "White" style of worship. Today the effects of assimilationist Indian missions and the breakdown of reservation monopolies are still being felt. Sister Gloria Davis, a Navajo-Choctaw nun and a participant in the 1992 Tekakwitha Conference, told Catherine Walsh (who covered the event for both the *New York Times* and a Jesuit publication): "The missionaries . . . said we had no religion, that we were pagans, even though we believed we were in harmony with the Creator and that he took care of us. But even now we are sometimes told by the church not to be too Indian."[5]

As a result, many Natives wonder whether Christianity, as the imported religion of their Amer-European colonizers, has anything to say to them. And although some, like William Wantland, Episcopal bishop of the Diocese of Eau Claire and a Seminole, dismiss such questions as "pure bunk," the effects are very real. They often include internal divisions and jealousies that have split even Native families. Donald Pelotte, the Abenaki bishop of Gallup, New Mexico and a member of the Tekakwitha Conference board of directors, can cite numerous examples of brothers and sisters not speaking to each other because of religious rivalries.

DIVIDES AND PARADIGMS

Cleavages exist not only between traditional spirituality (or neotraditional, syncretic religions such as peyotism) and Christianity but between Christian denominations as well. At issue is the degree of Indian culture and traditional practices that will be allowed in Christian practice and doctrine. Often the split is generational, between older persons reared under the old missionary system and younger Indians influenced by the reassertion of Native identity in the late 1960s.

The Episcopal Council of Indian Ministries, composed of both Native and non-Native members, has called for a new Christian paradigm— "with a Christ-centered focus and with spirituality at the center" as opposed to a missionary Christianity that would require acceptance of every item of orthodox Christian liturgy and dogma.[6] For Natives this means redeeming the biblical witness for those who, like Robert Warrior, know that Indians must read the Bible with Canaanite eyes. It means incorporating traditional spiritual practice and belief. It means acknowledging the power and truth contained in the old ways and stories.

Wantland says that if Christianity is going to speak to Indian people, it must do so through Native cultures. The result will be a Christianity "strange, if not alien to people of European background. It will be something far different from English and Scottish Christianity."[7] Pelotte agrees, seeing inculturation as the real issue. Commenting on Wantland's vision of a Native Christianity, he says, "I'm not sure where it's going to go in the Catholic community. It will happen very slowly, but it will happen."[8] According to Pelotte, "The irony of it all is that there is so much good that can come from both traditions, and we're missing it entirely."

According to Tinker, "a new day is emerging."[9] Emerging—but not yet emergent. Today the sacred pipe, the drum, sweat lodges, Native prayers and eagle feathers are becoming commonplace in Indian churches. Some congregations keep little of the Christian liturgy beyond the sacraments.

Steven Charleston, the former Episcopal bishop of Alaska and currently president of the Episcopal Divinity School, has called what is happening a Native Reformation. Pelotte says, "It's very serious, and we're only beginning to scratch the surface."

One thing is clear: If Christianity is going to survive among Native Americans, it will not be as a missionary faith. As Charleston points out, Natives have a prior "testament," another covenant with the Creator lived long before the coming of Europeans.[10] Native Christianity, moreover, must not only be rooted in Native cultures. It must be in the hands of Natives as well.

CHAPTER SIXTEEN

A BIBLICAL PARADIGM FOR
NATIVE LIBERATION

*Then the daughters of Zelophehad came forward. Zelophehad was the
son of Hepher son of Gilead son of Machir son of Manasseh son of
Joseph, a member of the Manassite clans. The names of his daughters
were: Mahlah, Noah, Hoglah, Milcah, and Tirzah. They stood before
Moses, Eleazar the priest, the leaders, and all the congregation, at the
entrance of the tent of meeting, and they said, "Our father died in
the wilderness; he was not among the company of those who gathered themselves together against the Lord in company of Korah, but
died for his own sin; and he had no sons. Why should the name of
our father be taken away from his clan because he had no son? Give
to us a possession among our father's brothers."*

*Moses brought their case before the Lord. And the Lord spoke to
Moses, saying: The daughters of Zelophehad are right in what they
are saying; you shall indeed let them possess an inheritance among
their father's brothers and pass the inheritance of their father on to
them."*

NUMBERS 27: 1–7

In the 11 September 1989 issue of the now-defunct journal *Christianity and
Crisis*, contributing editor Robert Warrior published an article entitled
"Canaanites, Cowboys and Indians." The piece, which went on to be widely
reprinted, likened the American Indian experience to that of the biblical

Canaanites, dispossessed of their homeland and annihilated by a foreign invader. Natives therefore read the Bible with "Canaanite eyes." Warrior's argument takes on added force in the case of the Cherokees, who were subjected to a genocidal reverse exodus from a country that was for them, literally, the "Promised Land."

Warrior goes on to maintain that the story of the Exodus, the paradigm for contemporary liberation theology, cannot be severed from the story of the conquest of Canaan and the destruction of the Canaanites. Exodus cannot be divorced from eisode. Colonialism and genocide are at the base of the texts themselves. Unless another paradigm can be found and the biblical witness redeemed, no Native Christian theology of liberation can exist.

Cherokee theologian William Baldridge responded shortly after publication of Warrior's article in a letter to the editor of *Christianity and Crisis*, stating that the essay had "precipitated an intellectual and spiritual crisis" for him as a Native Christian. He wrote, "Warrior's arguments had a powerful impact on me as I could dispute neither his emphasis on the story nor his reading of the story."[1]

As a means of redeeming the biblical text, Baldridge suggested the story of the Canaanite woman in Matthew 15. The woman approaches Jesus asking for healing for her daughter. Annoyed, the disciples urge him to send her away, and Jesus says to her, "I was sent only to the lost sheep of the house of Israel." The woman persists, and Jesus replies, "It is not fair to take the children's food and throw it to the dogs." But the woman will not be denied. She retorts, "Yes, Lord, yet even the little dogs eat the crumbs that fall from their master's table." According to Baldridge, "What happens next is a miracle: The Son of Yahweh is set free. The son of the god of Canaanite oppression repents. Jesus not only changes his mind, he changes his heart. He sees her as a human being and answers her as such. 'O woman, great is your faith! Be it done as you desire.' And her daughter was healed instantly . . . and so, I believe, were the wounds of bitterness in the Canaanite woman." The rift between Canaanite and oppressor is thus bridge for Baldridge.

Warrior considered Baldridge's position in a printed response. Ultimately, he rejected it, writing:

> I think it is important to note that in the story the woman does not become a follower of Jesus. Having received what she desired

from Jesus, she walks away and is never mentioned again. Yes, she changes Jesus, but she does not become a disciple. She seeks him out because he has something she needs. She is persistent to the point where he can no longer deny her humanity and the legitimacy of her pain. The question of what happened to her is left open. . . . The importance of the story is not whether she followed, but that without her, on Baldridge's reading, Jesus would have remained a narrow-minded bigot who viewed indigenous people as inhuman.

Isn't this where we American Indians find ourselves? Like the Canaanite woman, we must go begging to the people who colonized us in order to secure the bare minimum of justice. Like her, our healing has become wrapped up in changing the colonizer's mind about our right to be self-determined, legitimate nations of people. Thus we must confront them in strength with our humanity. We have been doing so for 500 years, to little avail. Yet we remain persistent and hope someday to change their minds, or at least their actions.

I am glad to have a fellow traveler in Bill Baldridge to join in the battle, and I respect his choice to follow the god he is trying to convert. But, if we are able to convert the son of the Christian god and his followers, my choice will still be to go home to the drum, the stomp dance, and the sweatlodge.[2]

Though I am today less certain than I was in 1990, when I took up the Warrior/Baldridge colloquy in what became my master's thesis, or even than in 1993, when my thoughts were finally published, I believe that a redemption of the biblical text, meeting Warrior's criteria, is possible. A biblical paradigm for Native American/Canaanite liberation can be found in the account of the daughters of Zelophehad in Numbers 27 and Joshua 17.

In Numbers, just as Moses and Eleazar have completed the census of the Israelites that will determine allocation of land in the Promised Land, Zelophehad's daughters approach. They say that their father has died in the wilderness, leaving no sons, only daughters. They are worried that, because women cannot inherit, they will be deprived of their place when land is allotted. Moses seeks the guidance of God, and God says, of course the daughters should have their place when land is apportioned.

Later, in the book of Joshua, when Eleazar and Joshua actually carry out the allocation, they forget about Zelophehad's children. The daughters step forward again, pointing out that God commanded Moses to allow them to inherit on the same basis as their male kin. Thus reminded, Joshua allots the promised portion to them.

The story illustrates that all, even the most powerless and oppressed of a society, have the right to share equally in the promise of God. It says also that the oppressed must not remain silent or inactive in the face of their oppression: At every turn it is incumbent to remind the oppressor of God's promise and to be the heralds of their own salvation. Zelophehad's daughters confront them in strength with their humanity. Where one might have faltered, five step forward together to demand what is theirs. Most important, the story has direct meaning for the story of the Canaanites.

The names of the five daughters (Mahlah, Noah, Hoglah, Milcah, and Tirzah) were, in fact, the names of five towns in northern Canaan in the land of Hepher. The names were taken from Numbers 26, where they were meant as towns, and reinterpreted for purposes of the allotment story. The Hepherites were not destroyed or dispossessed. Neither were they reduced to hewers of wood and drawers of water like the Gibeonites. Rather, they formed a religio-political alliance with the Israelites.

The story in Numbers and Joshua is the account of the maintenance of the Hepherites' cultural and territorial integrity—an integrity that, according to the biblical witness, survived at least until the time of Solomon.

American Indians are thus the Hepherites, Zelophehad's daughters, sharing a god with, and living in the midst of, a foreign people, yet preserving their own identity and self-determination.

CHAPTER SEVENTEEN

TRICKSTER

The Sacred Fool

Nanabohzo, the woodland tribal trickster, is a holotrope, *a comic holotrope, and a* sign *in a language game; a communal sign shared between, listeners and four points of view in third person narratives.*

The trickster is androgenous, a comic healer and liberator in literature; the whole figuration *that ties the unconscious to social experiences. The trickster sign is communal, an erotic shimmer in oral traditions; the narrative voices are holotropes in a discourse.*

GERALD VIZENOR,
"Trickster Discourse: Comic Holotropes and Language Games"

Loutish, lustful, puffed up with boasts and lies, ravenous for foolery and food, yet managing always to draw order from ordure, the trickster appears in myths and folktales of nearly every traditional society, sometimes as a god, more often as an animal. Seemingly trivial and altogether lawless, he arouses affection and even esteem wherever his stories are told, as he defies mythic seriousness and social logic. Just as skillfully, he has slipped out of our contemporary interpretive nets to thumb his nose at both scholarly and popular understanding of so-called primitive peoples. Yet these peoples too know their tricksters as the very embodiment of elusiveness.

ROBERT D. PELTON,
The Trickster in West Africa

One of the central arguments of the emerging Native Christian theological dialogue is that, if one is to consider Native American Christian theology—if one is to "talk" "God-talk" with a Native voice—then traditional theological categories must be reimagined and reformed consistent with Native experience, values, and worldview. This appropriation of the gospel is no different from what believers in any culture in any time have done. As Leonardo Boff reminds us, the gospel is never "naked"; it is always culturally clothed. Christians respond to the biblical witness because, to paraphrase Coleridge, there is something that "finds them" where they live their lives.[1] Unfortunately, too often Indians were told that to become Christian meant to adopt Western culture along with their baptism and to stop being Indian. The argument, however, goes beyond simply "revisioning" conventional categories of Western systematic theology. It also means considering new categories from Native thought-worlds. One such new category is that of Trickster.

Actually, Trickster discourse is not a wholly new category. In fact, it is not new at all but, rather, ancient. Many diverse cultures around the world have trickster figures. "Trickster" is, in fact, an anthropological categorization, an abstraction from particular embodiments in different cultures. In West Africa, it is Anansi the spider. For the Greeks and Romans, he was Hermes or Mercury. In northern Europe, numerous stories are told about the trickster Loki. Native Hawaiians know him as Maui. It is among the Native nations of the Americas, however, that Trickster plays his most important role, taking on many guises—Raven, Iktomi the spider, Wolverine, Rabbit, and the most familiar trickster of all, Coyote, among many others. Who is this Trickster? What role does he play in indigenous cultures? And what does he have to do with a Native American theology?

Lewis Hyde, in his book *Trickster Makes This World: Mischief, Myth, and Art*, states, "[A]ll tricksters are 'on the road.' They are the lords of in-between. A trickster does not live near the hearth; he does not live in the halls of justice, the soldier's tent, the shaman's hut, the monastery. He passes through each of these when there is a moment of silence, and he enlivens each with mischief, but he is not their guiding spirit. He is the spirit of the doorway leading out, and of the crossroad at the edge of town (the one where a little market springs up). He is the spirit of the road at dusk, the one that runs from one town to another and belongs to neither."[2] Trickster, as his name implies, is a mischief maker. Though he is usually referred to as he, he easily shapeshifts. He makes trouble for everyone, including himself. He comes to a bad end as often as he succeeds as a result of his actions. Trickster stories are thus teaching stories, imparting to listeners societal values and mores, through humor.

The biblical figure that most closely resembles Native tricksters is Jacob. The story of Jacob (Gen. 25:19–Gen. 37) is a trickster cycle, as any Indian reader immediately recognizes. Jacob contends with his twin, Esau, while still in the womb, grabbing his brother's heel to jockey for position in an attempt to be the firstborn. Later, he tricks a ravenous Esau into selling his birthright for a bowl of lentils. With the help of their mother, Rebekah, he poses as Esau to gain his father Isaac's blessing, rightly belonging to his brother. He deceives and cheats his father-in-law Laban out of his flock through a neat piece of trickery and then flees. Finally, he wrestles all night with Yahweh and comes away with a game hip as a result of the combat. Even his name implies trickery. In a reference to his prenatal shenanigans, Jacob translates as "heel thief."

The story of Jacob's duplicity in his dealings with Laban finds a resonance in a story told on the Atlantic Coast of Nicaragua, where the trickster of the Ashanti of Africa, Anansi, has melded with the culture of the Spanish and the local Miskito Indians and where today he is often called Hermano Anansi or Señor Anansi. As James De Sauza says of Anansi, "Sometimes he is a man; sometimes he is a spider. Sometimes he is good; sometimes he is bad. But he is always very, very tricky."[3] In the story, Anansi goes into the cattle business with Tiger—using Tiger's money. After a few years, they decide to split their large herd. After the division, Anansi tells his partner that it is too late to drive his herd away that night. He convinces Tiger to mark their respective cattle. Green leaves from the olive tree will be put on the ears of Tiger's cows, while dead brown leaves will be put on Anansi's. When the pair return, the fresh leaves have all turned brown, and Anansi departs with the entire herd, leaving Tiger broke and vowing revenge.

Trickster is a breaker of barriers and an eraser of boundaries. He moves between heaven and earth, between deity and mortals, between the living and the dead. According to Hyde, "Sometimes it happens that the road between heaven and earth is not open, whereon trickster travels not as a messenger [as Mercury/Hermes, the messenger of the gods] but as a thief, the one who steals from the gods the good things that humans need if they are to survive in this world." Raven, the trickster figure of the Northwest Coast, is a good example of Hyde's point. Before Raven, the world is in darkness. Through trickery, he steals light from the other world and returns to earth with it. True to form, however, he does this not out of any feeling for humanity but so that he will have light by which to feed.

The story illustrates Trickster's role as culture-hero, conveying benefit on humankind. He is a creative figure, but he does not create the world. Rather, he is a demiurge who shapes the world and gives it form. Among the Haidas, Raven is responsible for bringing the first humans into the world, changing his raucous cawing to a soft coo and coaxing them from a clamshell. He is the one who teaches them to hunt and fish and cook. He makes the first fishhook. He teaches the spider to weave a web and then tells humans how to make nets in imitation of the spider's lair. Coyote teaches the Crow how to hunt buffalo. He teaches the Nez Perce how to net salmon. Sometimes, he takes a more direct role in creation. Iktomi of the Sioux created time and space, language, and gave the animals their names. Glooskap, the Algonkian culture-hero, shapes the rocky coast of New England. Maui pulls the Hawaiian Islands up from the bottom of the ocean. And among the Innu, Wolverine is responsible for creation of the land in their earthdiver myth, in that he calls the meeting of the aquatic animals and urges them to bring up the land to the surface of the primordial waters.

While not evil, Trickster can be cruel. In a Menominee myth, for instance, Raccoon torments a pair of blind men. Coyote is said by the Maidus of California to be the inventor of the first lie, and the Sioux consider Iktomi the "grandfather of lies." Trickster can even be downright thuggish. Tseg'sgin', along with Jisdu the rabbit, one of the Cherokee tricksters, has few, if any, redeeming qualities. The same could be said about Veeho of the Cheyenne and Napi among the Blackfoot. It should be noted, however, that these tricksters are a relatively late development, postdating contact with Whites. Jack and Anna Kilpatrick, in fact, surmise that "Tseg'sgin" (pronounced "Jegsgin") is a corruption of "Jackson," for Andrew Jackson, the enemy of the Cherokees who set in motion their removal from their homes in what is now the American Southeast. *Veeho* means "white man" in Cheyenne.[4] So does *Napi* in Blackfoot.[5] Like the Cherokee, the Blackfoot have another, more creative trickster, Coyote. These stories testify to the lability and continued vitality of the trickster in

Native life. Among the Mayas of Guatemala, a newcomer is Maximon. Dressed in an ice-cream white suit, Panama hat, and dark glasses, he is known as the Lord of Looking Good.

Negative aspects of Trickster are, however, not the norm. If Trickster is the "god" of chance, chance or luck is sometimes bad, as we all know, "and more often than not, overweening pride or overreaching control is a contributing factor" in the downfall of Trickster's victims, including himself.[6]

Trickster can brook no pretension. He punctures pomposity. He turns the world upside down, disordering the normal patterns of tribal life and values and subverting expectations. In this way, he helps keep the world imaginatively in balance. Richard Erdoes and Alfonso Ortiz describe the Hopi trickster, Masau'u:

> The Hopi god Masau'u, the Skeleton Man, is a creator, a germinator, the protector of travelers, the god of life and death, the peacemaker, and the granter of fertility. But he is also a lecher, a thief, a liar, and sometimes a cross-dresser. Masau'u . . . is probably the strangest and most multifarious of all Native American trickster gods. He can assume any shape—human or animal—to lure a maiden to share his blanket. Ruler of the underworld, he is often shown as a skeleton but can also be depicted as a normal, handsome young man bedecked in turquoise. He is said to live in poverty, but he is lord of the land. . . .
>
> Masau'u is also the boundary maker and the god of planting and agriculture. During Hopi planting ceremonies, a Masau'u impersonator is the center of the action.[7]

In fact, in the Southwest, sacred clowns are common. These performers, such as the *koshare* and *kwerana* among the Keresan Pueblos, act a trickster function. They disrupt and mock the solemnity of ceremonies, often in bawdy and Rabelaisian ways. According to Hyde,

> Trickster the culture hero is always present; his seemingly asocial actions continue to keep our world lively and give it flexibility to endure. . . . I not only want to decribe the imagination figured in the trickster myth, I want to argue a paradox that the myth asserts: that the origins, liveliness, and durability of cultures require that there

be space for figures whose function is to uncover and disrupt the very things that cultures are based on. I hope to give some sense of how this can be, how *social life can depend on treating antisocial characters as a part of the sacred*.[8]

Thus Trickster serves as an important social regulator.

So there is a built-in contradiction in Trickster. He is sacred fool and sacred lecher. As the Sioux attest of Iktomi, he may be mischievous and ribald, but he is nonetheless *wakan*, holy. Howard Norman says of trickster myths, "[T]hese tales enlighten an audience about the sacredness of life. In the naturalness of their form, they turn away from forced conclusions, they animate and enact, they shape, and reshape the world."[9] These stories and their enacted form in ritual teach the naturalness of humanity, including human sexuality. These lessons are reinforced by the fact that Trickster is usually envisioned as an animal. Natives traditionally do not see themselves as separated from the rest of the created order but as part of it.

This fact is illustrated by the very figures that different Native cultures chose to embody Trickster—spider, rabbit, coyote, raccoon, etc. All are animals that live in close proximity to humans but liminal to their settlements and thrive in that space. They are usually fast, getting in and out of spaces of human habitation quickly, appearing to come out of nowhere. They are often stealthy, sneaky, and thieving. Coyotes, especially, have shown themselves to be highly adaptive to human presence. They have learned to thwart Amer-European traps. And in the early American West, they were more social animals, hunting in packs like their cousin, the wolf. Because wolves could not adapt to solitary hunts, they suffered, whereas the coyote adapted, able to hunt in either packs or alone, and flourished.

Lewis Hyde sums up:

> In short, trickster is a boundary-crosser. Every group has its edge, its sense of in and out, and trickster is always there, at the gates of the city and the gates of life, making sure there is commerce. He also attends the internal boundaries by which groups articulate their social life. We constantly distinguish—right and wrong, sacred and profane, clean and dirty, male and female, young and old, living and dead—and in every case trickster will cross the line and confuse the distinction. Trickster is the creative idiot, therefore, the wise fool, the

gray-haired baby, the cross-dresser, the speaker of sacred profani-
ties. When someone's honorable behavior has left him unable to act,
trickster will appear to suggest an an amoral action, something
right/wrong that will get life going again. Trickster is the mythic
embodiment of ambiguity and ambivalence, doubleness and duplicity, contradiction and paradox.[10]

He concludes, "Here we have come back in a roundabout way to the earlier point: trickster belongs to polytheism or, lacking that, he needs at least
a relationship to other powers, to people and institutions and traditions
that can manage the odd double attitude of both insisting that their boundaries be respected and recognizing that in the long run their liveliness
depends on having those boundaries regularly disturbed."[11] Can it be that
modern society/the church/those in power/the West abhor such ambiguity and thus flee it?

The history of Christian/Native encounter would seem to indicate that
this is, in fact, the case. Wakdjunkaga, the Winnebago trickster figure, may,
in his early adventures, carry his enormous penis around in a box (thus
literally being "led around by his dick"), but Christian missionaries were
appalled by such frank discussions of the earthiness of human existence.
This sexualized aspect of Trickster, coupled with his doubleness, led these
Christ-bearers to denounce the figure so central to Native cultures. In their
efforts to subvert and undermine traditional Native concepts of deity, they
equated and confused Trickster with Satan. Such was, calculated or not,
a misrepresentation. As Hyde points out, "The Devil is an agent of evil,
but trickster is *a*moral, not *im*moral. He embodies and enacts that large
portion of our experience where good and evil are hopelessly intertwined.
He represents the paradoxical category of sacred amorality."[12] Or according to Paul Radin, the early anthropologist who recorded the Winnebago
trickster cycle: "Trickster is at one and the same time creator and destroyer,
giver and negator, he who dupes others and is always duped himself. . . .
He knows neither good nor evil yet he is responsible for both. He possesses no values, moral or social . . . yet through his actions all values come
into being."[13] Hyde concludes,

> "It might be argued that the passing of such a seemingly confused
> figure marks an advance in the spiritual consciousness of the race,
> a finer tuning of moral judgment; but the opposite could be argued

as well—that the erasure of trickster figures, or unthinking confusion of them with the Devil, only serves to push the ambiguities of life into the background. We may well hope that our actions carry no moral ambiguity, but pretending that is the case when it isn't does not lead to greater clarity about right and wrong; it more likely leads to unconscious cruelty masked by inflated righteousness."[14]

Anyone familiar with the history of Christian/Native encounter over more than five centuries will find little to dispute in Hyde's assessment.[15]

The missionaries who branded the tricksters they encountered in Native cultures as demonic showed that they themselves were blind to the tricksters in the biblical tradition. Not only is there an ancient Israelite trickster in the person of Jacob, but there are aspects of trickster evident in Jesus himself.

Jesus' trickster qualities were well recognized by early Christian authors as they searched for stories and metaphors to explain the Christ event. According to Luke's gospel, when Jesus was twelve, his parents took him to Jerusalem for Passover. After the festival, they depart for home, but Jesus has slipped away from them. Returning to the city to search for him, they find him three days later sitting among the teachers in the temple, listening and questioning them. When Mary asks him, "Child, why have you treated us like this? Look, your father and I have been searching for you in great anxiety," Jesus replies, "Why were you searching for me? Did you not know that I must be in my Father's house?" (Luke 2: 41–51). The incident is meant to illustrate Jesus' messianic mission from an early age. It is also, however, a trickster story. Jesus stealthily evades his parents and goes to the temple. When found out, his answer to his mother's question—which his parents did not understand—plays upon the term *father*—his father being Joseph but also Yahweh. In the noncanonical Gospel of the Infancy of Jesus, Jesus molds birds out of clay. When Joseph discovers him, he is furious that the boy is making idols. Jesus calls the birds to life, and they fly away. For this gospel author, it is a sign of the Messiah who does not yet understand his powers. Yet it is also the action of Trickster: caught in illicit activity, Jesus destroys the evidence of his transgression. Though the actions of Jesus with the birds would not conform to the image of Christ formalized in the Christian canon, are they really that different from those of the young Jesus, just beginning his ministry, turns water into wine at the wedding at Cana? (See John 2: 1–11).

Other aspects of Jesus' career demonstrate his affinity with Trickster. Trickster is perpetually on the move, just as Jesus is perpetually on the road, with no place to lay his head. Jesus is the antisocial disrupter of religious norms. He subverts expectations about not only what the Messiah is but what a holy person in first-century Palestine should be like. He loved a good party. He exercised his appetites and ate and drank with sinners and publicans. He deigned to have interaction with a despised Samaritan woman and preached of the *good* Samaritan, scandalizing the pious of his generation. He even gave healing, albeit reluctantly, to the Cyro-Phoenician (Canaanite) woman's child.

Healing is an important, but seldom understood, feature of trickster stories. Gerald Vizenor, the Native author who more than any other understands Trickster and writes about him with extreme sophistication, highlights this healing power. He offers readers compassionate tricksters who heal through story and humor.[16] Trickster stories are even sometimes used in healing rituals. Among the Navajos, according to Barre Toelken, "to tell such a story without such moral or medicinal motives does a kind of violence to it, and to the community."[17] Jesus' many healings may be mighty signs and wonders, but they also help mark him as Trickster.

In Matthew's gospel, the Pharisees seek to entrap Jesus. They go to him and ask if it is lawful to pay taxes to Caesar. It is a seemingly classic "no-win" situation. If Jesus says to pay taxes to Rome, he will infuriate Jewish nationalist interests. If he condemns the practice, he will be reported to Roman authorities for preaching sedition. But Jesus will not so easily be caught in the trap they have laid. He asks them to produce a coin and asks whose image is on it. When they reply, "Caesar's," he offers his retort, "Give to Caesar the things that are Caesar's, and give to God the things that are God's." The slippery Trickster has once again eluded his enemies. He will not so easily be captured and rendered tame.

Trickster is a boundary-crosser who moves between heaven and earth, living and dead, opening up possibilities for humanity that would not exist but for his transgression of these limits. He is a god who "makes a way out of no way." In Jesus, Natives see the ultimate boundary-crosser, erasing the barriers between heaven and earth, life and death. In his resurrection, he becomes the *pontifex maximus*, literally the great bridge builder, building a bridge between life—and life. Like Trickster, who is the spirit of the doorway leading out and the road beyond, Jesus is described as the "door" and the "way."

Finally, in the promised *parousia*, we see affinities with the tricksters and culture-heroes of Native America. Such figures often departed, and their return is anticipated. Quetzalcoatl left the people of Mexico, and the Aztec initially believed the coming of Cortés to be his return. Similarly, Lono withdrew from Hawaiians, and they took the arrival of Captain Cook to be their culture-hero coming back to them. Passamaquoddy and Micmac stories document the withdrawal of Glooskap from his people. They make it clear, however, that he did not die but only retreated. In the Passamaquoddy story, he is in his lodge, making arrows; when the wigwam is filled with arrows, he will return to make war, signaling the *eschaton*. According to the Micmac, he will return to his people when Whites have departed. Though both stories are unmistakably post-Contact, there is little doubt that they reflect older traditions.

Tricksters do sometimes die. In one Cheyenne story, Veeho starves to death. Miguel Méndez, in his classic novel *Pilgrims in Aztlán*, gives us a Yaqui trickster, Rosario Cuamea, who dies trying to rape Death. Maui and Tseg'sgin' are reported to have perished in similar fashion. Yet, as Alan Velie points out, "[I]t is understood by teller and audience that trickster will be alive in the next episode."[18] To tell a story is to rehearse it, to reenact it so that mythic time and chronological time merge. Sacred time is always present—in Native traditions as in Christianity.

Amer-European scholars are always ready to pronounce the oral traditions of Native cultures as artifacts. Hyde writes, "Outside of traditional contexts there are no modern tricksters because trickster only comes to life in the complex terrain of polytheism. If the spiritual world is dominated by a single high god opposed to a single embodiment of evil, then the ancient trickster disappears."[19] Yet, Native oral traditions, including those of Trickster, are very much alive. As with the Glooskap myths cited previously, they, like the myths of all living cultures, are constantly changing. Thus, in a Sioux myth, Coyote cheats a sharp-trading White man. In the Nicaraguan story cited above, Tiger gets his fortune, of which Hermano Anansi relieves him, by winning the lottery.

Trickster is in fact everywhere. He is Brer Rabbit, a melding of West African traditions with the Cherokee's Jisdu. On a more mass-culture level, he is even Bugs Bunny. Writers like Vizenor and Thomas King write stories and novels involving Trickster, thus continuing and changing the oral tradition. Trickster stories continue to be told to educate and entertain. Once more, Trickster has slipped through the fingers of those who would seek to destroy him.

I am, of course, not the first to suggest affinities between Jesus and Trickster. Sister Charles Palm, for example, in her book *Stories That Jesus Told: Dakota Way of Life*, draws parallels between specific myths involving Iktomi and Coyote and particular parables told by Jesus. She also rather curiously equates an incident in the career of the great Cheyenne culture-hero and prophet Sweet Medicine, who gave his people the Sacred Arrows, with the parable of the sower and the seed.[20] Unlike her work, however, which drew simple and questionable equations in order to teach Sioux preschoolers Christian stories, I hope I am making a more nuanced and significant point. I affirm the sacrality of stories from the Native oral tradition. I am not suggesting simple parallels between trickster stories and incidents reported by the gospel writers about the life and work of Jesus. I only hope to show the importance of Trickster in Native cultures and open up a space for Native Christians to bring this part of their traditions into their Christian thinking and experience. By pointing out the trickster characteristics of Jacob or Jesus, I want to illustrate that trickster discourse has something vital and important to tell us about the nature of the Christ event and of ultimate reality itself.

Trickster is a transgressor of boundaries and limits. He is a liar and a thief. Yet even this is to a purpose. As Hyde observes:

> Our ideas about property and theft depend on a set of assumptions about how the world is divided up. Trickster's lies and thefts challenge those premises and in so doing reveal their artifice and suggest alternatives. One of the West African tricksters, Legba, has been well described in this regard as 'a mediator' who works 'by means of a lie that is really a truth, a deception that is in fact a revelation'.... It is in this sense that his lies subvert what seemed so clear a truth just moments ago. Suddenly the old verities are up for grabs.... Who gave all of Pennsylvania to William Penn?[21]

Who gave Josiah's cattle to the White rancher in Leslie Marmon Silko's novel *Ceremony*? Trickster opens up the space to ask all the nasty, unanswerable questions about Amer-European occupation of the Americas.

Trickster is a transgressor of boundaries and limits. He subverts expectations and disrupts social norms. Howard Norman writes, "His presence demands, cries out for, compassion and generosity toward existence itself. Trickster is a celebrator of life, a celebration of life, because by rallying against him a community discovers its own resilience and protective skills."[22] Jesus, too, came enjoying and proclaiming life, and that abundantly. Like Trickster, he indulged his appetites. He was a wine bibber and a glutton. Like those of Jesus, Trickster's exploits continue to be told. They still teach societal mores and taboos and the dangers of ignoring them. But they are also, above all, entertaining. Whitestream Christians acknowledge Jesus' healings and compassion. They affirm his life and his Passion. Can they also embrace and revel in his humor and his passions? Can they believe in God as both constant and capricious? Can they recognize deity for the trickster that it is?

CHAPTER EIGHTEEN

REACHING BEYOND LANGUAGE

Native American Eschatology and Apocalyptic Messianism

Without that deadly talent for being in the right place at the right time, evil must suffer defeat. And with each defeat, Doomsday is postponed . . . for at least one more day.

CONTROL,
"The Outer Limits"

How many of you, my readers, by a show of thoughts, believe that the world will end? In asking such a question, I am referring neither to an atomic or environmental cataclysm brought upon humanity by its own actions nor to some remote, entropic end, following our sun going nova millions or billions of years from now. I speak of some imminent, divinely hastened termination or cleansing, perhaps preceding a regeneration. If you are at all representative of the American public at large, between 30 and 50 percent of you believe in the end of history as supposedly foretold in the Bible.

Beyond any purely prurient or voyeuristic interest, however, that statistic alone makes the study of eschatology an important one. Further, besides Jewish-Christian traditions, other groups within the multicultural fabric of the United States have teachings or beliefs about an end-time. Islam, Buddhism, and numerous other religions all have their own forms of eschatological thinking. In addition, many Native American traditions preserve stories about the end of the world. Today, Native Christians, like their non-Native co-religionists, may await expectantly the *parousia* of

Christ and the accompanying judgment, as indeed they have since first conversion hundreds of years ago. Despite, however, what historian Homer Noley calls "the first White frost" (in his book of the same title), the imposition of Christianity upon Native American cultures, these hopes can take a decidedly Native spin. More than five hundred years of ongoing contact with Amer-European culture and Christianity has led to "fractured myths," as William McLoughlin terms them, accounts that reflect a syncretism of traditional beliefs with Christian mythology, creating new, blended accounts. And since contact, there have arisen numerous messianic movements among America's indigenes that look forward to an end of history on its current trajectory. Such streams of apocalyptic thought, however, are only parts of broader deltas of eschatological belief that long predate the advent of Europeans on this continent.

Despite the importance of eschatological thinking in many Native religious traditions, it has heretofore received very little in the way of analysis at either the popular or scholarly level. Creation myths have been the subject both of anthologies and academic study. Yet work on end-time beliefs has been almost totally lacking, despite the fact that, in many instances, creation and eschaton are homologues: the world had a beginning, so it will have an end. An exception is a fair amount of scattered work on Native apocalyptic movements, to which we will turn later.

The reasons for this dearth are not immediately apparent, especially given the close relationship of protology and eschatology. Study of Native end-time myths leads to two conclusions. The first concerns the relative prevalence of eschatologies across the many, diverse Native traditions in the Americas. Although nearly every tribe has at least one (and sometimes multiple) accounts of creation, not every culture has the concomitant eschatological myth. Second, creation myths are essentially positive in character. The world comes into being, and human history proceeds on its course from that event. By contrast, eschaton can be viewed as essentially negative. The world, or at least human history as we know it, terminates abruptly and, from a solely Western, humanist point of view, prematurely. Although Native myths about the beginning may make charming children's stories or be readily assimilable into New Age stews of spirituality, foretellings of the end are not so easily rendered tame. Put simply, such accounts are just not as much fun to contemplate. Further, since Christians view the impending apocalypse as essentially salvific in character, non-Christian eschatologies are not as instantly comparable to their Jewish-Christian counterparts as are origin stories.

These eschatological myths and apocalyptic movements operate on a semiotic field bounded alternately by knowledge and uncertainty. Human beings require knowledge and meaning. The end cannot be known, so eschatological or apocalyptic myths seek to complete knowledge, to fill it in, to do away with the uncertainty. If knowledge were, in fact, complete, there would be no need for such myths. So Natives extrapolated the end from what they did know—from the cycles of the seasons, the continual decay and rebirth of the earth and vegetation, the phases of the moon, the course of human life, and from their own creation myths. Creation and eschaton become homologues. Because the end is, by its very nature, in the future, it is what I term history *sans prenom*, that is to say, history without an historical antecedent. *Eschaton* or apocalypse is thus an historicized ahistory. It is creation projected forward, undone, perhaps only to be redone. As performance artist Laurie Anderson declared in "The Dream Before," "What is history? It is an angel, being blown backwards into the future."[1]

I have already noted that not every tribal tradition concerns itself with the end-times. For instance, in the Cherokee oral tradition, there is not a consideration of the end of the world. I believe, however, three stories reveal the eschatological imagination at work.

According to the Cherokee creation myth, the earth is an island fastened to the sky by four cords at its corners. If the cords break, the earth would sink back into the oceans. In the version included by Bierlein, there is some vague expectation of the event in the future and a promise of regeneration: "Some day, once the rawhide has grown old, it will crack and break and the earth will fall back into the waters and life will come to an end. Then, just like the last time, the creator will bring the earth back from the waters and recreate the world and life will start again."[2] Both expectation and foretold regenesis, however, are totally absent from other tellings, including Mooney.

The second concerns the theft of the eternal flame of the Cherokees. When the world was young, a conjurer stole the sacred fire and transformed it into quartz crystals in which the future could be seen. When the conjurer held the crystals in his hands, the sacred fire would come out of them and reveal the way of the Cherokees. The tribe sent a young boy to recover the fire. He tricked the thief by asking to see the People's future. As the flames sprang forth, the boy threw sacred tobacco onto the fire and the evildoer was consumed. Evil was imprisoned in the fire. As long as the sacred fire burns, the Cherokees will survive as a people.[3] The flame was carried to Oklahoma along the Trail of Tears.

Both stories have, I believe, within them what I term an unrealized eschatological potential, that is, myths that may hint at a potential end but where none is prophesied or necessarily expected. After all, it is possible to envision a time when the cords holding up the earth will fray and break or when the eternal flame will go out. A similar potential is witnessed in a story involving Tseg'sgin', one of the Cherokee trickster figures. The story is a model of concise storytelling, running only: "Tseg'sgin' tried to make love to Death. And he died. That's all." The story is recent in origin and can be traced, I believe, to the advent of AIDS. It has certain similarities to older stories, already noted in the previous chapter, told about Maui, the Native Hawaiian trickster, and the Yaqui Rosario Cuamea in Miguel Méndez's novel *Pilgrims in Aztlán*.[4] It encompasses both the universality of death and the possibility of annihilation due to the epidemic.

Other Indian traditions, as well, preserve stories with this unrealized eschatological potential, stories in which it is at least possible to contemplate imaginatively the end of the world. For instance, the Tshimshians believe that an Atlas-like strongman holds the world up on a hemlock pole. When the man shrugs or falters, earthquakes occur. Should he collapse, the world will be destroyed, and all will perish. Likewise, the Winnebago are not to speak about their Medicine Rite "until the world comes to an end." There is even an injunction that divulging the ritual to outsiders will *cause* the event.[5]

Most often this end of the world is seen as a natural event. It is viewed simply as a part of the order of the cosmos, the mirror image of creation. The world had a beginning, so it will have an end. As the Lakotas say, "Only the rocks and mountains last forever." An example of this natural conclusion is the Okanogan prophecy of the end of the world recorded by Ella Clark and reprinted by Paula Gunn Allen in *Spider Woman's Granddaughters*. According to Okanogan tradition, in the time to come the lakes will eventually melt the foundation of the world, and the rivers will cut it lose. The earth will float away, and that will be the end of the world.[6]

These are all examples of what I have called unrealized eschatological potential. There is no guarantee that any of these events will necessarily occur or when. Other tribes, however, have more developed eschatological traditions. It is often argued that these stories are post-Contact products, reflecting exposure to Jewish/Christian myths concerning the eschaton. We have too often seen, however, the overeagerness of non-Natives to attribute things in Indian cultures to contact with Europeans. While I agree that it is, at this late date, impossible to determine with certainty whether these stories were part of tribal cultures prior to the invasion by Europeans, I believe that the stronger case to be made is that they do reflect genuine pre-Contact tradition. There is no need to go to a diffusionist interpretation or to rehearse the old *kultukreis* debate.

I base this on a number of related considerations. First, very little, if anything, in many of these stories reflects an Amer-European worldview. Nor are there particular Jewish/Christian elements or motifs. Third, isn't it likely that similar cultural thanatic fears and hopes for something better would produce stories in the Native societies as well as in those of Europe or the so-called Middle East? Central to eschatological dis-ease is an understanding of the contingency of existence. To phrase the point differently, very few scholars today would contend that accounts of a flood, present in many diverse Indian cultures, were derived from the myth of Noah; why then must we assume that eschatological thinking is of European origin? Finally, there is a marked difference between accounts of "last things" that I would label pre-Contact and those which clearly are post-Contact. This, I would argue, demonstrates a discernible change caused by the very presence of the invader and exposure to that invader's myths, moving to a recognizable apocalyptic structure. So now I want to turn to examine Native eschatological and apocalyptic accounts, beginning first with those for which I believe the best case can be made for being part of tradition prior to Contact.

Pre-Contact myths, by my definition, can be grouped into two broad categories. These categories overlap, and it is sometimes hard to put a given myth in one class or the other. The first group is composed of what I call moral cautionary tales. The closest (though very much imperfect) equivalent to these stories in the Jewish-Christian tradition might be the biblical myth of Noah, wherein the world order is destroyed by Yahweh because of the irredeemable wickedness of humanity. The second category is the natural/cyclical, reflecting traditional Native concepts of the cyclical, circular nature of time and reality.

A Pomo creation story from California bridges unrealized eschatological potential with the first category. After Madumda creates humans, they began to misbehave, "killing each other and ignoring their children," so Madumda sweeps them away in a deluge. A second attempt at humanity fails, and he destroys them with fire. Two more tries end similarly, leading to destruction by ice and wind. After a fifth creation, Madumda gives the different peoples he has created their original instructions. He then departs, "warning the people to behave." The myth ends, "So this is our last chance."[7] Given the outcome of the four previous humanities, it is easy to contemplate yet another divine cleansing. Madumda's warning adds a moral cautionary element and a knowledge for humans that no more opportunities will be offered.

A Northern Cheyenne belief is more typical of the moral cautionary type. According to the Cheyennes, there is a pole in the far north upon which the world rests. At the base of the pole is a snow-white beaver. Whenever the people make the beaver angry, it gnaws at the pole. The pole is, according to the account of Mrs. Medicine Bull, already more than half-eaten away. When Grandfather Beaver chews through the last bit of post, "the earth will crash into a bottomless nothing. That will be the end of the people, of everything. The end of all ends." The myth also contains an aetiological component, explaining why Cheyennes do not eat beaver meat and even avoid touching a beaver pelt. A slightly different telling, minus the aetiological point, was mentioned by A. L. Kroeber in 1900.[8]

A Chiricahua Apache prophecy, recorded by Opler, relates that in time to come there will be severe droughts. The water will dry up until there are only springs at a few places. People will congregate at those places and begin to fight over water. This will continue until they all kill each other off. In this way the world ends. The anonymous Chiricahua informant adds that maybe "a few good people" will be left. He or she then adds a curious comment about this remnant: "When the new world comes after that the white people will be Indians and the Indians will be white people."[9] Opler also related an apparently more naturalistic end-time scenario from the Jicarilla Apache, absent the moral cautionary element. It states simply, "The heart of the world is also near Taos Pueblo. Some time, at the end of the world, that place will start to burn. The fire will spread to all the world."[10]

One of the most intriguing stories, fitting this category but moving into the apocalyptic, is a Passamaquoddy account concerning Glooskap, their culture-hero. After Glooskap's departure from the People, he takes up residence in a great lodge. There he spends all his time making arrows and allows no one to enter. One side of the structure is now filled with arrows. "When it is all quite full, he will come forth and make war. . . . He will make war on all, kill all; there will be no more world—world all gone." The battle will be against Glooskap's evil twin, Malsum the Wolf, and all the wicked. The storyteller states that it is not known when Glooskap will return for this final battle. It could be soon or distant.

The story was told by a Mrs. Le Cool and set down by Mrs. W. Wallace Brown, the wife of an Indian agent for the tribe, and is included by folklorist Charles G. Leland in his 1884 work, *The Algonquin Legends of New England*. Leland is so determined to find European antecedents for this story that he spends three pages to demonstrate that the Indians "have taken it from the Norse."[11] In this, though he fails to state it explicitly, Leland seems to be relying on Snorri Sturluson's account of the binding of Loki, the Norse trickster, which precedes the apocalypse of Ragnarök (and the account of Ragnarök itself) in Sturluson's prose *Edda*, written in the thirteenth century. If so, his source material is already corrupted: Sturluson was a Christian who disdained the older mythology, and his work reflects a strong Christian bias.[12]

According to Leland, the last battle will usher in "the eternal happy hunting-grounds."[13] But this is clearly an Amer-European imposition upon the text and, like Leland's conclusions as to the myth's origin, must be discounted. Thomas Parkhill does a credible job of deconstructing Leland in his recent book *Weaving Ourselves into the Land: Charles Godfrey Leland, "Indians," and the Study of Native American Religions*.[14]

According to Micmac variants, recorded by Jeanne Guillemin between 1969 and 1971, Glooskap (or Gluscap) withdrew from his people after European incursion ("He didn't die. He was just very angry with the English."). Guillemin, adding a universalist spin from the vantage point of late modernity, writes:

> *Gluscap* it must be noted, is not dead, only on retreat. I have been assured by a a good many Micmac storytellers that when White people have gone away, *Gluscap* will return once more and the Indians

will again thrive. This prophecy never seemed to me a vainglorious fantasy of Indian resurgency. The Micmac have never really had anything more than an unassuming, even diminutive claim on survival. The return of *Gluscap* is, to my mind, a metaphor for another truly postindustrial age when, corporations having disintegrated, everyone will be required to search out human-scale solutions to existence; we shall all be Indians then.[15]

The second category of eschatological myth is composed of those accounts in which there is a cycle of destruction and renewal. Such stories are familiar from the Mayan, Aztec, and other Meso-American civilizations. There were numerous accounts of world transformations at the passing of cyclical epochs. These epochs passed in great cataclysms followed by regenesis. The cycle was seen as continuous and was predicted for the future as well as described in the past. Interestingly, in the Mayan and Aztec instances, human agency could forestall the impending end, usually through sacrifice. In the case of the Aztec, Huitzilopotchli, their principal deity, the Sun and god of war, required blood if he were to continue to rise and the new epoch avoided.

Cyclical thinking was natural to indigenous peoples who saw the cycle of the seasons with its perpetual circle of degeneration, death, and new birth. The end of the world order then was seen in similar terms. Out of ekpyrosis comes metacomesis, or renewal. This is the mode of thought detailed by Mircea Eliade in his concept of "the myth of eternal return." It announces the triumph of cosmology over mere chronology. For the land-oriented Natives, it was the victory of place over history.

This mode of thinking can also be seen in several North American tribes. Tied to the cycle of nature is a Lakota description of the end of the world. According to an account given by Jenny Leading Cloud to Richard Erdoes in 1967, an old woman and her dog live in a hidden cave on the edge of the Badlands. The woman works at her quilling, making a blanket strip in the traditional manner. The dog, Shunka Sapa, never takes his eyes from the woman. Periodically, the woman must stop her work and get up to tend a pot of *wojapi*, berry soup, on a nearby fire. Whenever she turns her back, the dog undoes the work she has just accomplished: "This way she never makes any progress, and her quillwork remains forever unfinished." According to Leading Cloud, the old people used to say that if the woman ever finished her work "then at the very moment that she threads the last porcupine quill to complete the design, the world will come to an end."[16]

What at first impression may seem simple, naïve, merely clever is, in fact, complex. Much more is at work than meets the casual gaze. This Sioux dog story contains nothing teleological. It is *anti*-teleological. There is no need for the world to come to an end, an example of unrealized eschatological potential. According to Edward Ingebretsen in his book *Maps of Heaven, Maps of Hell*, "Although a thin line separates Holy and Horrific, it also joins them. The sacred and the taboo are necessarily linked at the edge, or beyond the edge, of speech. There culture sets up night watch over its boundaries."[17] The dog and the old woman are inexorably linked. Their fates are joined one to the other. Each needs the other in their eternal choreography. The myth depicts a struggle to hold a temporal but also a social boundary. The land that the dog and crone "patrol is the contested ideological space in which a society charts, and occasionally redraws, its cosmological, theological, and social maps."[18] Thanks to the dog, however, the map is never withdrawn.

A number of tribes have their origins in flood. For example, the Haidas trace their origins to a flood that covered the earth and forced the Indians to disperse into tribes. Likewise, the Pimas find their beginnings in a flood, after which the Hohokam people, ancestors of the Pimas, arose. These are not creation myths as much as they are also accounts of the destruction of one world order and the birth of a new. In both of the cited cases, there were people and a society before the floods came.

A similar story from the Sicangu Sioux was recorded by Erdoes from Leonard Crow Dog at Rosebud in 1974. The myth, much like the Pomo story limned earlier, details the creation and destruction of two previous worlds before this present reality. After creating this, the third world, the Creating Power says, "Now, if you have learned how to behave like human beings and how to live in peace with each other and with the other living things—the two-legged, the four-legged, the many-legged, the fliers, the no-legs, the green plants of this universe—then all will be well. But if you make this world bad and ugly, then I will destroy this world too. It's up to you." Then, according to Crow Dog, the Creating Power— not White Buffalo Calf Woman—gave them the pipe and enjoined them to live by it. "'Someday there might be a fourth world,' the Creating Power thought. Then he rested."[19]

Crow Dog is a traditional medicine man and a peyote road man. He is vocally anti-Christian. It is interesting, then, that a close reading of this story reveals it to be a fractured myth with clearly identifiable Christian tropes (e.g., the rainbow as a covenant that the world will not again be destroyed by flood as had the second world, an anthropomorphic "Creating Power," and that power "resting" after creative event). Even so, it also appears to contain pre-Contact elements. It stands in the eschatological tradition of periodic destruction and rebirth, and it also resembles the flood stories discussed previously, with the addition, however, of a moral cautionary element. There is also a striking similarity to the Hopi account of the four worlds, which will be discussed below.

These, then, in brief are the two main strands of Native eschatology in traditional myth, the moral cautionary and the natural/cyclical. This review was necessary to provide a framework for what follows. Both of these strains continue after Contact. Like much else about the life of America's indigenous persons, however, they would be inevitably and forever changed by that Contact. Let's turn, then, to examples of Native eschatology and apocalyptic that are definitely post-Contact.

The Wintus have developed strong eschatological traditions since Contact. In her autobiography, "Out of the Past" (published in 1941), Lucy Young told of a prophecy of her grandfather, who was gifted with the power of second sight. Before the coming of Whites, he had a dream in which a great White rabbit devoured the Indians' grass, seed, living. "We won't have nothing more, this world," the man said. Though scoffed at by his family, he predicted that his grandchildren would see it come to pass.[20] In the 1920s, years before the publication of Young's story, a Wintu medicine woman, Kate Luckie, told Cora DuBois, "When the Indians all die, then God will let the water come down from the north. Everyone will drown. That is because the white people never cared for land or deer or bear."[21] It is similar to the Sicangu story discussed above. Here the cautionary warning to care for the rest of creation is linked with an implicit admonition to Whites to encourage Indian survival.

This warning can also be seen by Ray Young Bear, a Mesquakie, in his book *Remnants of the First Earth*, already discussed in chapter 4. Speaking in a manner typical of world-renewal religions generally, Young Bear writes:

> Our sole obligation, my grandmother instructed, in having been created in the first place by the Holy Grandfather, is to maintain the Principal Religion of the Earthlodge clans. It was agreed eons and eons ago that if these ceremonies [for the renewal of the world] were not performed, the world would no longer be held together, the elements of wind and ice would whirl together and splinter us apart. Our forgetfulness, in other words, would become part of a chain of natural and man-made catastrophes—flag wars and ecological suffocation—leading to the end of the earth. And the people who so connivingly and viciously sought to make us forget ourselves by subjugating us, the Euro-Americans, would be the root cause.
>
> It is therefore prophesied that by making us forget who we are, they inevitably kill themselves.[22]

The Zuñis: Self-Portrayals, published in 1972, contains a warning that humanity will bring its end upon itself. Examining Amer-European values, it is a cautionary prophecy in which one can hear the ring of the Hebrew prophets. It is worth quoting at length:

> Many years ago when our grandparents foresaw what our future would be like, they spoke their prophecies among themselves and passed them on to the children before them.
>
> "Cities will progress and then decay to the ways of the lowest beings. Drinkers of dark liquids will come upon the land, speaking nonsense and filth. Then the end shall be nearer.
>
> "Population will increase until the land can hold no more. The tribes of men will mix. The dark liquids they drink will cause the people to fight among themselves. Families will break up: father against children and the children against one another.
>
> "Maybe when the people have outdone themselves, then maybe, the stars will fall upon the land, or drops of hot water will rain upon the earth. Or the land will turn under. Or our father, the sun, will not rise to start the day. Then our possessions will turn into beasts and devour us whole.

"If not, there will be an odor from gasses, which will fill the air we breathe, and the end for us shall come.

"But the people themselves will bring upon themselves what they receive. From what has resulted, time alone will tell what the future holds for us."[23]

A similar end is envisioned by Sioux holy man Asa Primeaux, Sr., in an article by Elizabeth Cook-Lynn. According to him, the end will be caused by the continued use of the earth in a non-sacred way for the increasing demands of technological society. He states, "Getting everything out of the earth, the gas and the oil, is making the world hollow, off-balance. One of these days the gases will be ignited and they will blow up the world."[24]

In 1974, Frank Fools Crow, a traditional Sioux medicine man, told T. E. Mails that "the end times are upon us." These thoughts began to come upon him during World War II. He said, "Sometimes we gathered together and sat up all night talking about the war, and about how the world might be coming to an end as our forefathers predicted it one day would. We were warned that when the end of the world comes, the entire earth would burn. And now strange things were happening. There were more and more people on earth every year, and the wars were more frequent and terrible." Then in 1965, Fools Crow was given a vision at Bear Butte. He stated that "God did tell me that the end of the world, as we have known it, is coming to a close." According to the prophecy, it will not end "exactly as the Bible says." Only the Creator knows how and when. Currently, said Fools Crow, White Buffalo Calf Woman, the savior-figure who gave the Lakota the sacred pipe and their sacred ceremonies, has returned and "in the company of another young lady is walking about our country."[25] This signals that the end of the world is not far off. Fools Crow's vision proves the truth of Ingebretsen's assertion, "While theological (apocalyptic) narratives of the Divine move to apparent confirmation—comfort and reassurance—in the *eschaton*, in actuality they provide ongoing examples of disconfirmation and imbalance."[26] There is never any actual closure. As Frank Kermode argues in *The Sense of an Ending*, "the end is always deferred; Jesus is always coming but never here."[27] White Buffalo Calf Woman and her mysterious companion are always about but never quite here any more than Christ is. Or any more than the raised-up ancestors of the Ghost Dance were. It demonstrates the terror of teleology.

The Hopi accounts of the destruction of the three previous worlds and the imminent this, the fourth world, are now fairly well known. This is due largely to the efforts of the Hopis themselves, since 1948, to disseminate the story and prophetically call the world to *metanoia*. Though the account may have its origins in pre-Contact times and fits in the natural/cyclical category described previously, Contact and recent world events, including ecological devastation, nuclear weapons, and overpopulation, have given the prophecy new interpretations and new urgency. These are chronicled by Danish scholar Armin Geertz in his book *The Invention of Prophecy*.[28]

The prophecy states that the present fourth world will end after slipping into a period of *koyaanisquatsi*, literally "life out of balance" and more generally "chaos." A complex set of omens will signal that the end is near. Many of these have already been fulfilled. These include the Hopis being surrounded by light (interpreted as the growth of the cities of Flagstaff and Winslow), the sun turning black (air pollution), the falling to the ground of a gourd of ashes (the use of the atomic bomb on Hiroshima and Nagasaki), the unbalancing of the seasons (general environmental imbalance and global warming), travel through the sky (airplanes), communication through a cobweb covering the earth (telecommunication, or perhaps the World Wide Web), futile attempts by Hopi elders to enter a house of mica (refusal to allow the Hopis to address the United Nations—they were finally permitted in 1993), and the dancing of the Blue Kachina—the only unfulfilled prophecy and, interestingly, the only uninterpreted one. When all these omens have come to pass, the world will enter a period known as the "Great Purification." After that, the world will be reborn out of Hopiland. Corn and water, both sacred to the Hopis, will be plentiful. But the path of White people disappears.

Syncretic Native religious movements have demonstrated the most profoundly apocalyptic caste, combining elements of both Native and Christian eschatology. These include the Prophet Dance, Tschaddam (or the Indian Shakers), and certain peyotist groups. Probably the foremost of these is the Ghost Dance. In the remainder of this chapter, I want to briefly look at a number of these.

As a rather peculiar way of entering into them, let me note that Paul Tillich claimed that the incident at Caesarea Philippi was the center of the gospel and the heart of the Christian faith. He places the heart in Peter's answer, "Thou art the Christ."[29] For Native Americans, however, the core is in the question itself, "Who do you say I am?" In 1925, E. Stanley Jones, a White missionary to India, wrote a book entitled *The Christ of the Indian Road*, dealing with "how Christ is becoming naturalized upon the Indian Road."[30] For Native Christians, and for adherents to the syncretic movements, the task is to discern the Christ of the Red Road. There are, in fact, many answers for Natives to Jesus' purported question at Caesarea Philippi. But, again, for my purposes, the answer is very specific. For these movements Jesus is the triumphant, eschatological Christ.

Before proceeding to these apocalyptic movements, it is necessary to note that there is a strain of messianic thought in Indian spiritual concepts independent of Jesus. By "messianic" I mean a hoped for deliverer or leader—as Vine Deloria, Jr., puts it, a "radical intervention by God in history"—a heavenly savior figure whose advent somehow brings the present age to a close. There are messianic elements, for instance, in the accounts of Quetzalcoatl of Meso-America, Degandawida and Hiawatha of the Iroquois, Pahana of the Hopi, in the Taki Onqoy (or Sickness Dance) of the Inca, and in historical leaders such as Popé of the Pueblo Revolt, Geronimo, Sweet Medicine, or Crazy Horse, among others. What sets these latter historical figures apart from Jesus, however, as Deloria points out, is that none of these culture-heroes ever "become the object of individual attention as to the efficacy in either the facts of their existence or their present supertemporal ability to affect events."[31]

I want to now highlight a few—and only a few—of the syncretic movements. Each of these is a crisis movement. Often they had a decidedly chiliastic aspect. As such, they belong to the strains of Native apocalyptic. Also, often, they are referred to together under the collective title *Ghost Dance movements*. However, for the sake of precision, I prefer to reserve that term for the 1870 and 1889–90 movements in the West, which were actually called that. I prefer to use the collective term *raising-up movements* for others, since the salient feature is generally the raising up of the dead ancestors.

In 1762, Neolin, also known simply as the Delaware Prophet, appeared among the Delawares, exhorting them to a confederation of all Indian nations to drive Whites back from the land from which they came. Indians were also to give up everything they had learned or received from Whites and return to the old ways. The prophet stated that he had received this vision from the Master of Life, who promised to give them success.

In the hands of Pontiac, an Ottawa, the prophecy led to a widespread Indian rebellion in the Great Lakes region.

In 1805, another prophet arose, this time among the Shawnees. Tenskwatawa, meaning "the open door," was the brother of Tecumseh. The prophet claimed to have a new revelation from the Master of Life. The message was essentially the same as that received by the Delaware Prophet. If Indians forsook White ways and drove Whites from their territory, they would find favor. Game would return to their land and their dead friends and relatives would be restored to them. The prophet was proclaimed to be the incarnation of Manabozho, the Algonkian culture-hero. His message received widespread acceptance among Native nations and gained adherents from Florida to Saskatchewan, undergoing local variations as it went.

It was particularly effective among the Cherokees, where, a medicine man named (according to Elias Boudinot) Tsali and two others received a vision of heavenly sent Indians who warned that Corn Mother was angry with the Cherokees for abandoning her ways and counseled a rejection of the White path; otherwise they would be destroyed. The prophet threatened to invoke a terrible storm, which would eradicate all but true believers in the new message. (Another sign mentioned by the prophets was that the earth would shake. And in 1811 the greatest earthquake ever to hit the North American continent struck on the New Madrid fault in Missouri. It was so powerful it caused the Mississippi River to flow backwards and rang church bells in Baltimore.) The story, related by James Mooney, of the "Removed Townhouses" probably dates from this period.

Long before Removal, the Cherokees heard the voices of the Nûñnehí, the immortal ones who were like the Cherokees, only invisible, warning of all the wars and misfortunes that were to come. They invited the Cherokees to come live with them and gave them detailed instructions about what they must do if they were to do so. Two towns followed the instructions and were borne away. When the Cherokees were removed from Georgia, they had the deepest regret because they were forced to leave behind their relatives who had gone to the Nûñnehí.[32]

In fact, many prophets and prophecies arose among the Cherokees at this time. According to McLoughlin, "Had the more immediate problem of war on their borders not forced attention to more mundane matters . . . this movement might eventually have produced a single charismatic prophet who, like Tenskwatawa among the Shawnees or Handsome Lake among the Senecas, could have correlated all the feelings and half-articulated hopes and fears of the believers into a single, coherent, and compelling message around which the nation might have rallied. But no such prophet appeared. Many minor prophets rose and fell as their prophecies failed to materialize," and power eventually returned to secular leadership.[33]

The Apaches have also experienced similar raising-up movements. In 1883, among the Cibecues, after confinement on reservations, a medicine man with Lightning power named Nakaidklini claimed to be able to raise the Apache dead to fight the Whites. He was killed after a short-lived uprising before the movement became widespread. From 1903 until 1907, they experienced a movement called dahgodi•yáh' ("rising upwards" or "they will be raised up"). A Lightning medicine man again led it. Called Daslahdn, he received a vision that he was to "lead the people up" into the sky after appropriate ceremonies. According to Jorge Noriega, there the people "would find a new world, and be free from the hatred, war and corruption of the old one," and there "wild fruits would be ripe all the time."[34] After the mysterious death of Daslahdn in 1906, the movement continued, spreading to the White Mountain Apaches from the Cibecues, but dwindled the following year. Also according to Noriega, the movement, though essentially traditionalist in origin, was the first to incorporate both Apache and Christian religions.[35]

Numerous syncretic religions, combining indigenous and Christian elements, contain distinctive messianic elements. Once again, only brief sketches of a few may be given.

Following the American Revolution, a reformer of the teachings of Hiawatha and Degandawida arose among the Senecas. In 1799, Ganiodayo, or Handsome Lake, an alcohol-ridden old man fell into a trance and was guided on a Dantesque journey, presumably by Teharonhiawagon, the primal being of life on earth. He emerged revived, preaching reform of the Iroquois religion. The trip included a White inferno and a meeting with Jesus, envisioned by him as an eschatological messiah who, rejected, has gone to bar the gates of heaven until his avenging return. Instead of a personal savior, however, Ganiodayo encounters Jesus as a fellow teacher, meeting him—to use biblical language—"face to face, as friend to friend."

Around the 1830s, a prophet named Bini, meaning *mind*, arose among the Wetsuwet'en people of what is now British Columbia. Repeatedly "lying as if dead" and returning to life, he could speak the language of the dead. He stated, "I went up to the sky and talked to God, who told me that his house would come down to this world and make it a happy place to live in. He ordered me to teach this song which you must continue to sing day after day, until the God's house descends."[36] He also delivered a variation on the Ten Commandments (one of which was: do not kill anyone by sorcery). According to Antonia Mills in *Eagle Down Is Our Law*, "The descent of God's house from the sky parallelled [sic] both the descent of a house which Sa (the Sun) had prepared for his earthly sons in an ancient Witsuwit'en kungax [oral tradition] and New Testament prophecies. In travelling to the sky world, Bini was becoming like the sons of Sa in the kungax as well as like the son of God in the New Testament—he was able to transcend the earth and to enter the kingdom of the heavenly father."[37] Unfortunately, instead of the bliss predicted by Bini, smallpox struck. When it did attack, he gathered the people together and had them dance. He ringed them with a rope, instructing that if the rope were broken many would die. According to contemporary accounts, one woman unintentionally touched and broke it, and shortly thereafter many of the village were stricken. Bini's vision eventually spread south, becoming the basis of the Prophet Dance on the Columbia Plateau and thus, at least indirectly, influencing the Ghost Dance.

Among the Natives of the Pacific Northwest, there is a syncretic religion with decidedly greater borrowings from Christianity. This is Tschaddam, or Indian Shaker religion. Having no relationship with the Christian sect of the same name, this is a revelatory, highly ritualized syncretic faith that considers itself a Christian denomination.

The church was founded by Squ-sacht-un (or John Slocum), a Squaxin, who, depending upon the account and point of view, either died or fell into a trance in 1881. He ascended to heaven where he was refused admittance because of his profligacy. Given the choice between going to hell or returning to earth and leading a righteous life and teaching others to do the same, he chose the latter.

Jesus occupies a leading place in Shakerism. He is affirmed as the Son of God, a member of the Trinity, and the Savior of humankind. His passion is fully accepted. His ultimate judgment is accepted, and such time will be a day of happiness and well-being when humanity will be healed. Shakers, however, do not accept the Bible as scripture. They believe

Slocum received direct revelation from Jesus Christ. The Bible is thus only history, an obsolete text for use only by Whites.[38]

One of the most unusual apocalyptic movements was that of Louis Riel during the Northwest Resistance in 1885. Louis Riel was the leader of the Métis, or mixed blood, people in the Red River country of western Canada. Continuing the resistance to the encroachments of the Hudson's Bay Company and the new Canadian government begun by his father, Riel led a revolt of Métis in 1870, seizing Fort Garry, a Hudson's Bay outpost in Manitoba, and establishing a provisional government. Negotiations promised the Métis amnesty and the ability to purchase land, but these terms were revoked when it was discovered that the Métis had executed a White captive. A military force was sent to retake Fort Garry, the Natives dispersed, and the rebellion ended. Riel eventually took refuge in the United States, becoming an American citizen.

Riel returned in 1885 and led the fight against White migration into present-day Saskatchewan, in what Canadians call the Northwest Rebellion and Métis term the Northwest Resistance. After initial success, the rebellion was quelled. Riel was captured and put on trial for treason. In an illegal (Riel was a U.S. citizen) and very probably rigged proceeding, the Métis leader was convicted. He was hung on November 16, 1885.[39]

Riel's rebellion had a millenarian caste to it. This stemmed from a vision Riel had in 1876. He identified himself with the biblical King David, and his vision was distinctly post-millenialist. Riel believed that humanity was living in the third and last epoch of the Kingdom of God, the epoch of the Holy Spirit (after the epochs of the Father and the Son). The new era dawned in 1876 (when he began his messianic mission). At that time spiritual leadership and authority passed from Rome to Montreal, the first residence of the Holy Spirit in the New World. After 457 years, it would move to St. Vital or St. Boniface in Manitoba. The Métis would be delivered from their present state of oppression. They would lead Manitoba, which would become the leading place in the new order. Catholics and Protestants would be reconciled and world peace established after a series of disastrous wars. The "true religion" would triumph. All of this would culminate in Christ's return. That return would take place after 457 plus 1876, or 2333 years. The date of Christ's parousia was thus set for 4209 CE.[40]

The most ambitious attempt to study Riel's religious thought is that of Thomas Flanagan in his book *Louis "David" Riel: Prophet of the New World.*

While informative, the work is nonetheless seriously flawed. Flanagan does not really take his subject seriously. To borrow Gertrude Stein's line about Oakland, he doesn't seem to believe there is a there there. He doesn't take the Métis seriously as Natives, a mistake in my opinion. Further, he sees Riel as only mentally ill and delusional. He views the Métis as ignoring or humoring his psychoses without believing in them, because of his value as a political leader. But Riel's vision and the Northwest Resistance are so inextricably intertwined that it is impossible to separate the two. Riel was leading a revolt to overthrow the perceived oppression of his people, and victory would usher in the Kingdom on earth.

Among the Apaches, a prophet known as Silas John rose to prominence in 1920 due to an increase in the number of "shooting witches" around the Fort Apache area. Dreams had revealed to Silas John that many of the old medicine men were false and that a new world was imminent. He possessed Lightning and Snake power, with the latter being dominant. The primary symbol of the new faith was the cross with a snake. This symbol had the power to ward off witches and evil. Silas John himself was recognized as the reincarnation of Monster Slayer, the son of Changing Woman, the progenitor of all humanity. Monster Slayer was then identified in English with Jesus.[41]

The central themes of Silas John's movement continued from the earlier dahgodi•ÿáh'. People were to dance in order to be "raised up" into a new world free from the evil of this present one. In order to distinguish those who were to be raised from those left behind, followers were to wear a silver medal on their chests consisting of the cross and the crescent moon. Silas John also gave adherents new names. This was of crucial importance because, when the time of dahgodi•ÿáh' arrived, only those who remembered their new names would be saved.[42]

According to Jorge Noriega, the last published documentation concerning Silas John's movement dates to 1954. At that time, the prophet had been in prison for more than twenty years, but the dances were still being performed. Noriega notes, "The lasting effects of the Silas John movement are unknown outside Apache circles."[43] There are, however, Apaches who still claim to be adherents of Silas John's religion.

The Ghost Dance religion that swept through Native communities in the late nineteenth century began with the mystical vision of one Indian, the Paiute Messiah Wovoka, of Jesus Christ. It was an eschatological vision of Christ's *parousia*, a coming that would wipe Amer-Europeans off the face of the North American continent. Dead ancestors would be raised up. After Christ's righteous judgment, the buffalo would return and all creation would be renewed. As Wovoka himself reported after his near-death experience in 1889:

> When I was in the other world with the Old Man, I saw all the people who have died. But they were not sad. They were happy while engaged in their old-time occupations and dancing, gambling, and playing ball. It was a pleasant land, level, without rocks or mountains, green all the time, and rich with an abundance of game and fish. Everyone was forever young.
>
> After showing me all of heaven, God told me to go back to earth and tell his people you must be good and love one another, have no quarreling, and live in peace with the whites; that you must work, and not lie or steal; and that you must put an end to the practice of war.
>
> If you faithfully obey your instructions from on high, you will at last be reunited with your friends in a renewed world where there would be no more death or sickness or old age. First, though, the earth must die. Indians should not be afraid, however. For it will come alive again, just like the sun died and came alive again [a reference to a total eclipse that occurred while Wovoka was in his coma]. In the hour of tribulation, a tremendous earthquake will shake the ground. Indians must gather on high ground. A mighty flood shall follow. The water and mud will sweep the white race and all Indian skeptics away to their deaths. Then the dead Indian ancestors will return, as will the vanished buffalo and other game, and everything on earth will once again be an Indian paradise.[44]

The movement had direct antecedents in the Ghost Dance of 1870, the Prophet Dance of Smohalla, and Bini's movement in Canada in the 1830s. Amer-European misunderstanding and fear of the Ghost Dance as a locus of political resistance led to the Wounded Knee Massacre. The Ghost Dance, banned since the time of Wounded Knee, was revived in the 1970s by Henry Crow Dog and Leonard Crow Dog.

The syncretic, messianic movement with by far the largest number of adherents is peyotism, which, in its various permutations, accounts for approximately 25 percent of the U.S. Indian population. Though peyote had been used in Mexico to induce visions for ten thousand years, peyotism in the U.S. grew in the wake of Wounded Knee. It was largely tolerated by authorities because it was perceived as a quietistic movement as compared to the Ghost Dance. There are a number of peyotist sects and denominations, varying in the number of Christian elements they embrace. However, the two primary rites within peyotism are the Half Moon way and the Cross Fire way.

In the Cross Fire way, the Bible is accepted, and water baptism is practiced. Jesus is accepted as Lord and Savior. His words are seen as eternal life, and there is healing through him. There is a strong emphasis on Christ's *parousia*, when there will be a judgment at which the good and bad of an individual will be weighed. Emerson Spider, Sr., a peyote roadman and a minister in the Native American Church, refers to himself as a "born-again Christian" and states, "The second coming of Christ is the only way to salvation."[45] There is strong emphasis on the atoning works of Christ. Spider wishes to merge the Native American Church with Christian beliefs and desires recognition as a Christian denomination, but he acknowledges that his views are not shared by all in the Native American Church.

Asa Primeaux explicitly criticizes Spider. He states, "You'll never make me believe that Jesus is the only one. No way. The Jesus Christ worshippers are nothing but murderers, idolaters, and thieves." Jesus is not the mediator between humanity and God because no such mediation is necessary. Yet in some of Primeaux's songs there is reference to the Savior and a last day of judgment. They also speak of the pity of God and note that the Savior alone has compassion.[46]

In the Half-Moon way, the Bible is not present, but Jesus is neither denied nor ignored, and prayers normally end with "in the name of Jesus. Amen." Christmas and Easter are celebrated with meetings. In practice, there is much interchange between the two rites with persons often attending both meetings. And although Jesus is deemphasized in the Half Moon rite, visions of Christ are not unheard of.[47]

The issue of power in these movements cannot be overlooked. The syncretic faiths discussed above are wholly in the hands of Natives themselves to define. They freely borrow and adapt elements of Christianity, turning them into distinctly Native things. They struggle to reach beyond language to articulate their visions. As for the ancient Israelites creation was Exodus projected backwards, so for Native Americans *eschaton* or apocalypse is creation projected forward and dissolved, then reconfigured, reconstructed, renewed. The late Audre Lorde declared, "The Master's tools will not dismantle his house." Native apocalyptic messianic movements remind us that it is a mistake to measure the Master's house with his yardstick as well.

These, then, are but a few of the eschatological and apocalyptic beliefs in Native cultures. Though it may seem an exhaustive survey, in this review I have only scratched the surface of what is indeed a very rich vein. Often the syncretic movements I discussed are viewed by scholars as backward or backward looking. This is both unfortunate and incorrect. As Lewis Carroll's White Queen says to Alice, "It's a poor sort of memory that only works backwards."

CHAPTER NINETEEN

FROM I-HERMENEUTICS TO
WE-HERMENEUTICS

Native Americans and the Post-Colonial

Vignette No. 1: *In 1782, Christian Delawares left their homes and their already planted fields in Gnadenhutten and moved into a new "praying town" organized by the Moravian missionary David Zeisberger at Sandusky. The move was voluntary, to avoid conflict with Amer-European farmers. When the Natives returned to harvest their crops, however, they were confronted by a patrol of one hundred militia from Fort Pitt. The peaceful band surrendered and explained their presence. The colonel in command ordered them bound and—in order to save ammunition—clubbed, scalped, and burned. According to eyewitness reports, the unresisting Natives sang hymns and prayed as the soldiers went about their grisly work. Twenty-nine men, twenty-seven women, and thirty-four children were killed.*[1]

Vignette No. 2: *In 1838, in one of the best remembered incidents of the Removal of Natives from the American Southeast, sixteen thousand Cherokees were forcibly marched nine hundred miles from Georgia to present-day Oklahoma. One-fourth of the Cherokee Nation died along the route that came to be called the Trail of Tears. As they walked, Christian Indians among them sang Christian hymns in their own language. The best known of these was an atonement hymn, "One Drop of Blood," which asks, "Jesus, what must I do for you to save me?" The reply is, "It only takes one drop of blood to wash away our sins. You are King of Kings, the Creator of all things." The Cherokee*

translation of "Guide Me, O Thou Great Jehovah," also sung on the
trail, is equally poignant:

Take me and guide me, Jehovah, as I am walking through this
    barren land.
I am weak, but thou art mighty. Ever help us.
Open unto us thy healing waters. Let the fiery cloud go before
    us and continue thy help.
Help us when we come to the Jordan River and we shall sing
    thy praise eternally.[2]

Christian Choctaws, enduring a similar trek, sang too. Theirs, a song
of Christian hope, promised that Jesus would save them and stated,
"For each of you the heavenly place where you shall dwell is there for
you. Follow Jesus to the heavenly place. You will see joy such as you
have never seen."[3] *Oklahoma proved a heavenly place for neither*
nation.

Vignette No. 3: *In 1862, 303 Sioux were sentenced to die for their*
roles in an uprising protesting their brutal treatment, led by Little
Crow, an Episcopalian. President Abraham Lincoln demanded to
review personally the records of the entire proceedings. In the end, he
authorized the hanging of thirty-nine men. On the day after Christ-
mas, in Mankato, Minnesota, thirty-eight men (one having received
a reprieve) quietly followed the provost marshal to the scaffold. They
showed no fear and stood calmly as the nooses were placed around
their necks. Then they broke into song. Contemporary newspaper
accounts reported that they had sung their Sioux death chant. In real-
ity, a good many were Christian. They were singing the hymn
"Many and Great, O God." As the trap dropped, they grabbed for
each others' hands and sang, saying "I'm here! I'm here!" It was the
largest mass execution in United States history.[4]

Vignette No. 4: *In his book* Custer Died for Your Sins, *Vine Delo-*
ria describes an encounter in 1967 with the Presbyterian minister in
charge of that denomination's Indian missions. Deloria listened to
the clergyman describe missionary work among the Shinnecocks of

New York's Long Island and then asked how long his church intended
to continue such work among a tribe that had lived as Christians for
more than 350 years. The impassive reply was, "Until the job is
done."[5]

Vignette No. 5: *From 1845 to 1848 it was a criminal offense in the*
Creek Nation to profess Christianity. The penalty for infraction was
thirty-nine lashes from a cowhide whip. When less than twenty years
old, Samuel Checote was so punished. According to one account,
"While blood flowed to his ankles, he was asked, 'Wilt you give up
Christ?' He replied 'You may kill me but you cannot separate me from
my Lord Christ.'" He later served as chief of the Nation and as a cler-
gyman. He was instrumental in having the ban on Christianity
lifted. Out of respect for his people, he never admitted having suf-
fered at the whipping post for his Christian confession.[6]

IRONIC HISTORIES: NATIVES AND CHRISTIANITY

These five brief vignettes, which could be replicated many times over, attest to what Marie Therese Archambault describes as the "terrible irony" of being both Native and Christian.[7] During the eighteenth and early nineteenth centuries, by necessity, Natives in the eastern United States made great efforts to adapt to and accommodate the Amer-European culture that had engulfed them. Many converted to Christianity, the borrowed religion of the foreign invader. They thought that these things would protect them from further depredations. They were wrong. The attempts at acculturation did not matter. The profession of Christianity did not matter. In the end, it only mattered that they were Indian. Their continued occupation of their homelands served as both a rankling reminder of a brutal conquest not yet complete and an impediment to its final completion. In the process by which Natives were dispossessed, Christian missionaries were often no less culpable than those wielding rifle or plow. As Homer Noley states, "On the one hand, church denominations geared themselves up to take the souls of Native American peoples into a brotherhood of love and peace; on the other, they were part of a white nationalist movement that geared itself up to take away the land and livelihood of Native American people by treachery and force."[8]

Though numerous non-Native historians have produced well-documented treatments of the Native/Christian encounter (most notably Henry Bowden's *American Indians and Christian Missions: Studies in Cultural Conflict* and John Webster Grant's *Moon of Wintertime: Missionaries and Canadian Indians in Encounter Since 1534*) scholarly discussion of these events by Natives has been lacking. In the early 1990s two volumes attempted to begin to fill this lacuna: *Missionary Conquest: The Gospel and Native American Cultural Genocide* by George Tinker and *First White Frost: Native Americans and United Methodism* by Homer Noley.[9] Although there are many areas of basic agreement between the two authors, a comparison of the two works yields important differences and provides an illustration of the complexity involved in rehearsing Native religious history.

While Tinker is willing, at least in the case of historic missions, to give missionaries the benefit of the doubt for their good intentions, Noley is less generous in his overall interpretation. Tinker declares, "To state the case baldly and dramatically, my thesis is that the Christian missionaries—of all denominations working among American Indian nations—were partners in genocide. Unwittingly no doubt, and always with the best of intentions, nevertheless the missionaries were guilty of complicity in the destruction of Indian cultures and tribal social structures—complicity in the devastating impoverishment and death of the people to whom they preached."[10] This was so because "the kerygmatic content of the missionary's Christian faith became confused with the accoutrements of the missionary's cultural experience and behavior."[11] Putting aside the difficulty of attributing intentionality, it must still be noted that the systemic nature of racism, of which Tinker himself makes quite a lot, organizes and structures personal intent (however good) so as to mask the racist ends it may serve. Tinker himself declares, "It would have been impossible for these earlier missionaries to see and acknowledge their own sin in this regard." Yet, elsewhere, he also states with regard to missionary cooperation in Amer-European economic and political power structures, "At some level, they must have known what they were about."[12] Tinker, it appears, wants to have it both ways. By contrast, Noley asks consistently how the missionaries, whose work, as Tinker notes, was clearly so destructive, could *not* have known what they were doing.[13] He declares, "Given the political intrigues that spanned most of the eighteenth century . . . the integrity of missionaries and their mission was in doubt. The biblical dictum

'You cannot serve God and Mammon' (Matt. 6:24) was set aside as missionaries, on the one hand, offered a religion of love and eternal life, and colonists, on the other hand, were forming militia to kill tribal people or drive them from their homes in order to take their lands and crops."[14] Intellectual and historiographic rigor force the question of how different the missiological experience would have to be before Tinker would surrender his assertion as to the "best intentions" of the missionaries, since such a belief cannot be reconcilable with *any* amount of Native suffering and *any* amount of culpability on the part of the evangelists. In the end, I suspect, Tinker's claim is intellectually empty because, given the grimness of the historical record and the role of missionaries in it, absent the improbable "smoking gun" stating baldly a divergence between stated and actual goals, it seems apparent there could be no circumstance, real or imaginary, that would dislodge Tinker from his much-repeated faith in the European and Amer-European bearers of the gospel.[15]

The second major difference between Tinker and Noley, dealing as it does with the way they approach their material, is more fundamental. Tinker limns the history of evangelical activities among Natives by focusing on the stories of four prominent missionaries from different regions and eras (John Eliot in Puritan New England; Pierre-Jean DeSmet in the Northwest; Junípero Serra in old California; and Henry Benjamin Whipple, Episcopalian bishop of Minnesota during the second half of the nineteenth century). Other exemplars could have been chosen, but, for Tinker, the unrelenting sameness of the stories makes further renditions unnecessary.[16] Tinker hopes that his study "becomes a contribution to our understanding of why Native American peoples have generally failed to enter the American mainstream and continue to live in poverty and oppression, marginalized on the periphery of society. By and large, Indian people have not found liberation in the gospel of Jesus Christ, but, rather, continued bondage to a culture that is both alien and alienating, and even genocidal against American Indian peoples."[17]

Tinker's method, however, has an unintended and unfortunate consequence. By concentrating exclusively on the four non-Natives of his case study, Natives are erased from the picture. In the process Native agency is destroyed and Native subjectivity is damaged. The missionaries are portrayed as the only actors in the story. Indians are passive recipients, merely acted upon.[18] Noley agrees—it would be impossible for him to do otherwise—that Natives were not involved in the preliminary discussions and planning sessions that took place prior to the deployment of missionaries to mission assignments. Their lot was to respond to the implementation of strategies that they had nothing to do with in the planning stages. They were not party to the assessments of their needs and the consequent decision making about how to go about meeting those needs. They were not involved in interdenominational agreements about who could work among which people. It is no wonder that they often became incredulous spectators of events that drastically affected their lives and reflected on their status as intelligent human beings.

From the very beginning of the major missionary movements, when the American Board of Commissioners for Foreign Missions debated heatedly on the subject of whether to "civilize" the Indian first and then "Christianize him," or vice versa, to Reconstruction Era top-to-bottom mission deployment, . . . Native people have generally been unwilling spectators of the frustrating results.[19]

In contrast to Tinker, however, Noley depicts the broad sweep of missiological history. He discusses the many prominent Native missionaries and clergy (e.g., Peter Jones, George Copway, John Sunday, Harry Long) who labored, and continue to labor, effectively among their own people. Natives were, of course, actors in the drama as well. A response was required of them. Remarkably, despite brutality, a great many Natives did willingly embrace the alien faith, and some of them went on to carry the message to others. This difference between Noley's and Tinker's accounts is crucial. In it lies the question of whether Natives were (and are) self-determined or selves-determined.[20]

Missionaries, in their colonialist drive to assimilate Natives, told those they converted that to become Christian meant to stop being Indian. An example is the experience of Natives after the purchase of Alaska by the United States. In 1897, Dr. Sheldon Jackson, a Presbyterian missionary, was appointed the first territorial commissioner of education. With the support of his colleague, Dr. S. Hall Young, Jackson set eradication of Native culture and language as a priority and established boarding schools along the Carlisle model. They encountered, however, a basic problem: these Natives did not fit their stereotypes of Indians. Instead of "rude savages," they found Alaska Natives who were already literate and multilingual, already educated in a Western sense, and already Christian and theologically astute. In fact, the Aleuts had been sending missionaries to other tribes for generations.[21] The first response of these "uncivilized" Natives was to send letters of protest to the Russian ambassador in Washington and to President McKinley. It did not work. In the place of the bilingual education system created by the Russians, Amer-Europeans taught the same self-hatred and internalized loathing that characterized American boarding schools.

Today, as already noted, only between 10 and 25 percent (depending on what set of statistics one chooses to believe) of Natives consider themselves Christian. Missions still often are conducted in a manner unchanged in over a hundred years. Natives are still taught that "Christian Indian" is an oxymoron. For all too many, to become Christian still means to cease being Indian. Because of the intimate connection between culture and religious traditions for indigenous peoples, an additional irony is that converts are often told the same thing by their traditional relatives. For those who choose to practice Christianity, the result can be ostracism and isolation from community, as illustrated by the story of Samuel Checote in the fifth vignette above. Referring to the brutal assimilationist methods of Christian evangelism, Lakota traditionalist and peyotist Leonard Crow Dog states, "Indians became Christian by force. Often they were killed if they did not convert. Indian Christians have a very hard time these days as they are caught between two ways of seeing the world. I feel sorry for those of you who don't know who you are."[22]

IRONIC READINGS: NATIVES AND BIBLICAL HERMENEUTICS

William Baldridge, a Cherokee, confirms these ironic histories as well as their continued contemporaneity:

> Many missionaries served as federal agents and in that role negotiated treaties which left us no land. Most missionaries taught us to hate anything Native American and that of necessity meant hating our friends, our families, and ourselves. Most refused to speak to us in any language but their own. The missionaries functioned as "Christ-bearing colonizers." If it were otherwise the missionaries would have come, shared the gospel, and left. We know, of course, that they stayed, and they continue to stay, and they continue to

insist that we submit to them and their definitions. The vast majority of Native people have experienced the missionary system as racist and colonial."[23]

Much of that racism can be traced to the biblical hermeneutics of those who came to colonize the Americas and the theological anthropology that flowed from those interpretive systems. From the outset of the invasion of the continent, the Bible was read in a manner oppressive of indigenous peoples and employed to justify conquest.

In his paper "Native Americans and the Hermeneutical Task," Homer Noley stresses the role of "theological presuppositions and constructions which were put in place by Colonial America to describe Native Americans in the nation's theological themes."[24] Jonathan Edwards was one of many who spoke of the Western hemisphere as a "promised land" whose inhabitants were "wholly possessed of Satan until the coming of Europeans." John Rolfe proclaimed in 1616 that the British were "a peculiar people, marked and chosen by the finger of God" for the colonial enterprise "to possess [the Americas], for undoubtedly he is with us."[25]

Both Alfred A. Cave, in "Canaanites in a Promised Land: The American Indian and the Providential Theory of Empire," and Djelal Kadir, in *Columbus and the Ends of the Earth: Europe's Prophetic Rhetoric as Conquering Ideology*, have demonstrated that biblical language was used to spawn and spur the colonial enterprise. Cave quotes Sir George Peckham, a prominent Catholic nobleman who envisioned America as a refuge for Catholics, as viewing the Native population as Canaanites inhibiting conquest of the Promised Land; these heathens would either be exterminated or, like the Gibeonites, submit "as drudges to hewe wood and carie water."[26] Kadir shows conclusively that colonizers crossed the Atlantic convinced that they were exercising their God-given right to lands held in escrow for them from the foundation of the world. Reverend Alexander Whitaker of Henrico, Virginia, exemplified this opinion when he wrote in 1613 that "this plantation, which the divill hath so often troden down, is by the miraculous blessing of God, revived. . . . God first shewed us the place, God first called us hither, and here God by his special providence hath maintained us."[27] Anders Stephanson shows in *Manifest Destiny* that such beliefs did not cease with the end of the colonial experience but persisted in the American Republic well into the nineteenth century.[28] When Natives were not conceptualized as Canaanites, they were viewed simply as part of a hostile landscape that needed to be ordered and tamed by European civilizers, little more than one more type of fauna to be either domesticated or driven toward extinction. Typical, and illustrative of such a mindset, was the declaration of Eliphalet Stark in a letter to a relative in 1797: "The Yankees have taken care of the wolves, bears, and Indians . . . and we'll build the Lord's temple yet, build it out of these great trees."[29] The roots of such racism were sunk deep in biblical exegesis.

In March 1493, the church was suddenly presented with a problem. Columbus returned home from the "New World" with captives who appeared to be human. The question immediately arose as to how to account for this when the biblical account of creation in Genesis clearly mentioned only three continents (Europe, Asia, and Africa), each populated by the progeny of a different son of Noah after the Deluge. In response, Pope Alexander VI issued his bull *Inter Caetera*. This bull sanctioned the Conquest, reading, "Among the works well pleasing to the Divine Majesty and cherished in our heart, this assuredly ranks highest, that in our times especially the Catholic faith and the Christian religion be exalted and everywhere increased and spread, that the health of souls be cared for and that the barbarous nations be overthrown and brought to the faith itself."[30]

The papal instruction did little, however, to answer the basic questions concerning the humanity and origins of the indigenes of the Americas. Some considered Natives merely human in form but devoid of a soul. Some contended that the newly discovered Natives must be "sons of Ham," the same stock as the "racially inferior" peoples of Africa.[31] Still others, observing the degree of civilization among their cultures, declared the Indians to be the lost tribes of Israel. Though all three ideas coexisted, the last gradually became dominant and persisted relatively unchallenged until well into the nineteenth century. John Wesley, for instance, echoed the prevailing opinions of the day when, addressing the urgency of Christian missions to Natives, he fretted:

> One thing has often given me concern. . . . The progeny of Shem (the Indians) seem to be quite forgotten. How few of these have seen the light of the glory of God since the English first settled among them! And now scarce one in fifty among whom we settled, perhaps scarce one in an hundred of them are left alive! Does it not seem as if God

had designed all the Indian natives not for reformation but for destruction? Undoubtedly with man it is impossible to help them. But is it too hard for God? Pray ye likewise of the Lord of the Harvest and he will send out more laborers into his Harvest.[32]

The argument over Native humanity itself was not finally resolved until 1512 when Pope Julius II, faced with "mounting evidence of man-like creatures inhabiting the Americas," declared that Native peoples were indeed human beings, descended from Adam and Eve through the Babylonians.[33] Thus by the grace of God and declaration of the Holy Pontiff, Indians were found to possess divine souls and were thus eligible for salvation. Europeans' first reaction to inhabitants of the Americas was thus not alterity but sameness. Behind the debate over origins was a belief not only in the literal truth of the biblical witness but also the notion that no people could attain any degree of civilization—even language—unless they could be shown as springing from the same roots as those of the known "Old World." They were not Other but Same. Yet, while the debate over the humanity of indigenes was settled, at least nominally, in the Natives' favor, questions as to the value of their cultures were not so resolved.

Edwards was hardly alone in proclaiming American Natives "wholly possessed of Satan" until the arrival of Europeans. Colonists and missionaries, regardless of the country from which they came, universally regarded Native cultures and religious traditions as pagan and diabolic, to be eradicated and replaced with Western values and ways of life. Even Russian missionaries, who on the whole were more sympathetic to the Native cultures they encountered, could not transcend and escape this Eurocentric bias. An 1894 letter from Orthodox Bishop Petr discussing the traditional beliefs of the Aleuts and Kodiaks states that the morality and religious views of these people "are in essence similar to the Bible stories." The cleric considers this proof of the common origins of all humanity from a single pair of progenitors as depicted in the Hebrew scriptures. He concludes:

> The incomplete and fragmentary nature of the religious views of the Kadiaks [sic] can simply be explained by the fact that they have been too long ... removed from the direct influence of God's Revelations, which alone can communicate to people in all its fullness the knowledge they need to have about God and the World, whereas originally God's Revelation was limited in all its purity to the European

peoples alone. It must be noted that in accordance with God's Holy Revelations the Aleuts and the Kadiaks were not completely bereft of God's Grace, as a result of which there remained with them a sense of morality which prevented them from falling into ultimate sin.[34]

In daring to admit that there was something of the divine in Native religious traditions, albeit fractured and diminished, Bishop Petr was affirming the classical doctrine of the *logos*, which had been interpreted so that the ancient Church could cast itself as the "heir of the pagans" and claim for itself the wisdom of the Greek philosophers—a doctrine that Edwards and others implicitly denied when they saw only deviltry in indigenous traditions. The Gospel according to John begins: "In the beginning was the Word [*logos*], and the Word was with God, and the Word was God." It then continues that this *logos is* "the true light, which enlightens everyone" and that it became flesh and lived among humanity (John 1:1, 9, 14). According to historian Justo González, "Since this Logos enlightens everyone, it follows, so the ancients said, that wherever people have any light, they have it because of this eternal Word of God, who became incarnate in Jesus Christ."[35] If the church had been consistent in its treatment of the *logos*, the doctrine should have provided a means to affirm indigenous cultures. Of course, it was not consistent. Gonzalez continues:

> If the Word incarnate in Christ is the true light which enlightens everyone, it follows that the Word of God can be found wherever humans have any light whatsoever. . . . Once it attained a position of power within the Roman Empire and Greco-Roman culture—partially through its use of the doctrine of the Logos—it did not even consider the possibility that the same Word may have illumined those whom the "best" of culture considered "barbarians." *They* had no Logos. The Word had to be taken from them. Ever since, Christians seem to have remembered the doctrine of the Logos only when approaching cultures and civilizations they had no possibility of overpowering. When, on the contrary, they faced cultures or civilizations they were determined to over run, or which had not advanced the art of killing as Western civilization had, they saw in those cultures and civilizations nothing but idolatry and ignorance.[36]

Not until the Second Vatican Council did significant theologians take seriously the notion that indigenous peoples might have something to contribute to the understanding of ultimate reality. In the wake of Vatican II, Italo-German theologian Romano Guardini queried whether truths might not "require their own soil in order to develop." Articulating a doctrine of division of labor among religions, he writes:

> Here too we might discern a kind of division of labor, by which, for example, certain truths became clear in India whereas Europeons had not yet grasped them. Hence we might find in the spiritual realm of the Vedas some insights which could be useful for a deepening of the doctrine of the Trinity, or it might be that in Buddhism—the strict Buddhism of the south—experiences emerged clearly which might be valuable for the problem of the "negative" knowledge of God.
>
> And what of the matter of mythology; indeed the whole question of myth? Shall we simply reject it, and shall those concerned about the purity of the message confine themselves to freeing this message from its mythical elements? Or is it not possible that a way of experiencing and thinking, in which all peoples lived for a time, should contain images which could contribute to a deepening of the Christian faith?[37]

Such expressions, while falling unfortunately short of setting Native traditions on an equal footing with Jewish/Christian traditions, are nonetheless far more accepting than earlier attitudes.

The older ideas, however, persist. Views that see Native religious traditions as worthless and demonic and Natives as the progeny of Ham remain staples of fundamentalist Christianity. The myth of the ten lost tribes remains alive in the Mormon description of American Indians as the Lamanites and continues to recur in popular discourse. Successionist, fulfillment, and anonymous Christ theologies continue to claim a superior position for Christianity over Native cultures. Even conceptualizations of Natives as Canaanites impeding the *eisode* have yet to die out completely. As Noley notes, Peter Marshall and David Manuel, in *The Light and the Glory*, claim that the divine scheme that America should be the "new Jerusalem" was "to be worked out in terms of the settlers' covenant with God and with each other." In such a plan Natives are listed along with droughts, smallpox, and wild animals as "enemies from which God delivered his people."[38] Worse yet, Amer-European missionaries, continuing the ironic history, still teach such theologies and the biblical interpretations that support them to their Native American charges. As George Tinker observes, it is not unusual for entire Indian congregations to remain faithful "to the very missionary theology that was first brought to them, even when the denomination has long ago abandoned that language for a more contemporary articulation of the gospel. One must at least suspect that the process of Christianization has involved some internalization of the larger illusion of Indian inferiority and the idealization of white culture and religion."[39] When such self-hatred has been internalized to its fullest extent, the Conquest will finally be complete.

IRONIC PHILOSOPHIES: NATIVES AND POST-COLONIALISM

For Native Americans, perhaps the most pervasive result of colonialism is that we cannot even begin a conversation without referencing our words to definitions imposed or rooted in 1492. The arrival of Columbus marks the beginning of colonial hubris in America, a pride so severe that it must answer the charge of blasphemy.[40]

The idea of the *post-colonial*, referring to "a general process of decolonisation which, like colonisation itself, has marked the colonising societies as powerfully as it has the colonised (of course, in different ways)," has gained a great deal of currency in academic circles and exerted an important influence on the developing discipline of cultural studies.[41] It has been most fully articulated by literary critics. To a certain extent this is natural because "literature offers one of the most important ways in which these new perceptions are expressed and it is in their writing, and through other arts such as painting, sculpture, music, and dance that the day-to-day realities experienced by colonized peoples have been most powerfully encoded and so profoundly influential."[42] Yet this also has posed a limitation for post-colonial analysis because these same literary scholars "have been reluctant to make the break across disciplinary (even post-disciplinary) boundaries required to advance the argument"[43] or, indeed, truly to test its utility as a way of apprehending the lived reality of persons and peoples. On its face, the concept has much to recommend it to Native scholars engaged in American Indian studies or religious studies, including biblical hermeneutics. As Bill Baldridge's statement above demonstrates, Native cultures were decisively different after the ruptures of invasion and colonization. It is self-evident that they were different from how they would have developed if left in isolation. New and extreme pressures, erratic and oppressive government policies, and the reduction of indigenes to less than 1 percent of the population have led to new constellations of identity.

Stuart Hall, a leading force in cultural studies, observes:

> The argument is not that, thereafter, everything has remained the Same—colonisation repeating itself in perpetuity to the end of time. It is, rather, that colonisation so refigured the terrain that, ever since, the very idea of a world of separate identities, of isolated or separable and self-sufficient cultures and economies, has been obliged to yield to a variety of paradigms designed to capture these different but related forms of relationship, interconnection and discontinuity.[44]

While I do not want to be accused of the charge of "banal reductionism," which Hall hurls at critic Arif Dirlik, I do believe that there are potentially troubling aspects of post-colonial discourse that must be seriously debated before American Natives can determine whether it is useful to hop aboard the post-colonial bandwagon. If Ella Shohat is correct about the ahistorical, universalizing, depoliticizing effects of the post-colonial, there is nothing in that analysis for Natives.[45] If Ruth Frankenberg and Lata Mani are right in their assertion that too often the sole function that post-colonial analysis seems to serve is as a critique of dominant, Western philosophical discourse—"merely a detour to return to the position of the Other as a resource for rethinking the Western self"—then Natives will want little part of it.[46] Unquestionably, as Dirlik states, "post-coloniality represents a response to a genuine need, the need to overcome a crisis of understanding produced by the inability of old categories to account for the world."[47] The "old categories" of Western discourse, however, never accounted for Native worldviews, and since the time of the first contact with Europeans, American Indians' reality has been all too monotonously the same, controlled by those who conquered them.

A basic question concerning post-coloniality is that raised by Hall in the title of his essay "When Was the 'Post-Colonial'? Thinking at the Limit." Shohat has pointed out the "problematic temporality" of the term. Bill

Ashcroft, Gareth Griffiths, and Helen Tiffin contend that the post-colonial is that period which commences at the moment of colonization and continues to the present day.[48] Hall, for his part, maintains that one thing the post-colonial is not is a periodization based on epochal stages "when everything is reversed at the same moment, all the old relations disappear for ever [*sic*] and entirely new ones come to replace them."[49] For him, the term is not merely descriptive of *there* versus *here* or *then* versus *now*. Nevertheless, for Hall, as for many post-colonial critics, the term has a temporal scope much more limited than that given to it by Ashcroft, Griffiths, and Tiffin. *Post-colonial* represents a time after colonialism and temporally means that time of post-independence of the former colonial world, even if the struggle for decolonization is not yet complete.

The problem is that for much of that two-thirds of the world colonialism is not dead. It is not living merely as "after-effects," as Hall implies. Native Americans remain a colonized people, victims of internal colonialism. *Internal colonialism* differs from classic colonialism (sometimes called "blue water" colonialism) in that in colonialism's classic form a small group of colonists occupy a land far from the colonial metropolis (*métropole*) and remain a minority, exercising control over a large indigenous population, whereas in internal colonialism, the native population is swamped by a large mass of colonial settlers who, after generations, no longer have a *métropole* to which to return. Today, Native American life is characterized by the same paternalistic colonialism that has marked it for over a century.

An ironic aspect of post-colonial critique for Natives is its relationship to postmodernism. Post-structuralist discourse provides its "philosophical and theoretical grounding," and like post-structuralism, it is "antifoundational."[50] To understand the irony of this predicament, one must turn back to the nineteenth century. Late in that century, two great rationalizing sciences rose to prominence, sociology and anthropology. The former purported to study what was normative in the dominant culture. The latter studied the Other and advised colonial masters in the manners and mores of native peoples that they might be more effectively controlled.[51] In like manner, in the late twentieth century two systems of critical thought arose to explain the world. It is no coincidence that just as the peoples of the Two-Thirds World began to find their voices and assert their own agency and subjectivity, postmodernism proclaimed the end of subjectivity. By finding its theoretical roots in European intellectual discourse, post-colonialism continues, by inadvertence, the philosophical hegemony of the West. Like postmodernism, post-colonialism is obsessed with the issues of identity and subjectivity. Hall writes that

> questions of hybridity, syncretism, of cultural undecidability and the complexities of diasporic identification . . . interrupt any "return" to ethnically closed and "centred" original histories. Understood in its global and transcultural context, colonisation has made ethnic absolutism an increasingly untenable cultural strategy. It made the "colonies" themselves, and even more, large tracts of the "post-colonial" world, always-already "diasporic" in relation to what might be thought of as their cultures of origin.[52]

Putting aside for the moment the diasporic nature of much of modern Native existence, one must nevertheless admit that there is something real, concrete, and centered in Native existence and identity. As I have argued in the opening chapter, Joseph Conrad can become a major figure of English letters and Léopold Sédar Senghor a member of the French Academy, but either one is Indian or one is not.[53] And certain genuine consequences flow from those accidents of birth and culture. It is part of the distinction drawn by Edward Said between filiation and affiliation.[54]

The problem is that at base post-colonial discourse is depoliticized. As Shohat notes, in its legitimate and sincere effort to escape essentialism, "post-colonial discourse sometimes seems to define any attempt to recover or inscribe a communal past as a form of idealisation, despite its significance as a site of resistance and collective identity."[55] Its error, like that of postmodernism, is that it mistakes having deconstructed something theoretically for having displaced it politically.[56] Jacqueline Rose, in her book *States of Fantasy*, observes that the postmodern in its "vision of free-wheeling identity . . . seems bereft of history and passion."[57] Said responds, "Just so, particularly at a moment when, all over the globe, identities, civilizations, religions, cultures seem more bloodily at odds than ever before. Postmodernism can do nothing to try to understand this."[58] The same case could be made against post-colonialism.

After more than five hundred years of ongoing colonialism, Native Americans wrestle with two different pulls of identity, one settled and the other diasporic.[59] The settled is that of traditional lands and a continent that was once wholly theirs. The diasporic is that of new homes to which they were exiled by their conquerors, of urban existence far removed from even those territories, and a grim realization that their colonizers are here to stay. Only the most winsome dreamer and the most prophetic visionary believe that Amer-Europeans are going anywhere—short of the success of the Ghost Dance or cataclysmic destruction brought upon Amer-Europeans by their own actions. Post-colonial critique provides a useful tool for analyzing Native literatures, which reflect these divergent pulls on identity, and for deconstructing the ironic and destructive biblical readings that have been imposed upon us. As long, however, as those readings and the theologies that spring from them are still taught, as long as denominational factionalism and Amer-European missionization continue to divide families and force Natives to choose between their communities and their religion, the post-colonial moment for Native Americans will not yet have arrived.

DISSOLVING IRONY:
SEARCHING FOR A COMMUNITY HERMENEUTIC

As outlined in Chapter 9, Reinhold Niebuhr delineates three types of history: the pathetic, the tragic, and the ironic. Pathos is that element of history that inspires pity but deserves neither admiration nor contrition. Suffering resulting from purely natural consequences is the clearest example of pathos. Tragedy is the conscious choice of evil for the sake of good. Irony "consists of apparently fortuitous incongruities of life which are discovered, upon closer examination, to be not merely fortuitous."[60] It is distinguished from the pathetic in that humans bear responsibility for it. It is distinguished from the tragic in that the responsibility rests on unconscious weakness rather than conscious choice. Irony, unlike pathos or tragedy, must dissolve when it is brought to light. It elicits laughter. American history for Niebuhr is ironic: there is a gap between the ideal of America's self-image and the reality of its history and existence.[61] Natives have been representing themselves in print for more than two hundred years and have striven to bring to light and thus dissolve the ironic histories, readings, and philosophies that have been imposed upon them by the dominant culture. Without falling into the post-colonial/postmodernist naiveté of believing that theoretical deconstruction necessarily means ultimate efficacy, they have asserted their own subjectivity and have attempted to develop and spell out their own histories, readings, and intellectual discourse in a way that affirms their personhood.

Noley states, "If the Native American clergy are satisfied with their training, there may not be an interest in a new basis for Native American ministries. If they are not satisfied, there is a place for Native American Biblical scholarship."[62] He remains skeptical, however, because most Native clergy "reflect the fundamentalism of rural white non-Indian Christianity."[63] His remarks are consonant with Tinker's contention that Natives often adhere to the missionary theology first brought to them generations ago. In point of fact, however, at least a few Native clergy and laity always have expressed their dissatisfaction with the transmitted biblical interpretation of the dominant culture.

The work of William Apess, a Pequot writing in the 1820s and 1830s, must be viewed as resistance literature, repeatedly employing indirection and signification to affirm Indian cultural and political identity over against the dominant culture. For example, in his autobiography, *Son of the Forest*, he rejects any use of the term *Indian* as a pejorative disgrace. Looking to the Bible, he finds no reference to "indians" and therefore deduces that it is "a word imported for the special purpose of degrading us." He concludes, "But the proper term which ought to be applied to our nation, to distinguish it from the rest of the human family, is that of 'Natives'—and I humbly conceive that the natives of this country are the only people under heaven who have a just title to the name, inasmuch as we are the only people who retain the original complexion of our father Adam."[64] Here Apess's subversion through rhetoric can be seen clearly. He invokes the language of evangelical Christianity with its appeal to the Bible. In all his writings, he constantly throws up the norms, language, and tools of Christianity into the face of Amer-Europeans in order to expose their racism and to subvert their use of the same material for racist ends.

A key example of Apess's use of signification can be found in his use of the contention that America's indigenes are the ten lost tribes of Israel. As quoted above, Apess states that Indians are the only people with Adam's original complexion, an assertion he repeats, a reference to his belief that Indians were the lost tribes. As such, they, like the Jews, whom he considers people of color, would be Semites and thus closer to Adam's coloring than the pale Anglo-Saxons. He includes a lengthy appendix to *Son of the Forest*, outlining all the various arguments in favor of this thesis.

He returns to the theme in a sermon, "The Indians: The Ten Lost Tribes." Far from using this myth of dominance to slur his own people, however, Apess uses it to claim their common humanity. If Natives are the ten lost tribes, they are every bit as human as their Amer-European invaders. If they are human, they are entitled to equal treatment. Beyond this, if they share a common ancestry with Amer-Europeans, how is there any basis for racism against them? In a scathing pun, Apess looks at Amer-Europeans' complexion and their treatment of Indians and concludes that their Christianity must be only "skin-deep."[65]

Likewise, Peter Jones, an Anishinaabe writing in the decades immediately after Apess, examines the biblical text and employs it against the established order. Jones concludes that Whites have more to atone for in their treatment of Natives than they will ever be able to achieve. In language reminiscent of Apess, he looks to the ultimate judgment, writing, "Oh, what an awful account at the day of judgment, must the unprincipled white man give, who has been the agent of Satan in the extermination of the original proprietors of the American soil! Will not the blood of the red man be required at *his* hands, who, for paltry gain, has impaired the minds, corrupted the morals, and ruined the constitution of a once hardy and numerous race?" Such judgment, however, extends to crimes far more numerous than the introduction of liquor. Jones declares sarcastically, "When I think of the long catalogue of evils entailed on my poor unhappy countrymen, my heart bleeds, not only on their account, but also for their destroyers, who, coming from a land of light and knowledge, are without excuse. Poor deluded beings! Whatever their pretensions to Christianity may have been, it is evident the love of God was not in their hearts; for that love extends to all mankind, and constrains to acts of mercy, but never impels to deeds of death."[66]

One hundred and fifty years later, Marie Therese Archambault declared: "When we read the Gospel, we must read it as *Native people* for this is who we are. We can no longer try to be what we think the dominant society wants us to be. . . . We must learn to subtract the chauvinism and cultural superiority with which this Gospel was often presented to our people. We must, as one author says, 'decolonize' the Gospel, which said we must become European in order to be Christian. We have to go beyond the *white gospel* in order to perceive its truth."[67]

For Robert Warrior, the Native experience is that of the biblical Canaanites, dispossessed of their homeland and annihilated by a foreign invader. His argument takes on added force in the case of the tribal groups who were subjected to a genocidal reverse Exodus from country that was for them, literally, the Promised Land. Thus, for Warrior, to read the biblical witness as a Native, as Archambault suggests, is to read it with "Canaanite eyes."[68]

Tinker, trained as a biblical scholar, contends that a Native biblical reading "presents an interesting challenge to the predominant, Eurocentric tradition of biblical scholarship." It will differ, he avers, from "Euro-American" hermeneutics in three ways: "First, the theological function of the Old Testament in a Native American context will differ. Second, the sociopolitical context of Native American peoples will characteristically generate interpretations that are particularly Native American. Moreover, the discrete cultural particularities of cognitive structures among Native Americans will necessarily generate 'normatively divergent' readings of scripture."[69] Each of these points requires some elaboration.

According to Justo González:

> The "modern" worldview is so prevalent, and so successful in its manipulation and the exploitation of the natural world, that in many circles it currently passes for the only rational or reasonable understanding of the world. The net result in theology, and in particular in biblical interpretation, has been the need to de-mythologize, as Bultmann correctly pointed out—or perhaps better, to re-mythologize into the myth patterns of the twentieth-century Western technocratic myth system. Passages in the Bible dealing with miracles, demons, and divine intervention in human and natural affairs, many of which have been sources of strength for believers throughout the centuries, have become problematic for many in the dominant culture—and, precisely because of the dominant power of that culture, for many in other cultures.[70]

Needless to say, however, the "modern" worldview is not the only possible way of seeing reality, nor is its logic as inescapable as its proponents would have us believe. Michael Oleska points out, "Traditional societies, as have existed since *homo sapiens* first appeared, have almost universally shared certain common attitudes toward fundamental experience. They perceive time, space, and nature in ways remarkably different from those of the post-Renaissance West."[71] Native worldviews are, in fact, much closer to the worldview of the ancient Israelites than that of the modern West. After all, Yahweh was first and foremost the tutelary, local tribal deity of the Hebrew people, whose acts they recognized in their lives. Stan McKay writes, "For those who come out of the Judeo-Christian background it might be helpful to view us as an 'Old Testament People.' We, like them, come out of an oral tradition which is rooted in the Creator and the creation. We, like Moses, know about the sacredness of the earth and the promise of land. Our creation stories also emphasize the power of the Creator and the goodness of creation. We can relate to the vision of Abraham and the laughter of Sarah. We have dreams like Ezekiel and have known people like the Pharaoh. We call ourselves 'the people' to reflect our sense of being chosen."[72]

These divergent worldviews will generate culturally relevant and specific interpretations of the biblical text. Native Christians give authority to scripture specifically because it resonates with their experience. Even while reading with Canaanite eyes, they locate themselves and their perceptual experience in the story. They report relating to Moses trudging up Sinai to meet the divine as one about to embark on a vision quest. They recognize Mary, the mother of Jesus, because she is *la Virgen de Guadalupe,* or White Buffalo Calf Woman, or Corn Mother, or *La llorona* refusing to be consoled at the death of her child. They can chuckle knowingly at the exploits of Jacob because he is the trickster familiar to them as Coyote, or Raven, or Iktomi. This is not the hermeneutics of professional exegetes. Rather, it is the folk theology upon which Christianity at the ground level has always thrived as a living faith. This process of appropriation of the text is no different than that which goes on in the lives of ordinary Christians anywhere in the world.

Any post-colonial biblical hermeneutic for Natives must affirm traditional religious expressions, which previously have been denied and denigrated. As Steven Charleston reminds us: Natives had a covenant with the Creator lived long before missionaries came to them. According to Charleston, and as alluded to previously herein, that original covenantal relationship forms the "Old Testament of Native America."[73] Yowa of the Cherokee, Wakan Tanka of the Lakota, the Great Energy of the Gwich'in, and countless other manifestations are as much *logoi* as any of the faces of deity in the Jewish-Christian tradition. Noley explicitly rejects the assimilationist, missionary hermeneutic that speaks of Native missions in terms of the parable of the tares (Mt 13:24–30, 36–43).[74] In such an interpretation, the tares sown by the enemy are Natives who continue to adhere to their indigenous religious traditions or those who practice religious dimorphism (a very common occurrence among Native peoples), whereby a person participates in Christianity but also still participates in his or her traditional culture and ways without mixing the two. A post-colonial hermeneutic rejects any interpretation that divides Native community.

A post-colonial hermeneutic also will take seriously the importance of land for Native peoples. This imperative has several layers. First, Natives tend to be spatially oriented rather than temporally oriented. Their cultures, spirituality, and identity are connected to the land—and not simply land in a generalized sense but *their* land. The act of creation is not so much what happened *then* as it is what happened *here*, it is the story of the formation of a specific land and a particular people. Thus, when Indian tribes were forcibly removed from their homes, they were robbed of more than territory. Taken from them was a numinous world where every mountain and lake holds meaning for their faith and identity. For example, the Cherokee word *eloh'*, sometimes translated as "religion," also means, at precisely the same time, "history," "culture," "law"—and "land."[75] George Tinker, in particular, has written repeatedly about this spatiality. He claims that a Native reading of the Greek scriptures "begins with a primarily spatial understanding of the *basileia*." In the predominant Western biblical scholarship, since the late nineteenth century when eschatology emerged as a central aspect of interpretation of the Greek scriptures, the *basileia tou theou* (the realm of God) has been seen almost exclusively in temporal terms. According to Tinker, "That is, the only appropriate question to ask about the *basileia* has been When?" For Natives, however, thinking spatially, "it is natural to read *basileia tou theou* as a creation metaphor." It is an image of the ideal of harmony and balance. Tinker concludes, "To this extent, the ideal world is the real world of creation in an ideal relationship of harmony and balance with the Creator. It is relational, first of all, because it implies a relationship between the created order of things and its Creator, and, second, because it implies a relationship between all of the things created." It is the real world within which we hope to realize the ideal world of harmony and balance.[76]

Naturally flowing from this is the question of humanity's relationship to the earth as a creation of the Creator. Natives traditionally do not relate to the land as landscape. Landscape is related to the German *landschaft*, "a territory shaped by people, a working country carved by axe and plough."[77] It is a word rooted in a belief that the earth must be subdued by human effort before it has worth. (Though many Natives have "tooled" the land, by irrigating it or clearing it for crops or pasture, for instance, there is not the concomitant view that it is inferior or worthless without such ministrations.) In that sense, it shares a common origin with the injunction of Genesis 1:28 to have dominion over the creation. By contrast, in traditional Native cultures the relationship to the creation is quite different. There is no superiority assumed or claimed for humanity, and humanity is, in some sense, undifferentiated from the rest of the created order. The world around the Native is a point of communion with the divine because it is a visible expression of the one who created it and still undergirds it.

Finally, when one speaks of land, the issue arises as to ownership. Before the advent of Europeans and the imposition of foreign notions of land tenure, which divided up the land that it might be rendered tame, land was not "owned" in a modern sense. It was held in common by all. It was not property but community. Once again, the affinity with the worldview of the ancient Hebrews is evident. Such a belief compares readily to that expressed in Leviticus 25:23: "And the land shall not be sold in perpetuity; for the land is mine: for ye are strangers and sojourners with me." When he attempted to rally the Native nations into a grand alliance to halt White expansionism, Tecumseh declared, "The only way to stop this evil is for all the red men to unite in claiming a common and equal right in the land, as it was at first, and should be now—for it never was divided, but belongs to all. No tribe has a right to sell, even to each other, much less to strangers, who demand all and will take no less."[78] This raises the ultimate question of ownership of land; namely, that of how it was wrested from its original occupants. Noley states the matter bluntly, "The fundamental question has never been addressed, even after two hundred years of white presence on this continent: namely, the validity of white presence on a continent already possessed and cultivated."[79] A postcolonial hermeneutic must take account of Native land claims.

The final fundamental, and most basic, element of a post-colonial hermeneutic is its communal character. As is often said, community is the highest value for Native peoples, and fidelity to it is a primary responsibility. Native religious traditions are not practiced for personal empowerment or fulfillment but rather to ensure the corporate good. And as already noted, there is generally no concept of salvation other than the continuance of the people, and the closest approximation of the Jewish-Christian doctrine of sin is a failure to live up to one's obligations to the people. A post-colonial hermeneutic for Natives rejects the individualistic interpretations brought by assimilationist missions in favor of more communal and communitarian methods and understandings.

No professional exegete or theologian can say what a text means, let alone *should mean*, for Native communities. Only the communities themselves, gathered in dialogue (though modern mass communications may permit them to be geographically distant), can perform that task. The community as the proper locus of the hermeneutical task means that what emerges resembles what Justo González, for Hispanics, labeled *Fuenteovejuna* (sheep trough) theology, "meaning . . . a theology undertaken with such a sense of community that it belongs to the community itself, and at the end no one knows who first proposed a particular idea."[80] In most traditional cultures the thought that an idea or a story could belong to an individual—belong to such an extent that he or she could have enforceable proprietary rights to it—would seem as irrational and bizarre as a single person owning the land.

A post-colonial Native hermeneutic, a "we-hermeneutic," however, "goes far beyond the proposal that Scripture is best understood within the circumstances of a community, and when interpreted by a community."[81] Community is not only a tool or a framework for the hermeneutical task but also its ultimate goal.

> Thus, the community is not just a hermeneutical tool and a necessary context in which to understand a text, but also the goal of every interpretation and every text to be interpreted. Without such a perspective, we fall into I-hermeneutics, which fails, not merely because it misinterprets its text, but also because it misinterprets its task. The task of hermeneutics is not merely for an individual—or even for a community—to understand a text, but is even more for building the community.[82]

I have called such an approach *communitist*. A truly post-colonial we-hermeneutic is communitist because it possesses an active commitment to

Native community. The community itself "stands at the very center" of such an interpretive system.[83]

Though such a hermeneutic will, of necessity, be culturally specific (Natives have too long been subjected to the universalizing impulses of Western discourse), as Hall claims for the post-colonial critique in general, it moves beyond the "clear-cut politics of binary oppositions," of "us" versus "them."[84] Though it seeks to be inclusive, as much as possible, of the entire Native American community, it does not stop there. Nor does it stop at the entire human community; rather, it seeks to embrace the entire created order, including plants, animals, Mother Earth herself.

In his book *Tribal Secrets*, Robert Warrior speaks of the need and ability of American Natives to assert their own "intellectual sovereignty."[85] What exactly a post-colonial we-hermeneutic will mean for Natives must emerge out of the community itself as we critically reflect upon our own communitist commitments. If, however, we are ever to dismantle the colonial paradigm and move to a place "after" and "beyond" colonialism[86] and the imperialist readings it engenders, we must have hermeneutical sovereignty as well.

NOTES

CHAPTER 1. IN OTHER'S WORDS

1. Leslie Marmon Silko, "Foreword," *Dancing with the Wind*, 4 (1992–93): 6–7. Emphasis in original.

2. N. Scott Momaday, "Foreword," *Dancing with the Wind*, 3 (1991): 6.

3. Louis Owens, *Other Destinies: Understanding the American Indian Novel* (Norman: University of Oklahoma Press, 1992), 3.

4. Gregory Gagnon, "American Indian Intellectuals: Are They above Reproach, or Easy Targets?" *Tribal College* (Summer 1995): 43.

5. Sherman Alexie, *Old Shirts and New Skins* (Los Angeles: American Indian Studies Center, University of California, 1993), 4.

6. See Ashis Nandy, *The Intimate Enemy: Loss and Recovery of Self under Colonialism* (Delhi: Oxford University Press, 1983), 102.

7. Wub-e-ke-niew [Francis Blake, Jr.], *We Have the Right to Exist* (New York: Black Thistle Press, 1995), xiv–xv, xxvi, xliii, xlvii. Blake also calls his volume, on Anishinaabe history and thought, the "first book ever published from an *Ahnishinahbæó±jibway* Perspective," despite numerous volumes by Gerald Vizenor and others.

8. Thomas King, ed., *All My Relations* (Toronto: McClelland & Stewart, 1990), xi.

9. Geary Hobson, *The Remembered Earth* (Albuquerque: University of New Mexico Press, 1979), 8.

10. A. T. Anderson, *Nations within a Nation: The American Indian and the Government of the United States* (Chappaqua, N.Y.: privately printed, 1976), 75–77.

11. Dennis McPherson and J. Douglas Rabb, *Indian from the Inside: A Study in Ethno-Metaphysics* (Thunder Bay: Ont.: Lakehead University, Centre for Northern Studies, 1993), 21–22.

12. N. Scott Momaday, *The Names: A Memoir* (New York: Harper & Row, 1976), 23–25.

13. Hobson, *Remembered Earth*, 8–9.

14. Ibid., 9.

15. Hobson could have added the example of Richard Fields, the chief of the Texas Cherokee who died leading the band in an abortive rebellion against its White oppressors, though only one-fourth Cherokee himself. See Richard Drinnon, *White Savage: The Case of John Dunn Hunter* (New York: Schocken Books, 1972), 183; Jace Weaver, "Poetry," Native Journal (January 1993): 23; Weaver, "Dreaming Fredonia," in Caroline Sullivan and Cynthia Stevens, eds., *Distinguished Poets of America* (Owings Mills: National Library of Poetry, 1993), 402.

16. Leslie Silko declares, "The community is tremendously important. That's where a person's identity has to come from, not from racial blood quantum levels." Silko, "Stories and Their Tellers: A Conversation with Leslie Marmon Silko," in Dexter Fisher, ed., *The Third Woman: Minority Women Writers of the United States* (New York: Houghton Mifflin, 1980), 19. For a discussion of this point in another colonial context, see Rob Nieuwenhuys, *Mirror of the Indies: A History of Dutch Colonial Literature* (Amherst: University of Massachusetts Press, 1982), 196.

17. Hobson, *Remembered Earth*, 9.

18. King, *All My Relations*, x–xi.

19. Arnold Krupat, *The Voice in the Margin: Native American Literature and the Canon* (Berkeley: University of California Press, 1989), 13–14; H. David Brumble III, *American Indian Autobiography* (Berkeley: University of California Press, 1988), 174; Paula Gunn Allen, ed., *Spider Woman's Granddaughters* (New York: Fawcett Columbine, 1989), 168, emphasis mine; Ngugi, *Decolonising the Mind*, 17.

20. David Murray, *Forked Tongues: Speech, Writing and Representation in North American Indian Texts* (Bloomington: Indiana University Press, 1991), 81.

21. King, *All My Relations*, x.

22. Edward W. Said, *The World, the Text, and the Critic* (Cambridge: Harvard University Press, 1983), 19–20.

23. See Roger Welsch, *Touching the Fire: Buffalo Dancers, the Sky Bundle, and Other Tales* (New York: Villard Books, 1992).

24. Achiel Peelman, *Christ Is a Native American* (Maryknoll, N.Y.: Orbis Books, 1995), 33. Emphasis mine.

25. Owens, *Other Destinies*, 12.

26. Vine Deloria, Jr., *We Talk, You Listen: New Tribes, New Turf* (New York: Macmillan, 1970).

27. Hobson, *Remembered Earth*, 10.

28. Lester Standiford writes, "Of course, a shortsighted view of the application of minorities literature would exclude even those members of a group whose place might be validated by blood heritage, but whose life experience lies largely outside the normal experience of the group: i.e., should the Anglo farmer be permitted to read *Moby Dick*?" See Standiford, "Worlds Made of Dawn: Characteris-

tic Image and Incident in Native American Imaginative Literature," in Wolodymyr T. Zyla and Wendell M. Aycock, eds., *Ethnic Literatures Since 1776: The Many Voices of America* (Lubbock: Texas Tech Press, 1978), 331. But should the Anglo farmer who knows nothing about whaling and who has never even seen the sea *write Moby Dick?*

29. D'Arcy McNickle, *Indian Man: A Life of Oliver La Farge* (Bloomington: Indiana University Press, 1971); John Joseph Mathews, *Life and Death of an Oilman: The Career of E. W. Marland* (Norman: University of Oklahoma Press, 1951); Jace Weaver, *Then to the Rock Let Me Fly: Luther Bohanon and Judicial Activism* (Norman: University of Oklahoma Press, 1993).

30. King, *All My Relations,* xi. Scott Momaday concurs: "The phrase 'American Indian Writer' I understand to indicate an American Indian who writes. It does not indicate anything more than that to me." See Standiford, "Worlds Made of Dawn," 332.

31. Martin William Smith [Martin Cruz Smith], *The Indians Won* (New York: Belmont, 1970); Robbie Robertson and the Red Road Ensemble, "Music for 'The Native Americans,'" (Hollywood, Cal.: Capitol Records, 1994); Robbie Robertson, interview on Canadian Broadcasting Corporation, October 14, 1994.

32. Forbes, "Colonialism," 19–20.

33. Krupat, *Voice in the Margin,* 207.

34. A. LaVonne Brown Ruoff, *American Indian Literatures: An Introduction, Bibliographic Review, and Selected Bibliography* (New York: Modern Language Association, 1990), vi.

35. Brian Swann, "Introduction: Only the Beginning," in Duane Niatum, ed., *Harper's Anthology of Twentieth Century Native American Poetry* (San Francisco: HarperSanFrancisco, 1988), xx.

36. King, *All My Relations,* x.

37. Bill Ashcroft, Gareth Griffiths, and Helen Tiffin, *The Empire Writes Back: Theory and Practice in Post-Colonial Literatures* (London: Routledge, 1989), 2.

38. In fairness to Ashcroft and his coauthors, they do define post-colonial as that period commencing with the moment of colonization and continuing to the present day, a time frame and definition that would encompass American Indians. Nevertheless, by their own admission, the only literatures they discuss are those of peoples who have already achieved political independence. See Ashcroft, Griffiths, and Tiffin, 2, 6. If we accept, rather, E. M. Beekman's definition of colonialism, in the preface to the English edition of Nieuwenhuys's *Mirror of the Indies,* as "the subjugation of an *entire* area, and [dating] from the time when the last independent domain was conquered," we would be forced to ask when colonialism took final hold in the area now called the United States. Nieuwenhuys, x. Emphasis in original.

39. See Michael Hector, *The Celtic Fringe in British National Development, 1536–1966* (Berkeley: University of California Press, 1975); Robert K. Thomas, "Colonialism: Classic and Internal," *New University Thought,* 4:4 (Winter 1966–67);

Ward Churchill, *Fantasies of the Master Race: Literature, Cinema and the Colonization of American Indians* (Monroe, Maine: Common Courage Press, 1993), 23–24, 31.

40. Of course, even in classic colonialism, a class of colonizer is created that is born in the colony and, while largely continuing to possess and identify with the values and worldview of the *métropole*, identifies the geographic area of the colony as their homeland. The French called such persons *pieds-noirs*. Nieuwenhuys describes the situation of such a class of persons when Dutch rule of Indonesia ended. He writes,

> The massive repatriation of people from Indonesia to the Netherlands, timely or not, forced a lot of those people to regard their past in the Indies as nothing but a memory. But memory is not quite the same thing as nostalgia or "a longing for that which has been lost." This nostalgia exists, naturally, among broad segments of the Indies community in the Netherlands, part of which—particularly its older members—considers itself to be in some kind of exile. This feeling of being cut off creates the nostalgia, which in turn colors people's memories. These memories can extend so far and so deep that they cause pain, even a great deal of pain.

According to Nieuwenhuys, it creates a distorted remembrance that is a familiar theme in romantic literature. See Nieuwenhuys, *Mirror of the Indies*, 298.

Such a "remembrance" may go part way toward explaining the increasing fascination of Amer-Europeans with idealized, romanticized, and fictive images of Indians and their spiritualities since the reassertion of Native tribal identity and sovereignty in the late sixties and early seventies.

41. Ashcroft, Griffiths, and Tiffin, *Empire Writes Back*, 25.

42. Edward W. Said, *Culture and Imperialism* (New York: Alfred A. Knopf, 1993), xxv.

43. Gerald Vizenor, *Manifest Manners: Postindian Warriors of Survivance* (Hanover, N.H.: Wesleyan University Press-University Press of New England, 1991), 69.

44. Tony Bennett and Valda Blundell, "First Peoples," *Cultural Studies* 9 (January 1995): 2.

45. Barbara Harlow, *Resistance Literature* (New York, Methuen, 1987), 2.

46. Menno Boldt, *Surviving as Indians* (Toronto: University of Toronto Press, 1993), 176.

47. Ibid., 175.

48. Ibid.

49. Edward W. Said, *The Pen and the Sword: Conversations with David Barsamian* (Monroe, Maine: Common Courage Press, 1994), 105.

50. Ashcroft, Griffiths, and Tiffin, *Empire Writes Back*, 25.

51. Ibid., 29–20; Nieuwenhuys, *Mirror of the Indies*, 307.

52. Quoted in Ashcroft, et al., *Empire Writes Back*, 30.

53. Homi K. Bhabha, *The Location of Culture* (New York: Routledge, 1944), 4.

54. Nandy, *Intimate Enemy*, xii, xix.

55. Ngugi, *Decolonising the Mind*, 14–16.

56. Quoted in Dana Milbank, "What's in a Name? For the Lumbees, Pride and Money," *Wall Street Journal*, November 13, 1995, 1.

57. Owens, *Other Destinies*, 7.

58. Ngugi, *Decolonising the Mind*, 9.

59. Isabelle Knockwood, *Out of the Depths* (Lockport, N.Y.: Roseway Publishing, 1992), 98.

60. Linda Cavanaugh and Tony Stizza, prods., "Strangers in Their Own Land" (Oklahoma City: Strangers in Their Own Land, Inc., 1993); Jim McKinney, interview with author, June 10, 1994; Quanah Tonemah, interview with author, June 10, 1994; Knockwood, *Out of the Depths*, 98. Knockwood also notes that Native languages were labeled routinely as "gibberish" and "mumbo jumbo" to denigrate them. This process continues to the present even in unlikely places. For a recent re-release of the ethnographic/colonialist film "In the Land of the Headhunters" (discreetly retitled "In the Land of the War Canoes") by Edward S. Curtis, the University of Washington and the Field Museum in Chicago provided a new sound-track for the silent film, recorded by Kwakiutl Indians. Though the track consists largely of spoken dialogue, no subtitles are provided for the viewer. What is being said is unimportant, merely colorful background noise, simply gibberish.

61. Joseph Bruchac, *Survival This Way: Interviews with American Indian Poets* (Tucson: University of Arizona Press, 1987), 284–85; Luci Tapahonso, *Sáanii Dahataal, The Women Are Singing* (Tucson: University of Arizona Press, 1993), x–xi. Beth Brant (Mohawk) observes:

> There are women who are writing bilingually. Salli Benedict, Lenore Keeshig-Tobias, Rita Joe, Beatrice Medicine, Anna Lee Walters, Luci Tapahonso, Mary TallMountain, Nia Francisco, Ofelia Zepeda, Donna Goodleaf are just some of the Native women who are choosing to use their own Nation's languages when English won't suffice or convey the integrity of the meaning. I find this an exciting movement. And an exciting consequence would be the development of *our own* critics, and publishing houses that do bilingual work. Our languages are rich, full of metaphor, nuance, and life. Our languages are not dead or conquered—like women's hearts, they are soaring and spreading the culture to our youth and our unborn.

See Beth Brant, *Writing as Witness* (Toronto: Women's Press, 1994). While Brant is correct that the movement is exciting and that bilingual publishing would be equally so, such a development is, at best, temporally remote and, at worst, highly unlikely.

62. Murray, *Forked Tongues*, 92.

63. Owens, *Other Destinies*, 6; Ashcroft, et al., *Empire Writes Back*, 11.

64. Bruchac, *Survival This Way*, 94; "The Spectrum of Other Languages: An Interview with Joy Harjo," *Tamaqua*, 3:1 (Spring 1992): 11–13.

65. Vizenor, *Manifest Manners*, 105–6.

66. McPherson and Rabb, *Indian from the Inside*, 14–15. Emphasis in original.

67. Ngugi, *Decolonising the Mind*, 29.

68. Nieuwenhuys, *Mirror of the Indies*, 177.

69. Peelman, *Christ Is a Native*, 59.

70. Ngugi, *Decolonising the Mind*, 3.

71. Enrique Dussel, *The Invention of the Americas: Eclipse of "the Other" and the Myth of Modernity* (New York: Continuum, 1995), 12.

72. Owens, *Other Destinies*, 7.

73. Homer Noley, *First White Frost* (Nashville: Abingdon Press, 1991), 18, citing Barry Fell, *America B.C.: Ancient Settlers in the New World* (New York: Quadrangle/New York Times, 1976), 15–16; John Ehle, *Trail of Tears: The Rise and Fall of the Cherokee Nation* (New York: Doubleday, 1988), 1; George Sanderlin, ed., *Witness: Writings of Bartolomé de Las Casas* (Maryknoll: Orbis Books, 1992), xvii; see generally, Ronald Sanders, *Lost Tribes and Promised Lands: The Origins of American Racism* (New York: Harper, 1978). The slur persists in Mormonism with its teachings about American Indians as Lamanites and continues to revive in both popular and scholarly discourse. See Gordon Bronitsky, "Jews and Indians: Old Myths and New Realities," *Jewish Spectator* (Winter 1991–92): 39.

74. Francis Jennings, *The Invasion of America: Indians, Colonialism, and the Cant of Conquest* (New York: W. W. Norton & Company, 1976), 10–11 (emphasis in original). And see Djelal Kadir, *Columbus and the Ends of the Earth: Europe's Prophetic Rhetoric as Conquering Ideology* (Berkeley: University of California Press, 1992); Reinhold Niebuhr, *Irony and American History* (New York: Charles Scribner's Sons, 1952), 24. Even Niebuhr, however, who spent much effort attempting to dispel the myth of American exceptionalism, was ultimately seduced by the myths of conquest. He writes that the European found here a "vast virgin continent, populated sparsely by Indians in a primitive state of culture." See Reinhold Niebuhr and Alan Heimert, *A Nation So Conceived* (London: Faber & Faber, 1964), 7. See also Weaver, "Original Simplicities": 206–7. As for the myths' codification in law, see James Kent, *Commentaries on American Law*, vol. 1 (New York: O. Halsted, 1826), 243; vol. 3 (New York: O. Halsted, 1828), 312.

75. Terry Goldie, *Fear and Temptation: The Image of the Indigene in Canadian, Australian, and New Zealand Literatures* (Kingston, Ont.: McGill-Queen's University Press, 1989), 100. See James O. Gump, *The Dust Rose Like Smoke: The Subjugation of the Zulu and the Sioux* (Lincoln: University of Nebraska Press, 1994).

76. Goldie, *Fear and Temptation*, 158, 149.

77. D. P. Kidder, "Missions," in John McClintock and James Strong, eds., *Cyclopedia of Biblical, Theological, and Ecclesiastical Literature*, vol. 6 (New York: Harper Brothers, c. 1877; reprint, Grand Rapids: Baker Book House, 1981), 375. See also Jace Weaver, "Missions and Missionaries," in Mary B. Davis, ed., *Native America in the Twentieth Century* (New York: Garland Publishing, 1994), 346. For general discussions of the "Vanishing Indian" or "doomed culture" and other

stereotypes of Native Americans, see Brian W. Dippie, *The Vanishing American: White Attitudes and U.S. Indian Policy* (Lawrence: University of Kansas Press, 1982); Robert F. Berkhofer, Jr., *The White Man's Indian: Images of the American Indian from Columbus to the Present* (New York: Vintage Books, 1978); and Daniel Francis, *The Imaginary Indian: The Image of the Indian in Canadian Culture* (Vancouver: Arsenal Pulp Press, 1992).

78. Elsie Clews Parsons, ed., *American Indian Life*, (1922; reprint, Lincoln: University of Nebraska Press, 1991), ix–x. It is interesting to note that even in Mark's modern discussion (introducing the reprint) one can see the imperialist impulse of anthropology at work. Changes in Native society are seen as akin to *biological species* becoming extinct! Bruce Trigger writes that early anthropologists "were also convinced that native cultures were disintegrating as a result of European contact; hence the primary aim of ethnologists was to record these cultures as thoroughly as possible before they disappeared completely." Bruce G. Trigger, "Ethnohistory: The Unfinished Edifice," *Ethnohistory* 33 (Summer 1986): 256, quoted in Margaret Connell Szasz, *Between Indian and White Worlds: The Cultural Broker* (Norman: University of Oklahoma Press, 1994), 7. In 1995, Achiel Peelman can still write, "Fifty years ago, many anthropologists, missionaries, medical doctors and politicians *rightly* described the Indians as 'vanishing peoples.' They did not hesitate to conclude that the only survival open to them was through total assimilation or individual integration into . . . North American society." Peelman also endorses the myth of the Vanishing Indian when he refers to "indigenous beliefs and values (the past). . . ." Peelman, *Christ Is a Native*, 21, 27.

79. Goldie, *Fear and Temptation*, 158, 155.

80. Quoted in Alvin Josephy, "New England Indians: Then and Now," in Laurence M. Hauptman and James D. Wherry, eds., *The Pequots in Southern New England: The Fall and Rise of an American Indian Nation* (Norman: University of Oklahoma Press, 1990), 7. Georges Sioui also speaks of non-Natives "crystallized perception" of Indians. Georges Sioui, *For an Amerindian Autohistory* (Montreal: McGill-Queen's University Press), 1992.

81. See, generally, Dussel, *Invention of the Americas*, and Edward W. Said, *Orientalism* (New York: Random House, 1978); Christopher Frayling, *Spaghetti Westerns: Cowboys and Europeans from Karl May to Sergio Leone* (London: Routledge & Kegan Paul, 1981), 103–4. Ngugi writes of the inferiority inculcated when Blacks read H. Rider Haggard. How much equally so the Indian child who reads pulp westerns, Cooper, or May?

82. Albert Memmi, *The Colonizer and the Colonized*, exp. ed. (Boston: Beacon Press, 1967), 52; Said, *Culture*, 237; Frantz Fanon, *The Wretched of the Earth* (New York: Grove, 1968), 210.

83. Howard Adams, 43; Jace Weaver, "American Indians and Native Americans: Reinhold Niebuhr, Historiography and Indigenous Peoples," in Sylvia O'Meara and Douglas A. West, eds., *From Our Eyes: Learning from Indigenous Peoples* (Toronto: Garamond Press, 1996), 29.

84. Sioui, *For an Amerindian Autohistory*, 101; Johannes Fabian, *Time and the Other: How Anthropology Makes Its Object* (New York: Columbia University Press, 1983), 17.

85. Said, *Culture*, 152; Sioui, *Amerindian Autohistory*, 101; Vizenor, *Manifest Manners*, 68–69; Ngugi, *Decolonising the Mind*, 16; George Tinker, *Missionary Conquest* (Minneapolis: Fortress Press, 1993), 118, 2; Sioui, *Amerindian Autohistory*, 32, 100; Jace Weaver, "Notes from a Miner's Canary," in Weaver, *Defending*, 16.

86. Leslie Marmon Silko, *Storyteller* (New York: Arcade Publishing, 1981), quoted on back cover.

87. Denise Lardner Carmody and John Tully Carmody, *Native American Religions: An Introduction* (New York: Paulist Press, 1993), 225, 67.

88. Karl Kroeber, ed., *Traditional Literatures of the American Indian* (Lincoln: University of Nebraska Press, 1981), 1, 2. Emphasis mine.

89. Penny Petrone, *Native Literature in Canada* (Toronto: Oxford University Press, 1990), 17, 9–34.

90. Vizenor, *Manifest Manners*, 72.

91. John Bierhorst, ed., *Four Masterworks of American Indian Literature* (New York: Farrar, Straus, and Giroux, 1974), xii.

92. Kroeber, *Traditional Literatures*, 2.

93. Gerald Vizenor, ed., *Narrative Chance: Postmodern Discourse on Native American Indian Literatures* (Albuquerque: University of New Mexico Press, 1989), 4.

94. Bill Ashcroft, Gareth Griffiths, and Helen Tiffin, eds., *The Post-Colonial Studies Reader* (London: Routledge, 1995), 2–3; Vizenor, *Manifest*, 77, 80; Owens, *Other Destinies*, 21.

95. Robert Allen Warrior, *Tribal Secrets: Recovering American Indian Intellectual Traditions* (Minneapolis: University of Minnesota Press, 1995), xviii–xix.

96. See Harlow, *Resistance Literature*, xvi. It should be noted that as internal Native criticism grows, some Amer-European critics accuse Natives, who merely are struggling to make their voices heard, of attempting to establish hegemony over Native studies. Arnold Krupat notes that Hertha Wong, for instance, was forced to assert tenuous claims to Native heritage in order to gain a hearing for her work on Native autobiography, calling the move "coy and potentially opportunistic." Elizabeth Cook-Lynn writes of the Wong volume that the "wannabee sentiment . . . clutters an otherwise tolerable piece of redundant scholarship" and that the "unnecessary claim . . . to be 'part Native American' is so absurd as to cast ridicule on the work itself." Gerald Vizenor notes that the "racialism of [Wong's] romantic notions [of identity] would bear minimal honor in tribal memories." See Robert Warrior, "A Marginal Voice," *Native Nations* (March–April 1991): 29–30; Daniel Littlefield, Jr., "American Indians, American Scholars and the American Literary Canon," *American Studies* 33 (1992): 96–108; Arnold Krupat, "Scholarship and Native American Studies: A Response to Daniel Littlefield, Jr.," *American Studies* 34 (1993): 91–92; Vizenor, *Manifest*, 61, 88. See also Hertha Dawn Wong, *Sending My*

Heart Back across the Years: Tradition and Innovation in Native American Autobiography (New York: Oxford University Press, 1992), v–vi.

97. Bierhorst, *Four Masterworks*, xi.

98. Krupat, *Voice in the Margin*, 209.

99. Gauri Viswanathan, *Masks of Conquest: Literary Study and British Rule in India* (New York: Columbia University Press, 1989), 166–67.

100. Goldie, *Fear and Temptation*, 108; Walter Ong, *Orality and Literacy: The Technologizing of the Word* (London: Methuen, 1982), 32.

101. Krupat, *Voice in the Margin*, 232.

102. Ibid., 17.

103. Ashcroft, Griffiths, and Tiffin, *Empire Writes Back*, 145.

104. Harlow, *Resistance Literature*, xvi; Owens, *Other Destinies*, 16.

105. Further, many Indian writers have written in a rather pan-Indian fashion stories set in tribal traditions other than their own. Thus Momaday and Ron Querry (Choctaw) have written about the Navajos and Pueblos, and Thomas King has written about the Bloods. See, for example, Ron Querry, *The Death of Bernadette Lefthand* (Santa Fe: Red Crane Books, 1993).

106. J. Hector St. John de Crèvecoeur, *Letters from an American Farmer* (reprint, New York: Penguin, 1981), 60–70, 120–24; Ashcroft, Griffiths, and Tiffin, *Empire Writes Back*, 136; Niebuhr and Heimert, *Nation So Conceived*, 11. In writing as he does, Niebuhr gives a perfect definition, not of indigeneity, but of Amer-Europeans.

107. Ashcroft, Griffiths, and Tiffin, *Empire*, 143. Such indigenizing strategies are reminiscent of the Jindyworobak movement in the 1930s and '40s in Australia, whose name is taken from an Aboriginal word meaning *to annex*. Concerning the indigenous response to such efforts, Goldie writes, "Many Aborigines have questioned the hubris of the Jindyworobak group in their attempts to transmute bourgeois white experience through the simple evocation of Aboriginal signifiers." Goldie, *Fear and Temptation*, 144.

108. Krupat, *Voice in the Margin*, 213–14. Emphasis in original.

109. Vizenor, *Manifest Manners*, 59.

110. James Ruppert, *Mediation in Contemporary Native American Fiction* (Norman: University of Oklahoma Press, 1995), 6–7. Emphasis mine.

111. Murray, *Forked Tongues*, 3, 80.

112. Goldie, *Fear and Temptation*, 217.

113. Simon Ortiz, "Toward a National Indian Literature: Cultural Authenticity in Nationalism," *MELUS* 8, no. 2 (1981): 9–10. Geary Hobson also maintains that it is Indian despite its written form. See Hobson, *Remembered Earth*, 4.

114. Paula Gunn Allen, *The Sacred Hoop: Recovering the Feminine in American Indian Traditions*, 2d ed. (Boston: Beacon Press, 1992), 79; Ortiz, "Toward a National Indian Literature," 8.

115. Ngugi, *Decolonising the Mind*, 67–69, 64–65, 85–86.

116. King, *All My Relations*, ix–x.

117. Ibid., xi.

118. Clifford E. Trafzer, ed., *Earth Song, Sky Spirit* (New York: Doubleday, 1993), 7; Ruoff, *American Indian Literatures*, 114; Petrone, *Native Literature*, 183–84. African post-colonial critic Abdul JanMohamed, who adapts Fanonian thought to literary criticism, writes, "The Third World's literary dialogue with Western cultures is marked by two broad characteristics: its attempt to negate the prior European negation of colonized cultures and its adoption and creative modification of Western languages and artistic forms in conjunction with indigenous languages and forms." Abdul R. JanMohamed, "The Economy of Manichean Allegory: The Function of Racial Difference in Colonialist Literature," *Critical Inquiry* 12, no. 1 (1985), quoted in Ashcroft, Griffiths, and Tiffin, *Post-colonial Studies*, 23.

119. Murray, *Forked Tongues*, 87–88.

120. Paula Gunn Allen, *Voice of the Turtle: American Indian Literature, 1900–1970* (New York: Ballantine, 1994), 7.

121. King, *All My Relations*, xii.

122. Warrior, *Tribal Secrets*, 117.

123. This is akin to what JanMohamed terms "Manichean aesthetics" and Ngugi calls the "aesthetic of oppression" versus that of "liberation." See Abdul R. JanMohamed, *Manichean Aesthetics: The Politics of Literature in Colonial Africa* (Amherst: University of Massachusetts Press, 1983); Ngugi wa Thiong'o, "Literature in Schools," in *Writers in Politics* (London: Heinemann, 1981), 38.

124. Owens, *Other Destinies*, 20.

125. Ruoff, *American Indian Literatures*, 2.

126. Calvin Martin, ed., *The American Indian and the Problem of History* (New York: Oxford University Press, 1987), 3–34, passim.

127. Rosemary McCombs Maxey, "Who Can Sit at the Lord's Table? The Experience of Indigenous Peoples," in Daniel L. Johnson and Charles Hambrick-Stowe, eds., *Theology and Identity: Traditions, Movements, and Polity in the United Church of Canada* (New York: Pilgrim Press, 1990), 54.

128. Johannes Olivier states, "There is as it were a veil between the natives and their European masters on account of which the essential character of the former remains almost entirely unknown to the latter." Quoted in Nieuwenhuys, *Mirror of the Indies*, 53. Eduardo and Bonnie Duran have attempted to redress this imbalance in a pychotherapeutic context. See Eduardo Duran and Bonnie Duran, *Native American Postcolonial Psychology* (Albany: State University of New York Press, 1995), 13–21.

129. Peelman, *Christ Is a Native*, 44.

130. Owens, *Other Destinies*, 8.

131. Sioui, *Amerindian Autohistory*, 31.

132. James Treat, ed., *Native and Christian: Indigenous Voices on Religious Identity in the United States and Canada* (New York: Routledge, 1996), 20.

133. Ruoff, *American Indian Literatures*, 2.

134. Åke Hultkrantz, *Native Religions of North America* (New York: Harper and Row, 1987), 20.

135. Carmody and Carmody, *Native American Religions*, 106–7.

136. David A. Rausch and Blair Schlepp, *Native American Voices* (Grand Rapids: Baker Books, 1994), 52, 51–53.

137. McPherson and Rabb, *Indian from the Inside*, 83ff.

138. Ngugi notes that a people's culture is an essential component in defining and revealing their worldview. Ngugi, *Decolonising*, 100.

139. Peelman, *Christ Is a Native*, 202; Carmody and Carmody, *Native American Religions*, 191–93.

140. M. A. Jaimes-Guerrero, "Native Womanism: The Organic Female Archetype—Kinship and Gender Identity within Sacred Indigenous Traditions," American Academy of Religion, November 20, 1995. Guerrero goes on to state, however, that Indians are "universal people" and that "cultural diversity derived from the environment is very different from saying that Indians were different cultures." She notes that indigenous peoples worldwide have a "universal connection with each other." As Robert Warrior notes, "Fourth World" and "indigenist" discourse, of which Jaimes-Guerrero is a leading exponent, has adhered to "idealism . . . and essentialism." Warrior, *Tribal Secrets*, xvii, xviii.

141. McPherson and Rabb, *Indian from the Inside*, i.

142. Ibid., 3.

143. Ibid.

144. Quoted in Sioui, *Amerindian Autohistory*, 69.

145. JanMohamed, "Economy of Manichean Allegory," 21–22. See also Ronald Takaki, *A Different Mirror: A History of Multicultural America* (Boston: Little, Brown and Company, 1993), 25–50. Takaki writes, "*The Tempest* can be approached as a fascinating tale that served as a masquerade for the creation of a new society in America. Seen in this light, the play invites us to view English expansion not only as imperialism, but also as a defining moment in the making of an English-American identity based on race." Takaki, 25–26.

146. Peelman, *Christ Is a Native*, 23.

147. Ibid. Emphasis in original.

148. Ibid.; Robert Allen Warrior, "Tribal Secrets" (Ph.D. diss., Union Theological Seminary, 1991), 8.

149. Peelman, *Christ Is a Native*, 23.

150. Vine Deloria, Jr., *God Is Red*, 2d ed. (Golden, Co.: Fulcrum Publishing, 1992), 79.

151. Peelman, *Christ Is a Native*, 46. See Allen, *Spider Woman's Granddaughters*: "Right relationship, or right kinship is fundamental to Native aesthetics" (9).

152. Moises Colop, interview with author, September 22, 1995.

153. Goldie, *Fear and Temptation*, 127.

154. McPherson and Rabb, *Indian from the Inside*, 10.

155. Ibid.

156. Richard Rorty, "Cosmopolitanism without Emancipation: A Response to Jean-François Lyotard," in *Objectivity, Relativism, and Truth: Philosophical Papers*, vol. 1 (Cambridge: Cambridge University Press, 1991), 213.

157. George Tinker, "An American Indian Response to Ecojustice," in Jace Weaver, ed., *Defending Mother Earth: Native American Perspectives on Environmental Justice* (Maryknoll: Orbis Books, 1966), 173.

158. Quoted in Goldie, *Fear and Temptation*, 221; Krim Benterrak, Stephen Muecke, and Paddy Roe, *Reading the Country: Introduction to Nomadology* (Fremantle: Fremantle Arts Centre, 1984), 126.

159. Aloysious Pieris, *An Asian Theology of Liberation* (Maryknoll: Orbis Books, 1988), xi–xii.

160. See, for example, Ashcroft, Griffiths, and Tiffin, *Empire Writes Back*, 8–9.

161. Han is a kind of existential angst that is a defining element of the Korean character. See Andrew Sung Park, *The Wounded Heart of God: The Asian Concept of Han and the Christian Doctrine of Sin* (Nashville: Abingdon, 1993); Chung Hyun-Kyung, *Struggle to Be the Sun Again* (Maryknoll: Orbis Books, 1990), 23, 44, 66, 99.

162. Philip Arnold, "Wampum, the Land, and the Abolition of Grief," American Academy of Religions, Philadelphia, Pa., November 20, 1995.

163. Noley, *First White Frost*, 79; Mary Churchill, "Native Struggles for Freedom in the Land," respondent, American Academy of Religion, Philadelphia, Pa., November 20, 1995. The title of Noley's book, *First White Frost* is a marvelous example of signification, possessing a double meaning. In an epigram at the book's opening, Noley explains, "Nitakechi, leader of the Choctaw Southern District, one of the most traditional of the Choctaw leaders, had the sad task of leading the people of his district on the forced march from Mississippi to Indian Territory. He said that three thousand Choctaw men, women, and children 'would be ready to start "the first white frost of October."' At the same time, Noley's title expresses the "covering" of Native spirituality with the "white frost" of the religion of the colonizer, Christianity.

164. Treat, *Native and Christian*, 12.

165. Greg Sarris, *Keeping Slug Woman Alive: A Holistic Approach to American Indian Texts* (Berkeley: University of California Press, 1993), 121.

166. Margaret Connell Szasz, ed., *Between Indian and White Worlds: The Cultural Broker* (Norman: University of Oklahoma Press, 1994); Dorothy R. Parker, "D'Arcy McNickle: Living a Broker's Life," in ibid.; Ruppert, *Mediation*; Murray, *Forked Tongues*, 1.

167. Ruppert, *Mediation*, 3, 20.

168. Ibid., 19–20, quoting Gerald Vizenor, *Earthdivers: Tribal Narratives on Mixed Descent* (Minneapolis: University of Minnesota Press, 1981), xvii.

169. Nieuwenhuys, *Mirror of the Indies*, 273, 324, 186.

170. Quoted in Treat, *Native and Christian*, 18.

171. Mourning Dove, *Cogewea, the Half-Blood* (Boston: Four Seas, 1927), 41. Emphasis in original. The work was actually completed in 1916 but remained unpublished for eleven years.

172. Owens, *Other Destinies*, 19.

173. Ibid.

174. Murray, *Forked Tongues*, 88–89.

175. Ruppert, *Mediation*, 19.

176. Ibid., 29.

177. Ibid., 32–33; see Paula Gunn Allen, *The Woman Who Owned the Shadows* (Spinsters, Ink, 1983; reprint, San Francisco: Aunt Lute Books, 1994).

178. Jace Weaver, "PW Interviews: Thomas King," *Publishers Weekly* (March 8, 1993), quoted in Vizenor, *Manifest Manners*, 174.

179. See Owens, *Other Destinies*, 14–15.

180. Petrone, *Native Literature*, 182.

181. Petrone here reveals a Eurocentric bias as she writes patronizingly, "Already many [Native writers] are able to deal with the culture clash and their own identity not only with perception but with some detachment and control, moving beyond the worst excesses of emotion and diction that marred much earlier protest writing." Ibid. In this regard, it is worth noting that one of my female students stated that to characterize what has occurred in the hemisphere as a "clash of cultures" is akin to calling rape a "clash of genders."

182. Vine Deloria, Jr., "Sacred Lands and Religious Freedom," *American Indian Religions* 1, no. 1 (Winter 1994): 75–76. Again, in Deloria's statement, one can recognize Said's distinction between filiation and affiliation.

183. William G. McLoughlin, *After the Trail of Tears: The Cherokees' Struggle for Sovereignty, 1839–1880* (Chapel Hill: University of North Carolina Press, 1993), xv.

184. In discussing whether the de-colonizing world had the wherewithal for democracy, Niebuhr and his coauthor Alan Heimert raise doubts about whether indigenous or traditional societies "possess the elementary preconditions of community, the cohesions of a common language and race, for instance, which European nations possessed at least two centuries before the rise of free institutions." Niebuhr and Heimert, *Nation So Conceived*, 149. For a critique of this wildly Eurocentric and ethnocentric query, see chapter 9, "Original Simplicities."

185. Carmody and Carmody, *Native American Religions*, 70.

186. King, *All My Relations*, xiii–xiv.

187. Warrior, *Tribal Secrets*, xxii–xxiii.

188. Hobson, *Remembered Earth*, 14

189. Pieris makes a distinction between what he calls "cosmic" religions, such as Native traditions, that have been pejoratively labeled *animism*, and "metacosmic" religions that possess an otherworldly soteriology. See Pieris, *Asian Theology*, 71–74; Peelman, *Christ Is a Native*, 44.

190. Goldie, *Fear and Temptation*, 120; David Thompson, *David Thompson's Narrative of His Explorations in Western America, 1784–1812*, ed. J. Tyrell (Toronto: Champlain Society, 1916), 362.

191. Allen, *Sacred Hoop*, 55. This relation of traditional religious practice to community is acknowledged even by many fundamentalist Native Christians otherwise opposed to traditional religion. Peelman notes that even the Pentecostal Native denomination, the Body of Christ Independent Church, which is radically

opposed to traditional Lakota religion and "rejects all traditional religious symbols as a means of true Lakota identity," nonetheless recognizes the importance of community in traditional cultural features like the *tiospaye*. Peelman, *Christ Is a Native*, 77.

192. Carmody and Carmody, *Native American Religions*, 51; Rausch and Schlepp, *Native American Voices*, 141–46.

193. Clifford Geertz, "From the Native's Point of View: On the Nature of Anthropological Understanding," in Richard Shweder and Robert LeVine, eds., *Culture Theory: Essays on Mind, Self and Emotion* (Cambridge: Cambridge University Press, 1984), 126.

194. Arnold Krupat, *Native American Autobiography: An Anthology* (Madison: University of Wisconsin Press, 1994), 4; Donald Fixico, *The Invasion of Indian Country in the Twentieth Century: American Capitalism and Tribal Natural Resources* (forthcoming). Fixico writes, "Traditional Native Americans believe that they are part of a whole. Indian people are not solitary. They historically have preferred a culture stressing community as more important than a single member of the group. The tendency is to see the whole or the group and want to be part of it. The group is seen as happiness of relatives and friends talking and laughing, the content of socialization among members, the security found among community and kinfolk. To want to be part of the whole and to see oneself as a small part of the 'one' refocuses the emphasis on group-ego rather than self-ego. In order to belong to the group and to be accepted by others, one places the needs of the group before the needs of the individual." See Donald Fixico, "The Struggle for Our Homes: Indian and White Values and Tribal Lands," in Weaver, *Defending Mother Earth*, 37–38.

195. Allen, *Sacred Hoop*, 55; McPherson and Rabb, *Indian from the Inside*, 100.

196. Fixico, "Struggle," 38.

197. McPherson and Rabb, *Indian from the Inside*, 6; King, *All My Relations*, ix. See also, Trafzer, *Earth Song*, 7.

198. Carmody and Carmody, *Native American Religions*, 100–101; Peelman, *Christ Is a Native*, 198. This split, of course, has been analyzed and critiqued by a number of Christian theologians. See, for instance, Paul Tillich, *Systematic Theology* (Welwyn: J. Nisbet, 1960), parts I and II; Karl Rahner, *Foundations of Christian Faith* (New York: Seabury Press, 1978), 44–89.

199. Peelman, *Christ Is a Native*, 54.

200. Christopher Ronwanièn:te Jocks, "Combing Out Snakes: Violence in the Longhouse Tradition," American Academy of Religion, Chicago, Ill., November 21, 1994. For a discussion of knowledge and power, see generally Gayatri Chakravorty Spivak, *Outside in the Teaching Machine* (New York: Routledge, 1993).

201. Leslie Marmon Silko, quoted in Trafzer, *Earth Song*, 21; see also Silko, "Foreword," 7–8.

202. Vizenor, *Manifest Manners*, 56.

203. Quoted in Vizenor, *Narrative Chance*, 3.

204. Alister McGrath, *Evangelicalism and the Future of Christianity* (Downers Grove, Ill.: InterVarsity Press, 1995), 18. For more information about the Kiowa Apaches, see Edward H. Spicer, *The American Indians* (Cambridge: Harvard University Press, 1980), 92–95.

205. Quoted in Kroeber, *Traditional Literatures*, 21–22. See also Krupat, *Voice in the Margin*, 220. Ngugi discusses the importance of story at Ngugi, *Decolonising the Mind*, 10–11.

206. Trafzer, *Earth Song*, 21. Vizenor writes, "Postindian simulations arise from the silence of heard stories, or the imagination of oral literature in translation, not the absence of the real in simulated realities; the critical distinction is that postindian warriors create a new tribal presence in stories." Vizenor, *Manifest Manners*, 12. In that book, he also contends, "This is a continuous turn in tribal narratives, the oral stories are dominated by those narratives that are translated, published, and read at unnamed distances." Thus once again the printed story is considered normative. The myth of conquest, of literacy over orature, must once again prove itself by conquering other stories.

207. Quoted in *Native Literature*, Petrone, 5. Emphasis mine.

208. See Ruppert, *Mediation*, 12.

209. Trafzer, *Earth Song*, 8. This is especially true for often displaced urban Indians. Thomas King is not alone among Native authors in receiving letters from Native readers thanking him for helping him make sense of contemporary Native experience. Thomas King, interview with author, Jan. 27, 1993. For a discussion of contemporary urban Natives, see Lynda Shorten, *Without Reserve: Stories from Urban Natives* (Edmonton: NeWest Press, 1991).

210. Allen, *Spider Woman's Granddaughters*, 5.

211. King, interview with author. King dedicates his anthology of contemporary Native fiction to Robinson. See King, *All My Relations*, v.

212. Allen, *Voice of the Turtle*, 6.

213. See Ruppert, *Mediation*, 25. Sioui (33) states, "Through their music and poetry and their arts in general, the . . . nations also express a keen awareness of their Amerindianness." Owens (5) notes that the "recovering or rearticulation of an identity, a process dependent upon a rediscovered sense of place as well as community" lies at the heart of contemporary Indian fiction. Similarly, Ruppert (28) observes that Native protagonists in current fiction are continually examining where they fit in and how they are seen by others. Their actions are judged by a "communal standard and definition of identity."

214. Quoted in Vizenor, *Manifest Manners*, 8.

215. Said, *Culture*, xii–xiii.

216. Owens, *Other Destinies*, 9; Trafzer, *Earth Song*, 4.

217. Owens, *Other Destinies*, 10.

218. Krupat, *Voice in the Margin*, 162–63. Emphasis mine.

219. Allen, *Spider Woman's Granddaughters*, 4. Of course, Allen resolves this existential dilemma by deciding that Indian writers are Indian.

220. Elizabeth Cook-Lynn, "You May Consider Speaking about Your Art . . .," in Brian Swann and Arnold Krupat, eds., *I Tell You Now: Autobiographical Essays by Native Americans* (Lincoln: University of Nebraska Press, 1987), 58. Emphasis in original.

221. Ashcroft, Griffiths, and Tiffin, *Empire Writes Back*, 5; Owens, *Other Destinies*, 11. See Robert Allen Warrior, "An Interview with Vine Deloria, Jr.," *The Progressive* (April 1990).

222. Hobson, *Remembered Earth*, 9, 10; Owens, *Other Destinies*, 11; Trafzer, *Earth Song*, 7. It may be that the discourse of other Others, of other oppositional literatures, carries this same sense of responsibility to community. It is not, however, generally true of writers from the dominant culture, who, pursuing the writers craft, follow Polonius's injunction to Laertes, "To thine ownself be true."

223. Hobson, *Remembered Earth*, 11. Thomas King notes that they may portray Indians outside of "traditional" contexts but "maintain their literary connection to Native culture." See King, *All My Relations*, xv.

224. Vizenor, *Manifest Manners*, 95. See also Ruppert, *Mediation*, 30.

225. Ruppert, *Mediation*, 28–29; Sioui, *Amerindian Autohistory*, 22.

226. Warrior, *Tribal Secrets*, xx.

227. For a discussion of mass humanity, see Romano Guardini, *The End of the Modern World*, trans. Joseph Theman and Herbert Burke (New York: Sheed & Ward, 1956).

228. Although Natives, as noted throughout, speak of Native community a lot, *communitist* is a word created by me. In coining such a term, I am not alone. Nieuwenhuys, to characterize a certain aspect of the Dutch Indies character, employs *d'artagnanism*, a certain "bravura and posturing" in the manner of Dumas's musketeer, when other terms are "unworkable." See Nieuwenhuys, *Mirror of the Indies*, 198. In like manner, Alice Walker coined *womanist* and the term has since been picked up by the community itself. See Delores S. Williams, *Sisters in the Wilderness: The Challenge of Womanist God-Talk* (Maryknoll: Orbis Books, 1993), 243.

229. Bhabha, *Location of Culture*, 3. Emphasis in original.

230. Linda Hogan, *The Book of Medicines* (Minneapolis: Coffee House Press, 1993). Robert Warrior also notes that poet Wendy Rose (Hopi/Miwok), in breaking her own silence, brings to the conversation "a stark reminder of the need for healing in Indian communities and presents a challenge for American Indian intellectuals to be more honest, more inclusive, and to recognize the profound challenges we face." Warrior, *Tribal Secrets*, 121. See also Bruchac, *Survival*, 254–58.

231. "Spectrum," 21; see also Joy Harjo, *The Woman Who Fell from the Sky* (New York: W. W. Norton, 1994), 19.

232. Tapahonso, *Sáanii Dahataal*, xii. Echoing this reversal of exile, Dennis Lee states that the "first necessity for the colonial writer" is for the imagination to "come home." Ngugi writes that the biggest problem for him as a writer is finding the appropriate fictional language to communicate with "the people I left

behind." Lee quoted in Ashcroft, Grifiths, and Tiffin, *Empire Writes Back*, 142. See also Ngugi, *Decolonising the Mind*, 75.

233. Warrior, *"Tribal Secrets,"* 118, 112–13.

234. Ibid., 125.

235. Cook-Lynn and Ortiz quoted in Vizenor, *Manifest Manners*, 93–94. Said declares that "criticism must think of itself as life-enhancing and constitutively opposed to every form of tyranny, domination, and abuse: its social goals are non-coercive knowledge produced in the interest of human freedom." Said, *World*, 29. Louis Owens contends, "The noble savage's refusal to perish throws a money wrench into the drama. . . . With few exceptions, American Indian novelists . . . are in their fiction rejecting the American gothic with its haunted, guilt-burdened wilderness and doomed Native and emphatically making the Indian the hero of other destinies, other plots." Owens, *Other Destinies*, 18.

236. Vizenor, *Manifest Manners*, 4.

237. Ngugi, *Decolonising of the Mind*, 87. It is this that Ngugi calls the "quest for relevance."

238. Ruppert, *Mediation*, xii.

239. See Owens, *Other Destinies*, 20; Ngugi, *Decolonising*, 82–83.

240. Bhabha, *Location of Culture*, 13. Emphasis in original.

241. See King, *All My Relations*, xiii–xiv. As an example of disagreement over means, one could note that Deloria decries Western education as making overeducated, deracinated Indians, whereas Warrior advocates it as a potential tool in the struggle for liberation in the dominant culture, a tool that need not *necessarily* lead to assimilation but can aid cultural survival. See Vine Deloria, Jr., *Red Earth, White Lies* (New York: Scribner's, 1995); Warrior, *"Tribal Secrets,"* 123.

242. In speaking so, it is not my intent to fetishize or romanticize pre-Contact society. There were conflicts and problems as in any other cultures. America was not some Edenic paradise. It was simply ours. Besides, as Trafzer notes, "Native Americans act as a community [to survive] even when individual members of the community refuse to cooperate in the maintenance of the people" (*Earth Song*, 20). See also Donald A. Grinde and Bruce E. Johansen, *Ecocide of Native America* (Santa Fe: Clear Light, 1995); Sioui, *Amerindian Autohistory*, 26.

243. Warrior, *Tribal Secrets*, 126. Penny Petrone touches upon the same theme and relates it to healing, but reflects a more decidedly Eurocentric bias that too often sees subaltern groups as whining. She writes, "Native writers will create their own forms, in responding to the fast-changing society they live in. Once the outrage has been exorcised, the self-pity and self-indulgence worked out, and the frictional heat of catharsis has subsided, new subjects and themes will take their place. In drawing upon traditional values to heal their scars, they will become liberated, and the victim syndrome will disappear" (*Native Literature*, 183). Despite her tone, by bringing together survival, healing, and liberation, she points at communitism and brings literature together with the religious enterprise. On this subject of whining and anger, see Standiford, ("Often, a native writer is overcome

with the urgency of his message and forsakes all concerns of craft in the effort to make his point," "Worlds Made of Dawn," 336). And see G. W. Haslam, *Forgotten Pages of American Literature* (Boston: Houghton Mifflin, 1970), 24. Haslam looks forward to "when Indian writers as a group forsake blatant protest and employ more imaginative—and probably more persuasive—forms; the pressure of their plight has tended to force Indian writers into desperate excoriations of conditions. Like Afro-Americans who have found that subtlety is often a more effective social weapon than shrill anger, native American artists are beginning to discover their own most moving modes of expression."

244. Vine Deloria, Jr., "It Is a Good Day to Die," *Katallagete* 4:2–3 (Fall–Winter 1972): 65.

CHAPTER 3. VENUS OF THE HALF-SHELL?

1. Trout is one of Kurt Vonnegut's favorite literary creations, appearing in several of his books, including *Slaughterhouse-Five* and *God Bless You, Mr. Rosewater*. Trout is a prolific but little-known writer of science fiction. His chief publisher is World Classics Library, which specializes in pornography. Without Trout's knowledge, the publisher put lurid covers on his novels and published his short stories in men's magazines. According to Vonnegut, *Venus on the Half-Shell* is Trout's great masterpiece.

2. Drew Hayden Taylor, *Only Drunks and Children Tell the Truth* (Burnaby, B.C.: Talonbooks, 1998); Thomas King, "Drums" (unpublished MS, 1999). As of this writing, "Drums" is still a work in progress and has yet be produced. Thanks go to its author for a copy of the manuscript discussed herein.

3. Vonnegut's novel *Cat's Cradle* even plays a minor role in the Taylor play.

4. Tonto interjects, "That was me. White people buy all this kind of stuff."

5. As in other King works, water imagery is important here. King's three novels all have aquatic allusions in their titles: *Medicine River, Green Grass, Running Water, Truth and Bright Water*. Here the agent of change is again linked to water.

CHAPTER 5. AN ÜBERMENSCH AMONG THE APACHE

1. Frederic Morton, "Tales of the Grand Teutons: Karl May among the Indians," *New York Times Book Review*, January 4, 1987, 15.

2. Ibid.

3. A. C. Ross, *Mitakuye Oyasin* (Denver: Bear, 1989), 1.

4. Ibid., 2.

5. Morton, "Tales of the Grand Teutons"; Christian F. Feest, "Europe's Indians," in James A. Clifton, ed., *The Invented Indian: Cultural Fictions and Government Policies* (New Brunswick, N.J.: Transaction Publishers, 1990), 326; Christopher Frayling, *Spaghetti Westerns: Cowboys and Europeans from Karl May to Sergio Leone* (London: Routledge & Kegan Paul, 1981), 105.

6. Quoted in Greg Langley, "A Fistful of Dreams: Taming the Wild West in the Old World" (*Munich Found Online*), 3–4.

7. Morton, "Tales of the Grand Teutons."

8. Langley, "Fistful of Dreams," 1.

9. Frayling, *Spaghetti Westerns*, 104, 106.

10. Julian Crandall Hollick and Dean Cappello, prods., "Winnetou and Old Shatterhand" ("Imagining America," Littleton, Mass.: Independent Broadcasting Associates, 1992), produced for National Public Radio in association with WGBH (Boston, Mass.); Morton, "Tales of the Grand Teutons"; Frayling, *Spaghetti Westerns*, 103–4.

11. Percy G. Adams, *Travelers and Travel Liars, 1660–1800* (New York: Dover, 1980), vii, 17.

12. Ibid., 4.

13. Morton, "Tales of the Grand Teutons."

14. Jack D. Forbes, *Columbus and Other Cannibals* (Brooklyn: Autonomedia, 1992), 37.

15. Francis, *Imaginary Indian*, 73.

16. Feest, "Europe's Indians," 316.

17. Ibid.

18. Ibid., 323–24.

19. Quoted in Hollick and Cappello, "Winnetou and Old Shatterhand," NPR.

20. Frayling, *Spaghetti Westerns*, 114.

21. Lisa Bartel-Winkler, "Das Drama des sterbenden Volkes," *Karl-May Jahrbuch* 7 (Radebeul: Karl May Verlag, 1924), quoted in Feest, "Europe's Indians," in *Indians and Europe*, Aachen: Edition Herodot/Rader Verlag, 1987), 612. Bartel-Winkler's remark on purity of blood is well-taken. Frayling remarks, "Throughout the 'Winnetou' stories, Shatterhand and his blood-brother represent a type of 'racial purity' in the face of May's favourite villains—half-breeds, Mormons and Yankees." See *Spaghetti Westerns*, 112. As I have written elsewhere, "An extension of the 'bad Indian' image, half-breeds have no redeeming virtues. They are neither White nor Indian. As such, they are the degenerate products of miscegenation, distrusted by both cultures and fitting in nowhere." Jace Weaver, *That the People Might Live: Native American Literatures and Native American Community* (New York: Oxford University Press, 1997), 104.

22. John F. Moffitt and Santiago Sebastián, *O Brave New People: The European Invention of the American Indian* (Albuquerque: University of New Mexico Press, 1996), 254–55.

23. Ibid., 256.

24. Morton, "Tales of the Grand Teutons."

25. Hollick and Cappello, "Winnetou and Old Shatterhand," NPR.

26. Morton, "Tales of the Grand Teutons."

27. Ibid.

28. Quoted in Hollick and Cappello, "Winnetou and Old Shatterhand," NPR.

29. Frayling, *Spaghetti Westerns*, 112.

30. Alfred Vagts, "The Germans and the Red Man," *American-German Review* 24 (1957): 17.

31. Jonathan Boyarin, "Europe's Indian, America's Jew," in Karl Kroeber, ed., *American Indian Persistence and Resurgence* (Durham: Duke University Press, 1994), 205.

32. See Weaver, *That the People*, 17.

33. Ibid., 18; see Dussel, *The Invention of the Americas*.

34. Berkhofer, *White Man's Indian*, 101.

35. Frayling, *Spaghetti Westerns*, 112.

36. Karl May, *Geographische Predigten*, quoted in Rudolf Conrad, "Mutual Fascination: Indians in Dresden and Leipzig," in Feest, *Indians and Europe*, 458.

37. Boyarin, "Europe's Indian," in Kroebar, *American Indian Persistence*, 206.

38. Ibid.

39. Hollick and Cappello, "Winnetou and Old Shatterhand," NPR.

40. Frayling, *Spaghetti Westerns*, 104.

41. Weaver, *That the People*, 18–19.

42. Hollick and Cappello, "Winnetou and Old Shatterhand," NPR. According to Eckehard Koch of the Karl-May-Gesellschaft, there are reasons for Germany's fascination with Indians, "the myth of the 'noble savage,' the discontent with civilization and the restricted freedom caused by the modern world, and the wish to escape from the narrowness of German life." Langley, "Fistful of Dreams," 3.

43. Quoted in Langley, 4–5.

44. Conrad, "Mutual Fascination," 455. Conrad does note, however, that when, on the trip, Lame Deer was asked for his opinion of Karl May, he responded, "Regardless of how things are set about and how people think, I would tend more to thank Karl May for writing about Indians, for he has kept alive the thought of Indians in the minds of all European people. . . . I wish we had had him in America at the turn of the century." Ibid., 455–56.

45. Quoted in "The Outside Prognosticator: Germanimo!" *Outside* (January 1996, retrieved from *Outside* magazine website).

46. Peter Bolz, "Life among the 'Hunkpapas': A Case Study in German Indian Lore," in Feest, *Indians and Europe*, 486.

47. Ibid., 482.

48. Feest, in Clifton, *Invented Indian*, 324.

49. Conrad, "Mutual Fascination," 469–70.

50. Ibid., 461.

51. Ibid., 464. Sarrasani had "supplemented" his Indian cast with Dresden locals, and they were among those who founded the first club.

52. Langley, "Fistful of Dreams," 4.

53. Ibid., 2.

54. Conrad, "Mutual Fascination," 458.

55. Frayling, *Spaghetti Westerns*, 113.

56. Weaver, *That the People*, 176.

57. King, *All My Relations*, xi–xii.

58. Though he admits May's fabrications, Ilmer, for instance, also claims truths for him. He states, "May's stories, while dramatic, are also full of inaccuracies and improbabilities. He wrote scenes based on events in the early 1800s but placed them in the 1860s and '70s. This is one reason May never became popular in the United States. His plots never rang true to the American ear. . . . May was a voracious reader and his portrayal of the American Indian was quite accurate. He revealed their noble character, their gifts as orators, their wildness, their savage and their heroic traits." Quoted in Langley, "Fistful of Dreams," 2.

59. Thomas King, *Truth and Bright Water* (Toronto: HarperCollins, 1999).

60. Gerald Vizenor, *Fugitive Poses: Native American Indian Scenes of Absence and Presence* (Lincoln: University of Nebraska Press, 1998), 89.

61. Vizenor, *Manifest Manners*, 31–32.

62. Vizenor has expressed interest in working further with May's representations in the future, perhaps playing with the images of May's world created in the films based on his work.

63. Frayling, *Spaghetti Westerns*, 103.

64. Langley, "Fistful of Dreams," 6.

65. James Fenimore Cooper, quoted in Adams, *Travelers*, 198–99.

CHAPTER 6. CLOWNS AND VILLAINS

1. Stan Le Roy Wilson, *Mass Media/Mass Culture: An Introduction*, updated 1993 ed. (New York: McGraw Hill, 1993), 4, 431.

2. Ibid., 4.

3. Vine Deloria, Jr., "Foreword: American Fantasy," in *The Pretend Indians: Images of Native Americans in the Movies*, Gretchen M. Bataille and Charles Silet, eds. (Ames: University of Iowa Press, 1980), xvi.

4. Berkhofer, *White Man's Indian*, 26–28.

5. Jan Elliott, "America to Indians: Stay in the Nineteenth Century," *Rethinking Columbus* (special issue of Rethinking Education (September 1991): 10.

6. Berkhofer, *White Man's Indian*, 30.

7. "Tammany Society," *World Book*, 1920 ed. (Chicago: Roach and Fowler).

8. Jennings C. Wise, *The Red Man in the New World Drama*, rev. and ed. by Vine Deloria, Jr. (New York: Macmillan Company, 1971), 88–93.

9. Gerald Bordman, *American Musical Theatre: A Chronicle*, 2d ed. (New York: Oxford University Press, 1992), 4.

10. Ward Churchill, *Fantasies of the Master Race: Literature, Cinema and the Colonization of American Indians*, 243–79.

11. Jill Lepore, *The Name of War: King Philip's War and the Origins of American Identity* (New York: Alfred A. Knopf, 1998), 191–210.

12. Ibid., 220.

13. Ibid., 221.

14. Ibid., 222–23.

15. Bordman, *American Musical Theatre*, 10.

16. Ibid., 52.

17. Ibid.

18. Ibid., 53.

19. Ibid., 98.

20. Dee Brown, *Bury My Heart at Wounded Knee* (New York: Holt, Rinehart & Winston, 1971), 414–18.

21. Bordman, *American Musical Theatre*, 127.

22. Ibid., 233.

23. Ibid., 231.

24. Ibid., 237.

25. Ben Bagley, *Unpublished Cole Porter* (New York: Painted Smile Records, 1972).

26. Bordman, *American Musical Theatre*, 391.

27. Ibid., 392.

28. James Robert Parish and Michael R. Pitts, *Film Directors: A Guide to Their American Films* (Metuchen, N.J.: Scarecrow Press, 1974), 397.

29. Bordman, *American Musical Theatre*, 430.

30. Ibid., 433–34.

31. Ibid., 445–46.

32. Guy Bolton, et al., *Girl Crazy* (Woodstock, Ill.: Dramatic Publishing Company, 1930), 19, 55.

33. Ibid., 66–68.

34. For a fuller discussion of my points with regard to Riggs and *Oklahoma!*, see Weaver, *That the People Might Live*, 95–103.

35. Lynn Riggs, *Green Grow the Lilacs* (New York: Samuel French, 1930), 1, 161, 64, 33–34, 19.

36. Brown, *Bury My Heart*, 402.

37. Peter Marks, "Rewrite a Classic Musical? Whatever Works Goes," *New York Times*, January 24, 1999, AR 1, 6.

38. Ibid., 6.

39. Ibid.

40. See J. M. Barrie, *Peter Pan* (New York: Samuel French, 1928).

41. Ron Castell, ed., *Blockbuster Entertainment Guide to Movies and Video 1997* (New York: Dell Publishing, 1996), 959.

42. Bordman, *American Musical Theatre*, 609–10.

43. In pleading with Dominick the bull, Joe entreats, "Move your little foot do." In so doing, he uses a double entendre, employing "foot" as a euphemism for penis.

44. Tom Jones and Harvey Schmidt, *The Fantasticks* (New York: Applause Theatre Book Publishers, 1960, 1990), 6.

45. Ibid., 63.
46. Ibid., 119–25.
47. Ibid., 67.

CHAPTER 7. INNOCENTS ABROAD

1. Quoted in Peter Høeg, *Smilla's Sense of Snow* (New York: Dell, 1997), front material. The book originally was published as *Frøken Smillas fornemmelse for sne* (Copenhagen: Rosinante/Munksgaard, 1992). Farrar, Straus and Giroux brought it out in the United States the following year.

2. Høeg, *Smilla's Sense*, 101. The author here discusses the "ritual significance" of meals for the Inuit, reinforcing the "feeling that practically everything in life is meant to be shared."

3. The same is true of the motion picture made from the novel in 1997, directed by Bille August and written for the screen by Ann Biderman.

4. An exception might be Ella Cara Deloria's *Waterlily* (Lincoln: University of Nebraska Press, 1988). Written around 1940 and based upon Deloria's research for anthropologist Franz Boas, the work comes close to a kind of ethnographic novel. In fact, it bears strong similarities to *Speaking of Indians*, a nonfiction volume by the same author.

5. Jack D. Forbes, *Africans and Native Americans: The Language of Race and the Evolution of Red-Black Peoples*, 2d ed. (Urbana: University of Illinois Press, 1993), 18–20; Forbes, *Columbus and Other Cannibals*, 37.

6. Robert Petersen, "Colonialism as Seen from a Former Colonized Area," plenary presentation, Eighth Inuit Studies Conference, Laval University, Montreal, Que., Oct. 25, 1992, 3, 14. The paper was subsequently published in *Arctic Anthropology*, 32, no. 2 (1995): 118–26. It should be noted that from 1380 to 1814, Norway and Denmark formed a single country. See Petersen, 3, for a discussion of the language deployed in both Greenlandic and Danish to describe the colonial relationship between Greenland and Denmark.

7. Høeg, *Smilla's Sense*, 13.

8. "Inuit: Greenland," *Global Prayer Digest* (July 6, 1987).

9. Jean Malaurie, *The Last Kings of Thule* (Chicago: University of Chicago Press, 1985).

10. Terrence Cole, Introduction to the 1999 Edition, Knud Rasmussen, *Across Arctic America* (Fairbanks: University of Alaska Press, 1999), xiv.

11. Ibid., xiv–xx.

12. Høeg, *Smilla's Sense*, 81.

13. Ibid., 203–4.

14. Cole, Introduction to *Across Arctic America*, xx. Note that the Greenlandic word for colony is *niuertogarfik*, or "trade center." See fn. 6, Petersen, "Colonialism."

15. Høeg, *Smilla's Sense*, 332.

16. "Inuit: Greenland," *Global Prayer Digest*.

17. Høeg, *Smilla's Sense*, 72–73. Cryolite is a mineral used in the smelting of aluminum. It was discovered in 1794 in Greenland and occurs almost nowhere else. In 1850, Denmark established a cryolite mine in Greenland, separate from the Greenland economy that extracted cryolite for over a century. See Petersen, "Colonialism," 4. Cryolite mining plays an important part in Høeg's novel. For information about American Indians and uranium mining, see Peter H. Eichstaedt, *If You Poison Us: Uranium and Native Americans* (Santa Fe: Red Crane, 1994).

18. Høeg, *Smilla's Sense*, 176–77.

19. Ibid., 125.

20. Ibid., 125, 134–35.

21. Petersen, "Colonialism," 5.

22. Ibid., 6. Echoing the tones of Høeg's book, Petersen writes, "The political consequences of this official situation were that a modernization of Greenland began, bringing about improvements in a number of areas. There was a campaign to reduce tuberculosis, the leading cause of death at the time, and the school system was reorganized and separated from the church. Many Danish teachers were engaged, and they introduced Danish-style schooling for children who were mainly monolingual Greenlandic speakers. . . . The housing program resulted in modernization of many dwellings, concentrating in the West Greenlandic open water area, in the towns where industrialization of the economy had begun." (pp. 5–6).

23. Ibid., 7.

24. Petersen describes the attitude of the assimilated Northern Danes, writing, "In Greenland, it was often the educated Greenlanders who accepted these ideas. But it is not only in Greenland that the people [Inuits] adopted the thoughts of the colonizers. Some groups were even thankful for having been colonized, for being Christianized, educated, and for having a subordinate job." Ibid., p. 8.

25. Høeg, *Smilla's Sense*, 14, 67.

26. Ibid., 95.

27. Quoted in Nieuwenhuys, *Mirror of the Indies*, 53.

28. Høeg, *Smilla's Sense*, 177.

29. Ibid., 454.

30. Maggie Siggins, *Riel: A Life of Revolution* (Toronto: HarperCollins Publishers, 1994), 184.

31. Ibid., 195.

32. Louis Jackson, *Our Caughnawagas in Egypt* (Montreal: W. Drysdale & Co., 1885), 5/1. This slim volume has long been out of print. I brought it back in print in 1998 by including it in my book on CD-ROM, *American Journey*. See Jace Weaver, *American Journey: The Native American Experience* (Woodbridge, Conn.: Research Publications, 1998). In order to make this text as accessible as possible, I include herein citations to both editions of the work. Thus a footnote "Jackson, 5/1" designates that the information or quotation appears on page 5 of the original book and on page 1 of the version on CD-ROM.

33. Jackson, *Our Caughnawagas*, 4/1.

34. Hilton Obenzinger, *American Palestine: Melville, Twain, and the Holy Land Mania* (Princeton: Princeton University Press, 1999), 138–39. Obenzinger principally analyzes two texts, Melville's *Clarel* and Mark Twain's travel narrative, *The Innocents Abroad: or, The New Pilgrim's Progress*. As to the presence of someone like Melville's Ungar in Egypt, it is not wholly implausible. The American Civil War split the Five Civilized Tribes, including the Cherokees. Approximately 2200 Cherokees fought in the Union Army, while 1600 served the Confederacy. One Cherokee, Stand Watie, rose to the rank of brigadier and was reported to be the last Confederate general to surrender.

35. Jackson, *Our Caughnawagas*, 4/1.

36. Ibid., 6–7/2.

37. Ibid., 18/5.

38. Ibid., 32/10.

39. Ibid., 33/10.

40. Ibid., 13–14/4.

41. Ibid., 34/11.

42. Ibid., 9/3.

43. Ibid., 4/1.

44. Ibid., 7–9/2.

45. Ibid., 26/8.

46. Ibid., 12/4.

47. Ibid., 29–30/9.

48. Ibid., 31/10.

49. Ibid., 33/10.

50. Ibid., 4/1.

51. Ibid., 34–35/11.

52. Ibid., 34/11.

CHAPTER 8. HELL AND HIGHWATER

1. Vizenor, *Fugitive Poses*, 15.

2. Ibid. Emphasis in original.

3. Weaver, *That the People Might Live*, 164.

4. Vizenor, *Manifest Manners*, 61.

5. Welsch, *Touching the Fire*, xv.

6. Ibid., xxi.

7. Ibid., xx–xxi. Emphasis in original.

8. Ibid., xxv.

9. Jay Miller, *Earthmaker: Tribal Stories from Native North America* (New York: Putnam Publishing Group, 1992), 8.

10. Ibid., 164, 121.

11. Of course, there is equally an issue here of the lability of the oral tradition. Stories often vary from storyteller to storyteller and telling to telling, not just

from tribe to tribe. The oral tradition was—and is—always evolving. It was only with the advent of ethnologists that the written myth was valorized above the oral performance, and the written text was canonized and considered normative.

12. Bill Wahlberg, *Star Warrior: The Story of SwiftDeer* (Santa Fe: Bear & Company, 1993), xix. Reagan's Ph.D. is from the Pacific Cultural Institute for Advanced Studies in Hollywood, California.

13. Ibid., xx.

14. Ibid., xxi.

15. Ibid., xxii.

16. Ibid., xxv.

17. Ibid., 172.

18. Ibid., 115.

19. Ibid., 233.

20. Ibid., 232–33.

21. Ibid., xiv–xv.

22. Jamake Highwater, *Kill Hole* (New York: Grove Press, 1992).

23. Jamake Highwater, *The Primal Mind: Vision and Reality in Indian America* (New York: Harper & Row, 1981), xvii.

24. Vizenor, *Fugitive Poses*, 68.

25. Jamake Highwater, "Second-Class Indians," *American Indian Journal* (July 1980): 9.

26. Quoted in Vizenor, *Manifest Manners*, 61.

27. Beverly Slapin and Doris Seale, eds., *Through Indian Eyes: The Native Experience in Books for Children* (Philadelphia: New Society Publishers, 1992), 167.

CHAPTER 9. ORIGINAL SIMPLICITIES AND PRESENT COMPLEXITIES

1. Fetterman, his death, and his lionizing in some recitations of Western history is in many ways a precursor to the "Custer Myth," accurately described by Native writer James Welch in his book *Killing Custer*. See Welch, with Paul Stekler, *Killing Custer* (New York: W. W. Norton, 1994), 21, 42–43, 245–47.

2. As will be seen later in this chapter, the war also caused changes in Niebuhr's own thinking about the nation and its history. He died, however, before the conflict came to an end and thus missed seeing the full impact of the war on U.S. society.

3. The Korean War would also come to be included in this category. In both cases, those who most fervently defended the myth of American exceptionalism would speak of a betrayal by subversive elements that prevented victory. Such a view also ignores, as does much of American scholarship, America's indigenous peoples. Red Cloud's War, of which the Fetterman engagement was but one skirmish, ended with the defeat of the United States, the forced closure of the Bozeman Trail, and the signing of the Fort Laramie Treaty of 1868.

4. Reinhold Niebuhr, *The Nature and Destiny of Man*, vol. 2 (New York: Charles Scribner's Sons, 1943), 306–7.

5. Reinhold Niebuhr, *The Children of Light and the Children of Darkness* (New York: Charles Scribner's Sons, 1944), 166–67.

6. As Niebuhr scholar Richard Reinitz states, "In Niebuhr's vast output there are a number of works on history in general, and many on America, but few that purport to deal with American history." See Reinitz, *Irony and Consciousness: American Historiography and Reinhold Niebuhr's Vision* (Lewisburg, Penn.: Bucknell University Press, 1980), 112. Because *The Irony of American History* and *A Nation So Conceived* are Niebuhr's only full-length treatments of the subject, this chapter, necessarily, will focus principally on them. Other works will, however, be discussed to the extent that they shed light upon Niebuhr's thought.

7. Niebuhr, *Irony*, vii–viii.

8. One can question whether it is possible to speak of "responsibility" for unconscious weakness at all—or whether responsibility, and hence culpability, is purely a matter of things within conscious control.

9. Niebuhr and Heimert, *Nation So Conceived*, 123.

10. Niebuhr, *Irony*, 51.

11. Niebuhr notes that the British have demonstrated the same sense of messianism, acquired according to him and Heimert at the time of the Glorious Revolution (see Niebuhr, *Nature and Destiny*, 306–7; Niebuhr and Heimert, *Nation So Conceived*, 123). John Rolfe, writing in 1616, claimed that the British were "a peculiar people, marked and chosen by the finger of God" for the colonial enterprise "to possess [the Americas], for undoubtedly he is with us." Perry Miller, *Errand into the Wilderness* (Cambridge, Mass.: Harvard University Press, 1957), 119.

12. Alfred A. Cave, "Canaanites in a Promised Land: The American Indians and the Providential Theory of Empire," *American Indian Quarterly* (Fall 1988): 282. This reference to the Gibeonites is by Sir George Peckham, a prominent Catholic nobleman who saw America as a refuge for English Catholics.

13. This theory was elaborated upon by William Strachey, secretary to the Virginia colony, in a tract written in 1612. That it was used against both Africans and Indians is an example of what I have termed "the consistency of racism." It continues to be seen today. W. A. Criswell, *The Criswell Study Bible* (Nashville: Thomas Nelson, 1988), 19.

14. It is little wonder Robert Warrior states, in "Canaanites, Cowboys, and Indians," that, given this history, America's indigenous peoples must read the biblical witness with "Canaanite eyes." See Warrior's, article in *Christianity and Crisis* (Sept. 11, 1989): 262. I offer my own extension of Warrior's remarks in two articles, "Native Reformation in Indian Country?" and "A Biblical Paradigm for Native Liberation," both reworked in this book.

15. Niebuhr, *Irony*, 24.

16. Djelal Kadir notes that Herman Melville "sang, now splenetically, now in elegy, America's prophetic allegory." See *Columbus and the Ends of the Earth:*

Europe's Prophetic Rhetoric as Conquering Ideology (Norman: University of Oklahoma Press, 1992), 108.

17. Herman Melville, *White Jacket* (1850), 153.

18. Niebuhr and Heimert, *Nation So Conceived*, 145–50.

19. Niebuhr, *Irony*, 38.

20. Ibid., 35–36.

21. In his most famous work, *Magnalia Christi Americana*, published in 1702, Cotton Mather wrote of "covenant-mercies" given and "covenant-duties" imposed upon the chosen people in their colonial endeavor (14).

22. Niebuhr and Heimert, *Nation So Conceived*, 149–50.

23. Niebuhr, *Irony*, 52.

24. Niebuhr and Heimert, *Nation So Conceived*, 7.

25. Robert Dahlin, "PW Interviews: Richard Slotkin," *Publishers Weekly* (Dec. 28, 1992): 49.

26. Niebuhr and Heimert, *Nation So Conceived*, 32.

27. Miller, *Errand*, 107–10.

28. Niebuhr, *Irony*, 35.

29. Ibid.

30. Reinitz, *Irony and Consciousness*, 99.

31. Ibid.

32. Reinhold Niebuhr, *Pius [sic] and Secular America* (New York: Charles Scribner's Sons, 1958), 76. In *An Ethic for Enemies: Forgiveness in Politics*, ethicist Donald Shriver writes, "One should remember that the truly original issue of multiethnic political relation came with the meeting on these shores of Europeans with Native Americans. The latter were the first to face the new modern issue of whether immigrants can or should become members of an earlier established society. Many Native Americans today ruefully tell stories of the tradition of hospitality in their cultures on grounds of which their ancestors welcomed the first Europeans to set foot in this, a 'New World' to them." See Shriver, *An Ethic for Enemies: Forgiveness in Politics* (New York: Oxford University Press, 1995), 171. Yet, despite such a sensitive discussion, Shriver can, in Niebuhrian fashion, refer to the United States' treatment of African Americans as "the oldest American civic injustice."

33. Niebuhr, *Pius [sic] and Secular America*, 78.

34. That is to say that the worst anti-Communist is the former Communist. Niebuhr, as the German-speaking son of a German immigrant, fully accepted American values and became more American than those he refers to as "natives."

35. Niebuhr and Heimert, *Nation So Conceived*, 45.

36. Ibid., 11.

37. For a full discussion of this important concept, see Vizenor, *Manifest Manners*, 144.

38. Niebuhr and Heimert, *Nation So Conceived*, 46–47. In so speaking, they are quoting Oscar Handlin, *Race and Nationality in American Life* (Garden City, N.Y.: Anchor Books, 1957), 145.

39. Niebuhr and Heimert, *Nation So Conceived*, 130.

40. John Lukacs, "1918," *American Heritage* (Nov. 1993): 46.

41. Ibid.

42. Ibid.

43. Richard Fox, *Reinhold Niebuhr: A Biography* (New York: Pantheon, 1985), p. 57.

44. Niebuhr and Heimert, *Nation So Conceived*, 127.

45. Niebuhr, *Irony*, 69.

46. Niebuhr and Heimert, *Nation So Conceived*, 138–39.

47. Ibid., 148–49.

48. Ibid., 150.

49. Ibid., 139, 149. This ignores, once again, America's original inhabitants, many of whom had highly developed democratic institutions, some of which may have influenced the founders of the Republic. For a fuller discussion, see Donald Grinde, Jr., and Bruce Johansen, *Exemplar of Liberty: Native America and the Evolution of Democracy* (Los Angeles: American Indian Center, University of California, Los Angeles, 1991), 141–216.

50. This temporary blessing later turned into a curse as America's aging industrial plant was surpassed by the more modern technologies of those nations, like Germany and Japan, that had to rebuild from the ruins of war.

51. Niebuhr, *Irony*, 38–39.

52. Niebuhr and Heimert, *Nation So Conceived*, 154.

53. Ibid., 154.

54. Reinitz, *Irony and Consciousness*, 91.

55. Ibid.

56. Ibid., 112.

57. Ibid., 116.

58. Reinhold Niebuhr, "The Social Myths of the Cold War," *Journal of International Affairs* 21 (1967): 46, 47.

59. Reinhold Niebuhr, "Vietnam: Studies in Ironies," *New Republic* (June 24, 1967): 11. Emphasis in original.

60. Quoted in Reinitz, *Irony and Consciousness*, 120.

61. Ibid., 121.

62. Quoted in Ibid.

63. Reinhold Niebuhr, "Redeemer Nation to Super-Power," *New York Times*, Dec. 4, 1970, 47.

64. Reinitz, 122.

65. Charles C. Brown, *Niebuhr and His Age* (Philadelphia: Trinity Press International, 1992) 236.

66. Edward Said, *Culture and Imperialism* (New York: Alfred A. Knopf, 1993), 4–5.

67. Niebuhr, *Nature and Destiny*, 307.

68. Shriver, *Ethic for Enemies*, 74.

69. That history is still written in this manner thirty years after Niebuhr co-wrote *A Nation So Conceived* can be seen in the work of numerous non-Native scholars. For instance, historian and sociologist Franz Schurmann, like Niebuhr the son of immigrants, produces a rendering of American history remarkably like Niebuhr's in his volume *American Soul* (San Francisco: Mercury House, 1995), from which Indians are almost totally absent and in which the nativist designation "native American" denotes Euro-Americans born in the United States.

70. Quoted in Grinde and Johansen, *Exemplar*, ix.

71. Quoted in Bataille and Silet, *Pretend Indians*, xvi.

72. Luther Standing Bear, *Land of the Spotted Eagle* (1933; reprint, Lincoln: University of Nebraska Press, 1978), 248.

CHAPTER 10. INDIAN PRESENCE WITH NO INDIANS PRESENT

1. Walter R. Echo-Hawk and Roger C. Echo-Hawk, "Repatriation, Reburial, and Religious Rights," in *Handbook of American Indian Religious Freedom*, ed. Christopher Vecsey (New York: Crossroad, 1991), 67.

2. Ibid.

3. Edward Said states, "Of all the modern sciences, anthropology is the one historically most tied to colonialism, since it was often the case that anthropologists and ethnologists advised colonial rulers on the manners and mores of native people." See *Culture and Imperialism*, 152.

4. Ibid., 152.

5. Echo-Hawk and Echo-Hawk, "Repatriation," in Vecsey, *Handbook*, 67.

6. U.S. Department of Interior, *Federal Agencies Task Force Report, American Indian Religious Freedom Act Report* (Washington: 1979), 64.

7. Echo-Hawk and Echo-Hawk, "Repatriation," in Vecsey, *Handbook*, 68.

8. 16 U.S.C. § 432 (1906); 16 U.S.C. §§ 470aa–470ll (1988).

9. 20 U.S.C. §§ 80q-9, 80q-9(c) (1990).

10. 25 U.S.C. §§ 3001–3013 (1991).

11. David H. Getches, Charles F. Wilkinson, and Robert A. Williams, Jr., *Cases and Materials on Federal Indian Law*, 3d ed. (St. Paul: West Publishing Company, 1993), 772–73.

12. Lynne Goldstein, "Archaeology," in Davis, *Native America*, 53.

13. Echo-Hawk and Echo-Hawk, "Repatriation," in Vecsey, *Handbook*, 64.

14. Quoted in George Johnson, "Indian Tribes' Creationists Thwart Archeologists," *New York Times*, Oct. 22, 1996, C13. For Bonnichsen's account of the find and the resulting controversy, see Robson Bonnichsen and Alan L. Schneider, "Roots," *The Sciences* (May-June 1995): 26–31.

15. Quoted in Valerie Henderson, "Five Tribes Seek Remains of 'The Ancient One,'" *Indian Country Today* (Nov. 25–Dec. 2, 1996): B1.

16. Quoted in Timothy Egan, "Tribe Stops Study of Bones That Challenge History," *New York Times*, Sept. 30, 1996, A12.

17. Quoted in "Mistaken Man," *New York Times Magazine* (Dec. 1, 1996): 31.

18. Egan, "Tribe Stops Study," A12; Danyelle Robinson, "Ancient Remains Relative to Many," *Indian Country Today* (Jan. 20–27, 1997), A7; Robinson, "Tribes, Scientists Base Claims on Separate Acts," *Indian Country Today* (Jan. 20–27, 1997): A8.

19. Robinson, "Tribes," A8; Egan, "Tribe Stops Study," A12.

20. Quoted in Egan, A12.

21. Quoted in Danyelle Robinson, "Ancient Remains Linked to American Indian Tribes," *Indian Country Today* (Feb. 17–24, 1997): A1.

22. Johnson, "Indian, Tribes' Creationists," A1.

23. Quoted in Ibid., C13.

24. Ibid.

25. "Science and the Native American Cosmos," *New York Times* (Oct. 25, 1996), A38. One of the two letters under this collective caption was from me.

26. N. Scott Momaday, "Disturbing the Spirits," *New York Times*, Nov. 2, 1996, A15.

27. Quoted in Egan, "Tribe Stops Study," A12.

28. Quoted in Henderson, "Five Tribes Seek Remains," B1.

29. Robinson, "Ancient Remains Relative to Many," A7.

30. See Johnson, "Indian Tribes' Creationists," C13.

31. See my essay "From I-Hermeneutics to We-Hermeneutics: Native Americans and the Post-Colonial," Chapter 19.

32. Clark Wissler, *Indians of the United States*, rev. ed. with revisions by Lucy Wales Kluckhohn (Garden City, N.Y.: Doubleday, 1966), 4.

33. Deloria, *Red Earth*, 82.

34. Ibid.

35. Russell Thornton, "Repatriation of Human Remains and Artifacts," in Davis, *Native America in the Twentieth Century*, 543.

36. Wissler, *Indians of the United States*, 8–9; Olivia Vlahos, *New World Beginnings: Indian Cultures in the Americas* (New York: Viking Press, 1970), 16; Peter Farb, *Man's Rise to Civilization as Shown by the Indians of North America from Primeval Times to the Coming of the Industrial State* (New York: E. P. Dutton, 1968), 199.

37. Thomas D. Dillehay, "The Battle of Monte Verde," *The Sciences* (Jan.-Feb. 1997): 32.

38. Ibid.: 33.

39. John Noble Wilford, "Human Presence in Americas Is Pushed Back a Millenium," *New York Times*, Feb. 11, 1997, C4.

40. Deloria, *Red Earth*, 68–69.

41. Quoted in Johnson, "Indian Tribes' Creationists," C13.

42. Karen Freeman, "9,700-Year-Old Bones Back Theory of Coastal Migration," *New York Times*, Oct. 6, 1996, 32.

43. "Prehistory of Languages," *Archaeology* (July-Aug. 1994): 17.

44. John Noble Wilford, "Ancient Spears Tell of Mighty Hunters of Stone Age," *New York Times*, March 4, 1997, C6.

45. John Noble Wilford, "'American' Arrowhead Found in Siberia," *New York Times*, Aug. 2, 1996, A6.

46. Noley, *First White Frost*, 17–18.

47. Quoted in Bruce Shiamberg, "American-Indians Choose Spirit over Science," *New York Times*, Nov. 11, 1996, A14.

48. Noley, *First White Frost*, 16–17.

49. Deloria, *Red Earth*, 107.

50. Daniel Riegel, "On the Origins of Native Americans: A Synthesis of Ideas," unpub. paper (Yale University, Dec. 23, 1996), 5; Thomas D. Dillehay and David J. Meltzer, eds., *The First Americans: Search and Research* (Boston: CRC Press, 1991), 144.

51. Dillehay, "Battle of Monte Verde," 33.

52. Billy M. Jones and Odie B. Faulk, *Cherokees: An Illustrated History* (Muskogee, Okla.: The Five Civilized Tribes Museum, 1984), 10; see, generally, David McCutchen, *The Red Record: The Wallum Olum of the Lenni Lenape, the Delaware Indians, a Translation and Study* (Garden City Park, N.Y.: Avery Publishing Group, 1993).

53. Deloria, *Red Earth*, 97.

54. Goldstein, "Archaeology," in Davis, *Native America*, 50.

55. J. Douglas McDonald, Larry J. Zimmerman, A. L. McDonald, William Tall Bull, and Ted Rising Sun, "The Northern Cheyenne Outbreak of 1879: Using Oral History and Archaeology as Tools of Resistance," in *The Archaeology of Inequality*, ed. Randall H. McGuire and Robert Paynter (Oxford: Blackwell, 1991), 64, 77.

56. William D. Lipe, "For the Good of All, Study Those Ancient Bones," *New York Times*, Oct. 4, 1996, A14.

57. Scott L. Malcomson, "The Color of Bones," *New York Times Magazine* (April 2, 2000): 45.

58. Ibid.

59. Quoted in James Brooke, "Body of Ancient Man Found in West Canada Glacier," *New York Times*, Aug. 25, 1999, A13.

60. See, for example, James Brooke, "Lost Worlds Rediscovered as Canadian Glaciers Melt," *New York Times*, Oct. 5, 1999, F5; John Noble Wilford, "New Answers to an Old Question: Who Got Here First," *New York Times*, Nov. 9, 1999, F1; Mark K. Stengel, "The Diffusionists Have Landed," *Atlantic Monthly* (Jan. 2000): 35; John Noble Wilford, "The New World's Earliest People," *New York Times*, Apr. 11, 2000, F2.

CHAPTER 11. LOSING MY RELIGION

1. *Lyng v. Northwest Indian Cemetery Protective Association*, 485 U.S. 439 (1988); *Employment Division v. Smith*, 494 U.S. 872 (1990).

2. *Church of Lukumi Babalu Aye v. Hialeah*, 113 S.Ct. 2217 (1993).

3. President Clinton finally responded with an Executive Order that offered some protection to sacred sites on federal lands. This was recently used successfully to protect lands sacred to the Quechan in California from destruction by mining. In

the Quechan case, the Department of the Interior seemed to articulate a broad policy for protection of Native sacred sites.

4. Quoted in Jeffrey L. Sheler and Ted Gest, "How Big Is God's Tent?" *U.S. News and World Report* (Feb. 24, 1997): 44–45.

5. Jace Weaver, ed. *Native American Religious Identity: Unforgotten Gods* (Maryknoll, N.Y.: Orbis Books, 1998), 227.

6. *Sherbert v. Verner*, 374 U.S. 398 (1963).

7. *Cantwell v. Connecticut*, 310 U.S. 296 (1939).

8. *Reynolds v. U.S.*, 98 U.S. 145 (1879). For good discussions of the Court and religious liberty in both the Native and non-Native contexts, see John R. Wunder, *"Retained by the People": A History of American Indians and the Bill of Rights* (New York: Oxford University Press, 1994); Ronald B. Flowers, *That Godless Court?: Supreme Court Decisions on Church-State Relationships* (Louisville: Westminster/John Know Press, 1994); David E. Wilkins, *American Indian Sovereignty and the U.S. Supreme Court* (Austin: University of Texas Press, 1997).

9. Fortunately, in 1998, I was wrong about the case's possible impact on a pending suit by non-Native rock climbers who were suing the National Park Service. At issue was the Service's ban on Wyoming's Devil's Tower (a sacred site known as Bear Lodge to Natives) during the month of June, when it is used by Natives for religious ceremonies. The plaintiffs contended that the ban violated the First Amendment as an establishment of religion. Though *Smith* and *Boerne* were not directly applicable, I worried that they might have an indirect impact. I helped draft an amicus brief for a group of scholars, including Vine Deloria and myself, in support of the position of the Service and Natives at the level of the Tenth Circuit Court of Appeals. The appellate court dismissed the suit based on a lack of standing, and in the Spring of 2000, the Supreme Court denied certiorari.

10. Weaver, *Then to the Rock Let Me Fly*, 138; *Choctaw Nation v. Oklahoma*, 397 U.S. 620 (1970).

11. Stephen Carter, *The Culture of Disbelief: How American Law and Politics Trivialize Religious Devotion* (New York: BasicBooks, 1993), 9.

12. Vine Deloria, Jr., and Clifford Lytle, *American Indians, American Justice* (Austin: University of Texas Press, 1983), 131.

13. James M. Washington, "The Crisis in the Sanctity of Conscience in American Jurisprudence," 42 De Paul L. Rev. 11 (1992); see Rudolf Otto, *The Idea of the Holy* (London: Oxford University Press, 1923).

14. Kent, *Commentaries*, vol. 3, 312–13.

15. Luther Lee Bohanon, "The Autobiography of Judge Luther L. Bohanon," unpub. MS, 1988, vi–3.; Weaver, *Then to the Rock*, 47. For a more detailed discussion of the Otoe and Missouria, by a scholar involved in the case on their behalf, see Berlin Basil Chapman, *The Otoe and Missourias: A Study of Indian Removal and the Legal Aftermath* (Oklahoma City: Times Journal Publishing Co., 1965).

16. Don Monet and Skanu'u (Ardythe Wilson), *Colonialism on Trial: Indigenous Land Rights and the Gitksan and Wet'suwet'en Sovereignty Case* (Philadelphia:

New Society Publishers, 1992), 188. See *Delgam Uukw v. the Queen*, 79 D.L.R. 4th 185 (1991).

17. McEachern quoted in Monet and Skanu'u, *Colonialism on Trial*, 188.

18. Ibid., 189.

19. Ken MacQueen, "A Landmark Ruling Shocks Anthropologists," *Vancouver Sun*, July 13, 1991, 1.

20. Milluak (Alice Jeffrey), "Remove Not the Landmark," in *Aboriginal Title in British Columbia: Delgam Uukw v. the Queen*, ed. Frank Cassidy (Montreal: Institute for Research on Public Policy, 1992), 58. For other statements by the hereditary chiefs, see Gisday Wa and Delgam Uukw, *The Spirit in the Land: Statements of the Gitksan and Wet'suwet'en Hereditary Chiefs in the Supreme Court of British Columbia, 1987–1990* (Gabriola, B.C.: Reflections, 1992). The 1991 McEachern decision was overturned by the Supreme Court of Canada. Oral tradition was ruled admissible as evidence. As of this writing, the Canadian and British Columbia governments are negotiating a land settlement with the tribes. *Delgamuukw v. the Queen*, 1997 Can. Sup. Ct. LEXIS 96.

21. John Petoskey, "Indians and the First Amendment," in *American Indian Policy in the Twentieth Century*, ed. Vine Deloria, Jr. (Norman: University of Oklahoma Press, 1985), 221.

22. *Lyng*, 485 U.S. at 442.

23. Id. at 452.

24. *Northwest Indian Cemetery Protective Association v. Peterson*, 795 F.2d 688, 701 (9th Cir. 1986) (Beezer, C.J., dissenting).

25. *Reynolds*, 98 U.S. at 166–67.

26. Deward E. Walker, Jr., "Protection of American Indian Sacred Geography," in Vecsey, *Indian Religious Freedom*, 112.

27. Ibid., 112–13.

28. *Van der Peet v. the Queen*, 1996 Can. Sup. Ct. LEXIS 63.

29. Rudy Platiel and Ross Howard, "Indians Don't Have Right to Sell Catch, Court Rules," *Toronto Globe and Mail*, Aug. 22, 1996, A1.

30. Jeffrey Simpson, "Aboriginal Rights Are Different Things to Judges and Politicians," *Toronto Globe and Mail*, Sept. 4, 1996, A20.

31. Platiel and Howard, "Indians Don't Have Right," A1.

32. Ibid., A16; Simpson, "Aboriginal Rights," A20; Jace Weaver, "Natives Will Challenge Authority," *Toronto Globe and Mail*, Sept. 7, 1996, A21.

33. Note Justice O'Connor's admission that the site was "an integral and necessary part" of the Indians' religious systems.

34. See note 3, above.

35. Elizabeth Cook-Lynn, "Editor's Editorial," *Wicazo Sa Review* (Spring 1997): 7.

36. *Lukumi*, 113 S. Ct. at 2249 (Souter, J., concurring).

37. *Smith*, 494 U.S. at 921 (Blackmun, J., dissenting).

CHAPTER 12. TRIANGULATED POWER AND THE ENVIRONMENT

1. John Winthrop, "General Considerations for the Plantation in New England, with an Answer to Several Objections" (c. 1631); see also, Wise, *Red Man in the New World Drama*, 78–79.

2. John Winthrop, *Winthrop Papers*, vol. 2 (Boston: Massachusetts Historical Society, 1931), 141; Robert F. Berkhofer, *White Man's Indian*, 120–21; Neal Salisbury, *Manitou and Providence: Indians, Europeans, and the Making of New England 1500–1643* (New York: Oxford University Press, 1982), 183; Takaki, *Different Mirror*, 42.

3. *Johnson v. McIntosh*, 8 Wheat. 543 (1823). Marshall later backtracked on this notion in *Worcester v. Georgia*, 6 Pet. 515 (1832), calling it an "extravagant and absurd idea, that feeble settlements made on the sea coast . . . acquired legitimate power by them to govern the people."

4. Actually, despite his seeming demurer, Marshall proceeded at some length to discuss at least a variation of that same issue, seemingly in agreement with Vattel.

5. Kent, *Commentaries*, vol. 3, 312; vol. 1, 243.

6. *Washington Department of Ecology v. United States Environmental Protection Agency*, 752 F.2d 1465 (9th Cir., 1985).

7. Dick and Wimpfen, "Oil Mining," *Scientific American* (October 1980): 185A; see *Pennsylvania Coal v. Mahon*, 260 U.S. 393 (1922). In oil mining, which exploits petroleum by excavating a series of tunnels either above or below deposits and then by draining or pumping oil into the tunnels rather than by surface drilling, the amount of excavated material brought to the surface and later disposed of is small compared with that brought up by conventional mineral extraction. The prospect of subsidence is slight. Further, water can be injected into the oil reservoir, thus reducing the risk further. Dick and Wimpfen: 183–85.

8. Ibid.: 188.

9. Ibid.: 187.

10. Shapiro, "Energy Development on the Public Domain: Federal/State Cooperation and Conflict Regarding Environmental Land Use Control," 9 *Nat. Resources Law.* 397, 398 (1976).

11. Ibid.

12. Articles of Confederation, art. 9.

13. U.S. Const., art. I, §8, cl. 3.

14. *Cherokee Nation v. Georgia*, 5 Pet. 1 (1831).

15. Getches, Wilkinson, and Williams, *Cases and Materials*, 325.

16. *United States v. Kagama*, 118 U.S. 375 (1886); *Lone Wolf v. Hitchcock*, 187 U.S. 553 (1903).

17. U.S. Const., art. IV, §3, cl. 2.

18. *Griffin v. United States*, 168 F.2d 457, 460 (8th Cir., 1948).

19. 73 C.J.S. "Public Lands" sec. (1967); see also *Kleppe v. New Mexico*, 426 U.S. 529, 543 (1976).

20. *Camfield v. United States*, 167 U.S. 518, 526 (1897).

21. Felix Cohen, *Handbook of Federal Indian Law* (Washington: G.P.O., 1942), 122, quoted in Getches, Wilkinson, and Williams, *Cases and Materials*, 227.

22. Cohen, *Handbook*, 122; *United States v. Winans*, 198 U.S. 371 (1905); see also, Lloyd Burton, *American Indian Water Rights and the Limits of Law* (Lawrence: University Press of Kansas, 1991), 21.

23. See "Clipped Sovereignty," *Black's Law Dictionary*, 5th ed. (St. Paul: West Publishing, 1979), 231.

24. Getches, Wilkinson, and Williams, *Cases and Materials*, 325.

25. For a discussion of the situation on the federal public domain, see *Utah Power & Light Co. v. United States*, 243 U.S. 389, 404–5 (1917).

26. For example, Okla. Stat. Ann. tit. 52, §87.1 (West 1969 & Supp. 1980); Wyo. Stat. §30-5-109 (1977).

27. The limitation of production of crude oil or gas to some fraction of total productive capacity.

28. See, Richard W. Hemingway, *The Law of Oil and Gas* (St. Paul: West Publishing, 1971), 421, 423.

29. R. M. Williams, "Relationship between State and Federal Government with Respect to Oil and Gas Matters," 19 *Oil & Gas Inst.* 239, 253–54 (1968); see also I. R. Myers, *The Law of Pooling and Unitization* 390–91 (2d ed. 1967).

30. Myers, *Law of Pooling*, 389.

31. Controlled lands are federally owned lands in the public domain and other lands controlled or supervised by the federal government, including the trust lands of Indian tribes.

32. Williams, "Relationship between State and Federal": 254; see also, Terry Wilson, *The Underground Reservation: Osage Oil* (Lincoln: University of Nebraska Press, 1985).

33. Williams, "Relationship between State and Federal": 255.

34. Shapiro, "Energy Development": 418–22.

35. Ibid.

36. For a complete discussion of these challenges, see Jace Weaver, "Federal Lands: Energy, Environment and the States," *Columbia Journal of Environmental Law* 7, no. 2, (1982): 213–26.

37. *Andrus v. Click*, 97 Idaho 791, 796, 554 P.2d 969, 974 (1976).

38. *Cox v. Hibbard*, 31 Or.App. 269, 274, 570 P.2d 1190, 1193 (1977).

39. *Ventura County v. Gulf Oil Corp.*, 601 F2d 1080, 1083 (9th Cir. 1979), *aff'd mem.*, 100 S. Ct. 1593 (1980).

40. Nicholas J. Spaeth, Julie Wrend, and Clay Smith, eds., *American Indian Law Deskbook: Conference of Western Attorneys General* (Niwot: University of Colorado, 1993), 263–300.

41. Ibid., 269.

42. Act of Feb. 8, 1887, ch. 119, 24 Stat. 388.

43. *Montana v. United States*, 450 U.S. 544, 567 (1981).

44. Spaeth, Wrend, and Smith, *American Indian Law Deskbook*, 265; see, for example, *Cardin v. De La Cruz*, 671 F.2d 363 (9th cir. 1982), *cert. denied*, 459 U.S. 967 (1982); *Confederated Salish and Kootenai Tribes v. Namen*, 665 F.2d 951 (9th Cir. 1982), *cert. denied*, 459 U.S. 977 (1982); *Knight v. Shoshone and Arapahoe Indian Tribes*, 670 F.2d 900 (10th Cir. 1982).

45. *Brendale v. Confederated Tribes & Bands of Yakima*, 492 U.S. 408 (1989).

46. Getches, Wilkinson, and Williams, *Cases and Materials*, 713–14.

47. Spaeth, Wrend, and Smith, *American Indian Law Deskbook*, 289–90.

48. Ibid., 289; see also, 265–66, 291.

49. Ibid., 291.

50. Joseph Singer, "Sovereignty and Property," 86 *Nw.U.L.Rev.* 1, 4–5 (1991). Emphasis in original.

51. Getches, Wilkinson, and Williams, *Cases and Materials*, 731.

52. Spaeth, Wrend, and Smith, *American Indian Law Deskbook*, 286–87.

53. Ibid., 287.

54. Ibid., 288.

55. *Washington*, 752 F.2d at 1469.

56. *New Mexico v. Mescalero Apache Tribe*, 462 U.S. 324, 334–35 (1983).

57. Spaeth, Wrend, and Smith, *American Indian Law Deskbook*, 274.

58. Getches, Wilkinson, and Williams, *Cases and Materials*, 730. These laws include the Federal Water Pollution Control Act (commonly called the Clean Water Act); the Clean Air Act; the Safe Drinking Water Act; the Endangered Species Act; the Resource Conservation and Recovery Act; the Comprehensive Environmental Response, Compensation and Liability Act (commonly referred to as Superfund); the Surface Mining Control and Reclamation Act; and the Federal Insecticide, Fungicide and Rodenticide Act.

59. Judith Royster and Rory Fausett, "Control of the Reservation Environment: Tribal Primacy, Federal Delegation, and the Limits of State Intrusion," 64 *Wash.L.Rev.* 581, 583–96 (1989).

60. *Nance v. EPA*, 645 F.2d 701, 714-15 (9th Cir.), *cert. denied*, 454 U.S. 1081 (1981).

61. *Washington*, 752 F.2d at 1469. States' rights advocates point to the fact that the *Washington* case was decided prior to *Brendale* and that a different outcome would probably appertain today. Such an expansive reading of *Brendale* is, however, unwarranted, and given traditional judicial deference to administrative determinations, a different decision seems unlikely.

62. Getches, Wilkinson, and Williams, *Cases and Materials*, 731.

63. 33 U.S.C. §1377(e)(2).

64. "Indian Tribes: Water Quality Planning and Management, Interim Final Rule," 54 Fed. Reg. 14,354, 14,355 (1989); Spaeth, Wrend, and Smith, *American Indian Law Deskbook*, 282.

65. Spaeth, Wrend, and Smith, *American Indian Law Deskbook*, 282.

66. Ibid., 290.

67. Royster and Fausett, "Control of the Reservation Environment," 635; Spaeth, Wrend, and Smith, *American Indian Law Deskbook,* 270.

68. Getches, Wilkinson, and Williams, *Cases and Materials,* 732–33.

69. Spaeth, Wrend, and Smith, *American Indian Law Deskbook,* 291–92; *Solem v. Bartlett,* 465 U.S. 463, 468 (1984).

70. *Washington,* quoted in Getches, Wilkinson, and Williams, *Cases and Materials,* 728 n. 1.

71. Spaeth, Wrend, and Smith, *American Indian Law Deskbook,* 292.

72. See "The Endangered West," *New York Times,* June 18, 1995, 14.

73. Getches, Wilkinson, and Williams, *Cases and Materials,* 731–32; see also Teresa A. Williams, "Pollution and Hazardous Waste on Indian Lands: Do Federal Laws Apply and Who May Enforce Them?" 17 *Am.Ind.L.Rev.* 269 (1992); Richard A. Du Bey, et al., "Protection of the Reservation Environment: Hazardous Waste Management on Indian Lands," 18 *Envtl.L.* 449 (1988).

74. See *Washington,* quoted in Getches, Wilkinson, and Williams, *Cases and Materials,* 729.

75. See Weaver, *Defending Mother Earth,* 117.

CHAPTER 13. SCALING RÍOS MONTT

1. Weaver, *Then to the Rock Let Me Fly,* 31.

2. Request to Question Augusto Pinochet Ugarte, Criminal Investigation 19/97 L, Central Investigating Court Number 5, Audiencia Nacional, Madrid (October 14, 1998).

3. Request to Arrest Augusto Pinochet Ugarte, Criminal Investigation 19/97 L, Central Investigating Court Number 5, Audiencia Nacional, Madrid (October 16, 1998).

4. *Ex Parte Pinochet,* 3 W.L.R. 1456 (House of Lords, 25 Nov. 1998); *Ex Parte Pinochet,* 2 W.LR. 827 (House of Lords, 24 Mar. 1999).

5. *Pinochet,* 3 W.L.R. 1456.

6. Order Affirming Jurisdiction in the Criminal Proceeding, Appeal 173/98, Criminal Investigation 1/98, Central Investigating Court Number 6, Criminal Chamber, Audiencia Nacional, Madrid (Nov. 5, 1998).

7. *Pinochet,* 2 W.LR. 827; Warren Hoge, "Britain's High Court Supports Move to Release Pinochet," *New York Times,* February 1, 2000, A8.

8. Hoge, "Britain's High Court," A8.

9. Ibid.

10. *Xuncax v. Gramajo,* 886 F.Supp. 162 (D.Mass., 1995).

11. *Paul v. Avril,* 901 F.Supp. 330, 336 (S.D.Fla. 1994).

12. Chitra Ragavan, "A Safe Haven, but for Whom?" *U.S. News and World Report* (*www.usnews.com*) (Nov. 15, 1999).

13. "15 to Sue Japan in U.S. over Sex Slavery," *New York Times,* Sept. 16, 2000, p. A5.

14. *Attorney General of Israel v. Eichmann,* 36 I.L.R. 5 (Israel, D.C. Jerusalem, 1961), *aff'd* 136 I.L.R. 277 (Supr. Ct., 1962).

15. *Demanjanjuk v. Petrovsky,* 776 F2d 571 (6th Cir., 1985).

16. See *U.S. v. Noriega,* 776 F.Supp. 1506 (S.D. Fla. 1990).

17. Lacabe, "Criminal Procedures," 7.

18. Elisabetta Povoledo, "Argentines Sentenced," *New York Times* (Dec. 7, 2000), p. A12.

19. Ibid. Argentina refused to extradite Astiz. An international warrant has been issued for his arrest.

20. Tim Weiner and Gunger Thompson, "Wide Net in Argentine Torture Case," *New York Times* (Sept. 11, 2000), A6.

21. *Filartiga v. Pena-Irala,* 577 F. Supp. 860, 862-863 (E.D. NY 1984).

22. *Pinochet,* 2 W.L.R. 827.

23. Id., quoting Quincy Wright, (1947) 41 A.J.I.L. at 71.

24. *Schooner Exchange v. McFaddon,* 11 U.S. (7 Cranch) 116, 139 (1812).

25. Sheldon Glueck, The Nuremberg Trial and Aggressive War, 59 Harv. L. J. 396, 426 (1946).

26. Id. at 427.

27. *Pinochet,* 2 W.L.R. 827.

28. Id. (per Lord Hutton).

29. Id. (per Lord Millett).

30. *Demanjanjuk,* 603 F.Supp. 1468 (N.D. Oh., 1985); 776 F.2d 571 (6th Cir., 1985).

31. *Pinochet,* 2 W.L.R. 827 (per Lord Hutton).

32. See, *Demanjanjuk,* 776 F.2d at 581.

33. *Siderman de Blake v. Republic of Argentina,* 965 F.2d 699, 718 (9th Cir. 1992).

34. *Pinochet,* 2 W.L.R. 827 (per Lord Hutton).

35. Emphasis mine.

36. Burgers and Danielius, *Handbook of the Convention against Torture and Other Cruel, Inhuman or Degrading Treatment or Punishment,* 1. Emphasis mine.

37. Lacabe, "Criminal Procedures," 27–28.

38. *Gramajo,* 886 F. Supp. at 169–71, 176–80. In *Filartiga,* the plaintiffs, citizens of Paraguay, were awarded over $10,000,000 in the torture and murder of Joelito Filartiga by Pena, the inspector general of police in Asunción in Paraguay. *Filartiga,* 577 F. Supp. at 867. The Second Circuit had confirmed jurisdiction in 1980. *Filartiga v. Pena-Irala,* 630 F.2d 876 (2d Cir., 1980).

39. *Pinochet,* 2 W.L.R. 827 (per Lord Millett). In *Prosecutor v. Furundzija,* the tribunal declared, "Clearly, the jus cogens nature of the international crime of torture articulates the notion that the prohibition has now become one of the most fundamental standards of the international community. Furthermore, this prohibition is designed to produce a deterrent effect, in that it signals to all members of the international community and the individuals over whom they wield authority that the prohibition of torture is an absolute value from which nobody must

deviate." *Prosecutor v. Ferundzija*, Tribunal for Former Yugoslavia, Case No. 17-95-17/1~T, para. 153.

40. Reuters, Fiona Ortiz, "Guatemalan Group Hopes to Emulate Pinochet Case with Lawsuit against Former Dictator." November 26, 1998, 1. http://www.nandotimes.com.

41. Reuters, "Spanish Court to Probe Guatemalan Human Rights Abuses." March 27, 2000, 1. http://www.cnn.com.

42. See Greg Grandin, "No Victory for Dictators," *New York Times*, March 7, 2000, A25.

43. Reuters, "Guatemalan Human Rights Abuses," 2.

44. Andrew Reding, *Democracy and Human Rights in Guatemala* (World Policy Institute: 1997), 7–8. http://www.world policy.org.

45. Ibid., 8–9.

46. Ibid., 9.

47. Susanne Jonas, *The Battle for Guatemala: Rebels, Death Squads, and U.S. Power* (Boulder, Colo.: Westview Press, 1991), 153.

48. Jennifer Schirmer, *Guatemalan Military Project: A Violence Called Democracy* (Philadelphia: University of Pennsylvania Press, 1998), 18.

49. Ibid.

50. Jonas, *Battle for Guatemala*, 127–28. In Guatemala, the term *Indian* carries pejorative connotations. In this essay, it will be used only in direct quotations from others. The Native population themselves prefer the term *indigena*.

51. Reding, *Democracy and Human Rights*, 40; Jonas, *Battle for Guatemala*, 128.

52. Jonas, *Battle for Guatemala*, 147.

53. Schirmer, *Guatemalan Military Project*, 83, 43–44.

54. Reding, *Democracy and Human Rights*, 9; "Guatemala," *Human Rights Watch World Report 1998*, 3. http://www.igc.apc.org.

55. Jonas, *Battle for Guatemala*, 148; Schirmer, *Guatemalan Military Project*, 18–19.

56. Schirmer, *Guatemalan Military Project*, 45.

57. Ibid., 45–46.

58. See, generally, Victor Montejo, *Voices from Exile: Violence and Survival in Modern Maya History* (Norman: University of Oklahoma Press, 1999).

59. Schirmer, *Guatemalan Military Project*, 57.

60. Jonas, *Battle for Guatemala*, 148–49.

61. Schirmer, *Guatemalan Military Project*, 45.

62. Ibid. Emphasis in original.

63. Ibid., 52, 57.

64. Ibid., 35.

65. Ibid., 145.

66. Ibid., 143–44.

67. Ibid., 136.

68. Ethnic identification in Guatemala is complex. There is an element of class in these identifications, and no fixed lines exist between the three groups. There are, of course, linguistic and cultural factors involved as well.

69. Schirmer, *Guatemalan Military Project*, 59.

70. Ibid., 56.

71. Ibid.

72. Reding, *Democracy and Human Rights*, 9.

73. *Pinochet*, 2 W.L.R. 827.

74. Schirmer, *Guatemalan Military Project*, 137.

75. See chapter 6, "Clowns and Villains."

76. Schirmer, *Guatemalan Military Project*, 61. Emphasis in original.

77. Jonas, *Battle for Guatemala*, 154.

78. Reuters, "Spanish Court to Probe Accusations of Genocide in Guatemala." March 22, 2000, 1–2. http://cnn.com. The article reports that anthropologists have unearthed the remains of fifteen campesinos at Choyomche, believed to be those from a 1984 army massacre.

79. Schirmer, *Guatemalan Military Project*, 75.

80. Ibid., 144.

81. Schirmer, *Guatemalan Military Project*, 91; Jonas, *Battle for Guatemala*, 150.

82. Not subject to forced enlistment into the Civil Patrol, women continued to wear traditional dress. This came to be seen as a sign of resistance.

83. Schirmer, *Guatemalan Military Project*, 64–65.

84. Jonas, *Battle for Guatemala*, 149.

85. Schirmer, *Guatemalan Military Project*, 60.

86. See note 8, Order Affirming Jurisdiction.

87. Lacabe, "Criminal Procedures," 14.

88. *Pinochet*, 3 W.L.R. 1456. Lord Lloyd cites *Oppenheim's International Law*: "The application of international law as part of the law of the land means that, subject to the overriding effect of statute law, rights and duties flowing from the rules of customary international law will be recognized and given effect by English courts without the need of any specific Act adopting those rules into English law." 9th ed. (1992), 57. The U.S. Supreme Court has recognized a similar principle in the *Paquete Habana* case, declaring, "International law is our law." *Paquete Habana*, 175 U.S. 677, 700 (1900).

89. See note 8 above, Order Affirming Jurisdiction.

90. Id.

91. Id.

92. Lacabe, "Criminal Procedures," 18–19.

93. See Richard Wilson, *Mayan Resurgence in Guatemala* (Norman: University of Oklahoma Press, 1999); Estuardo Zapeta, "Guatemala: Maya Movement at the Political Crossroads," *Abya Yala News*, 8, no. 3 (Fall 1994). Garzón found that destruction of a group based on religious motivations was tantamount to the destruction of a religious group. Lacabe, "Criminal Procedures," 22.

94. Lacabe, "Criminal Procedures," 26.

95. Ibid.

96. See note 8 above, Order Affirming Jurisdiction.

97. Lacabe, "Criminal Procedures," 27–28.

98. See note 8 above, Order Affirming Jurisdiction.

99. Convention against Torture and Other Cruel, Inhuman or Degrading Treatment or Punishment 1(1) (1984).

100. *Pinochet*, 2 W.L.R. 827 (per Lord Millett).

101. *Pinochet*, 3 W.L.R. 1456 (per Lord Steyn).

102. Id. (per Lord Nicholls).

103. Id. (per Lord Steyn).

104. Once again, in its November 5 opinion regarding jurisdiction in the case of Pinochet, the Criminal Chamber concurred. Order Affirming Jurisdiction, see note 8 above.

105. John Ward Anderson, "Guatemala Swears in New President," *Washington Post* (washingtonpost.com) (January 14, 2000), 1–3. CACIF is the Comité Coordinador de Asociaciones Agrícolas, Commerciales, Industriales y Financieras. Part chamber of commerce, part cartel, and part quasi-governmental instrumentality, CACIF accounts for approximately 90 percent of the wealth of Guatemala. Portillo's relationship to Ríos Montt is complex. His vice president and foreign minister are staunch Ríos Montt supporters. The former dictator reportedly vetoed the president's first choice for defense minister, a general involved in the Mejía coup. Yet Portillo also turned down Ríos Montt's first choice for foreign minister, his own daughter. The new president has also brought leftists, human rights activists, and *indigenas* into his cabinet.

106. "Spanish Prosecutors Oppose Guatemalan Charges Urged by Nobel Laureate." March 31, 2000, pp. 1–2. http://www.cnn.com.

107. "Guatemala to Offer Spanish Court Information on Killings." April 12, 2000, p. 1. http://www.cnn.com.

108. *Pinochet*, 2 W.L.R. 827 (per Lord Phillips).

109. Ortiz, "Guatemalan Group Hopes," 1–2.

110. Reuters, "Spanish Court to Probe Accusations," p. 2.

111. Reuters, "Spanish Court to Probe Guatemalan," p. 2; "Guatemala Ex-dictator Under Investigation in Spain Cancels Trip to France." April 18, 2000, p. 1. http://www.cnn.com.

112. "Spanish Prosecutors," pp. 1–2.

113. Jayson Blair, "Pinochet's Revenge: Oliver North, You Better Watch Out," *New York Times*, March 26, 2000, p. WK 5.

114. Quoted in Telford Taylor, *Nuremberg and Vietnam: An American Tragedy* (Chicago: Quadrangle Books, 1970), 11–12.

115. Barbara Crossette, "Canada Tries to Define Line between Human and National Rights," *New York Times*, Sept. 14, 2000, A11.

116. *Pinochet*, 2 W.L.R. 827 (per Lord Millett).

117. *In re Piracy Jure Gentium* [1934] A.C. 586 at 597; see also, *Gramajo*, 886 F. Supp. at 180.

118. Glueck, "Nuremberg Trial," 398.

CHAPTER 14. IT CAME FROM OUTER SPACE

1. "Oregon Tribe Claims Meteorite," Nov. 17, 1999, p. 2, www.koin.com; Courtenay Thompson, "Tribes Claim Willamette Meteorite," *Oregonian*, Nov. 17, 1999, pp. 3–4. www.oregonlive.com; *Oregon Iron Co. v. Hughes*, 47 Or. 313, 316–17 (Or. Sup. Ct., 1905).

2. *Oregon Iron*, 47 Or. at 322; Robert D. McFadden, "Meteorite Dispute Greets Opening of Planetarium," *New York Times* Feb. 19, 2000, A1, B2.

3. In the mid-nineteenth century, the government began to consolidate Indian tribes onto reservations in the Willamette Valley. Grand Ronde was set aside in 1857 by executive order. The Confederated Tribes is composed of the Shasta, Kalapuya, Rogue River, Mollala, and Umpqua. It also includes members from other area tribes, including the Chinooks and the Clackamas, the latter of which gave its name to the county where the meteorite was found by Hughes. Tracy Olson, "Confederated Tribes of Grand Ronde," in Davis, *Native America*, 135–36.

4. McFadden, "Meteorite Dispute": A1, B2; Benjamin Weiser, "Museum Sues to Keep Meteorite Sought by Indian Group," *New York Times*, Feb. 29, 2000, B3; John Bacon, "Indian Tribes Argue for Meteorite Rights," *USA Today*, Feb. 29, 2000, 3A.

5. Weiser, "Museum Sues," B3.

6. Jack F. Trope, "The Native American Graves Protection and Repatriation Act: Implementing Regulations (and 1996 Museum Act Amendment)," in *Mending the Circle: A Native American Repatriation Guide*, eds. Walter Echo-Hawk, Elizabeth Sackler, and Jack Trope (New York: American Indian Ritual Object Repatriation Foundation, 1996), 206.

7. *Oregon Iron*, 47 Or. at 318–19.

8. Id. Scientists believe that it could have landed somewhere in Canada or Washington state and was moved to the West Linn site by glacial ice approximately ten thousand years ago.

9. Id. at 321.

10. Id. at 321–22.

11. Weiser, "Museum Sues," B3.

12. Thompson, "Tribes Claim Willamette Meteorite," 3.

13. Ibid.; *Oregon Iron*, 47 Or. at 320.

14. *Oregon Iron*, 47 Or. at 320.

15. Zachariah Atwell Mudge, *Sketches of Mission Life among the Indians of Oregon* (New York: Carlton & Porter, 1854), 19–20.

16. Ibid., 20–21.

17. See, Jay Miller, "North Pacific Ethnoastronomy: Tsimshian and Others," in *Earth and Sky: Visions of the Cosmos in Native American Folklore*, eds. Ray A. Williamson and Claire R. Farrer (Albuquerque: University of New Mexico Press, 1992), 193–205. See also Ray A. Williamson, *Living the Sky: The Cosmos of the American Indian* (Boston: Houghton Mifflin, 1984).

18. Carter, *Culture of Disbelief,* 9

19. Quoted in Thompson, "Tribes Claim Willamette Meteorite," 1–3.

20. Jack Trope, "Native American Graves Protection and Repatriation Act," in Echo-Hawk, Sackler, and Trope, *Mending the Circle,* 10.

21. Ibid., 13.

22. There are exceptions for competing claims (which does not seem to be an issue in the instant case) and for objects that are "indispensable for completion of a specific scientific study, the outcome of which would be of major benefit to the United States." The museum, though it has alleged a general benefit to science and the public, has not claimed the ongoing use of its lobby centerpiece for a *specific* study. At any rate, museums are required by the act to turn over objects within ninety days after the end of the specific study.

23. Other tribes or bands party to the 1855 treaty were the Kalapuya, Molalla, and Tumwater.

24. It is a basic principle of federal Indian law that whatever rights are not ceded by Native nations (or taken away by Congress) are retained as part of the nations' preexisting sovereignty.

25. Olson, "Tribes of Grand Ronde," in Davis, *Native America,* 136. According to Tracy Olson, a member of Grand Ronde, termination signified a loss of "home" and "identity" for elders and caused the youth of the tribe to struggle with "identity and heritage."

26. Trope, "Native American Graves Protection and Repatriation Act," in Echo-Hawk, *Mending the Circle,* 13.

27. *Oregon Iron,* 47 Or. at 320.

28. These examples are only meant to be suggestive. There may be additional grounds for questioning the museum's right of possession.

29. McFadden, "Meteorite Dispute," A1.

CHAPTER 15. NATIVE REFORMATION IN INDIAN COUNTRY?

1. Vine Deloria, Jr., *Custer Died for Your Sins,* 2d. ed. Norman: University of Oklahoma Press, 1988), 112.

2. Interview with Marie-Therese Archambault in Jace Weaver, "Native Reformation in Indian Country," *Christianity and Crisis* (Feb. 15, 1993).

3. George Tinker, *A Missionary Conquest* (Minneapolis: Fortress Press, 1993).

4. Quoted in Weaver, "Native Reformation, *Christianity and Crisis.*

5. Ibid.

6. Ibid.

7. Ibid.

8. Ibid.

9. George E. Tinker, "Natives and the Land: 'The End of Living, and the Beginning of Survival,'" in *Lift Every Voice: Constructing Christian Theology from the*

Underside, ed. Susan Brooks Thistlethwaite and Mary Potter Engel (San Franscisco: Harper & Row, 1990), p. 143.

10. Steven Charleston, "The Old Testament of Native America," in Thistlethwaite and Engel, pp. 49–50.

CHAPTER 16. A BIBLICAL PARADIGM FOR NATIVE LIBERATION

1. William Baldridge, "Native American Theology: A Biblical Basis," *Christianity and Crisis*, quoted in Treat, *Native and Christian*, p. 100.

2. Robert Warrior, "Robert Allen Warrior Responds," *Christianity and Crisis*, quoted in Treat, pp. 102–3.

CHAPTER 17. TRICKSTER

1. See chapter 19, "From I-Hermeneutics to We-Hermeneutics: Native Americans and the Post-Colonial."

2. Lewis Hyde, *Trickster Makes This World: Mischief, Myth, and Art* (New York: Farrar, Strauss and Giroux, 1998), 6.

3. James De Sauza and Harriet Rohmer, *Brother Anansi and the Cattle Ranch* (San Francisco: Children's Book Press, 1989), 5.

4. Richard Erdoes and Alfonso Ortiz, eds. *American Indian Trickster Tales* (New York: Viking, 1998), xvi.

5. Ibid., xviii.

6. Hyde, *Trickster Makes This World*, 130.

7. Erdoes and Ortiz, *American Indian Trickster*, xviii.

8. Hyde, *Trickster Makes This World*, 9. Emphasis mine.

9. Quoted in Erdoes and Ortiz., *American Indian Trickster*, xix.

10. Hyde, *Trickster Makes This World*, 9.

11. Ibid., 13.

12. Ibid., 10.

13. Paul Radin, *The Trickster* (New York: Schocken Books, 1972), xxiii.

14. Hyde, *Trickster Makes This World*, 10–11.

15. See, generally, Noley, *First White Frost*.

16. See Vizenor, *Manifest Manners*, 122; Louis Owens, "'Ecstatic Strategies': Gerald Vizenor's Darkness in Saint Louis Bearheart," in Vizenor, *Narrative Chance*, 141–53.

17. Quoted in Hyde, *Trickster Makes This World*, 12.

18. Alan Velie, "The Trickster Novel," in Vizenor, *Narrative Chance*, 136.

19. Hyde, *Trickster Makes This World*, 9–10.

20. Sister Charles Palm, *Stories Jesus Told: Dakota Way of Life* (Sioux Falls, S.D.: American Indian Research Center, Blue Cloud Abbey, 1985), 50–58. For an account of the life of Sweet Medicine, see, Peter J. Powell, *Sweet Medicine*, vol. 2 (Norman: University of Oklahoma Press, 1969), 460–66. See also, Jace Weaver,

"Native Americans and Religious Education," in *Multicultural Religious Education* ed. Barbara Wilkerson (Birmingham: Religious Education Press, 1997), 282.

21. Hyde, *Trickster Makes This World*, 72.

22. Quoted in Erdoes and Ortiz, *American Indian Trickster*, xxi.

CHAPTER 18. REACHING BEYOND LANGUAGE

1. Laurie Anderson, "The Dream Before" (1989), quoted in Roselee Goldberg, "Hitching a Ride on the Great White Whale," *New York Times*, Oct. 3, 1999, Arts & Leisure, 39.

2. J. F. Bierlein, *Parallel Myths* (New York: Ballantine, 1994), 249; quoted in David Leeming and Jake Page, *The Mythology of Native North America* (Norman: University of Oklahoma Press, 1998), 143.

3. Rennard Strickland, *Fire and the Spirits: Cherokee Law from Clan to Court* (Norman: University of Oklahoma Press, 1975), 189.

4. See Steven Goldsberry, *Maui the Demigod* (New York: Poseidon Press, 1984), 391–99, and Miguel Méndez, *Pilgrims in Aztlán* (Tempe: Bilingual Press, 1992), 143–45, 169.

5. Paul Radin, *The Road of Life and Death* (Princeton: Princeton University Press, 1945), xiv.

6. Allen, *Spider Woman's Granddaughters*, 126.

7. Leeming and Page, *Mythology*, 112–13.

8. See Richard Erdoes and Alfonso Ortiz, eds. *American Indian Myths and Legends* (New York: Pantheon, 1984), 484–85; Gretchen Will Mayo, *North American Indian Stories: More Earthmaker Tales* (New York: Walker and Company, 1990), 41, 43.

9. Morris Opler, *Myths and Tales of the Chiricahua Apache Indians*, vol. 37, *Memoirs of the American Folklore Society*, (1942), quoted in Peter Nabokov, ed., *Native American Testimony*. Exp. ed. (New York: Viking, 1991), 440.

10. Morris Opler, *Myths and Tales of the Jicarilla Apache Indians*, vol. 31, *Memoirs of the American Folklore Society*, 1938, p. 336.

11. Charles G. Leland, *The Algonquin Legends of New England; or, Myths and Folk Lore of the Micmac, Passamaquoddy, and Penobscot Tribes* (Boston: Houghton, Mifflin, 1884), pp. 130-134.

12. Hyde, *Trickster Makes This World*, 100–107; see also, generally, H. A. Guerber, *Myths of the Norsemen* (London: George G. Harrap & Co., 1908).

13. Leland, *Algonquin Legends*, 131.

14. Thomas C. Parkhill, *Weaving Ourselves into the Land: Charles Godfrey Leland, "Indians," and the Study of Native American Religions* (Albany: State University of New York Press, 1997).

15. Jeanne Guillemin, *Urban Renegades: The Cultural Strategy of American Indians* (New York: Columbia University Press, 1975), 108–10.

16. Erdoes and Ortiz, *American Indian Myths*, 485–86.

17. Edward J. Ingebretsen, *Maps of Heaven, Maps of Hell: Religious Terror as Memory from the Puritans to Stephen King* (Armonk, N.Y.: M.E. Sharpe, 1996), 98.

18. Ibid., 104.

19. Erdoes and Ortiz, *American Indian Myths*, 496–99.

20. Lucy Young, told to Edith V. A. Murphey, "Out of the Past: A True Indian Story," *California Historical Society Quarterly*, vol. 20, no. 4 (Dec. 1941).

21. Cora DuBois, "Wintu Ethnography," *University of California Publications in American Archaeology and Ethnology*, vol. 36, 1935–39, 75–76.

22. Young Bear, *Remnants of the First Earth*, xii.

23. Zuñi People, *The Zuñis: Self-Portrayals* (Albuquerque: University of New Mexico Press, 1972), quoted in Nabokov, *Native American Testimony*, 439–40.

24. Elizabeth Cook-Lynn, "A Monograph of a Peyote Singer: Asa Primeaux, Sr." *Wicazo Sa Review* (Spring 1991): 9.

25. Thomas E. Mails, *Fools Crow* (Lincoln: University of Nebraska Press, 1979), 55, 152, 196–97.

26. Ingebretsen, *Maps of Heaven*, 197.

27. Quoted in ibid.

28. Armin W. Geertz, *The Invention of Prophecy: Continuity and Meaning in Hopi Indian Religion* (Berkeley: University of California Press, 1994).

29. Paul Tillich, *Shaking the Foundations* (New York: Charles Scribner's Sons, 1948), 141–42.

30. E. Stanley Jones, *The Christ of the Indian Road* (New York: Abingdon Press, 1925), 5.

31. Deloria, *God Is Red*, 192, 185

32. James Mooney, *History, Myths, and Sacred Formulas of the Cherokees.* (Reprint, Asheville, N.C.: Historical Images, 1992), 335–36.

33. William G. McLoughlin, *Cherokee Renascence in the New Republic* (Princeton: Princeton University Press, 1986), 184–85.

34. Jorge Noriega, "The Shadows of Power: An Ethnographic Account of Apache Shamanism" (unpub. paper, 1994), 40–41, 43.

35. Ibid., 41.

36. Antonia Mills, *Eagle Down Is Our Law: Witsuwit'en Law, Feasts, and Land Claims* (Vancouver: University of British Columbia Press, 1994), 168.

37. Ibid.

38. James Mooney, *The Ghost Dance Religion and the Sioux Outbreak of 1890*, Smithsonian Institution, Bureau of American Ethnology Bulletin no. 14, pt. 2 (Washington, D.C.: 1896), 749–56; Vittorio Lanternari, *The Religions of the Oppressed: A Study of Modern Messianic Cults* (New York: Alfred A. Knopf, 1963), 124–28.

39. Weaver, *American Journey*, 1998.

40. See, generally, Thomas Flanagan, *Louis "David" Riel: Prophet of the New World* (Toronto: University of Toronto Press, 1996).

41. Noriega, "Shadows of Power," 42–43.

42. Ibid., 43.

43. Ibid.

44. Quoted in Scott Peterson, *Native American Prophecies* (New York: Paragon House, 1990), 99.

45. Emerson Spider, Sr., "The Native American Church of Jesus Christ," in Raymond J. DeMallie and Douglas R. Parks, eds., *Sioux Indian Religion* (Norman: University of Oklahoma Press, 1987), 189–209.

46. Cook-Lynn, "Monograph of a Peyote Singer": 10–15.

47. Vincent Catches, "Native American Church: The Half-Moon Way," *Wicazo Sa Review* (Spring 1991): 17–23.

CHAPTER 19. FROM I-HERMENEUTICS TO WE-HERMENEUTICS

1. Rausch and Schlepp, *Native American Voices*, 130–31.

2. Marilyn M. Hofstra, ed., *Voices: Native American Hymns and Worship Resources* (Nashville: Discipleship Resources, 1992), 14–15.

3. Ibid., 39.

4. Noley, *First White Frost*, 165–66.

5. Deloria, *Custer Died for Your Sins*, 112.

6. Noley, *First White Frost*, 198–200.

7. Quoted in Jace Weaver, "Native Reformation in Indian Country?" in *Chrùtianity and Crisis* (Feb. 15, 1993): 40.

8. Noley, *First White Frost*, 85.

9. Although the history of Natives and Methodism is Noley's primary focus, the volume is much fuller, providing a broad history of Native/Christian interaction.

10. Tinker, *Missionary Conquest*, 4; Tinker, "Reading the Bible as Native Americans," *New Interpreters Bible*, vol. 1 (Nashville: Abingdon Press, 1994), 174.

11. Tinker, *Missionary Conquest*, 4.

12. Ibid., 10, 18.

13. Noley, *First White Frost*, 191.

14. Ibid., 43.

15. See Anthony Flew, "Theology and Falsification," in *New Essays in Philosophical Theology*, ed. A. G. N. Flew and A. C. MacIntyre (London: S.C.M., 1950), 96ff.

16. Tinker, *Missionary Conquest*, 125–26.

17. Ibid., 5.

18. See John Webster Grant, *Moon of Wintertime: Missionaries and the Indians of Canada in Encounter Since 1534* (Toronto: University of Toronto Press, 1984), 239.

19. Noley, *First White Frost*, 205–6.

20. See Holly Folk, "Indian Missionaries among the Anishinaabe Tribes of the Great Lakes Region: Selves-Determined or Self-Determining," unpub. paper, Columbia University, Spring 1996.

21. Michael Oleska, ed., *Alaskan Missionary Spirituality* (New York: Paulist Press, 1987), 21–24. The Russian Revolution of 1917 threw Russian Orthodox missions in America into a turmoil that would not end fully until fifty-three years later when the Russian Patriarch recognized the American church as autocephalous.

22. Quoted in Treat, *Native and Christian: Indigenous Voices*, 18.

23. William Baldridge, "Reclaiming Our Histories," in *New Visons for the Americas: Religious Engagement and Social Transformation*, ed. David Batstone (Minneapolis: Fortress Press, 1993), 25. Baldridge's original title for the article in which this statement appeared was "Christianity after Colonialism."

24. Homer Noley, "Native Americans and the Hermeneutical Task," unpub. paper, delivered at the Roundtable of Ethnic Theologians, 1988.

25. Quoted in Miller, *Errand into the Wilderness*, 119.

26. Cave, "Canaanites in a Promised Land," 287.

27. Quoted in ibid.: 288.

28. Anders Stephanson, *Manifest Destiny: American Expansion and the Empire of Right* (New York: Hill and Wang, 1995), 15–65.

29. Letter quoted in Grinde and Johansen, *Ecocide in Native America*, 7; Weaver, *Defending Mother Earth*, 14–15.

30. Papal bull quoted by Terry Tafoya and Roy De Boer, "Comments on the Involvement of Christian Churches in Native American Affairs," in Marilyn Bode, *Christians and Native Americans in the Late Twentieth Century* (Seattle: Church Council of Greater Seattle, 1981), 17.

31. Jace Weaver, "Original Simplicities and Present Complexities: Reinhold Niebuhr, Ethnocentrism, and the Myth of American Exceptionalism," *Journal of the American Academy of Religion*, 63, no. 2 (1995): 234–35.

32. Noley, *First White Frost*, 43–44.

33. Ibid., 18.

34. Quoted in Oleska, *Alaskan Missionary*, 71.

35. Justo González, *Out of Every Tribe and Nation: Christian Theology at the Ethnic Roundtable* (Nashville: Abingdon Press, 1992), 43.

36. Ibid.

37. Romano Guardini, *The Church of the Lord: On the Nature and Mission of the Church* (Chicago: Henry Regnery Company, 1966), 8–9.

38. See Noley, "Native Americans."

39. Tinker, *Missionary Conquest*, 3.

40. Baldridge, "Reclaiming Our Histories," in Batstone, *Visions*, 24.

41. Stuart Hall, "When Was 'the Post-Colonial'? Thinking at the Limit," in *The Post-Colonial Question: Common Skies, Divided Horizons*, ed. Iain Chambers and Lidia Curti (London: Routledge, 1996), 246.

42. Ashcroft, Griffiths, and Tiffin, *The Empire Writes Back*, 1.

43. Hall, "'Post-Colonial' Thinking," in Chambers and Curti, *Post-Colonial Question*, 258.

44. Ibid., 252–53.

45. See Ella Shohat, "Notes on the Postcolonial," *Social Text* 31-32 (1992).

46. Ruth Frankenberg and Lata Mani, "Crosscurrents, Crosstalk: Race, 'Post-coloniality' and the Politics of Location," *Cultural Studies* 7:2 (1992): 101; Hall, "'Post-Colonial' Thinking," in Chambers and Curti, *Post-Colonial Question*, 248–49.

47. Arif Dirlik, "The Postcolonial Aura: Third World Criticism in the Age of Global Capitalism," *Critical Inquiry* (Winter 1992): 353.

48. Ashcroft, Griffiths, and Tiffin, *Empire Writes Back*, 2, 6.

49. Hall, "'Post-Colonial' Thinking," in Chambers and Curti, *Post-Colonial Question*, 247.

50. Ibid., 255–56.

51. Said, *Culture and Imperialism*, 152.

52. Hall, "'Post-Colonial' Thinking," in Chambers and Curti, *Post-Colonial Question*, 250.

53. See King, *All My Relations*, x.

54. Said, *The World, the Text, and the Critic*, 19–20.

55. Hall, Quoted in "'Post-Colonial' Thinking," in Chambers and Curti, *Post-Colonial Question*, 251.

56. Ibid., 249.

57. Jacqueline Rose, *States of Fantasy* (New York: Oxford University Press. 1996).

58. Edward Said, "Fantasy's Role in the Making of Nations," *Times Literary Supplement* (Aug. 9, 1996), p. 7.

59. Ibid.

60. Reinhold Niebuhr, *The Irony of American History*, vii–viii.

61. Weaver, "Original Simplicities," 233–34.

62. Noley, "Native Americans."

63. Ibid.

64. William Apess, *On Our Own Ground: The Complete Writings of William Apess, a Pequot*, ed. Barry O'Connell (Amherst: University of Massachusetts Press, 1992), 10.

65. Ibid., 34 ff.

66. Peter Jones, *History of the Ojebway Indians: With Especial Reference to Their Conversion to Christianity* (London: A. W. Bennett, 1861), 29–30.

67. Quoted in Treat, *Native and Christian*, 135.

68. In Jace Weaver, "A Biblical Paradigm for Native Liberation," *Christianity and Crisis* (Feb. 15, 1993): 40.

69. Tinker, "Reading the Bible as Native Americans," 174.

70. González, *Out of Every Tribe*, 48.

71. Oleska, *Alaskan Missionary*, 7–8.

72. Quoted in Treat, *Native and Christian*, 52.

73. Steven Charleston, "The Old Testament of Native America," in Thistlethwaite and Engel, *Lift Every Voice*, 54–55.

74. Noley, *First White Frost*, 187

75. Weaver, *Defending Mother Earth*, 12.

76. Tinker, "Reading the Bible as Native Americans," 176–80.

77. Stephen Daniels, "This Land Was Made for Us," [*London*] *Times Literary Supplement*, Aug. 9, 1996, 8.

78. Noley, *First White Frost*, 71–72.

79. Ibid.

80. González, *Out of Every Tribe*, 53.

81. Ibid., 54; see also Kim.

82. González, *Out of Every Tribe*, 54.

83. Ibid.

84. Hall, "'Post-Colonial' Thinking," in Chambers and Curti, *Post-Colonial Question*, 244.

85. Warrior, *Tribal Secrets*, 97–98.

86. Hall, "'Post-Colonial' Thinking," 253–54.

Bibliography

Adams, Howard. *Prison of Grass: Canada from a Native Point of View.* Rev. ed. Saskatoon: Fifth House, 1989.

Adams, Percy G. *Travelers and Travel Liars, 1660–1800.* New York: Dover, 1980.

Alexie, Sherman. *Old Shirts and New Skins.* Los Angeles: American Indian Studies Center, University of California, Los Angeles, 1993.

Allen, Paula Gunn. *The Sacred Hoop: Recovering the Feminine in American Indian Traditions.* 2d ed. Boston: Beacon Press, 1992.

———. *The Woman Who Owned the Shadows.* Reprint, San Francisco: Aunt Lute Books, 1994.

———, ed. *Spider Woman's Granddaughters.* New York: Fawcett Columbine, 1989.

———, ed. *Voice of the Turtle: American Indian Literature, 1900–1970.* New York: Ballantine, 1994.

Anderson, A. T. *Nations within a Nation: The American Indian and the Government of the States.* Chappaqua, N.Y.: Privately printed, 1976.

Anderson, John Ward. "Guatemala Swears in New President." *Washington Post,* January 14, 2000.

Apess, William. *On Our Own Ground: The Complete Writings of William Apess, a Pequot.* Ed. Barry O'Connell. Amherst: University of Massachusetts Press, 1992.

Arnold, Philip P. "Wampum, the Land, and the Abolition of Grief." Unpublished paper. American Academy of Religion, Philadelphia, November 20, 1995.

Ashcroft, Bill, Gareth Griffiths and Helen Tiffin. *The Empire Writes Back: Theory and Practice in Post-Colonial Literatures.* London: Routledge, 1989.

———, eds. *The Post-Colonial Studies Reader.* London: Routledge, 1995.

Bacon, John. "Indian Tribes Argue for Meteorite Rights." *USA Today,* Feb. 29, 2000.

Bagley, Ben. *Unpublished Cole Porter.* New York: Painted Smile Records, 1972.

Barrie, J. M. *Peter Pan.* New York: Samuel French, 1928.

Bartel-Winkler, Lisa. "Das Drama des sterbenden Volkes." *Karl-May Jahrbuch 7*. Radebeul, Germany: Karl-May-Verlag, 1924.

Bataille, Gretchen M. and Charles P. Silet, eds. *The Pretend Indians: Images of Native Americans in the Movies*. Ames: University of Iowa Press, 1980.

Batstone, David, ed. *New Visions for the Americas: Religious Engagement and Social Transformation*. Minneapolis: Fortress Press, 1993.

Bennett, Tony and Valda Blundell. "First Peoples." *Cultural Studies* 9 (January 1995).

Benterrak, Krim, Stephen Muecke, and Paddy Roe. *Reading the Country: Introduction to Nomadology*. Freemantle: Freemantle Arts Centre, 1984.

Berkhofer, Robert F., Jr. *The White Man's Indian: Images of the American Indian from Columbus to the Present*. New York: Vintage Books, 1978.

Bhabha, Homi K. *The Location of Culture*. New York: Routledge, 1994.

Bierhorst, John, ed. *Four Masterworks of American Indian Literature*. New York: Farrar, Straus, and Giroux, 1974.

Bierlein, J. F. *Parallel Myths*. New York: Ballantine, 1994.

Blair, Jayson. "Pinochet's Revenge: Oliver North, You Better Watch Out." *New York Times*, Mar. 26, 2000.

Bode, Marilyn. *Christians and Native Americans in the Late Twentieth Century*. Seattle: Church Council of Greater Seattle, 1981.

Bohanon, Luther Lee. "The Autobiography of Luther L. Bohanon." Unpublished MS, 1988.

Boldt, Menno. *Surviving as Indian*. Toronto: University of Toronto Press, 1993.

Bolton, Guy, et al. *Girl Crazy*. Woodstock, Ill.: Dramatic Publishing Company, 1930.

Bonnichsen, Robson and Alan L. Schneider. "Roots." *The Sciences* (May-June 1995).

Bordman, Gerald. *American Musical Theatre: A Chronicle*, 2d ed. New York: Oxford University Press, 1992.

Bowden, Henry Warner. *American Indians and Christian Missions: Studies in Cultural Conflict*. Chicago: University of Chicago Press, 1981.

Brant, Beth. *Writing as Witness*. Toronto: Women's Press, 1994.

Bronitsky, Gordon. "Jews and Indians: Old Myths and New Realities." *Jewish Spectator* (Winter 1991–92).

Brooke, James. "Body of Ancient Man Found in West Canada Glacier." *New York Times*, Aug. 25, 1999.

———. "Lost Worlds Rediscovered as Canadian Glaciers Melt." *New York Times*, Oct. 5, 1999.

Brown, Charles C. *Niebuhr and His Age*. Philadelphia: Trinity Press International, 1992.

Brown, Dee. *Bury My Heart at Wounded Knee*. New York: Holt, Rinehart & Winston, 1971.

Bruchac, Joseph. *Survival This Way: Interviews with American Indian Poets*. Tucson: University of Arizona Press, 1987.

Brumble, H. David, III. *American Indian Autobiography*. Berkeley: University of California Press, 1988.

Burton, Lloyd. *American Indian Water Rights and the Limits of Law*. Lawrence: University Press of Kansas, 1991.

Carmody, Denise Lardner, and John Tully Carmody. *Native American Religions: An Introduction*. New York: Paulist Press, 1993.

Carter, Stephen. *The Culture of Disbelief: How American Law and Politics Trivialize Religious Devotion*. New York: BasicBooks, 1993.

Cassidy, Frank, ed. *Aboriginal Title in British Columbia: Delgam Uukw v. the Queen*. Montreal: Institute for Research on Public Policy, 1992.

Castell, Ron, ed. *Blockbuster Entertainment Guide to Movies and Video 1997*. New York: Dell, 1996.

Catches, Vincent. "Native American Church: The Half-Moon Way." *Wicazo Sa Review* (Spring 1991).

Cavanaugh, Linda, and Tony Stizza, prods. "Strangers in Their Own Land." Oklahoma City: Strangers in Their Own Land, Inc., 1993.

Cave, Alfred A. "Canaanites in a Promised Land: The American Indians and the Providential Theory of Empire." *American Indian Quarterly* (Fall 1988).

Chambers, Iain, and Lidia Curti, eds. *The Post-Colonial Question: Common Skies, Divided Horizons*. London: Routledge, 1996.

Chapman, Berlin Basil. *The Otoes and Missourias: A Study of Indian Removal and the Legal Aftermath*. Oklahoma City: Times Journal Publishing Co., 1965.

Charles Palm (Sister). *Stories Jesus Told: Dakota Way of Life*. Sioux Falls, S.D.: American Indian Research Center, Blue Cloud Abbey, 1985.

Chung Hyun-Kyung. *Struggle to Be the Sun Again*. Maryknoll, N.Y.: Orbis Books, 1990.

Churchill, Mary. "Native Struggles for Freedom in the Land." Respondent. American Academy of Religion, Philadelphia, November 20, 1995.

Churchill, Ward. *Fantasies of the Master Race: Literature, Cinema and the Colonization of American Indians*. Monroe, Maine: Common Courage Press, 1993.

Clifton, James, ed. *The Invented Indian: Cultural Fictions and Government Policies*. New Brunswick, N.J.: Transaction Publishers, 1990.

Cohen, Felix. *Handbook of Federal Indian Law*. Washington: G.P.O., 1942.

Cook-Lynn, Elizabeth. "Editor's Editorial." *Wicazo Sa Review* (Spring 1997).

———. "A Monograph of a Peyote Singer: Asa Primeaux, Sr." *Wicazo Sa Review* (Spring 1991).

Crèvecoeur, Michel Guillaume Jean de [Hector St. John]. *Letters from an American Farmer*. Reprint, New York: Penguin, 1981.

Criswell, W. A. *The Criswell Study Bible*. Nashville: Thomas Nelson, 1988.

Dahlin, Robert. "PW Interviews: Richard Slotkin." *Publishers Weekly* (Dec. 28, 1992).

Daniels, Stephens. "This Land Was Made for Us." [*London*] *Times Literary Supplement*, Aug. 9, 1996.

Davis, Mary B., ed. *Native America in the Twentieth Century, An Encyclopedia*. New York: Garland Publishing, 1994.

De Sauza, James and Harriet Rohmer. *Brother Anansi and the Cattle Ranch.* San Francisco: Children's Book Press, 1989.

Deloria, Ella Cara. *Waterlily.* Lincoln: University of Nebraska Press, 1988.

Deloria, Vine, Jr. *Custer Died for Your Sins*, 2d ed. Norman: University of Oklahoma Press, 1988.

———. *God Is Red*, 2d ed. Golden, Colo.: Fulcrum Publishing, 1992.

———. "It Is a Good Day to Die." *Katallagete* 4: (Fall–Winter 1972): 1–3.

———. *Red Earth, White Lies.* New York: Scribner's, 1995.

———. "Sacred Lands and Religious Freedom." *American Indian Religions* 1:1 (Winter 1994).

———. *We Talk, You Listen: New Tribes, New Turf.* New York: Macmillan, 1970.

———, ed. *American Indian Policy in the Twentieth Century.* Norman: University of Oklahoma Press, 1985.

Deloria, Vine, Jr., and Clifford Lytle. *American Indians, American Justice.* Austin: University of Texas Press, 1983.

DeMallie, Raymond J., and Douglas R. Parks, eds. *Sioux Indian Religion.* Norman: University of Oklahoma Press, 1987.

Dillehay, Thomas D. "The Battle of Monte Verde." *The Sciences* (Jan.-Feb. 1997).

Dillehay, Thomas D., and David J. Meltzer, eds. *The First Americans: Search and Research.* Boston: CRC Press, 1991.

Dippie, Brian W. *The Vanishing American: White Attitudes and U.S. Indian Policy.* Lawrence: University of Kansas Press, 1982.

Dirlik, Arif. "The Postcolonial Aura: Third World Criticism in the Age of Global Calitalism." *Critical Inquiry* (Winter 1992).

Drinnon, Richard. *White Savage: The Case of John Dunn Hunter.* New York: Schocken Books, 1972.

Du Bey, Richard A., et al. "Protection of the Reservation Environment: Hazardous Waste Management on Indian Lands." 19 Envtl. L. (1988).

DuBois, Cora. "Wintu Ethnography." *University of California Publications in American Archaeology and Ethnology.* Vol. 36, 1935–1939.

Duran, Eduardo, and Bonnie Duran. *Native American Postcolonial Psychology.* Albany: State University of New York Press, 1995.

Dussel, Enrique. *The Invention of the Americas: Eclipse of "the Other" and the Myth of Modernity.* New York: Continuum, 1995.

Echo-Hawk, Walter, Elizabeth Sackler, and Jack Trope, eds. *Mending the Circle: A Native American Repatriation Guide.* New York: American Indian Ritual Object Repatriation Foundation, 1996.

Egan, Timothy. "Tribe Stops Study of Bones That Challenge History." *New York Times*, Sept. 30, 1996.

Ehle, John. *Trail of Tears: The Rise and Fall of the Cherokee Nation.* New York: Doubleday, 1988.

Eichstaedt, Peter H. *If You Poison Us: Uranium and Native Americans.* Santa Fe: Red Crane, 1994.

Elliott, Jan. "America to Indians: Stay in the Nineteenth Century." *Rethinking Columbus* (special edition of *Rethinking Education*), Sept. 1991.

"The Endangered West." *New York Times,* June 18, 1995.

Erdoes, Richard and Alfonso Ortiz, eds. *American Indian Myths and Legends.* New York: Pantheon, 1984.

———. *American Indian Trickster Tales.* New York: Viking 1998.

Fabian, Johannes. *Time and the Other: How Anthropology Makes Its Object.* New York: Columbia University Press, 1983.

Fanon, Frantz. *The Wretched of the Earth.* New York: Grove, 1968.

Farb, Peter. *Man's Rise to Civilization as Shown by the Indians of North America from Primeval Times to the Coming of the Industrial State.* New York: E. P. Dutton, 1968.

Feest, Christian, ed. *Indians and Europe.* Aachen: Edition Herodot/Rader Verlag, 1987.

Fisher, Dexter, ed. *The Third Woman: Minority Women Writers of the United States.* New York: Houghton Mifflin, 1980.

Flanagan, Thomas. *Louis "David" Riel: Prophet of the New World.* Toronto: University of Toronto Press, 1996.

Flew, A. G. N., and A. C. MacIntyre, eds. *New Essays in Philosophical Theology.* London: S.C.M., 1950.

Flowers, Ronald B. *That Godless Court?: Supreme Court Decisions on Church-State Relationships.* Louisville: Westminster/John Knox Press, 1994.

Folk, Holly. "Indian Missionaries among the Anishinaabe Tribes of the Great Lakes Region: Selves-Determined or Self-Determining." Unpublished paper. Columbia University, 1996.

Forbes, Jack D. *Africans and Native Americans: The Language of Race and the Evolution of Red-Black Peoples.* 2d ed. Urbana: University of Illinois Press, 1993.

———. *Columbus and Other Cannibals.* Brooklyn: Autonomedia, 1992.

Fox, Richard. *Reinhold Niebuhr: A Biography.* New York: Pantheon, 1985.

Francis, Daniel. *The Imaginary Indian: The Image of the Indian in Canadian Culture.* Vancouver: Arsenal Pulp Press, 1992.

Frankenberg, Ruth, and Lata Mani. "Crosscurrents, Crosstalk: Race, 'Postcoloniality' And the Politics of Location." *Cultural Studies* 7, no. 2 (1992).

Frayling, Christopher. *Spaghetti Westerns: Cowboys and Europeans from Karl May to Sergio Leone.* London: Routledge & Kegan Paul, 1981.

Freeman, Karen. "9,700-Year-Old Bones Back Theory of Coastal Migration." *New York Times,* Oct. 6, 1996.

Gagnon, Gregory. "American Indian Intellectuals: Are They Above Reproach, or Easy Targets?" *Tribal College* (Summer 1995).

Geertz, Armin W. *The Invention of Prophecy: Continuity and Meaning in Hopi Indian Religion.* Berkeley: University of California Press, 1994.

Getches, David H., Charles F. Wilkinson and Robert A. Williams, Jr. *Cases and Materials on Federal Indian Law.* 3d ed. St. Paul: West Publishing Company, 1993.

Gisday Wa and Delgam Uukw. *The Spirit in the Land: Statements of the Gitksan and Wet'suwet'en Hereditary Chiefs in the Supreme Court of British Columbia, 1987–1990.* Gabriola, B.C.: Reflections, 1992.

Glueck, Sheldon. "The Nuremberg Trial and Aggressive War." 59 Harv. L. Rev. (1946).

Goldberg, Roselee. "Hitching a Ride on the Great White Whale." *New York Times,* Oct. 3, 1999.

Goldie, Terry. *Fear and Temptation: The Image of the Indigene in Canadian, Australian, and New Zealand Literatures.* Kingston, Ont.: McGill-Queen's University Press, 1989.

Goldsberry, Steven. *Maui the Demigod.* New York: Poseidon Press, 1984.

González, Justo. *Out of Every Tribe and Nation: Christian Theology at the Ethnic Roundtable.* Nashville: Abingdon Press, 1992.

Grandin, Greg. "No Victory for Dictators." *New York Times,* March 7, 2000.

Grant, John Webster. *Moon of Wintertime: Missionaries and the Indians of Canada in Encounter since 1534.* Toronto: University of Toronto Press, 1984.

Grinde, Donald A. and Bruce E. Johansen. *Ecocide of Native America.* Santa Fe: Clear Light, 1995.

———. *Exemplar of Liberty: Native America and the Evolution of Democracy.* Los Angeles: American Indian Center, University of California, Los Angeles, 1991.

Guerber, H. A. *Myths of the Norsemen.* London: George G. Harrap & Co., 1908.

Guardini, Romano. *The Church of the Lord: On the Nature and Mission of the Church.* Chicago: Henry Regnery Company, 1966.

———. *The End of the Modern World.* Joseph Theman and Herbert Burke, trans. New York: Sheed & Ward, 1956.

"Guatemala Ex-dictator under Investigation in Spain Cancels Trip to France." Apr. 18, 2000. http://www.cnn.com.

"Guatemala to Offer Spanish Court Information on Killings." Apr. 12, 2000. http://www.cnn.com.

Guillemin, Jeanne. *Urban Renegades: The Cultural Strategy of American Indians.* New York: Columbia University Press, 1975.

Gump, James. *The Dust Rose Like Smoke: The Subjugation of the Zulu and the Sioux.* Lincoln: University of Nebraska Press, 1994.

Handlin, Oscar. *Race and Nationality in American Life.* Garden City, N.Y.: Anchor Books, 1957.

Harjo, Joy. *The Woman Who Fell from the Sky.* New York: W.W. Norton, 1994.

Harlow, Barbara. *Resistance Literature.* New York: Metheun, 1987.

Haslam, G. W. *Forgotten Pages of American Literature.* Boston: Houghton Mifflin, 1970.

Hauptmann, Laurence M. and James D. Wherry, eds. *The Pequots in Southern New England: The Fall and Rise of an American Indian Nation.* Norman: University of Oklahoma Press, 1990.

Hector, Michael. *The Celtic Fringe in British National Development, 1536–1966.* Berkeley: University of California Press, 1975.

Hemingway, Richard W. *The Law of Oil and Gas*. St. Paul: West Publishing, 1971.

Henderson, Valerie. "Five Tribes Seek Remains of 'The Ancient One.'" *Indian Country Today*, Nov. 25–Dec. 2, 1996.

Highwater, Jamake. *Kill Hole*. New York: Grove Press, 1992.

———. *The Primal Mind: Vision and Reality in Indian America*. New York: Harper & Row, 1981.

———. "Second-Class Indians." *American Indian Journal*, July 1980.

Hobson, Geary, ed. *The Remembered Earth*. Albuquerque: University of New Mexico Press, 1979.

Hofstra, Marilyn M., ed. *Voices: Native American Hymns and Worship Resources*. Nashville: Discipleship Resources, 1992.

Hogan, Linda. *The Book of Medicines*. Minneapolis: Coffee House Press, 1993.

Hoge, Warren. "Britain's High Court Supports Move to Release Pinochet." *New York Times*, Feb. 1, 2000.

Hollick, Julian Crandall, and Dean Cappello, prods. "Winnetou and Shatterhand." "Imagining America." Littleton, Mass.: Independent Broadcasting Associates, 1992.

Høeg, Peter. *Smilla's Sense of Snow*. New York: Dell, 1997.

Hultkrantz, Åke. *Native Religions of North America*. New York: Harper & Row, 1987.

Human Rights Watch World Report 1998. http://www.igc.apc.org.

Hyde, Lewis. *Trickster Makes This World: Mischief, Myth, and Art*. New York: Farrar, Strauss and Giroux, 1998.

Ingebretsen, Edward J. *Maps of Heaven, Maps of Hell: Religious Terror as Memory from the Puritans to Stephen King*. Armonk, N.Y.: M. E. Sharpe, 1996.

"Inuit: Greenland." *Global Prayer Digest*. Pasadena: Frontier Fellowship, July 6, 1987.

Jackson, Louis. *Our Caughnawagas in Egypt*. Montreal: W. Drysdale & Co., 1885.

Jaimes-Guerrero, M. A. "Native Womanism: The Organic Female Archetype—Kinship and Gender Identity within Sacred Indigenous Traditions." Unpublished paper. American Academy of Religion, Philadelphia, November 20, 1995.

JanMohamed, Abdul. "The Economy of Manichean Allegory: The Function of Racial Difference in Colonialist Literature." *Critical Inquiry* 12, no. 1 (1985).

———. *Manichean Aesthetics: The Politics of Literature in Colonial Africa*. Amherst: University of Massachusetts Press, 1983.

Jennings, Francis. *The Invasion of America: Indians, Colonialism, and the Cant of Conquest*. New York: W. W. Norton & Company, 1976.

Jocks, Christopher Ronwanièn:te. "Combing Out Snakes: Violence in the Longhouse Tradition." Unpublished paper. American Academy of Religion, Chicago, November 21, 1994.

Johnson, Daniel L., and Charles Hambrick-Stowe, eds. *Theology and Identity: Traditions, Movements, and Polity in the United Church of Canada*. New York: Pilgrim Press, 1990.

Johnson, George. "Indian Tribes' Creationists Thwart Archaeologists." *New York Times*, Oct. 22, 1996.

Jonas, Susanne. *The Battle for Guatemala: Rebels, Death Squads, and U.S. Power*. Boulder, Colo.: Westview Press, 1991.

Jones, Billy M., and Odie B. Faulk. *Cherokees: An Illustrated History*. Muskogee, Okla.: The Five Civilized Tribes Museum, 1984.

Jones, E. Stanley. *Christ of the Indian Road*. New York: Abingdon Press, 1925.

Jones, Peter. *History of the Ojebway Indians: With Especial Reference to Their Conversion to Christianity*. London: A. W. Bennett, 1861.

Jones, Tom, and Harvey Schmidt. "The Fantasticks." New York: Applause Theatre Book Publishers, 1960.

Kadir, Djelal. *Columbus and the Ends of the Earth: Europe's Prophetic Rhetoric as Conquering Ideology*. Berkeley: University of California Press, 1992.

Kent, James. *Commentaries on American Law*. Vol. 1. New York: O. Halsted, 1826.

———. *Commentaries on American Law*. Vol. 3. New York: O. Halsted, 1828.

King, Thomas. *Drums*. Unpublished play. 1999.

———. *Truth and Bright Water*. Toronto: HarperCollins, 1999.

———, ed. *All My Relations*. Toronto: McClelland & Stewart, 1990.

Knockwood, Isabelle. *Out of the Depths*. Lockport, Nova Scotia: Roseway Publishing, 1992.

Kroeber, Karl, ed. *American Indian Persistence and Resurgence*. Durham, N.C.: Duke University Press, 1994.

———, ed. *Traditional Literatures of the American Indian*. Lincoln: University of Nebraska Press, 1981.

Krupat, Arnold. *Native American Autobiography: An Anthology*. Madison: University of Wisconsin Press, 1994.

———. "Scholarship and Native American Studies: A Response to Daniel Littlefield, Jr." *American Studies* 34 (1993).

———. *The Voice in the Margin: Native American Literature and the Canon*. Berkeley: University of California Press, 1988.

Lacabe, Margarita. "The Criminal Procedures against Chilean and Argentinean Repressors in Spain: A Short Summary." Derechos Human Rights, 1999. http://www.derechos.org.

Langley, Greg. "A Fistful of Dreams: Taming the Wild West in the Old World." *Munich Found Online*.

Lanternari, Vittorio. *The Religions of the Oppressed: A Study of Modern Messianic Cults*. New York: Alfred A. Knopf, 1963.

Leeming, David, and Jake Page. *The Mythology of Native North America*. Norman: University of Oklahoma Press, 1998.

Leland, Charles G. *The Algonquin Legends of New England; or, Myths and Folk Lore of the Micmac, Passamaquoddy, and Penobscot Tribes*. Boston: Houghton, Mifflin, 1884.

Lepore, Jill. *The Name of War: King Philip's War and the Origins of American Identity*. New York: Alfred A. Knopf, 1998.

Lipe, William D. "For the Good of All, Study Those Bones." *New York Times*, Oct. 4, 1996.

Littlefield, Daniel, Jr. "American Indians, American Scholars and the American Literary Canon." *American Studies* 33 (1992).

Luckas, John. "1918." *American Heritage* (Nov. 1993).

MacQueen, Ken. "A Landmark Ruling Shocks Anthropologists." *Vancouver Sun*, July 13, 1991.

McClintock, John, and James Strong, eds. *Cyclopedia of Biblical, Theological, and Ecclesiastical Literature*. New York: Harper Brothers. Reprint, Grand Rapids: Baker Book House, 1981.

McCutchen, David. *The Red Record: The Wallum Olum of the Lenni Lenape, the Delaware Indians, a Translation and Study*. Garden City Park, N.Y.: Avery Publishing Group, 1993.

McFadden, Robert D. "Meteorite Dispute Greets Opening of Planetarium." *New York Times*, Feb. 19, 2000.

McGrath, Alister. *Evangelicalism and the Future of Christianity*. Downers Grove, Ill.: InterVarsity Press, 1995.

McGuire, Randall H., and Robert Paynter, eds. *The Archaeology of Inequality*. Oxford, England: Blackwell, 1991.

McLoughlin, William G. *After the Trail of Tears: The Cherokees' Struggle for Sovereignty, 1839–1880*. Chapel Hill: University of North Carolina Press, 1993.

————. *Cherokee Renascence in the New Republic*. Princeton, N.J.: Princeton University Press, 1986.

McNickle, D'Arcy. *Indian Man: A Life of Oliver La Farge*. Bloomington: Indiana University Press, 1971.

————. *Wind from an Enemy Sky*. New York: Harper & Row, 1978.

McPherson, Dennis, and J. Douglas Rabb. *Indian from the Inside: A Study in Ethno-Metaphysics*. Thunder Bay, Ont.: Lakehead University, Centre for Northern Studies, 1993.

Mails, Thomas E. *Fools Crow*. Lincoln: University of Nebraska Press, 1979.

Malcomson, Scott L. "The Color of Bones." *New York Times Magazine* (Apr. 2, 2000).

Malaurie, Jean. *The Last Kings of Thule*. Chicago: University of Chicago Press, 1985.

Marks, Peter. "Rewrite a Classic Musical? Whatever Works Goes." *New York Times*, January 24, 1999.

Martin, Calvin, ed. *The American Indian and the Problem of Time*. New York: Oxford University press, 1987.

Mathews, John Joseph. *Life and Death of an Oilman: The Career of E. W. Marland*. Norman: University of Oklahoma Press, 1951.

May, Karl. *Winnetou I*. Bamberg, Germany: Karl-May-Verlag, 1951.

————. *Winnetou II*. Bamberg: Karl-May-Verlag, 1951.

————. *Winnetou III*. Bamberg: Karl-May-Verlag, 1951.

Mayo, Gretchen Will. *North American Indian Stories: More Earthmaker Tales*. New York: Walker and Company, 1990.

Memmi, Albert. *The Colonizer and the Colonized.* Exp. ed. Boston: Beacon Press, 1967.

Méndez, Miguel. *Pilgrims in Aztlán.* Tempe, Ariz.: Bilingual Press, 1992.

Milbank, Dana. "What's in a Name? For Lumbees, Pride and Money." *Wall Street Journal,* November 13, 1995.

Miller, Jay. *Earthmaker: Tribal Stories from Native North America.* New York: Putnam, 1992.

Miller, Perry. *Errand into the Wilderness.* Cambridge, Mass.: Harvard University Press, 1957.

Mills, Antonia. *Eagle Down is Our Law: Witsuwit'en Law, Feasts, and Land Claims.* Vancouver: UBC Press, 1994.

"Mistaken Man." *New York Times Magazine* (Dec. 1, 1996).

Moffitt, John F., and Santiago Sebastián. *O Brave New People: The European Invention of the American Indian.* Albuquerque: University of New Mexico Press, 1996.

Momaday, N. Scott. "Disturbing the Spirits." *New York Times,* Nov. 2, 1996.

———. "Foreword." *Dancing with the Wind.* Vol. 3: 1991.

———. *The Names: A Memoir.* New York; Harper & Row, 1976.

Monet, Don and Skanu'u (Ardythe Wilson). *Colonialism on Trial: Indigenous Land Rights and the Gitksan and We'suwet'en Sovereignty Case.* Philadelphia: New Society Publishers, 1992.

Montejo, Victor. *Voices from Exile: Violence and Survival in Modern Maya History.* Norman: University of Oklahoma Press, 1999).

Mooney, James. *The Ghost Dance Religion and the Sioux Outbreak of 1890.* Washington, D.C.: Smithsonian Institution, Bureau of American Ethnology Bulletin no. 14, pt. 2, 1896.

———. *History, Myths, and Sacred Formulas of the Cherokees.* Reprint, Asheville, N.C.: Historical Images, 1992.

Morton, Frederic. "Tales of the Grand Teutons: Karl May among the Indians." *New York Times Book Review,* January 4, 1987.

Mourning Dove. *Cogewea, the Half-Blood.* Boston: Four Seas, 1927.

Mudge, Zachariah Atwell. *Sketches of Mission Life among the Indians of Oregon.* New York: Carlton & Porter, 1854.

Murray, David. *Forked Tongues: Speech, Writing and Representation in North American Indian Texts.* Bloomington: Indiana University Press, 1991.

Nabokov, Peter, ed. *Native American Testimony.* Exp. ed. New York: Viking, 1991.

Nandy, Ashis. *The Intimate Enemy: Loss and Recovery of Self under Colonialism.* Delhi: Oxford University Press, 1983.

Ngugi wa Thiong'o. *Decolonising the Mind: The Politics of Language in African Literature.* London: James Currey, 1986.

———. "Literature in Schools." In *Writers in Politics.* London: Heinemann, 1981.

Niatum, Duane, ed. *Harper's Anthology of Twentieth Century Native American Poetry.* San Francisco: HarperSanFrancisco, 1998.

Niebuhr, Reinhold. *The Children of Light and the Children of Darkness.* New York: Charles Scribner's Sons, 1944.

———. *Irony of American History*. New York: Charles Scribner's Sons, 1952.

———. *The Nature and Destiny of Man*. Vol. II. New York: Charles Scribner's Sons, 1943.

———. *Pius [sic] and Secular America*. New York: Charles Scribner's Sons, 1958.

———. "The Presidency and the Irony of American History." In Reinitz, *Irony and Consciousness*.

———. "Redeemer Nation to Super-Power." *New York Times*, Dec. 4, 1970.

———. "The Social Myths of the Cold War." *Journal of International Affairs* 21 (1967).

———. "Vietnam: Studies in Ironies." *New Republic* (June 24, 1967).

Niebuhr, Reinhold, and Alan Heimert. *A Nation So Conceived*. London: Faber & Faber, 1964.

Nieuwenhuys, Rob. *Mirror of the Indies: A History of Dutch Colonial Literature*. Amherst: University of Massachusetts Press, 1982.

Noley, Homer. *First White Frost*. Nashville: Abingdon Press, 1991.

———. "Native Americans and the Hermeneutical Task." Unpublished paper, 1988.

Noriega, Jorge. "The Shadows of Power: An Ethnographic Account of Apache Shamanism." Unpublished paper, 1994.

O'Meara, Sylvia and Douglas A. West, eds. *From Our Eyes: Learning from Indigenous Peoples*. Toronto: Garamond Press, 1996.

Obenzinger, Hilton. *American Palestine: Melville, Twain, and the Holy Land Mania*. Princeton: Princeton University Press, 1999.

Oleska, Michael, ed. *Alaskan Missionary Spirituality*. New York: Paulist Press, 1987.

Ong, Walter. *Orality and Literacy: The Technologizing of the Word*. London: Methuen, 1982.

Opler, Morris. *Myths and Tales of the Chiricahua Apache Indians*. Memoirs of the American Folklore Society. Vol. 37, 1942.

———. *Myths and Legends of the Jicarilla Apache Indians*. Memoirs of the American Folklore Society. Vol. 31, 1938.

"Oregon Tribe Claims Meteorite." Nov. 17, 1999. http://www.koin.com.

Ortiz, Fiona. "Guatemalan Group Hopes to Emulate Pinochet Case with Lawsuit Against Former Dictator." Reuters News Service Nov. 26, 1998. http://www.nandotimes.com.

Ortiz, Simon. "Toward a National Indian Literature: Cultural Authenticity in Nationalism." *MELUS*, 8, no. 2, 1981.

Otto, Rudolf. *The Idea of the Holy*. London: Oxford University Press, 1923.

"The Outside Prognosticator: Germanimo!" *Outside*, (January 1966).

Owens, Louis. *Other Destinies: Understanding the American Indian Novel*. Norman: University of Oklahoma Press, 1992.

Parish, James Robert, and Michael R. Pitts. *Film Directors: A Guide to Their American Films*. Metuchen, N.J.: Scarecrow Press, 1974.

Park, Andrew Sung. *The Wounded Heart of God: The Asian Concept of Han and the Christian Doctrine of Sin*. Nashville: Abingdon, 1993.

Parkhill, Thomas C. *Weaving Ourselves into the Land: Charles Godfrey Leland, "Indians," and the Study of Native American Religions*. Albany: State University of New York Press, 1997.

Parsons, Elsie Clews, ed. *American Indian Life*. 1922. Reprint, Lincoln: University of Nebraska Press, 1991.

Peelman, Achiel. *Christ Is a Native American*. Maryknoll, N.Y.: Orbis Books, 1995.

Petersen, Robert. "Colonialism as Seen from a Former Colonized Area." Eighth Inuit Studies Conference. Laval University, Montreal, Que., Oct. 25, 1992.

Peterson, Scott. *Native American Prophecies*. New York: Paragon House, 1990.

Petrone, Penny. *Native Literature in Canada*. Toronto: Oxford University Press, 1990.

Pieris, Aloysious. *An Asian Theology of Liberation*. Maryknoll, N.Y.: Orbis Books, 1988.

Platiel, Rudy, and Ross Howard. "Indians Don't Have Right to Sell Catch, Court Rules." *Toronto Globe and Mail*, Aug. 22, 1996.

"Prehistory of Languages." *Archaeology* (July-Aug. 1994).

Powell, Peter J. *Sweet Medicine*. Norman: University of Oklahoma Press, 1969.

Querry, Ron. *The Death of Bernadette Lefthand*. Santa Fe: Red Crane Books, 1993.

Radin, Paul. *The Road of Life and Death*. Princeton: Princeton University Press, 1945.

———. *The Trickster*. New York: Schocken Books, 1972.

Ragavan, Chitra. "A Safe Haven, but for Whom?" *U.S. News and World Report*. Nov. 15, 1999. http://www.usnews.com.

Rahner, Karl. *Foundations of Christian Faith*. New York: Seabury Press, 1978.

Ramussen, Knud. *Across Arctic America*. 1999 ed. Fairbanks: University of Alaska Press, 1999.

Rausch, David A., and Blair Schlepp. *Native American Voices*. Grand Rapids: Baker Books, 1994.

Reding, Andrew. *Democracy and Human Rights in Guatemala*. World Policy Institute, 1997. http://www.worldpolicy.org.

Reinitz, Richard. *Irony and Consciousness: American Historiography and Reinhold Niebuhr's Vision*. Lewisburg, Penn.: Bucknell University Press, 1980.

Reuters News Service. "Spanish Court to Probe Guatemalan Human Rights Abuses." March 27, 2000. http://www.cnn.com.

———. "Spanish Court to Probe Accusations of Genocide in Guatemala." March 22, 2000. http://www.cnn.com.

Riegel, Daniel. "On the Origins of Native Americans: A Synthesis of Ideas." Unpublished paper. Yale University, Dec. 23, 1996.

Riggs, Lynn. *Green Grow the Lilacs*. New York: Samuel French, 1930.

Robertson, Robbie, and the Red Road Ensemble, "Music for 'The Native Americans.'" Hollywood, Calif.: Capital Records, 1994.

Robinson, Danyelle. "Ancient Remains Linked to American Indian Tribes." *Indian Country Today* (Feb. 17–24, 1997).

———. "Ancient Remains Relative to Many." *Indian Country Today*, January 20–27, 1997.

————. "Tribes, Scientists Base Claims on Separate Acts." *Indian Country Today*, Jan. 20–27, 1997.

Rorty, Richard. "Cosmopolitanism without Emancipation: A Response to Jean-François Lyotard." In *Objectivity, Relativism, and Truth: Philosophical Papers*, Volume 1. Cambridge, Mass.: Cambridge University Press, 1991.

Rose, Jacqueline. *States of Fantasy*. New York: Oxford University Press, 1996.

Ross, A. C. *Mitakuye Oyasin*. Denver: Bear, 1989.

Royster, Judith, and Rory Fausett. "Control of the Reservation Environment: Tribal Primacy, Federal Delegation, and the Limits of State Intrusion." 64 Wash. L. Rev. (1989).

Ruoff, A. LaVonne Brown. *American Indian Literature: An Introduction, Bibliographic Review, and Selected Bibliography*. New York: Modern Language Association, 1990.

Ruppert, James. *Mediation in Contemporary Native American Fiction*. Norman: University of Oklahoma Press, 1995.

Said, Edward. *Culture and Imperialism*. New York: Alfred A. Knopf, 1993.

————. "Fantasy's Role in the Making of Nations." [*London*] *Times Literary Supplement*, Aug. 9, 1996.

————. *Orientalism*. New York: Random House, 1978.

————. *The Pen and the Sword: Conversations with David Barsamian*. Monroe, Maine: Common Courage Press, 1994.

————. *The World, the Text, and the Critic*. Cambridge: Harvard University Press, 1983.

Salisbury, Neal. *Manitou and Providence: Indians, Europeans, and the Making of New England 1500–1643*. New York, Oxford University Press, 1982.

Sanderlin, George, ed. *Witness: Writings of Bartolomé de Las Casas*. Maryknoll, N.Y.: Orbis Books, 1992.

Sanders, Ronald. *Lost Tribes and Promised Lands: The Origins of American Racism*. New York: Harper, 1978.

Sarris, Greg. *Keeping Slug Woman Alive: A Holistic Approach to American Indian Texts*. Berkeley: University of California Press, 1994.

Schirmer, Jennifer. *The Guatemalan Military Project: A Violence Called Democracy*. Philadelphia: University of Pennsylvania Press, 1998.

Schurmann, Franz. *American Soul*. San Francisco: Mercury House, 1995.

"Science and the Native American Cosmos." *New York Times*, Oct. 25, 1996.

Sheler, Jeffrey L., and Ted Gest. "How Big Is God's Tent?" *U.S. News and World Report* (Feb. 24, 1997).

Shiamberg, Bruce. "American Indians Choose Spirit over Science." *New York Times*, Nov. 11, 1996.

Shohat, Ella. "Notes on the Postcolonial." *Social Text* 31-32 (1992).

Shorten, Lynda. *Without Reserve: Stories from Urban Natives*. Edmonton: NeWest Press, 1991.

Shriver, Donald. *An Ethic for Enemies: Forgiveness in Politics*. New York: Oxford University Press, 1995.

Shweder, Richard and Robert LeVine, eds. *Culture Theory: Essays on Mind, Self and Emotion*. Cambridge, Mass.: Cambridge University Press, 1984.

Siggins, Maggie. *Riel: A Life of Revolution*. Toronto: HarperCollins, 1994.

Silko, Leslie Marmon. "Foreword." *Dancing with the Wind*. Vol. 4: 1992–93.

———. *Storyteller*. New York: Arcade Publishing, 1981.

Simpson, Jeffrey. "Aboriginal Rights Are Different Things to Judges and Politicians." *Toronto Globe and Mail*, Sept. 4, 1996.

Singer, Joseph. "Sovereignty and Property." 86 Nw. U. L. Rev. 1 (1991).

Sioui, Georges. *For an Amerindian Autohistory*. Montreal: McGill-Queen's University Press, 1992.

Slapin, Beverly, and Doris Seale, eds. *Through Indian Eyes: The Native Experience in Books for Children*. Philadelphia: New Society Publishers, 1992.

Smith, Martin William [Martin Cruz Smith]. *The Indians Won*. New York: Belmont, 1970.

Spaeth, Nicholas J., Julie Wrend, and Clay Smith, eds. *American Indian Law Deskbook: Conference of Western Attorneys General*. Niwot: University of Colorado, 1993.

"Spanish Prosecutors Oppose Guatemalan Charges Urged by Nobel Laureate." Mar. 31, 2000. http://www.cnn.com.

"The Spectrum of Other Languages: An Interview with Joy Harjo." *Tamaqua* 3, no. 1, Spring 1992.

Spicer, Edward H. *The American Indians*. Cambridge: Harvard University Press, 1980.

Spivak, Gayatri Chakravorty. *Outside in the Teaching Machine*. New York: Routledge, 1993.

Standing Bear, Luther. *Land of the Spotted Eagle*. 1933. Reprint, Lincoln: University of Nebraska Press, 1978.

Stengel, Mark K. "The Diffusionists Have Landed." *Atlantic Monthly* (Jan. 2000).

Stephanson, Anders. *Manifest Destiny: American Expansion and the Empire of Right*. New York: Hill and Wang, 1995.

Strickland, Rennard. *Fire and the Spirits: Cherokee Law from Clan to Court*. Norman: University of Oklahoma Press, 1975.

Sullivan, Caroline and Cynthia Stevens, eds. *Distinguished Poets of America*. Owings Mills: National Library of Poetry, 1993.

Swann, Brian, and Arnold Krupat, eds. *I Tell You Now: Autobiographical Essays by Native Americans*. Lincoln: University of Nebraska Press, 1987.

Szasz, Margaret Connell. *Between Indian and White Worlds: The Cultural Broker*. Norman: University of Oklahoma Press, 1994.

Takaki, Ronald. *A Different Mirror: A History of Multicultural America*. Boston: Little, Brown and Company, 1993.

Tapahonso, Luci. *Sáanii Dahataal, The Women Are Singing*. Tucson: University of Arizona Press, 1993.

Taylor, Drew Hayden. *Only Drunks and Children Tell the Truth*. Burnaby, B.C.: Talonbooks, 1998.

Taylor, Telford. *Nuremberg and Vietnam: An American Tragedy*. Chicago: Quadrangle Books, 1970.

Thistlethwait, Susan Brooks, and Mary Potter Engel. *Lift Every Voice: Constructing Christian Theology from the Underside*. San Francisco: Harper & Row, 1990.

Thomas, Robert K. "Colonialism: Classic and Internal." *New University Thought* 4, no. 4 (Winter 1966–67).

Thompson, Courtenay. "Tribes Claim Willamette Meteorite." *Portland Oregonian*, Nov. 17, 1999.

Thompson, David. *David Thompson's Narrative of His Explorations in Western America, 1784–1812*. Ed. J. Tyrell. Toronto: Champlain Society, 1916.

Tillich, Paul. *Shaking the Foundations*. New York: Charles Scribner's Sons, 1948.

———. *Systematic Theology*. Welwyn: J. Nisbet, 1960.

Tinker, George. *Missionary Conquest*. Minneapolis: Fortress Press, 1993.

———. "Reading the Bible as Native Americans." *New Interpreters Bible*. Vol. I. Nashville: Abingdon Press, 1994.

Trafzer, Clifford, ed. *Earth Song, Sky Spirit*. New York: Doubleday, 1993.

Treat, James, ed. *Native and Christian: Indigenous Voices on Religious Identity in the United States and Canada*. New York: Routledge, 1996.

Trigger, Bruce G. "Ethnohistory: The Unfinished Edifice." *Ethnohistory* 33 (Summer 1986).

U.S. Department of Interior. *Federal Agencies Task Force Report, American Indian Religious Freedom Act Report*. Washington, D.C.: 1979.

Vagts, Alfred. "The Germans and the Red Man." *American-German Review*, vol. 24, 1957.

Vanderwerth, W.C. *Indian Oratory*. Norman: University of Oklahoma Press, 1971.

Vecsey, Christopher, ed. *Handbook of American Indian Religious Freedom*. New York: Crossroad, 1991.

Viswanathan, Gauri. *Masks of Conquest: Literary Study and British Rule in India*. New York: Columbia University Press, 1989.

Vizenor, Gerald. *Dead Voices*. Norman: University of Oklahoma Press, 1992.

———. *Earthdivers: Tribal Narratives on Mixed Descent*. Minneapolis: University of Minnesota Press, 1981.

———. *Fugitive Poses: Native American Indian Scenes of Absence and Presence*. Lincoln: University of Nebraska Press, 1998.

———. *The Heirs of Columbus*. Hanover, N.H.: Wesleyan University Press–University Press of New England, 1991.

———. *Hotline Healers: An Almost Browne Novel*. Hanover, N.H.: Wesleyan University Press–University Press of New England, 1991.

———. *Landfill Meditation*. Hanover, N.H.: Wesleyan University Press–University Press of New England, 1991.

———. *Manifest Manners: Postindian Warriors of Survivance*. Hanover, N.H.: Wesleyan University Press–University Press of New England, 1991.

————, ed. *Narrative Chance: Postmodern Discourse on Native American Literatures.* Albuquerque: University of New Mexico Press, 1989.

Vlahos, Olivia. *New World Beginnings: Indian Cultures in the Americas.* New York: Viking Press, 1970.

Wahlberg, Bill. *Star Warrior: The Story of SwiftDeer.* Santa Fe: Bear & Company, 1993.

Warrior, Robert. "Canaanites, Cowboys, and Indians." *Christianity and Crisis* (Sept. 11, 1989).

————. "An Interview with Vine Deloria, Jr." *The Progressive*, April 1990.

————. "A Marginal Voice." *Native Nations* (March-April 1991).

————. "Tribal Secrets." Ph.D. Diss. Union Theological Seminary, 1991.

————. *Tribal Secrets: Recovering American Indian Intellectual Traditions.* Minneapolis: University of Minnesota Press, 1995.

Washington, James M. "The Crisis in the Sanctity of Conscience in American Jurisprudence." 42 De Paul L. Rev. 11 (1992).

Weaver, Jace. *American Journey: The Native American Experience.* Woodbridge, Conn.: Research Publications, 1998.

————. "Federal Lands: Energy, Environment and the States." *Columbia Journal of Environmental Law* 7, no. 2 (1982).

————. "Native Americans and Religious Education." In *Multicultural Religious Education*, ed. Barbara Wilkerson. Birmingham: Religious Education Press, 1997.

————. "Natives Will Challenge Authority." *Toronto Globe and Mail*, Sept. 7, 1996.

————. "Poetry." *Native Journal.* (January 1993).

————. "PW Interviews: Thomas King." *Publishers Weekly*, March 8, 1993.

————. *That the People Might Live: Native American Literatures and Native American Community.* New York: Oxford University Press, 1997.

————. *Then to the Rock Let Me Fly: Luther Bohanon and Judicial Activism.* Norman: University of Oklahoma Press, 1993.

————, ed. *Defending Mother Earth: Native American Perspectives on Environmental Justice.* Maryknoll, N.Y.: Orbis Books, 1996.

————, ed. *Native American Religious Identity: Unforgotten Gods.* Maryknoll, N.Y.: Orbis Books, 1998.

Weiser, Benjamin. "Museum Sues to Keep Meteorite Sought by Indian Group." *New York Times*, Feb. 29, 2000.

Welch, James. *The Heartsong of Charging Elk.* New York: Doubleday, 2000.

Welch, James (with Paul Stekler). *Killing Custer.* New York: W. W. Norton, 1994.

Welsch, Roger. *Touching the Fire: Buffalo Dancers, the Sky Bundle, and Other Tales.* New York: Villard Books, 1992.

Wilford, John Noble. "'American' Arrowhead Found in Siberia." *New York Times*, Aug. 2, 1996.

————. "Ancient Spears Tell of Mighty Hunters of Stone Age." *New York Times*, Mar. 4, 1997.

―――. "Human Presence in Americas Is Pushed Back a Millenium." *New York Times*, Feb. 11, 1997.

―――. "New Answers to an Old Question: Who Got Here First." *New York Times*, Nov. 9, 1999.

―――. "The New World's Earliest People." *New York Times*, Apr. 11, 2000.

Wilkins, David E. *American Indian Sovereignty and the U.S. Supreme Court*. Austin: University of Texas Press, 1997.

Williams, Delores S. *Sisters in the Wilderness: The Challenge of Womanist God-Talk*. Maryknoll, N.Y.: Orbis Books, 1993.

Williams, R. M. "Relationship between State and Federal Government with Respect to Oil and Gas Matters." 19 Oil & Gas Inst., 1968.

Williams, Teresa A. "Pollution and Hazardous Waste on Indian Lands: Do Federal Laws Apply and Who May Enforce Them?" 17 Am. Ind. L. Rev. (1992).

Williamson, Ray A., and Claire R. Farrer, eds. *Earth and Sky: Visions of the Cosmos in Native American Folklore*. Albuquerque: University of New Mexico Press, 1992.

Williamson, Ray A. *Living the Sky: The Cosmos of the American Indian*. Boston: Houghton Mifflin, 1984.

Wilson, Richard. *Mayan Resurgence in Guatemala*. Norman: University of Oklahoma Press, 1999.

Wilson, Stan Le Roy. *Mass Media/Mass Culture: An Introduction*. Updated and expanded ed. New York: McGraw Hill, 1993.

Wilson, Terry P. *The Underground Reservation: Osage Oil*. Lincoln: University of Nebraska Press, 1985.

Winthrop, John. *Winthrop Papers*. Vol. 2. Boston: Massachusetts Historical Society, 1931.

Wise, Jennings. *The Red Man in the New World Drama*. Ed. and rev. by Vine Deloria, Jr. New York: Macmillan, 1971.

Wissler, Clark. *Indians of the United States*. Rev. by Lucy Wales Kluckohn. Garden City, N.Y.: Doubleday, 1966.

Wong, Hertha Dawn. *Sending My Heart Back across the Years: Tradition and Innovation in Native American Autobiography*. New York: Oxford University Press, 1992.

Wub-e-ke-niew [Francis Blake, Jr.]. *We Have the Right to Exist*. New York: Black Thistle Press, 1995.

Wunder, John R. *"Retained by the People": A History of American Indians and the Bill of Rights*. New York: Oxford University Press, 1994.

Young, Lucy (told to Edith V. A. Murphey). "Out of the Past: A True Indian Story." *California Historical Society Quarterly* 20, no. 4 (Dec. 1941).

Young Bear, Ray A. *Black Eagle Child: The Facepaint Narratives*. Iowa City: University of Iowa Press, 1992.

―――. *Remnants of the First Earth*. New York: Grove Press, 1996.

Zapeta, Estuardo. "Guatemala: Maya Movement at the Political Crossroads." *Abya Yala News* (Fall 1994).

Zuñi People. *The Zuñis: Self-Portrayals*. Albuquerque: University of New Mexico Press, 1972.

Zyla, Wolodymyr T., and Wendell M. Aycock, eds. *Ethnic Literatures Since 1776: The Many Voices of America*. Lubbock: Texas Tech Press, 1978.

INDEX